P9-EEU-743

Writing About Literature

Ninth Edition

Edgar V. Roberts

Prentice Hall, Upper Saddle River, New Jersey 07458

Library of Congress Cataloging-in-Publication Data

Roberts, Edgar V.
   Writing about literature / by Edgar V. Roberts.—9th ed.
     p.   cm.
   Includes indexes.
   ISBN 0–13–081430–X
   1. English language—Rhetoric. 2. Literature—History and
criticism—Theory, etc. 3. Criticism—Authorship. 4. Academic
writing. I. Title.
PE1479.C7R59 1998
808'.0668—dc21   98–17503
                                            CIP

Editor-in-chief: Charlyce Jones-Owen
Acquisitions editor: Carrie Brandon
Editorial assistant: Gianna Caradonna
Managing editor: Bonnie Biller
Production liaison: Fran Russello
Editorial/production supervision: Bruce Hobart (Pine Tree Composition)
Cover director: Jayne Conte
Cover designer: Kiwi Design
Prepress and manufacturing buyer: Mary Ann Gloriande
Marketing manager: Rob Mejia

This book was set in 10/12 Palatino by Pine Tree
Composition, Inc., and was printed and bound by Courier
Companies, Inc. The cover was printed by Phoenix Color Corp.

For permission to use copyrighted material please refer to p. xvi which
is hereby made part of this copyright page.

 ©1999, 1995, 1991, 1988, 1983, 1977, 1973, 1969, 1964 by Prentice-Hall, Inc.
Simon & Schuster/A Viacom Company
Upper Saddle River, New Jersey 07458

Printed in the United States of America
10 9 8 7 6 5 4 3 2 1

ISBN: 0-13-081430-X

Prentice-Hall International (UK) Limited, *London*
Prentice-Hall of Australia Pty. Limited, *Sydney*
Prentice-Hall Canada Inc., *Toronto*
Prentice-Hall Hispanoamericana, S.A., *Mexico*
Prentice-Hall of India Private Limited, *New Delhi*
Prentice-Hall of Japan, Inc., *Tokyo*
Simon and Schuster Asia Pte. Ltd., *Singapore*
Editora Prentice-Hall do Brasil, Ltda., *Rio de Janiero*

Contents

To the Instructor

In the Ninth Edition of *Writing About Literature*, I have kept and strengthened those features that so many of you have valued over the years. As in the past, I base my approach not on genres, with specific assignments to be determined, but rather on topics for full-length essays on texts in any genre. While the constant emphasis is on writing complete essays about literature, the chapters may also be used as starting points for classroom study and discussion, and they may also be adapted for shorter writing assignments. In a one-semester course the book is extensive enough to offer selective choices for study and writing; whereas in a two- or three-semester sequence, it offers the possibility of complete or close-to-complete use.

Organization

As in each past edition of *Writing About Literature*, the chapters consist of two parts. The first is a discussion of a literary approach, and the second consists of suggestions for writing, together with a sample essay or essays showing how students might deal with the approach.

A major characteristic preserved in this edition is that, after the preliminary discussion in Chapter 1, the chapters are arranged in a loose order of increasing difficulty. Beginning with Chapter 2, which helps students connect their reading with their responses and preferences, the chapters contain topics relevant to all the genres. The comparison-contrast chapter, for example (Chapter 13), illustrates the ways in which the earlier techniques may be focused on any of the topics in the book. The later chapters, such as those on prosody, film, and research, are increasingly involved; but they also combine and build on the various techniques of analysis presented in the earlier chapters.

Although you might assign the chapters in sequence throughout your course, you may also choose them according to your objectives and needs. One instructor, for example, might pass over the earlier chapters and go directly to the later ones. Another might choose the chapter on comparison-contrast for separate assignments such as comparative studies of imagery, structure, character, and point of view. Still another might use just a few of the chapters, assigning them two or more times until students overcome initial difficulties. No matter how the chapters are used, the two parts—discussion and illustration—enable students to improve their writing.

The illustrative parts of the chapters—the sample essays—are presented in the belief that the word *imitation* need not be preceded by adjectives like *slavish* and *mere*. These sample essays represent suggestions and guidance for thematic development, and therefore represent a full treatment of each of the various topics. Nevertheless, they have been kept within the approximate lengths of most assignments in undergraduate courses. If students are writing outside of class, they can readily create essays as full as the samples. And even though the samples treat three or more aspects of particular topics, there is nothing to prevent assigning only one aspect, either for an impromptu or for an outside-class essay. Thus, using the chapter on setting, you might assign a paragraph about the use of setting in only the first scene of a story, or a paragraph about interior settings, colors, or shades of light.

I emphasize that the purpose of the sample essays is to show what *might* be done—not what *must* be done—on particular assignments. It is clear that students writing about literary works are facing a complex task. First, they must read a new work for the first time; second, they must attempt to understand it; and third, they must then apply new or unfamiliar concepts to that work as they begin to write about it. By guiding them in developing a thematic form in which to express their ideas, the sample essays are intended to help them overcome the third difficulty. *Guidance* is key here, *not* prescription. At first, of course, some students may follow the samples closely, whereas others may adapt them or else use them as points of departure. My hope is that students will free themselves to go their own ways as they become more experienced as writers.

Following the sample essays are commentaries, something students recommended that I include in the Fourth Edition that I have kept ever since. These are designed to connect the precepts in the first parts of the chapters to the sample writing in the second parts.

Additions, Revisions, Other Changes, and Retentions

All changes in the Ninth Edition of *Writing About Literature,* as in earlier editions, are designed to help students read, study, think, plan, draft, and write. I have left no part of the book untouched. A number of chapters are extensively revised; some are almost entirely rewritten. Of particular note is the new chapter, Chapter 17, on the writing of reviews. The reason for this addition is a practical one: Of all the writing about literature that students may be called upon to do in their lives and future careers, the writing of a review is the most likely, whether for general audiences or for audiences united by a common concern.

Another major change is the repositioning of Chapters 3 through 6. These four chapters, all of which are suitable for fiction and three of which are suitable for drama, are now arranged in the order of *character, setting, plot and structure,* and *point of view.* The chapters on prosody and rhyme of the Eighth Edition are merged into a single chapter—Chapter 14—but the revised chapter contains the substance of the earlier two chapters. As in the Eighth Edition, the discussion of the extended comparison-contrast essay in Chapter 13 is removed to make room for the extensive chapter on research (Chapter 18). This circumstance makes it possible to include the discussion of documentation in Chapter 18 and also to preserve the unique nature of the material in Appendix B, which remains as "The Integration of Quotations and Other Important Details, and the Use of Tenses in Writing about Literature."

There are many other changes designed to improve the Ninth Edition. In making the many revisions, alterations, repositionings, and additions (and subtractions), I have tried to clarify, improve, and freshen the underlying information and examples. Many of the titles, headings, and subheadings have been revised as sentences so as to make them encapsulate the material they precede. My hope is that the sharper headings will assist students in their understanding of the various topics. The writing sections now headed "Raise Questions to Discover Ideas" are expanded, and to the various "Special Writing Topics" sections I have added topics designed to help students do library research.

Of the major sections retained from the Eighth Edition, Appendix A is worthy of note. This appendix contains brief descriptions of important critical approaches such as New Criticism, structuralism, feminism, deconstructionism, and reader-response criticism. Also of major importance in the Ninth Edition are the lists of "Special Writing Topics" at the ends of the chapters. These are mainly keyed to the works anthologized in Appendix C, but you are encouraged to adapt them to the selections in whatever anthologies you may be using. In a number of the chapters, there are short related topics that are boxed and shaded to set them apart for emphasis. These discussions, such as "A Note on Handwriting and Word Processing" and "Important Considerations about Computer-Aided Research," are designed as short notes to help students think about and develop their own writing. Users of previous editions have singled out these short boxed discussions for praise.

Aside from the extensive revisions and improvements, the chapters are internally different because of a number of changes in Appendix C ("Works Used for Sample Essays and References"). Readers have suggested the retention of Poe's "The Cask of Amontillado" and Bierce's "An Occurrence at Owl Creek Bridge," added in the Eighth Edition. Also added here are Chopin's "The Story of an Hour" and Hardy's "The Three Strangers." In addition, Blake's "The Tyger," Hughes's "Negro," and Wagner's "The Boxes" have been added. Accordingly, a small number of stories and poems that were included in the Eighth Edition have been omitted. To accompany these changes, there are also a number of changes in the topics of the sample essays. I hope that these will make the book richer and, within the confines of the short number of selections, timely. With all the changes, the Ninth Edition of *Writing About Literature* remains a useful and comprehensive guide for composition courses in which literature is introduced, and also for literature courses at any level.

An innovation of the Sixth Edition that has been retained in all subsequent editions is the glossary, which is based on the terms set in boldface in the text. The increasing number of students taking entrance examinations and GREs has justified this continuation. A student may consult the glossary, which includes definitions and page numbers for further reference, and thereby develop full and systematic knowledge of many important literary concepts.

A particular word is in order about the works included in Appendix C. At one time I believed that clarifying references could be drawn from a pool of works commonly known by advanced high school and college students, and I therefore thought that no reference anthology was necessary. I presented a small number of works in the Second Edition, keyed to some but not all of the sample essays, but reviewers recommended against it for the next editions. Recently, however, readers have emphasized that references to unknown works, even complete and self-explanatory ones, do not fully explain and clarify. Therefore, after the Fifth Edition, I have made the book almost completely self-contained with the increased number of works in Appendix C.[1] The result is that both references and sample essays may be easily verified by a reading of the works included in the book. Experience has shown that the unity and coherence provided by these works help students understand and develop their own assignments.

Writing and Literature

The Ninth Edition brings into focus something that has been true of *Writing About Literature* since it first appeared in 1964. The book is primarily a practical guide for writing; the stress throughout is on how the reading of literature may improve writing. This emphasis is made to help students not only in composition and literature but also in most of their classes. In other subjects such as psychology, economics, sociology, biology, and political science, instructors use texts and ask students to develop raw data, and they assign writing on this basis. Writing is on external, written materials, not on the student's own experiences or on opinions. Writing is about reading.

Yet instructors of composition face the problems we have always faced. On the one hand, the needs of other departments, recently thrown into renewed focus by studies about "writing across the curriculum," cause wide diversification of subject matter, straining the general knowledge of the staff and also creating a certain topical and thematic disunity. On the other hand, programs stressing internalized subject matter, such as personal experiences or occasional topic materials, have little bearing on writing for

---

[1]For the chapter on problems, however, I have continued to assume that students are acquainted with Shakespeare's *Hamlet;* and for the essay on film I have assumed that they might know or learn to know Welles's *Citizen Kane*

other courses. We as English faculty, with a background in literature, have the task of meeting the service needs of our institutions without compromising our own disciplinary commitment.

The approach in this book is aimed at this dilemma. Teachers can work with their own discipline—literature—while also fulfilling their primary and often required responsibility of teaching writing that is externally, not internally, directed. The book thus keeps the following issues in perspective:

- The requirement of the institution for composition
- The need of students to develop writing skills based on written texts
- The responsibility of the English faculty to teach writing while still working within their own expertise

It is therefore gratifying to claim that, for more than three decades, *Writing About Literature* has been offering assistance to meet these needs. The approach works, but it is still novel. It gives coherence to the sometimes fragmented composition course. It also provides for adaptation and, as I have stressed, variety. Using the book, you can develop a virtually endless number of new topics for essays. One obvious benefit is the possibility of entirely eliminating not only the traditional "theme barrels" of infamous memory in fraternity and sorority houses but also the newer interference from business "enterprises" that provide critical essays to order.

Although *Writing About Literature* is designed, as I have said in the past, as a rhetoric of practical criticism for students, it is based on profoundly held convictions. I believe that true liberation in a liberal arts curriculum is achieved only through clearly defined goals. Just to make assignments and let students do with them what they can is to encourage frustration and mental enslavement. If students develop a deep knowledge of specific approaches to subject material, however, they can begin to develop some of that expertness that is essential to freedom. As Pope said,

> True Ease in Writing comes from Art, not Chance,
> As those move easiest who have learn'd to dance.

It is almost axiomatic that the development of writing skill in one area (in this instance the interpretation of literature) has an enabling effect for skills in other areas. The search for information with a particular goal in mind, the asking of pointed questions, the testing, rephrasing, and developing of ideas—all these and more are transferable skills for students to build on throughout their college years and beyond.

I have one concluding article of faith. Those of us whose careers have been established in the study of literature have made commitments to our belief in its value. The study of literature is valid in and for itself; but literature as an art form employs techniques and creates problems for readers that can be dealt with only through analysis, and analysis means work.

Thus the immediate aim of *Writing About Literature* is to help students to read and write about individual literary works. The ultimate objective (in the past I wrote "primary objective") is to promote the pleasurable study and, finally, the love, of literature.

Acknowledgments

As I complete the Ninth Edition of *Writing About Literature*, I renew my deepest thanks to all of you who have been loyal to the earlier editions. Your approval of the book is a great honor. As I think about the revisions for the Ninth Edition, I am impressed with how much *Writing About Literature* has been influenced by the collective wisdom of many students and teachers. Those who have been particularly helpful for the ninth edition are Professors Isabella Devere, Santa Fe Community College; Vera Froelich, Bryant College; and David Sudol, Arizona State University. Conversations and discussions with other have influenced my changes in innumerable and immeasurable ways.

I thank Carrie Brandon, English Editor of Prentice Hall, for her thoughtfulness, encouragement, and helpfulness. Phil Miller of Prentice Hall has given me firm and friendly support over a number of years. I should also like to thank Maggie Barbieri, Bonnie Biller, Gianna Caradonna, Irene Fraga, Barbara Kittle, Rob Mejia, Fran Russello, and Gina Sluss, all of Prentice Hall. In addition, I thank Bruce Hobart of Pine Tree Composition, and especially, Carolyn Ingalls, who copyedited the manuscript and who offered many, many corrections and improvements. I particularly thank Jonathan Roberts for his skilled and unfailing help in preparing the manuscripts and disks of the halting and tentative drafts leading to the final copy. Thank you all.

I would also like to thank the following copyright holders for their permission to quote from their work.

Robert Frost, "Desert Places" from *The Poetry of Robert Frost*, edited by Edward Connery Lathem. Copyright 1936 by Robert Frost. Copyright © 1964 by Lesley Frost Ballantine. Copyright © 1969 by Henry Holt and Co., Inc. Reprinted with the permission of Henry Holt and Company, Inc.

Irving Layton, "Rhine Boat Trip" from *The Selected Poems of Irving Layton*. Copyright © 1977 by New Directions Publishing Corporation. Reprinted with the permission of the publishers.

John Masefield, "Cargoes" from *Selected Poems* (New York: Macmillan Publishing Company, 1978). Reprinted with the permission of The Society of Authors as the Literary Representatives of the Estate of John Masefield.

Frank O'Connor, "First Confession" from *Collected Stories*. Copyright 1950 by Frank O'Connor. Reprinted with the permission of Alfred A. Knopf, Inc.

Shelly Wagner, "The Boxes" from *The Andrew Poems*. Copyright © 1994 by Shelly Wagner. Reprinted with the permission of Texas Tech University Press.

Edgar V. Roberts

chapter 1

Preliminary:

The Process of Reading, Responding to, and Writing About Literature

The following chapters introduce a number of analytical approaches important in the study of literature, along with guidance for writing informative and well-focused essays based on these approaches. The chapters will help you fulfill two goals of composition and English courses: (1) to write good essays; and (2) to understand and assimilate great works of literature.

The premise of the book is that no educational process is complete until you can *apply* what you study. That is, you have not learned something—really *learned* it—until you talk or write about it. This does not mean that you retell a story, state an undeveloped opinion, or describe an author's life, but rather that you deal directly with topical and artistic issues about individual works. The need to write requires that you strengthen your understanding and knowledge through the recognition of where your original study might have fallen short. Thus, it is easy for you to read the chapter on point of view (Chapter 6), and it is also easy to read Bierce's story "An Occurrence at Owl Creek Bridge." Your grasp of point of view as a concept will not be complete, however, nor will your appreciation of the technical artistry of "An Occurrence at Owl Creek Bridge" be complete, until you have *written* about the technique. As you prepare your essay, you need to reread parts of the work, study your notes, and apply your knowledge to the problem at hand; you must check facts, grasp relationships, develop insights, and express yourself with as much exactness and certainty as possible.

Primarily, then, this book aims to help you improve your writing skills through the use of literature as subject matter. After you have finished a number of essays derived from the following chapters, you will be able to approach just about any literary work with the confidence that you can understand it and write about it.

ॐ WHAT IS LITERATURE, AND WHY DO WE STUDY IT?

We use the word *literature,* in a broad sense, to mean compositions that tell stories, dramatize situations, express emotions, and analyze and advocate ideas. Before the invention of writing thousands of years ago, literary works were necessarily spoken or sung, and were retained only as long as living people continued to repeat them. In some societies, the oral tradition of literature still exists, with many poems and stories designed exclusively for spoken delivery. Even in our modern age of writing and printing, much literature is still heard aloud rather than read silently. Parents delight their children with stories and poems; poets and story writers read their works directly before live audiences; plays and scripts are interpreted on stages and before moving-picture cameras for the benefit of a vast public.

No matter how we assimilate literature, we gain much from it. In truth, readers often cannot explain why they enjoy reading, for goals and ideals are not easily articulated. There are, however, areas of general agreement about the value of systematic and extensive reading.

Literature helps us grow, both personally and intellectually. It provides an objective base for knowledge and understanding. It links us with the cultural, philosophic, and religious world of which we are a part. It enables us to recognize human dreams and struggles in different places and times that we otherwise would never know existed. It helps us develop mature sensibility and compassion for the condition of *all* living things—human, animal, and vegetable. It gives us the knowledge and perception to appreciate the beauty of order and arrangement, which a well-structured song or a beautifully painted canvas also gives us. It provides the comparative basis from which to see worthiness in the aims of all people, and it therefore helps us see beauty in the world around us. It exercises our emotions through interest, concern, sympathy, tension, excitement, regret, fear, laughter, and hope. It encourages us to assist creative and talented people who need recognition and support. Through our cumulative experience in reading, literature shapes our goals and values by clarifying our own identities—both positively, through acceptance of the admirable in human beings, and negatively, through rejection of the sinister. It enables us to develop perspectives on events occurring locally and globally, and thereby it gives us understanding and control. It is one of the shaping influences of life. It makes us human.

☃ TYPES OF LITERATURE: THE GENRES

Literature may be classified into four categories or *genres:* (1) prose fiction, (2) poetry, (3) drama, and (4) nonfiction prose. Usually the first three are classed as **imaginative literature**.

The genres of imaginative literature have much in common, but they also have distinguishing characteristics. **Prose fiction,** or **narrative fiction,** includes **myths, parables, romances, novels**, and **short stories.** Originally, *fiction* meant anything made up, crafted, or shaped, but today the word refers to prose stories based in the imaginations of authors. The essence of fiction is **narration,** the relating or recounting of a sequence of events or actions. Fictional works usually focus on one or a few major characters who change and grow (in their ability to make decisions, awareness and insight, attitude toward others, sensitivity, and moral capacity) as a result of how they deal with other characters and how they attempt to solve their problems. Although fiction, like all imaginative literature, may introduce true historical details, it is not real history. Its main purpose is to interest, stimulate, instruct, and divert, not to create a precise historical record.

Poetry expresses a monologue or a conversation grounded in the most deeply felt experiences of human beings. It exists in many formal and informal shapes, from the brief **haiku** to the extensive **epic.** More economical than prose fiction in its use of words, poetry relies heavily on **imagery, figurative language,** and **sound.**

Drama is literature designed to be performed by actors for the benefit and delight of an audience. Like fiction, drama may focus on a single character or a small number of characters, and it enacts fictional events as if they were happening in the present. The audience therefore becomes a direct witness to the events as they occur, from start to finish. Although most modern plays use prose dialogue, on the principle that the language of drama should resemble the language of ordinary persons as much as possible, many plays from the past, such as those of ancient Greece and Renaissance England, are in poetic form.

Nonfiction prose consists of news reports, feature articles, essays, editorials, textbooks, historical and biographical works, and the like, all of which describe or interpret facts and present judgments and opinions. In nonfiction prose the goal is to present truths and logical conclusions about the factual world of history, science, and current events. Imaginative literature, although also grounded in facts, is less concerned with the factual record than with the revelation of truths about life and human nature.

▼ READING LITERATURE AND RESPONDING TO IT ACTIVELY

Regrettably, our first readings of works do not provide us with full understanding. After we have finished reading a work, we may find it embarrassingly difficult to answer pointed questions or to say anything intelligent about it at all. But more active and thoughtful readings give us the understanding to develop well-considered answers. Obviously, we need to follow the work and to understand its details, but just as important, we need to respond to the words, get at the ideas, and understand the implications of what is happening. We rely on our own fund of knowledge and experience to verify the accuracy and truth of situations and incidents, and we try to articulate our own emotional responses to the characters and their problems.

To illustrate such active responding, the following story, "The Necklace" (1884), by the French writer Guy de Maupassant,[1] is printed with marginal annotations like those that any reader might make during original and follow-up readings. Many observations, particularly at the beginning, are *assimilative*; that is, they do little more than record details about the action. But as the story progresses, the comments begin to reflect conclusions about the story's meaning. Toward the end, the comments are full rather than minimal; they result not only from first responses but also from considered thought. Here, then, is Maupassant's "The Necklace."

---

[1]Maupassant, an apostle of Gustave Flaubert, was one of the major nineteenth-century French naturalists. He was an especially careful writer, devoting great attention to reality and economy of detail. His stories are focused on the difficulties and ironies of existence among not only the Parisian middle class, as in "The Necklace," but also both peasants and higher society. Two of his better-known novels are *A Life* (1883) and *A Good Friend* (1885). Among his other famous stories are "The Rendez-vous" and "The Umbrella." "The Necklace" is notable for its concluding ironic twist, and for this reason it is perhaps the best known of his stories.

Guy de Maupassant (1850–1893)

The Necklace   1884

Translated by Edgar V. Roberts

She was one of those pretty and charming women, born, as if by an error of destiny, into a family of clerks and copyists. She had no dowry, no prospects, no way of getting known, courted, loved, married by a rich and distinguished man. She finally settled for a marriage with a minor clerk in the Ministry of Education.

She was a simple person, without the money to dress well, but she was as unhappy as if she had gone through bankruptcy, for women have neither rank nor race. In place of high birth or important family connections, they can rely only on their beauty, their grace, and their charm. Their inborn finesse, their elegant taste, their engaging personalities, which are their only power, make working-class women the equals of the grandest ladies.

She suffered constantly, feeling herself destined for all delicacies and luxuries. She suffered because of her grim apartment with its drab walls, threadbare furniture, ugly curtains. All such things, which most other women in her situation would not even have noticed, tortured her and filled her with despair. The sight of the young country girl who did her simple housework awakened in her only a sense of desolation and lost hopes. She daydreamed of large, silent anterooms, decorated with oriental tapestries and lighted by high bronze floor lamps, with two elegant valets in short culottes dozing in large armchairs under the effects of forced-air heaters. She imagined large drawing rooms draped in the most expensive silks, with fine end tables on which were placed knick-knacks of inestimable value. She dreamed of the perfume of dainty private rooms, which were designed only for intimate tête-à-têtes with the closest friends, who because of their achievements and fame would make her the envy of all other women.

When she sat down to dinner at her round little table covered with a cloth that had not been washed for three days, in front of her husband who opened the kettle while declaring ecstatically, "Ah,

"She" is pretty but poor. Apparently there is no other life for her than marriage. Without connections, she has no entry into high society, and marries an insignificant clerk.

She is unhappy.

A view of women that excludes the possibility of a career. In 1884, women had little else than their personalities to get ahead.

She suffers because of her cheap belongings, wanting expensive things. She dreams of wealth and of how other women would envy her if she had all these fine things. But these luxuries are unrealistic and unattainable for her.

Her husband's taste is for plain things, while she dreams of expensive gourmet food. He has adjusted to his status. She has not.

good old boiled beef! I don't know anything better," she dreamed of expensive banquets with shining placesettings, and wall hangings portraying ancient heroes and exotic birds in an enchanted
forest. She imagined a gourmet-prepared main
course carried on the most exquisite trays and
served on the most beautiful dishes, with whispered gallantries which she would hear with a
sphinxlike smile as she dined on the pink meat of a
trout or the delicate wing of a quail.

5   She had no decent dresses, no jewels, nothing. And she loved nothing but these; she believed
herself born only for these. She burned with the desire to please, to be envied, to be attractive and
sought after.

She had a rich friend, a comrade from convent days, whom she did not want to see anymore
because she suffered so much when she returned
home. She would weep for the entire day afterward with sorrow, regret, despair, and misery.

Well, one evening, her husband came home
glowing and carrying a large envelope.

"Here," he said, "this is something for you."

She quickly tore open the envelope and took
out a card engraved with these words:

> *The Chancellor of Education and Mrs. George
> Ramponneau request that Mr. and Mrs. Loisel
> do them the honor of coming to dinner at the
> Ministry of Education on the evening of Janu-
> ary 8.*

10   Instead of being delighted, as her husband
had hoped, she threw the invitation spitefully on
the table, muttering:

"What do you expect me to do with this?"

"But honey, I thought you'd be glad. You
never get to go out, and this is a special occasion! I
had a lot of trouble getting the invitation. Everyone
wants one. The demand is high and not many
clerks get invited. Everyone important will be
there."

She looked at him angrily and stated impatiently:

"What do you want me to wear to go there?"

15   He had not thought of that. He stammered:

"But your theater dress. That seems nice to
me . . . "

She lives for her unrealistic dreams, and these increase her frustration.

She even thinks of giving up a rich friend because she is so depressed after visiting her.

A new section in the story.

An invitation to dinner at the Ministry of Education. A big plum.

It only upsets her.

She declares that she hasn't anything to wear.

He tries to persuade her that her theater dress might do for the occasion.

He stopped, amazed and bewildered, as his wife began to cry. Large tears fell slowly from the corners of her eyes to her mouth. He said falteringly:

"What's wrong? What's the matter?"

But with a strong effort she had recovered, and she answered calmly as she wiped her damp cheeks:

"Nothing, except that I have nothing to wear and therefore can't go to the party. Give your invitation to someone else at the office whose wife will have nicer clothes than mine."

Distressed, he responded:

"Well, all right, Mathilde. How much would a new dress cost, something you could use at other times, but not anything fancy?"

She thought for a few moments, adding things up and thinking also of an amount that she could ask without getting an immediate refusal and a frightened outcry from the frugal clerk.

Finally she responded tentatively:

"I don't know exactly, but it seems to me that I could get by on four hundred francs."

He blanched slightly at this, because he had set aside just that amount to buy a shotgun for Sunday lark-hunts the next summer with a few friends in the Plain of Nanterre.

However, he said:

"All right, you've got four hundred francs, but make it a pretty dress."

As the day of the party drew near, Mrs. Loisel seemed sad, uneasy, anxious, even though her gown was all ready. One evening her husband said to her:

"What's the matter? You've been acting funny for several days."

She answered:

"It's awful, but I don't have any jewels to wear, not a single gem, nothing to dress up my outfit. I'll look like a beggar. I'd almost rather not go to the party."

He responded:

"You can wear a corsage of cut flowers. This year it's all the rage. For only ten francs you can get two or three gorgeous roses."

She was not convinced.

"No . . . there's nothing more humiliating than looking shabby in the company of rich women."

But her husband exclaimed:

(margin notes)

20

Her name is Mathilde.

He volunteers to pay for a new dress.

She is manipulating him.

25

The dress will cost him his next summer's vacation. (He doesn't seem to have included her in his plans.)

A new section, the third in the story. The day of the party is near.

30

Now she complains that she doesn't have any nice jewelry. She is manipulating him again.

35

She has a good point, but there seems to be no way out.

"God, but you're silly! Go to your friend Mrs. Forrestier, and ask her to lend you some jewelry. You know her well enough to do that."

She uttered a cry of joy:

40 "That's right. I hadn't thought of that."

The next day she went to her friend's house and described her problem.

Mrs. Forrestier went to her mirrored wardrobe, took out a large jewel box, opened it, and said to Mrs. Loisel:

"Choose, my dear."

She saw bracelets, then a pearl necklace, then a Venetian cross of finely worked gold and gems. She tried on the jewelry in front of a mirror, and hesitated, unable to make up her mind about each one. She kept asking:

45 "Do you have anything else?"

"Certainly. Look to your heart's content. I don't know what you'd like best."

Suddenly she found a superb diamond necklace in a black satin box, and her heart throbbed with desire for it. Her hands shook as she picked it up. She fastened it around her neck, watched it gleam at her throat, and looked at herself ecstatically.

Then she asked, haltingly and anxiously:

"Could you lend me this, nothing but this?"

50 "Why yes, certainly."

She jumped up, hugged her friend joyfully, then hurried away with her treasure.

The day of the party came. Mrs. Loisel was a success. She was prettier than anyone else, stylish, graceful, smiling and wild with joy. All the men saw her, asked her name, sought to be introduced. All the important administrators stood in line to waltz with her. The Chancellor himself eyed her.

She danced joyfully, passionately, intoxicated with pleasure, thinking of nothing but the moment, in the triumph of her beauty, in the glory of her success, on cloud nine with happiness made up of all the admiration, of all the aroused desire, of this victory so complete and so sweet to the heart of any woman.

She did not leave until four o'clock in the morning. Her husband, since midnight, had been sleeping in a little empty room with three other men whose wives had also been enjoying themselves.

55 He threw, over her shoulders, the shawl that he had brought for the trip home—a modest everyday wrap, the poverty of which contrasted sharply

---

He proposes a solution: borrow jewelry from Mrs. Forrestier, who is apparently the rich friend mentioned earlier.

Mathilde will have her choice of jewels.

A "superb" diamond necklace.

This is what she wants, just this.

She leaves with the "treasure."

A new section.

The Party. Mathilde is a huge success.

Another judgment about women. Does the author mean that only women want to be admired? Don't men want admiration, too?

Loisel, with other husbands, is bored, while the wives are having a ball.

Ashamed of her shabby wrap, she rushes away to avoid being seen.

with the elegance of her evening gown. She felt it and hurried away to avoid being noticed by the other women who luxuriated in rich furs.

Loisel tried to hold her back:

"Wait a minute. You'll catch cold outdoors. I'll call a cab."

But she paid no attention and hurried down the stairs. When they reached the street they found no carriages. They began to look for one, shouting at cabmen passing by at a distance.

They walked toward the Seine, desperate, shivering. Finally, on a quay, they found one of those old night-going buggies that are seen in Paris only after dark, as if they were ashamed of their wretched appearance in daylight.

A comedown after the nice evening. They take a wretched-looking buggy home.

It took them to their door, on the Street of Martyrs, and they sadly climbed the stairs to their flat. For her, it was finished. As for him, he could think only that he had to begin work at the Ministry of Education at ten o'clock.

"Street of Martyrs." Is this name significant?   60

Loisel is down-to-earth.

She took the shawl off her shoulders, in front of the mirror, to see herself once more in her glory. But suddenly she cried out. The necklace was no longer around her neck!

SHE HAS LOST THE NECK-LACE!

Her husband, already half undressed, asked:

"What's wrong?"

She turned toward him frantically:

"I . . . I . . . I no longer have Mrs. Forrestier's necklace."   65

He stood up, bewildered:

"What! . . . How! . . . It's not possible!"

And they looked in the folds of the gown, in the folds of the shawl, in the pockets, everywhere. They found nothing.

They can't find it.

He asked:

"You're sure you still had it when you left the party?"   70

"Yes. I checked it in the vestibule of the Ministry."

"But if you'd lost it in the street, we would've heard it fall. It must be in the cab."

"Yes, probably. Did you notice the number?"

"No. Did you see it?"

"No."   75

Overwhelmed, they looked at each other. Finally, Loisel got dressed again:

"I'm going out to retrace all our steps," he said, "to see if I can find the necklace that way."

And he went out. She stayed in her evening dress, without the energy to get ready for bed, stretched out in a chair, drained of strength and thought.

He goes out to search for the necklace.

Her husband came back at about seven o'clock. He had found nothing.

80 He went to Police Headquarters and to the newspapers to announce a reward. He went to the small cab companies, and finally he followed up even the slightest hopeful lead.

She waited the entire day in the same enervated state, in the face of this frightful disaster.

Loisel came back in the evening, his face pale and haggard. He had found nothing.

"You'll have to write to your friend," he said, "that you broke a clasp on her necklace and that you're having it fixed. That'll give us time to look around."

She wrote as he dictated.

85 By the end of the week they had lost all hope.

And Loisel, looking five years older, declared:

"We'll have to see about replacing the jewels."

The next day they took the case which had contained the necklace and went to the jeweler whose name was inside. He looked at his books:

"I wasn't the one, Madam, who sold the necklace. I only made the case."

90 Then they went from jeweler to jeweler, searching for a necklace like the other one, racking their memories, both of them sick with worry and anguish.

In a shop in the Palais-Royal, they found a necklace of diamonds that seemed to them exactly like the one they were looking for. It was priced at forty thousand francs. They could buy it for thirty-six thousand.

They got the jeweler to promise not to sell it for three days. And they made an agreement that he would buy it back for thirty-four thousand francs if the original was recovered before the end of February.

Loisel had saved eighteen thousand francs that his father had left him. He would have to borrow the rest.

He borrowed, asking a thousand francs from one, five hundred from another, five louis* here, three louis there. He wrote promissory notes, undertook ruinous obligations, did business with finance companies and the whole tribe of loan sharks. He compromised himself for the remainder of his days, risked his signature without knowing whether he would be able to honor it; and, terrified by anguish over the future, by the black misery

*louis: a gold coin worth twenty francs.

But is unsuccessful.

He really tries. He's doing his best.

Loisel's plan to explain delaying the return. He takes charge, is resourceful.

Things are hopeless.

They hunt for a replacement.

A new diamond necklace will cost 36,000 francs, a monumental amount.

They make a deal with the jeweler. (Is Maupassant hinting that things might work out for them?)

It will take all of Loisel's inheritance . . .

. . . plus another 18,000 francs that must be borrowed at enormous rates of interest.

that was about to descend on him, by the prospect of all kinds of physical deprivations and moral tortures, he went to get the new necklace, and put down thirty-six thousand francs on the jeweler's counter.

Mrs. Loisel took the necklace back to Mrs. Forrestier, who said with an offended tone:

"You should have brought it back sooner; I might have needed it."

She did not open the case, as her friend feared she might. If she had noticed the substitution, what would she have thought? What would she have said? Would she not have taken her for a thief?

Mrs. Loisel soon discovered the horrible life of the needy. She did her share, however, completely, heroically. That horrifying debt had to be paid. She would pay. They dismissed the maid; they changed their address; they rented an attic flat.

She learned to do the heavy housework, dirty kitchen jobs. She washed the dishes, wearing away her manicured fingernails on greasy pots and encrusted baking dishes. She handwashed dirty linen, shirts, and dish towels that she hung out on the line to dry. Each morning, she took the garbage down to the street, and she carried up water, stopping at each floor to catch her breath. And, dressed in cheap house dresses, she went to the fruit dealer, the grocer, the butchers, with her basket under her arms, haggling, insulting, defending her measly cash penny by penny.

They had to make installment payments every month, and, to buy more time, to refinance loans.

The husband worked evenings to make fair copies of tradesmen's accounts, and late into the night he made copies at five cents a page.

And this life lasted ten years.

At the end of ten years, they had paid back everything—everything—including the extra charges imposed by loan sharks and the accumulation of compound interest.

Mrs. Loisel looked old now. She had become the strong, hard, and rude woman of poor households. Her hair unkempt, with uneven skirts and rough, red hands, she spoke loudly, washed floors with large buckets of water. But sometimes, when her husband was at work, she sat down near the window, and she dreamed of that evening so long ago, of that party, where she had been so beautiful and so admired.

95

Mrs. Forrestier complains about the delay.

Is this enough justification for not telling the truth? It seems to be for the Loisels.

A new section, the fifth.

They suffer to repay their debts. Loisel works late at night. Mathilde accepts a cheap attic flat, and does all the heavy housework herself to save on domestic help.

She pinches pennies, and haggles with the local tradesmen.

They struggle to meet payments. *100*

Mr. Loisel moonlights to make extra money.

For ten years they struggle, but they endure.

They are successful, and have finally paid back the entire debt.

Mrs. Loisel (how come the narrator does not say "Mathilde"?) is roughened and aged by the work. But she has behaved "heroically" (¶ 98), and has shown her mettle.

105 What would life have been like if she had not lost that necklace? Who knows? Who knows? Life is so peculiar, so uncertain. How little a thing it takes to destroy you or to save you!

A moral? Our lives are shaped by small, uncertain things; we hang by a thread.

Well, one Sunday, when she had gone for a stroll along the Champs-Elysées to relax from the cares of the week, she suddenly noticed a woman walking with a child. It was Mrs. Forrestier, still youthful, still beautiful, still attractive.

A scene on the Champs-Elysées. She sees Jeanne Forrestier, after ten years.

Mrs. Loisel felt moved. Would she speak to her? Yes, certainly. And now that she had paid, she could tell all. Why not?

She walked closer.

"Hello, Jeanne."

110 The other gave no sign of recognition and was astonished to be addressed so familiarly by this working-class woman. She stammered:

"But . . . Madam! . . . I don't know. . . . You must have made a mistake."

"No. I'm Mathilde Loisel."

Her friend cried out:

"Oh! . . . My poor Mathilde, you've changed so much."

Jeanne notes Mathilde's changed appearance.

115 "Yes. I've had some tough times since I saw you last; in fact hardships . . . and all because of you! . . ."

"Of me . . . how so?"

"You remember the diamond necklace that you lent me to go to the party at the Ministry of Education?"

"Yes. What then?"

"Well, I lost it."

120 "How, since you gave it back to me?"

"I returned another exactly like it. And for ten years we've been paying for it. You understand this wasn't easy for us, who have nothing. . . . Finally it's over, and I'm damned glad."

Mathilde tells Jeanne everything.

Mrs. Forrestier stopped her.

"You say that you bought a diamond necklace to replace mine?"

"Yes, you didn't notice it, eh? It was exactly like yours."

125 And she smiled with proud and childish joy.

Mrs. Forrestier, deeply moved, took both her hands.

"Oh, my poor Mathilde! But mine was only costume jewelry. At most, it was worth only five hundred francs! . . ."

SURPRISE! The lost necklace was *not* real diamonds, and the Loisels slaved for no reason at all. But hard work and sacrifice probably brought out better qualities in Mathilde than she otherwise might have shown. Is this the moral of the story?

☙ READING AND RESPONDING IN A JOURNAL

The comments included alongside the story demonstrate the active reading-responding process you should apply to everything you read. Use the margins in your text to record your comments and questions, but, in addition, plan to keep a *journal* for lengthier responses. Your journal, which may consist of a notebook, note cards, separate sheets of paper, or a computer file, will be immensely useful to you as you move from your initial impressions toward more carefully considered thought.

In keeping your journal, your objective should be to learn assigned works inside and out and then to say perceptive things about them. To achieve this goal, you need to read the work more than once. You will need a good note-taking system so that as you read, you can develop a "memory bank" of your own knowledge about a work. You can draw from this fund of ideas when you begin to write. As an aid in developing your own procedures for reading and "depositing" your ideas, you may wish to begin with the following "Guidelines for Reading." Of course, you will want to modify these suggestions and to add to them, as you become a more experienced, disciplined reader.

Guidelines for Reading

1. **Observations for Basic Understanding**
   a. Explain words, situations, and concepts. Write down words that are new or not immediately clear. If you find a passage that you do not quickly understand, decide whether the problem arises from unknown words. Use your dictionary, and record the relevant meanings in your journal, but be sure that these meanings clarify your understanding. Make note of special difficulties so that you may ask your instructor about them.
   b. Determine what is happening. For a story or play, where do the actions take place? What do they show? Who is involved? Who is the major figure? Why is he or she major? What relationships do the characters have with one another? What concerns do the characters have? What do they do? Who says what to whom? How do the speeches advance the action and reveal the characters? For a poem, what is the situation? Who is talking, and to whom? What does the speaker say about the situation? Why does the poem end as it does and where it does?

2. **Notes on First Impressions**
   a. Make a record of your reactions and responses, which you may derive from your marginal notations. What did you think was memorable, noteworthy, funny, or otherwise striking? Did you worry, get scared, laugh, smile, feel a thrill, learn a great deal, feel proud, find a lot to think about? In your journal, record these responses and explain them more fully.
   b. Describe interesting characterizations, events, techniques, and ideas. If you like a character or an idea, explain what you like, and do the same for char-

acters and ideas you don't like. Is there anything else in the work that you especially like or dislike? Are parts easy or difficult to understand? Why? Are there any surprises? What was your reaction to them? Be sure to use *your own* words when writing your explanations.

3. **Development of Ideas and Enlargement of Responses**

   a. Trace developing patterns. Make an outline or a scheme: What conflicts appear? Do these conflicts exist between people, groups, or ideas? How does the author resolve them? Is one force, idea, or side the winner? Why? How do you respond to the winner or to the loser?

   b. Write expanded notes about characters, situations, and actions. What explanations need to be made about the characters? Which actions, scenes, and situations invite interpretation? What assumptions do the characters and speakers reveal about life and humanity generally; about themselves, the people around them, their families, and their friends; and about work, the economy, religion, politics, philosophy, and the state of the world and the universe? What manners or customs do they exhibit? What sort of language do they use? What literary conventions and devices have you noticed, and what do these contribute to the action and ideas of the story?

   c. Write a paragraph or several paragraphs describing your reactions and thoughts. If you have an assignment, your paragraphs may be useful later because you might transfer them directly as early drafts. Even if you are making only a general preparation, however, always write down your thoughts.

   d. Memorize interesting, well-written, and important passages. Use note cards to write them out in full, and keep them in your pocket or purse. When walking to class, riding public transportation, or otherwise not occupying your time, learn them by heart.

   e. Always write down questions that arise as you read. You may raise these in class, and they may also aid your own study.

Specimen Journal Entries

The following entries illustrate how you may use the guidelines in your first writing attempts. You should try to develop enough observations and responses to be useful later, both for additional study and for developing essays. Notice that the entries are not only comments but also questions.

Journal Entries on Maupassant's "The Necklace"

Early in the story, Mathilde seems spoiled. She is poor, or at least lower-middle class, but is unable to face her own situation.

She is a dreamer and seems harmless. Her daydreams about a fancy home, with all the expensive belongings, are not unusual. Most people dream about being well off.

She is embarrassed by her husband's taste for plain food. The story contrasts her taste for trout and quail with Loisel's cheaper favorites.

When the Loisels get the invitation, Mathilde gets especially difficult. Her wish for an expensive dress (the cost of Loisel's summer weekends) and then her wanting the jewelry are problems.

Her success at the party shows that she has the charm the storyteller talks about in paragraph 2. She seems never to have had any other chance to exert her power.

The worst part of her personality is shown when she hurries away from the party because she is ashamed of her everyday shawl. It is Mathilde's unhappiness and unwillingness to adjust to her modest means that cause the financial downfall of the Loisels. This disaster is her fault.

Borrowing the money to replace the necklace shows that both Loisel and Mathilde have a strong sense of honor. Making up for the loss is good, even if it destroys them financially.

There are some nice touches, like Loisel's seeming to be five years older (paragraph 86), and his staying with the other husbands of women enjoying themselves (paragraph 54). These are well done.

It's too bad that Loisel and Mathilde don't confess to Jeanne that the jewels are lost. Their pride or their honor stops them—or perhaps their fear of being accused of theft.

Their ten years of slavish work (paragraphs 98–102) show how they have come down in life. Mathilde does all her work by hand, so she really does pitch in, and is, as the narrator says, heroic.

Mathilde becomes loud and frumpy when living in the attic flat (paragraph 99), but she also develops strength. She does what she has to. The earlier apartment and the elegance of her imaginary rooms had brought out her limitations.

The setting of the Champs-Elysées also reflects her character, for she feels free there to tell Jeanne about the disastrous loss and sacrifice (paragraph 121), producing the surprise ending.

The narrator's thought about how "little a thing it takes to destroy you or save you" (paragraph 105) is full of thought. The necklace is little, but it makes a huge problem. This creates the story's irony.

Questions: Is this story more about the surprise ending or about the character of Mathilde? Is she to be condemned or admired? Does the outcome stem from the little things that make us or break us, as the narrator suggests, or from the difficulty of rising above one's economic class, which seems true, or both? What do the speaker's remarks about women's status mean? (Remember, the story was published in 1884.) This probably isn't relevant, but wouldn't Jeanne, after hearing about the substitution, give the full value of the necklace to the Loisels, and wouldn't they then be pretty well off?

These are reasonable, if fairly full, remarks and observations about "The Necklace." Use your journal similarly for *all* reading assignments. If your assignment is simply to learn about a work, general notes like these should be enough. If you are preparing for a test, you might write pointed observations more in line with what is happening in your class and also might write and answer your own questions (see Chapter 19, "Writing Examinations on Literature"). If you have a writing assignment, these entries will help you focus more closely on your topic—such as character, idea, or setting. Whatever your purpose, always use a journal when you read, and put into it as many details and responses as you can. Your journal will then be invaluable in helping you develop your ideas and refresh your memory.

ॐ WRITING ESSAYS ON LITERARY TOPICS

Writing is the sharpened, focused expression of thought and study. It begins with the search for something to say—an idea. Not all ideas are equal; some are better than others, and getting good ideas is an ability that you will develop the more you think and write. As you discover ideas and write them down, you will also improve your perceptions and increase your critical faculties.

In addition, because literature itself contains the subject material, though not in a systematic way, of philosophy, religion, psychology, sociology, and politics, learning to analyze literature and to write about it will also improve your capacity to deal with these and other disciplines.

Writing Does Not Come Easily: Don't Worry—Just Do It

At the outset, it is important to realize that writing is a process that begins in uncertainty and hesitation, and that becomes certain and confident only as a result of diligent thought and considerable care. When you read a complete, polished, well-formed piece of writing, you might believe at first that the writer wrote this perfect version in only one draft and never needed to make any changes and improvements in it at all. Nothing could be further from the truth.

If you could see the early drafts of writing you admire, you would be surprised and startled—and also encouraged—to see that good writers are also human and that what they first write is often uncertain, vague, tangential, tentative, incomplete, and messy. Usually, they do not like these first drafts, but nevertheless they work with their efforts and build upon them: They discard some details, add others, chop paragraphs in half, reassemble the parts elsewhere, throw out much (and then maybe recover some of it), revise or completely rewrite sentences, change words, correct misspellings, and add new material to tie all the parts together and make them flow smoothly.

There Are Three Major Stages of Thinking and Writing

For good and not-so-good writers alike, the writing task follows three basic stages. (1) The first stage—*discovering ideas*—shares many of the qualities of ordinary conversation. Usually, conversation is random and disorganized. It shifts from topic to topic, often without any apparent cause, and it is repetitive. In discovering ideas for writing, your process is much the same, for you jump from idea to idea, and do not necessarily identify the connections or bridges between them. (2) By the second step, however—*creating an early, rough draft of a critical paper*—your thought should be less like ordinary conversation and more like classroom discussion. Such discussions generally stick to a point, but they are also free and spontaneous, and digressions often occur. (3) At the third stage—*preparing a finished essay*—your thinking must be sharply focused, and your writing must be organized, definite, concise, and connected.

If you find that trying to write an essay gets you into difficulties like false starts, dead ends, total cessation of thought, digressions, despair, hopelessness, and other such frustrations, remember that *it is important just to start.* Just simply write anything at all—no matter how unacceptable your first efforts may seem—and force yourself to come to grips with the materials. Beginning to write does not commit you to your first ideas. They are not untouchable and holy just because they are on paper or on your computer screen. You may throw them out in favor of new ideas. You may also cross out words or move sections around, as you wish. However, if you keep your first thoughts buried in your mind, you will have nothing to work with. It is essential to accept the uncertainties in the writing process and make them work *for* you rather than *against* you.

𝔹 DISCOVERING IDEAS

You cannot know your own ideas fully until you write them down. Thus, the first thing to do in the writing process is to dig deeply into your mind and drag out all your responses and ideas about the story. Write anything and everything that occurs to you. Don't be embarrassed if things do not look great at first, but keep working toward improvement. If you have questions you can't answer, write them down and plan to answer them later. In your attempts to discover ideas, use the following prewriting techniques.

Brainstorming or Freewriting
Gets Your Mind Going

Brainstorming or **freewriting** is an informal way to describe your own written but private no-holds-barred conversation with yourself. It is your first step in writing. When you begin freewriting, you do not know what is going to happen, so you let your mind play over all the possibilities that you generate as you consider the work, or a particular element of the work, or your own early responses to it. In effect, you are talking to yourself and writing down all your thoughts, whether they fall into patterns or seem disjointed, beside the point, or even foolish. At this time, do not try to organize or criticize your thoughts. Later you can decide which ideas to keep and which to throw out. For now, *the goal is to get all your ideas on paper or on the computer screen*. As you are developing your essay later on, you may, *at any time*, return to the brainstorming or freewriting process to initiate and develop new ideas.

Focus on Specific Topics

1. DEVELOP SUBJECTS YOU CREATE WHEN TAKING NOTES AND BRAIN-STORMING. Although the goal of brainstorming is to be totally free about the topics, you should recognize that you are trying to think creatively. You will therefore need to start directing your mind into specific channels. Once you start focusing on definite topics, your thinking, as we have noted, is analogous to classroom discussion. Let us assume that in freewriting, you produce a topic that you find especially interesting. You might then start to focus on this topic and to write as much as you can about it. The following examples from early thoughts about Maupassant's "The Necklace" show how a writer may zero in on such a topic—in this case, "honor"—once the word comes up in freewriting:

> Mathilde could have gone to her friend and told her she had lost the necklace. But she didn't. Was she overcome with shame? Would she have felt a loss of honor by confessing the loss of the necklace?
>
> What is honor? Doing what you think you should even if you don't want to, or if it's hard? Or is it pride? Was Mathilde too proud or too honorable to tell her friend? Does having honor mean going a harder way, when either way would probably be okay? Do you have to suffer to be honorable? Does pride or honor produce a choice for suffering?
>
> Mathilde wants others to envy her, to find her attractive. Later she tells Loisel that she would feel humiliated at the party with rich women unless she wore jewelry. Maybe she is more concerned about being admired than about the

necklace. Having a high self-esteem has something to do with honor, but more with pride.

Duty. Is it the same as honor? Is it Mathilde's duty to work so hard? Certainly her pride causes her to do her duty and behave honorably, and therefore pride is a step towards honor.

Honor is a major part of life, I think. It seems bigger than any one life or person. Honor is just an idea or a feeling—can an idea of honor be larger than a life, take over someone's life? Should it?

These paragraphs do not represent finished writing, but they do demonstrate how a writer may attempt to define a term and determine the degree to which it applies to a major character or circumstance. Although the last paragraph departs from the story, this digression is perfectly acceptable because in the freewriting stage, writers treat ideas as they arise. If the ideas amount to something, they may be used in the developing essay; but if they don't, they can be thrown away. The important principle in brainstorming is to record *all* ideas, with no initial concern about how they might seem to a reader. The results of freewriting are for the eyes of the writer only. (A student once began a freewriting exercise by indicating his desire for a large bowl of ice cream. Although the wish had nothing to do with the topic, it did cause the student to begin writing and to express more germane ideas. Needless to say, the original wish did not get into the final essay.)

2. BUILD ON YOUR ORIGINAL NOTES. An essential way to focus your mind is to mine your journal notes for relevant topics. For example, let us assume that you have made an original note on "The Necklace" about the importance of the attic flat where Mathilde and her husband live after they paid for the replacement necklace. With this note as a start, you can develop a number of ideas, as in the following:

The attic flat is important. Before, in her apartment, Mathilde was dreamy and impractical. She was delicate, but after losing the necklace, no way. She becomes a worker when in the flat. She can do a lot more now.

M. gives up her servant, climbs stairs carrying buckets of water, washes greasy pots, throws water around to clean floors, does all the wash by hand.

While she gets stronger, she also gets loud and frumpy—argues with shopkeepers to get the lowest prices. She stops caring for herself. A reversal here, from incapable and well groomed to coarse but capable. All this change happens in the attic flat.

Notice that no more than a brief original note can help you discover thoughts that you did not originally have. This act of stretching your mind leads you to put elements of the story together in ways that create support for ideas that you may use to build good essays. Even in an assertion as basic as "The attic flat is important," the process itself, which is a form of concentrated thought, leads you creatively forward.

3. RAISE AND ANSWER YOUR OWN QUESTIONS.   A major way to discover ideas about a work is to raise and answer questions as you read. The "Guidelines for Reading" will help you formulate questions (page 13), but you may also raise specific questions like these (assuming that you are considering a story):

- What explanations are needed for the characters? Which actions, scenes, and situations invite interpretation? Why?
- What assumptions do the characters and speakers reveal about life and humanity generally; about themselves, the people around them, their families, and their friends; and about work, the economy, religion, politics, and the state of the world?
- What are their manners or customs?
- What kinds of words do they use: formal or informal words, slang or profanity?
- What literary conventions and devices have you discovered, and how do these add to the work? (When an author addresses readers directly, for example, that is a **convention**; when a comparison is used, that is a **device**, which might be either a **metaphor** or a **simile**.)

Of course you may raise other questions as you reread the piece, or you may be left with one or two major questions that you decide to pursue.

4. USE THE PLUS-MINUS, PRO-CON, OR EITHER-OR METHOD TO PUT IDEAS TOGETHER.   A common method of discovering ideas is to develop a set of contrasts: plus-minus, pro-con, either-or. Let us suppose a plus-minus method of considering the character of Mathilde in "The Necklace": Should she be "admired" (plus) or "condemned" (minus)?

Plus: Admired?	Minus: Condemned?
After she cries when they get the invitation, she recovers with a "strong effort"—maybe she doesn't want her husband to feel bad.	She wants only to be envied and admired for being attractive (end of first part), not for more important qualities.
She really scores a great victory at the dance. She does have the power to charm and captivate.	She wastes her time in daydreaming about things she can't have, and whines because she is unhappy.
Once she loses the necklace, she and her husband become impoverished. But she does "her share . . . completely, heroically" (paragraph 98) to make up for the loss.	She manipulates her husband into giving her a lot of money for a party dress, but they live poorly.
	She assumes that her friend would think she was a thief if she knew she was returning a different necklace.

Plus: Admired?	Minus: Condemned?
Even when she is poor, she still dreams about that marvelous, shining moment. She gets worse than she deserves.	Shouldn't she have had more confidence in the friend?
At the end, she confesses the loss to her friend.	She gets loud and coarse, and haggles about pennies, thus undergoing a total cheapening of her character.

Once you put contrasting ideas side by side, as in this example, you will get new ideas. Filling the columns almost demands that you list as many contrasting positions as you can and that you think about how material in the work supports each position. It is in this way that true, genuine thinking takes place.

Your notes will therefore be useful regardless of how you finally organize your essay. You may develop either column in a full essay, or you might use the notes to support the idea that Mathilde is too complex to be either wholly admired or wholly condemned. You might even introduce an entirely new idea, such as that Mathilde should be pitied rather than condemned or admired. In short, arranging materials in the plus-minus pattern is a powerful way to discover ideas that can lead to ways of development that you might not otherwise find.

5. **TRACE DEVELOPING PATTERNS.** You can also discover ideas by making a list or scheme for the story or main idea. What conflicts appear? Do these conflicts exist between people, groups, or ideas? How does the author resolve them? Is one force, idea, or side the winner? Why? How do you respond to the winner or to the loser?

Using this method, you might make a list similar to this one:

Beginning: M. is a fish out of water. She dreams of wealth, but her life is drab and her husband is ordinary.

Fantasies—make her even more dissatisfied—punishes herself by thinking of a wealthy life.

Her character relates to the places in the story: the Street of the Martyrs, the dinner party scene, the attic flat. Also the places she dreams of—she fills them with the most expensive things she can imagine.

They get the dinner invitation—she pouts and whines. Her husband feels discomfort, but she doesn't really harm him. She manipulates him into buying her an expensive party dress, though.

Her dream world hurts her real life when her desire for wealth causes her to borrow the necklace. Losing the necklace is just plain bad luck.

The attic flat brings out her potential coarseness. But she also develops a spirit of sacrifice and cooperation. She loses, but she's really a winner.

These observations all focus on Mathilde's character, but you may wish to trace other patterns you find in the story. If you start planning an essay about another pattern, be sure to account for all the actions and scenes that relate to your topic. Otherwise, you may miss a piece of evidence that can lead you to new conclusions.

6. LET YOUR WRITING HELP YOU DEVELOP YOUR THINKING. No matter what method of discovering ideas you use, it is important to realize that *unwritten thought is incomplete thought.* Make a practice of writing notes about your reactions and any questions that occur to you. Very likely they will lead you to the most startling discoveries that you finally make about a work.

❦ DRAFTING YOUR ESSAY

As you use the brainstorming and focusing techniques for discovering ideas, you are also beginning to draft your essay. You will need to revise your ideas as connections among them become more clear, and as you reexamine the work for support for the ideas you are developing, but you already have many of the raw materials you need for developing your topic.

Create a Central Idea

By definition, an essay is *a fully developed and organized set of paragraphs that develop and enlarge a central idea.* All parts of an essay should contribute to the reader's understanding of the idea. To achieve unity and completeness, each paragraph refers to the central idea and demonstrates how selected details from the work relate to it and support it. The central idea will help you control and shape your essay, and it will provide guidance for your reader.

A successful essay about literature is a brief but thorough (not exhaustive) examination of a literary work in light of a particular element, such as **character, point of view,** or **symbolism.** Typical central ideas might be (1) that a character is strong and tenacious, (2) that the point of view makes the action seem "distant and objective," or (3) that a major symbol governs the actions and thoughts of the major characters. In essays on these topics, all points must be tied to such central ideas. Thus, it is a fact that Mathilde Loisel in "The Necklace" endures ten years of slavish work and sacrifice. This fact is not relevant to an essay on her character, however, unless you connect it by showing how it demonstrates one of her major traits—in this case, her growing strength and perseverance.

Look through all of your ideas for one or two that catch your eye for development. If you have used more than one prewriting technique, the

---

WRITING BY HAND, TYPEWRITER, OR WORD PROCESSOR

It is important for you to realize that writing is an inseparable part of thinking and that unwritten thought is incomplete thought.

Because thinking and writing are so interdependent, it is essential to get ideas into a visible form so that you may develop them further. For many students, it is psychologically necessary to carry out this process by writing down ideas by hand or by typewriter. If you are one of these students, make your written or typed responses on only one side of your paper or note cards. Doing this will enable you to spread your materials out and get an actual physical overview of them when you begin writing. Everything will be open to you; none of your ideas will be hidden on the back of the paper.

Today, word processing is thoroughly established as an indispensable tool for writers. The word processor can help you develop ideas, for it enables you to eliminate unworkable thoughts and replace them with others. You can move sentences and paragraphs tentatively into new contexts, test out how they look, and move them somewhere else if you choose.

In addition, with the rapid printers available today, you can print drafts even in the initial and tentative stages of writing. Using your printed draft, you can make additional notes, marginal corrections, and suggestions for further development. With the marked-up draft for guidance, you can go back to your word processor and fill in your changes and improvements, repeating this procedure as often as you can. This facility makes the machine an additional incentive for improvement, right up to your final draft.

Word processing also helps you in the final preparation of your essays. Studies have shown that errors and awkward sentences are frequently found at the bottoms of pages prepared by hand or with a conventional typewriter. The reason is that writers hesitate to make improvements when they get near the end of a page because they shun the dreariness of starting the page over. Word processors eliminate this difficulty completely. Changes can be made anywhere in the draft, at any time, without damage to the appearance of the final draft.

Regardless of your writing method, it is important to realize that *unwritten thought is incomplete thought.* Even with the word processor's screen, you cannot lay everything out at once. You can see only a small part of what you are writing. Therefore, somewhere in your writing process, prepare a complete draft of what you have written. A clean, readable draft permits you to gather everything together and to make even more improvements through the act of revision.

---

chances are that you have already discovered at least a few ideas that are more thought-provoking, or important, than the others.

Once you choose an idea that you think you can work with, write it as a complete sentence. A *complete sentence* is important: A simple phrase, such as "setting and character," does not focus thought the way a sentence does.

A sentence moves the topic toward new exploration and discovery because it combines a topic with an outcome, such as "The setting of 'The Necklace' reflects Mathilde's character." You may choose to be even more specific: "Mathilde's strengths and weaknesses are reflected in the real and imaginary places in 'The Necklace.'"

With a single, central idea for your essay, you have a standard for accepting, rejecting, rearranging, and changing the ideas you have been developing. You may now draft a few paragraphs to see whether your idea seems valid, or you may decide that it would be more helpful to make an outline or a list before you attempt to support your ideas in a rough draft. In either case, you should use your notes for evidence to connect to your central idea. If you need more ideas, use any of the brainstorming-prewriting techniques to discover them. If you need to bolster your argument by including more details that are relevant, jot them down as you reread the work.

Using the central idea that *the changes in the story's settings reflect Mathilde's character* might produce a paragraph like the following, which stresses her negative qualities:

> The original apartment in the Street of Martyrs and the dream world of wealthy places both show negative sides of Mathilde's character. The real-life apartment, though livable, is shabby. The furnishings all bring out her discontent. The shabbiness makes her think only of luxuriousness, and her one servant girl causes her to dream of having many servants. The luxury of her dream life heightens her unhappiness with what she actually has.

Even in such a discovery draft, however, where the purpose is to write initial thoughts about the central idea, many details from the story are used in support. In the final draft, this kind of support will be absolutely essential.

Create a Thesis Sentence

With your central idea to guide you, you can now decide which of the earlier observations and ideas can be developed further. Your goal is to establish a number of major topics to support the central idea, and to express them in a **thesis sentence**—an organizing sentence that plans or forecasts the major topics you will treat in your essay. Suppose you choose three ideas from your discovery stage of development. If you put the central idea at the left and the list of topics at the right, you have the shape of the thesis sentence. Note that the first two topics have been taken from the discovery paragraph.

Central Idea	Topics
The setting of "The Necklace" reflects Mathilde's character.	1. Real-life apartment
	2. Dream surroundings
	3. Attic flat

This arrangement leads to the following thesis statement:

> Mathilde's character growth is related to her first apartment, her dream-life mansion rooms, and her attic flat.

You can revise the thesis statement at any stage of the writing process if you find that you do not have enough evidence from the work to support it. Perhaps a new topic may occur to you, and you can include it, appropriately, as a part of your thesis sentence.

As we have seen, the central idea is the glue of the essay. The thesis sentence *lists the parts to be fastened together*—that is, the topics in which the central idea is to be demonstrated and argued. To alert your readers to your essay's structure, the thesis sentence is often placed at the end of the introductory paragraph, just before the body of the essay begins.

☞ WRITE A FIRST DRAFT

To write a first draft, you support the points of your thesis sentence with your notes and discovery materials. You may alter, reject, and rearrange ideas and details as you wish, as long as you change your thesis sentence to account for the changes (a major reason why most writers write their introductions last). The thesis sentence shown earlier contains three topics (it could be two, or four, or more), to be used in forming the body of the essay.

BEGIN EACH PARAGRAPH WITH A TOPIC SENTENCE. Just as the organization of the entire essay is based on the thesis, the form of each paragraph is based on its **topic sentence.** A topic sentence is an assertion about how a topic from the predicate of the thesis statement supports the central idea. The first topic in our example is the relationship of Mathilde's character to her first apartment, and the resulting paragraph should emphasize this relationship. If you choose the coarsening of her character during the ten-year travail, you can then form a topic sentence by connecting the trait with the location, as follows:

> The attic flat reflects the coarsening of Mathilde's character.

Beginning with this sentence, the paragraph can show how Mathide's rough, heavy housework has a direct effect on her behavior, appearance, and general outlook.

USE ONLY ONE TOPIC—NO MORE—IN EACH PARAGRAPH. Usually you should treat each separate topic in a single paragraph. However, if a topic seems especially difficult, long, and heavily detailed, you may divide it into two or more subtopics, each receiving a separate paragraph of its own.

Should you make this division, your topic then is really a section, and each paragraph in the section should have its own topic sentence.

WRITE SO THAT YOUR PARAGRAPHS DEVELOP OUT OF YOUR TOPIC SENTENCES.   Once you choose your thesis sentence, you can use it to focus your observations and conclusions. Let us see how our topic about the attic flat may be developed as a paragraph:

> <u>The attic flat reflects the coarsening of Mathilde's character</u>. Maupassant emphasizes the burdens she endures to save money, such as mopping floors, cleaning greasy and encrusted pots and pans, taking out the garbage, and handwashing clothes and dishes. This work makes her rough and coarse, an effect that is heightened by her giving up care of her hair and hands, wearing the cheapest dresses possible, and becoming loud and penny-pinching in haggling with the local shopkeepers. If at the beginning she is delicate and attractive, at the end she is unpleasant and coarse.

Notice that details from the story are introduced to provide support for the topic sentence. All the subjects—the hard work, the lack of personal care, the wearing of cheap dresses, and the haggling with the shopkeepers—are introduced not to retell the story but rather to exemplify the claim the writer is making about Mathilde's character.

Develop an Outline

So far we have been developing an **outline**—that is, a skeletal plan of organization for your essay. Some writers never use formal outlines at all, preferring to make informal lists of ideas, whereas others rely on them constantly. Still other writers insist that they cannot make an outline until they have finished their essays. Regardless of your preference, *your finished essay should have a tight structure*. Therefore, you should create a guiding outline to develop or to shape your essay.

The outline we have been developing here is the **analytical sentence outline.** This type is easier to create than it sounds. It consists of (1) an *introduction,* including the central idea and the thesis sentence, together with (2) *topic sentences* that are to be used in each paragraph of the body, followed by (3) a *conclusion.*

When applied to the subject we have been developing, such an outline looks like this:

TITLE: How Setting in "The Necklace" Is Related to the Character of Mathilde

1. **INTRODUCTION**
   a. *Central idea:* Maupassant uses his setting to show Mathilde's character.

    b. *Thesis statement:* Her character growth is related to her first apartment, her daydreams about elegant rooms in a mansion, and her attic flat.

2. **BODY**—*Topic sentences* a, b, and c (and d, e, and f, if necessary)

    a. Details about her first apartment explain her dissatisfaction and depression.

    b. Her daydreams about mansion rooms are like the apartment because they too make her unhappy.

    c. The attic flat reflects the coarsening of her character.

3. **CONCLUSION**—*Topic sentence*

    a. All details in the story, particularly the setting, are focused on the character of Mathilde.

The *conclusion* may be a summary of the body; it may evaluate the main idea; it may briefly suggest further points of discussion; or it may be a reflection on the details of the body.

Use the Outline in Developing Your Essay

The sample essays included throughout this book are organized according to the principles of the analytical sentence outline. To emphasize the shaping effect of these outlines, all central ideas, thesis sentences, and topic sentences are underlined. In your own writing, you may underline or italicize these "skeletal" sentences as a check on your organization. Unless your instructor requires such markings, however, remove them in your final drafts.

🦌 SAMPLE ESSAY, FIRST DRAFT

The following sample essay is a first draft of the topic we have been developing. The essay follows the outline presented here and includes details from the story in support of the various topics. It is by no means, however, as good a piece of writing as it can be. The draft omits a topic, some additional details, and some new insights that are included in the final draft (pages 39–40). It therefore reveals the need to make improvements through additional brainstorming and discovery-prewriting techniques.

How Setting in "The Necklace" Is Related to the Character of Mathilde°

[1]
In "The Necklace" Guy de Maupassant does not give much detail about the setting. He does not even describe the necklace itself, which is the central object in his plot, but he says only that it is "superb" (paragraph 47). Rather, he uses the setting to reflect the character of the central figure, Mathilde Loisel.* All his details are presented to bring out her traits. Her character growth is related to her first apartment, her daydreams about mansion rooms, and her attic flat. [†]

[2]
Details about her first apartment explain her dissatisfaction and depression. The walls are "drab," the furniture "threadbare," and the curtains "ugly" (paragraph 3). There is only a simple country girl to do the housework. The tablecloth is not changed daily, and the best dinner dish is boiled beef. Mathilde has no evening clothes, only a theater dress that she does not like. These details show her dissatisfaction about her life with her low-salaried husband.

[3]
Her dream-life images of wealth are like the apartment because they too make her unhappy. In her daydreams about life in a mansion, the rooms are large, filled with expensive furniture and bric-a-brac, and draped in silk. She imagines private rooms for intimate talks, and big dinners with delicacies like trout and quail. With dreams of such a rich home, she feels even more despair about her modest apartment on the Street of Martyrs in Paris.

[4]
The attic flat reflects the coarsening of Mathilde's character. Maupassant emphasizes the burdens she endures to save money, such as mopping floors, cleaning greasy and encrusted pots and pans, taking out the garbage, and hand-washing clothes and dishes. This work makes her rough and coarse, a fact also shown by her giving up care of her hair and hands, wearing the cheapest dresses possible, haggling with local shopkeepers, and becoming loud and penny-pinching. If at the beginning she is delicate and attractive, at the end she is unpleasant and coarse.

[5]
In summary, Maupassant focuses everything in the story, including the setting, on the character of Mathilde. Anything extra is not needed, and he does not include it. Thus he says little about the big party scene, but emphasizes the necessary detail that Mathilde was a great "success" (paragraph 52). It is this detail that brings out some of her early attractiveness and charm (despite her more usual unhappiness). Thus in "The Necklace," Maupassant uses setting as a means to his end—the story of Mathilde and her needless sacrifice.

°See pages 5–12 for this story.
*Central idea.
†Thesis sentence.

☞ DEVELOP AND STRENGTHEN YOUR ESSAY THROUGH REVISION

After finishing a first draft like this one, you may wonder what more you can do. You have read the work several times, discovered ideas to write about through brainstorming techniques, made an outline of your ideas, and written a full draft. How can you do better?

The best way to begin is to observe that *a major mistake writers make when writing about literature is to do no more than retell a story or reword an idea.* Retelling a story shows only that you have read it, not that you have thought about it. Writing a good essay requires you to arrange your thoughts into a pattern that can be followed by a perceptive reader.

Use Your Own Order of References

There are many ways to escape the trap of summarizing stories and to set up your own pattern of development. One way is to stress *your own* order when referring to parts of a work. Do not treat details as they happen, but rearrange them to suit your own thematic plans. Rarely, if ever, should you begin by talking about a work's opening; it is better to talk first about the conclusion or middle. As you examine your first draft, if you find that you have followed the chronological order of the work instead of stressing your own order, you may use one of the prewriting techniques to figure out new ways to connect your materials. The principle is that you should introduce references to the work to support the points you wish to make, and only these points.

Use Literary Material as Evidence in Your Argument

Whenever you write, your position is like that of a detective using clues as evidence for building a case, or of a lawyer using evidence as support for an *argument*. Your goal should be to convince your readers of your own knowledge and the reasonableness of your conclusions.

It is vital to use evidence convincingly so that your readers can follow your ideas. Let us look briefly at two drafts of a new example to see how writing may be improved by the pointed use of details. These are from drafts of a longer essay on the character of Mathilde.

1	2
The major extenuating detail about Mathilde is that she seems to be iso-	The major flaw of Mathilde's character is that she is withdrawn and

1	2
lated, locked away from other people. She and her husband do not talk to each other much, except about external things. He speaks about his liking for boiled beef, and she states that she cannot accept the big invitation because she has no nice dresses. Once she gets the dress, she complains because she has no jewelry. Even when borrowing the necklace from Jeanne Forrestier, she does not say much. When she and her husband discover that the necklace is lost, they simply go over the details, and Loisel dictates a letter of explanation, which she writes in her own hand. Even when she meets Jeanne on the Champs-Elysées, she does not say a great deal about her life but only goes through enough details about the loss and replacement of the necklace to make Jeanne exclaim about the needlessness of the ten-year sacrifice.	uncommunicative, apparently unwilling or unable to form an intimate relationship. For example, she and her husband do not talk to each other much, except about external things such as his taste for boiled beef and her lack of a party dress and jewelry. With such an uncommunicative marriage, one might suppose that she would be more open with her close friend, Jeanne Forrestier, but Mathilde does not say much even to her. This flaw hurts her greatly, because if she were more open, she might have explained the loss and so have avoided the horrible sacrifice. This lack of openness, along with her self-indulgent dreaminess, is her biggest defect.

A comparison of these paragraphs shows that the first has more words than the second (158 to 122), but that it is more appropriate for a rough than a final draft because the writer does little more than retell the story. The paragraph is cluttered with details that do not support any conclusions. If you examine it for what you might learn about Maupassant's actual use of Mathilde's solitary traits in "The Necklace," you will find that it gives you but little help. The writer needs to consider why these details should be shared, and to revise the paragraph according to the central idea.

On the other hand, the details in the second paragraph all support the declared topic. Phrases such as "for example," "with such," and "this lack" show that the writer of paragraph 2 has assumed that the audience knows the story and now wants help in interpretation. Paragraph 2 therefore guides readers *by connecting the details to the topic.* It uses these details *as evidence,* not as a retelling of actions. By contrast, paragraph 1 recounts a number of relevant actions but does not *connect* them to the topic. More details, of course, could have been added to the second paragraph, but they are unnecessary because the paragraph demonstrates the point with the details used. There are many qualities that make good writing good, but one of the most important is shown in a comparison of the two paragraphs: *In good writing, no details are included unless they are used as supporting evidence in a pattern of thought.*

Keep to Your Point

To show another distinction between first- and second-draft writing, let us consider a third example. The following paragraph, in which the writer assumes an audience that is interested in the relationship of economics and politics to literature, is drawn from an essay on "The Idea of Economic Determinism in 'The Necklace.'" In this paragraph, the writer shows how economics are related to a number of incidents from the story. The idea is to assert that Mathilde's difficulties result not from character but rather from financial restrictions:

> More important than chance in governing life is the idea that people are controlled by economic circumstances. Mathilde, as is shown at the story's opening, is born poor. Therefore, she doesn't get the right doors opened for her, and her marriage is to a minor clerk. With a vivid imagination and a burning desire for luxury, seeming to be born only for the wealthy life, her poor home brings out her daydreams of expensive surroundings. She taunts her husband, Loisel, when he brings the big invitation, because she does not have a suitable (read "expensive") dress. Once she gets the dress, it is jewelry that she lacks, and she borrows that and loses it. The loss of the necklace is the greatest trouble, because it forces the Loisels to borrow deeply and to lead an impoverished life for ten years.

This paragraph begins with an effective topic sentence, indicating that the writer has a good plan. The remaining part, however, shows how easily writers may be diverted from their objective. The flaw is that the material of the paragraph, while accurate, *is not tied to the topic*. Once the second sentence is under way, the paragraph gets lost in a retelling of events, and the fine opening sentence is left behind. The paragraph therefore shows that writers cannot assume that detail alone will make an intended meaning clear. They must do the connecting themselves, to make sure that all relationships are explicitly clear. *This point cannot be overstressed.*

Let us see how the problem may be treated. If the ideal paragraph can be schematized with line drawings, we might say that the paragraph's topic should be a straight line, moving toward and reaching a specific goal (explicit meaning), with an exemplifying line moving away from the straight line briefly to bring in evidence, but returning to the line after each new fact in order to demonstrate the relevance of the fact. Thus, the ideal scheme looks like this, with a straight line touched a number of times by an undulating line:

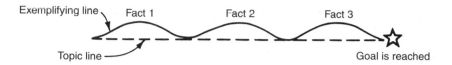

Notice that the exemplifying line, waving to illustrate how documentation or exemplification is to be used, always returns to the topic line. A scheme for the faulty paragraph on "The Necklace," however, would look like this, with the line never returning, but flying out into space:

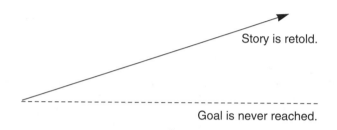

How might the faulty paragraph be improved? The best way is to remind the reader again and again of the topic, and to use examples from the text in support.

As our model wavy-line diagram indicates, each time a topic is mentioned, the undulating line merges with the straight, or central-idea, line. This relationship of topic to illustrative examples should prevail no matter what subject you write about. If you are analyzing *point of view*, for example, you should keep connecting your material to the speaker, or narrator, and the same applies to topics like character, theme, or setting. According to this principle, we might revise the paragraph on economic determinism in "The Necklace" as follows. (Parts of sentences stressing the relationship of the examples to the topic of the paragraph are underlined.)

> More important than chance in governing life is the idea that people are controlled by economic circumstances. <u>As illustration</u>, the speaker begins by emphasizing that Mathilde, the main character, is born poor. Therefore, she doesn't get the right doors opened for her, and her marriage is to a minor clerk. <u>In keeping with the idea</u>, her vivid imagination and burning desire for luxury (she seems to have been born only for the wealthy life) feed on her weakness of character as she feels deep unhappiness and depression because of the contrast between her daydreams of expensive surroundings and the poor home she actually has. <u>These straitened economic circumstances</u> inhibit her relationship with her husband, and she taunts him when he brings the big invitation because she does not have a suitable (read "expensive") dress. As a merging of

her unrealistic dream life with actual reality, <u>her borrowing of the necklace</u> <u>suggests the impossibility of overcoming economic restrictions</u>. In the context of the idea, the ten-year sacrifice to pay for the lost necklace <u>demonstrates that</u> <u>lack of money keeps people down, destroying their dreams and hopes of a</u> <u>better life.</u>

The paragraph now reaches the goal of the topic sentence. While it has also been lengthened, the length has been caused not by inessential detail but by phrases and sentences that give form and direction. You might object that if you lengthened all your paragraphs in this way, your essays would grow too bulky. The answer is to reduce the number of major points and paragraphs, on the theory that *it is better to develop a few topics pointedly than to develop many pointlessly*. Revising for the purpose of strengthening central and topic ideas requires that you either throw out some topics or else incorporate them as subpoints in the topics you keep. To control your writing in this way can result only in improvement.

☞ CHECK THE DEVELOPMENT AND ORGANIZATION OF YOUR IDEAS

It bears repeating over and over again that the first requirement of a good essay is to introduce a point or main idea and then stick to it. Another major step toward excellence is to make your central idea expand and grow. The word *growth* is a metaphor describing the creation of new insights, the disclosure of ideas that were not at first noticeable, and the expression of original, new, and fresh interpretations.

Try to Be Original

In everything you ever write, it is important that you try to be original. You might initially claim that you cannot be original when you are writing about someone else's work. "The author has said everything," might go your argument, "and therefore I can do little more than follow the story." This claim presupposes that you have no choice in selecting material and no opportunity to make individual thoughts and original contributions.

But you do have choices and opportunities to be original. One obvious area of originality is *the development and formulation of your central idea*. For example, a natural first response to "The Necklace" is "The story is about a woman who loses a borrowed necklace and endures hardship to help pay for it." Because this response refers only to events in the story and not to any idea, an area of thought might be introduced if the hardship is called "needless." Just the use of this word alone demands that you explain the differences between *needed* and *unneeded* hardships, and your application of these differences to the heroine's plight would produce an original essay. Even better and more original insights could result if the topic of the budding essay were to connect the dreamy, withdrawn traits of the main character to her misfortunes and also to general misfortunes. A resulting central idea might be "People themselves create their own difficulties." Such an idea would require you to define not only the personal but also the representative nature of Mathilde's experiences, an avenue of exploration that could produce much in the way of a fresh, original essay about "The Necklace."

You can also develop your ability to treat your subject freshly and originally if you plan the body of the essay *to build up to what you think is your most important and incisive idea.* As examples of such planning, the following brief outline suggests how a central idea may be widened and expanded:

SUBJECT: Mathilde as a Growing Character

1. Mathilde has normal daydreams about a better life.
2. She takes a risk and then loses, in trying to make her daydreams seem real.
3. She develops by facing her mistake and working hard to correct it.

The list shows how a subject may be enlarged if you treat your exemplifying topic in an increasing order of importance. In this case, the order moves from Mathilde's habit of daydreaming to the development of her character strength. The pattern shows how you can meet two primary standards of excellence in writing—organization and growth.

Clearly, you should always try to develop your central idea. Constantly adhere to your topic, and constantly develop it. Nurture it and make it grow. Admittedly, in a short essay you will be able to move only a short distance with an idea, but you *should never be satisfied to leave the idea exactly where you found it.* To the degree that you can learn to develop your ideas, you will receive recognition for increasingly original writing.

Write with Your Readers in Mind

Whenever you write, you must decide how much detail to discuss. Usually you base this decision on your judgment of your readers. For example, if you assume that they have not read the work you are writing about, you will need to include a short summary as background. Otherwise, they may not understand your argument.

Consider, too, whether your readers have any special interests or concerns. If they are particularly interested in politics, sociology, religion, or psychology, for example, you may need to select and develop your materials accordingly.

Your instructor will let you know who your audience is. Usually, it will be your instructor or your fellow students. They will be familiar with the work and will not expect you to retell a story or summarize an argument. Rather, they will look to you as an *explainer* or *interpreter*. Thus, you may omit details from the work that do not exemplify and support your central idea, even if the details are important parts of the work. What you write should always be based on your developing idea together with your assessment of your readers.

Use Exact, Comprehensive, and Forceful Language

In addition to being original, organized, and well developed, the best writing is expressed in *exact, comprehensive,* and *forceful* language. At any stage of the composition process, you should try to correct your earliest sentences and paragraphs, which usually need to be rethought, reworded, and rearranged.

TRY TO MAKE YOUR SENTENCES MEANINGFUL. First of all, ask yourself whether your sentences really *mean* what you intend, or whether you can make them more exact and therefore stronger. For example, consider these two sentences from essays about "The Necklace":

> It seems as though the main character's dreams of luxury cause her to respond as she does in the story.

> This incident, although it may seem trivial or unimportant, has substantial significance in the creation of the story; by this I mean the incident that occurred is essentially what the story is all about.

These sentences are inexact and vague, and therefore unhelpful; neither of them goes anywhere. The first sentence is satisfactory up to the verb "cause," but then it falls apart because the writer has lost sight of the meaning. It is best to describe *what* that response is, rather than to be satisfied with nothing more than that there *is* a response. To make the sentence more exact, we may make the following revision:

> Mathilde's dreams of luxury make it impossible for her to accept her own possessions, and therefore she goes beyond her means in order to attend the party.

With this revision, the writer could consider the meaning of the story's early passages and could contrast the ideas there with those in the latter part. Without the revision, it is not clear where the writer might go.

The second sentence is vague because again the writer has lost sight of the topic. If we adopt the principle of trying to be exact, however, we may bring the dead sentence to life:

> The accidental loss of the necklace, which is trivial though costly, supports the narrator's claim that major turns in life are produced not by earthshaking events, but rather by minor ones.

TRY TO MAKE YOUR SENTENCES COMPLETE AND COMPREHENSIVE. Second, in addition to being exact, it is vital to make sentences—all sentences, but particularly thesis and topic sentences—complete and comprehensive. As an example, consider the following sentence from an essay about "The Necklace":

> The idea in "The Necklace" is that Mathilde and her husband work hard to pay for the lost necklace.

This sentence does not offer us any ideas about the story. It needs additional rethinking and rephrasing to make it more comprehensive, as in the these two revisions:

> In "The Necklace" Maupassant shows that hard work and responsibility are basic and necessary in life.
>
> Maupassant's surprise ending of "The Necklace" symbolizes the need for always being truthful.

Both new sentences are connected to the action described by the original phrasing, "Mathilde and her husband work hard to pay for the lost necklace," although they point toward differing treatments. The first sentence concerns the virtue shown by the Loisels in their sacrifice. Because the second sentence includes the word *symbolizes,* an essay stemming from it would stress the Loisels' mistake in not confessing the loss. In dealing with the symbolic meaning of their failure, an essay developed along the lines of the sentence would focus on the negative aspects of their characters, and an essay developed from the first sentence would stress their positive aspects. Either of the revised sentences, therefore, is more comprehensive than the original sentence and thus would help a writer get on the track toward an accurate and thoughtful essay.

Of course it is never easy to create fine sentences, but as a mode of improvement, you might create some self-testing mechanisms:

- *For treating story materials.* Always relate the materials to an idea or a point. Do not say simply that "Mathilde works constantly for ten years to help pay off

---

**USING THE NAMES OF AUTHORS WHEN WRITING
ABOUT LITERATURE**

For both men and women writers, you should typically include the author's *full
name* in the *first sentence* of your essay. Here are a few model first sentences:

> Ambrose Bierce's "An Occurrence at Owl Creek Bridge"
> is a story featuring both pathos and suspense.

> "An Occurrence at Owl Creek Bridge," by Ambrose Bierce,
> is a story featuring both pathos and suspense.

For all later references, use only last names, such as *Bierce, Chekhov,* or
Hardy. However, for the "giants" of literature, you should use the last names
exclusively. In referring to writers like Shakespeare and Milton, for example,
there is no need to include *William* or *John.*

In spite of today's informal standards, do not use an author's first name,
as in "*Ambrose* skillfully creates pathos and suspense in 'An Occurrence at
Owl Creek Bridge.'" Also, do not use a familiar title before the names of dead
authors, such as "*Mr.* Bierce's 'An Occurrence at Owl Creek Bridge' is a suspenseful
and pathetic story." Use the last name alone.

As with all conventions, of course, there are exceptions. If you are referring
to a childhood work of a writer, the first name is appropriate, but shift to
the last name when referring to the writer's mature works. If your writer has a
professional or a noble title, such as "*Judge* O'Connor," "*Governor* Cross,
"*Lord* Byron" or "*Lady* Winchelsea," it is not improper to use the title. Even
then, however, the titles are commonly omitted for males, so that most references
to Lord Byron and Lord Tennyson should be simply to "Byron" and
"Tennyson."

Referring to living authors is somewhat problematical. Some journals and
newspapers, like the *New York Times,* use the respectful titles *Mr.* and *Ms.* in
their reviews. However, scholarly journals, which are likely to remain on library
shelves for many decades, follow the general principle of beginning with the
entire name and then using only the last name for subsequent references.

---

the debt." Instead, blend the material into a point, like this: "Mathilde's ten-year
effort shows *the horror of indebtedness*," or "Mathilde's ten-year effort
demonstrates the emergence of her strength of character."

- *For responses and impressions.* Do not say simply, "The story's ending left me
  with a definite impression," but *state* what the impression is: "The story's ending
  surprised me and also made me sympathetic to the major character."
- *For ideas.* Try to make the idea clear and direct. Do not say, "Mathilde is living
  in a poor household," but rather get at an idea like this one: "The story of
  Mathilde shows that living in poverty reduces the quality of life."

- *For critical commentary.* Do not be satisfied with a statement such as "I found 'The Necklace' interesting," but try to describe *what* was interesting and *why* it was interesting: "I found 'The Necklace' interesting because it shows how chance and bad luck may either make or destroy people's lives."

Good writing begins with attempts, like these, to rephrase sentences to make them really say something. If you always name and pin down descriptions, responses, and judgments, no matter how difficult the task seems, your sentences can be strong because you will be making them exact.

✿ SAMPLE ESSAY, SECOND DRAFT

If you refer again to the first draft of the essay about Maupassant's use of setting to illustrate Mathilde's character (page 28), you might notice that several parts of the draft need extensive reworking and revising. For example, paragraph 2 contains a series of short, unconnected comments, and the last sentence of that paragraph implies that Mathilde's dissatisfaction relates mainly to her husband rather than to her general circumstances. Paragraph 4 focuses too much on Mathilde's coarseness and not enough on her sacrifice and cooperation. The draft also ignores the fact that the story ends in another location, the Champs Elysées, where Maupassant continues to demonstrate the nature of Mathilde's character. Finally, there is not enough support in this draft for the contention (in paragraph 5) that *everything* in the story is related to the character of Mathilde.

To discover how these issues may be more fully considered, the following revision of the earlier draft creates more introductory detail, includes an additional paragraph, and reshapes each of the paragraphs to stress the relationship of central idea to topic. Within the limits of a short assignment, the essay illustrates all the principles of organization and unity that we have been discussing here.

Maupassant's Use of Setting in "The Necklace"
to Show the Character of Mathilde

[1] In "The Necklace" Guy de Maupassant uses setting to reflect the character and development of the main character, Mathilde Loisel.* As a result, his setting is not particularly vivid or detailed. He does not even describe the ill-fated necklace—the central object in the story—but states only that it is "superb" (paragraph 47). In fact, however, he includes descriptions of setting only if they illuminate qualities about Mathilde. Her changing character may be related to the first apartment, the dream-life mansion rooms, the attic flat, and the public street.†

[2] Details about the modest apartment of the Loisels on the Street of Martyrs indicate Mathilde's peevish lack of adjustment to life. Though everything is serviceable, she is unhappy with the "drab" walls, "threadbare" furniture, and "ugly" curtains (paragraph 3). She has domestic help, but wants more servants than the simple country girl who does the household chores in the apartment. Her embarrassment and dissatisfaction are shown by details of her irregularly cleaned tablecloth and the plain and inelegant boiled beef that her husband adores. Even her best theater dress, which is appropriate for apartment life but which is inappropriate for more wealthy surroundings, makes her unhappy. All these details of the apartment establish that Mathilde's dominant character trait at the story's beginning is maladjustment. She therefore seems unpleasant and unsympathetic.

[3] Like the real-life apartment, the impossibly expensive setting of her daydreams about living in a mansion strengthens her unhappiness and her avoidance of reality. All the rooms of her fantasies are large and expensive, draped in silk and filled with nothing but the best furniture and bric-a-brac. Maupassant gives us the following description of her dream world:

> She imagined a gourmet-prepared main course carried on the most exquisite trays and served on the most beautiful dishes, with whispered gallantries which she would hear with a sphinxlike smile as she dined on the pink meat of a trout or the delicate wing of a quail. (paragraph 4)

With impossible dreams like this one, her despair is complete. Ironically, this despair, together with her inability to live with reality, brings about her undoing. It makes her agree to borrow the necklace (which is just as unreal as her daydreams of wealth), and losing the necklace drives her into the reality of giving up her apartment and moving into the attic flat.

[4] Also ironically, the attic flat is related to the coarsening of her character while at the same time it brings out her best qualities of cooperativeness and honesty. Maupassant emphasizes the drudgery of the work Mathilde endures to maintain the flat, such as walking up many stairs, washing floors with large

*Central idea.
†Thesis sentence.

[4] buckets of water, cleaning greasy and encrusted pots and pans, taking out the garbage, hand-washing clothes, and haggling loudly with local tradespeople. All this reflects her coarsening and loss of sensibility, also shown by her giving up hair and hand care, and wearing the cheapest dresses. The work she performs, however, makes her heroic (paragraph 98). As she cooperates to help her husband pay back the loans, her dreams of a mansion fade, and all she has left is the memory of her triumphant appearance at the Minister of Education's party. Thus the attic flat brings out her physical change for the worse at the same time that it also brings out her psychological and moral change for the better.

[5] Her walk on the Champs-Elysées illustrates another combination of traits—self-indulgence and frankness. The Champs-Elysées is the most fashionable street in Paris, and her walk to it is similar to her earlier indulgences in her daydreams of upper-class wealth. But it is on this street where she meets Jeanne, and it is Mathilde's frankness in confessing the loss and replacement to Jeanne that makes Mathilde completely honest. While the walk thus serves as the occasion for the story's concluding surprise and irony, Mathilde's being on the Champs-Elysées is totally in character, in keeping with her earlier reveries about luxury.

[6] Other details in the story also have a similar bearing on Mathilde's character. For example, the story presents little detail about the party scene beyond the statement that Mathilde is a great "success" (paragraph 52)—a judgment that shows her ability to shine if given the chance. After she and Loisel accept the fact that the necklace cannot be found, Maupassant includes details about the Parisian streets, about the visits to loan sharks, and about the jewelry shops in order to bring out Mathilde's sense of honesty and pride as she "heroically" prepares to live her new life of poverty. Thus, in "The Necklace," Maupassant uses setting to highlight Mathilde's maladjustment, her needless misfortune, her loss of youth and beauty, and finally her growth as a responsible human being.

☙ COMMENTARY ON THE ESSAY

Several improvements to the first draft may be seen here. The language of paragraph 2 has been revised to show more clearly the inappropriateness of Mathilde's dissatisfaction. In paragraph 3, the irony of the story is brought out, and the writer has connected the details to the central idea in a richer pattern of ideas, showing the effects of Mathilde's despair. Paragraph 5— new in this revision—includes additional details about how Mathilde's walk on the Champs-Elysées is related to her character. In paragraph 6, the fact that Mathilde is able "to shine" at the dinner party is interpreted according to the central idea. Finally, the conclusion is now much more specific, summarizing the change in Mathilde's character rather than saying simply that the setting reveals her "needless misfortune." In short, the second draft reflects the complexity of "The Necklace" better than the first draft. Because the writer has revised the first-draft ideas about the story, the final essay is tightly structured, insightful, and forceful.

☞ ESSAY COMMENTARIES

Throughout this book, the sample essays are followed by short commentaries that show how the essays embody the chapter's instruction and guidelines. For each essay in which a number of possible approaches are suggested, the commentary points out which one is employed; and when a sample essay uses two or more approaches, the commentary makes this fact clear. In addition, each commentary singles out one of the paragraphs for detailed analysis of its strategy and use of detail. It is hoped that the commentaries will help you develop the insight necessary to use the essays as aids in your own study and writing.

To sum up, follow these guidelines whenever you write about a story or any kind of literature:

- Never just retell the story. Use story materials only to support your central idea or argument.
- Throughout your essay, keep reminding your reader of your central idea. Keep returning to your points.
- Within each paragraph, make sure that you stress your topic idea.
- Develop your topic. Make it bigger than it was when you began.
- Always make your statements exact, comprehensive, and forceful.
- **Never just retell the story.**

☞ SPECIAL WRITING TOPICS FOR STUDYING THE WRITING PROCESS

1. Write a brainstorming paragraph on the topic of anything in a literary work that you find especially good or interesting. Write as the thoughts occur to you; do not slow yourself down in an effort to make your writing seem perfect; you may make corrections and improvements later.

2. Using marginal and journal notations, together with any additional thoughts, describe the way in which the author of a particular work has resolved particularly important ideas and difficulties.

3. Create a plus-minus table to list your responses about a character or ideas in a work.

4. Raise questions about the actions of characters in a story or play in order to determine the various customs and manners of the society out of which the work is derived.

5. Analyze and explain the way in which the conflicts in a story or play are developed. What pattern or patterns seem to develop? How does the work grow out of the conflicts?

6. Basing your ideas on your marginal and journal notations, select an idea and develop a thesis sentence from it, using your idea and a list of possible topics for the development of an essay.

7. Using the thesis sentence that you write for exercise 6, develop a brief topical outline for an essay.

8. What effect do the minor characters in "The Necklace" (Loisel and Jeanne Forrestier) have upon your perception of Mathilde?

9. A critic has said that the disaster befalling Mathilde and Loisel results not so much from their losing the necklace as from their not telling Jeanne about the loss. How true is this judgment? Be sure to consider what they themselves think might have happened if they had confessed the loss to Jeanne.

10. Write a brief story of your own in which you show how a chance event has a major impact on the lives of your character or characters. In what ways is your chance event similar to or different from what happens to Mathilde? What view of life and reality do you think is represented by the consequences of the chance event?

chapter 2

Writing About Likes and Dislikes:

Responding to Literature

People read for many reasons. In the course of daily affairs, they read signs, labels, price tags, recipes, or directions for assembling a piece of furniture or a toy. They read newspapers to learn about national, international, and local events. They might read magazines to learn about important issues, celebrities, political figures, and biographical details about significant persons. Sometimes they might read to pass the time, or to take their minds off pressing problems or situations. Also, people regularly read out of necessity—in school and in their work. They study for examinations in chemistry, biology, psychology, and political science. They go over noun paradigms and verb forms in a foreign language. They read to acquire knowledge in many areas, and they read to learn new skills, new information, and new ways to do their jobs better.

But, aside from incidental, leisurely, and obligatory reading, many people turn to imaginative literature, which they read because they like it and find it interesting. Even if they don't equally like all the things that they read, they nevertheless enjoy reading and usually pick out authors and types of literature that they like.

It is therefore worth considering those qualities of imaginative literature that at the primary level produce responses of pleasure (and also of displeasure). You either like or dislike a story, poem, or play. If you say no more than this, however, you have not said much. Analyzing and explaining your likes and dislikes requires you to describe the reasons for your responses. The goal should be to form your responses as judgments, which are usually *informed* and *informative,* rather than as simple reactions, which may be *uninformed* and *unexplained.*

Sometimes a reader's first responses are that a story or poem is either "okay" or "boring." These reactions usually mask an incomplete and superficial first reading. They are neither informative nor informed. As you study most works, however, you will be drawn into them and become *interested* and *involved.* To be interested in a poem, play, or story is to be taken into it emotionally; to be involved suggests that your emotions become almost wrapped up in the characters, problems, outcomes, ideas, and expressions of opinion and emotion. Both "interest" and "involvement" describe genuine responses to reading. Once you get interested and involved, your reading ceases to be a task or an assignment and grows into a pleasure.

☙ USE YOUR JOURNAL TO RECORD YOUR RESPONSES

No one can tell you what you should or should not like, for liking is your own concern. While your reading is still fresh, therefore, you should use your journal to record your responses to a work in addition to your observations about it. Be frank in your judgment. Write down what you like or dislike, and explain the reasons for your responses, even if these are brief and incomplete. If, after later thought and fuller understanding, you change or modify your impressions, write down these changes too. Here is a journal entry that explains a favorable response to Guy de Maupassant's "The Necklace":

> I like "The Necklace" because of the surprise ending. It isn't that I like Mathilde's bad luck, but I like the way Maupassant hides the most important fact in the story until the end. Mathilde does all that work and sacrifice for no reason at all, and the surprise ending makes this point strongly.

This paragraph could be developed as part of an essay. It is a clear statement of liking, followed by references to likable things in the story. This response pattern, which can be simply phrased as "I like [dislike] this work because . . . ," is a useful way to begin journal entries because it always requires an explanation of responses. If at first you cannot explain the causes of your responses, at least make a brief list of the things you like or dislike. If you write nothing, you will probably forget your reactions. Recovering them later, either for discussion or writing, will be difficult.

❦ STATE REASONS FOR YOUR FAVORABLE RESPONSES

Usually you can equate your interest in a work with liking it. You can be more specific about favorable responses by citing one or more of the following:

- You like and admire the characters and what they do and stand for. You get involved with them. When they are in danger, you are concerned; when they succeed, you are happy; when they speak, you like what they say.
- After you have read the last word in a story or play, you are sorry to part with these characters and wish that there were more to read about them and their activities.
- Even if you do not particularly like a character or the characters, you are nevertheless interested in the reasons for and outcomes of their actions.
- You get so interested and involved in the actions or ideas in the work that you do not want to put the work down until you have finished it.
- You like to follow the pattern of action or the development of the author's thoughts, so that you respond with appreciation upon finishing the work.
- You find that reading enables you to relax or to take your mind off a problem or a pressing responsibility.
- You learn something new—something you had never before known or thought about human beings and their ways of handling their problems.
- You learn about customs and ways of life in different places and times.
- You gain new insights into aspects of life that you thought you already understood.
- You feel happy or thrilled because of reading the work.
- You are amused, and you laugh often as you read.
- You like the author's ways of describing scenes, actions, ideas, and feelings.
- You find that many of the expressions are remarkable and beautiful, and are therefore worth remembering.

❦ STATE REASONS FOR YOUR UNFAVORABLE RESPONSES

Although so far we have dismissed *okay* and *boring* and have stressed *interest*, *involvement*, and *liking*, it is important to know that disliking all or part of a work is normal and acceptable. You do not need to hide this response. Here, for example, are two short journal responses expressing dislike for Maupassant's "The Necklace":

1. I do not like "The Necklace" because Mathilde seems spoiled, and I don't think she is worth reading about.

2. "The Necklace" is not an adventure story, and I like reading only adventure stories.

These are both legitimate responses because they are based on a clear standard of judgment. The first response stems from a distaste for one of the main character's unlikable traits, and the second from a preference for rapidly moving stories that evoke interest in the dangers that main characters face and overcome.

Here is a paragraph-length journal entry that might be developed from the first response. Notice that the reasons for dislike are explained. They would need only slightly more development for use in an essay:

> I dislike "The Necklace" because Mathilde seems spoiled, and I don't think she is worth reading about. She is a phony. She nags her husband because he is not rich. She never tells the truth. I dislike her for hurrying away from the party because she is afraid of being seen in her shabby coat. She is foolish and dishonest for not telling Jeanne Forrestier about losing the necklace. It's true that she works hard to pay the debt, but she also puts her husband through ten years of hardship. If Mathilde had faced facts, she might have had a better life. I do not like her and cannot like the story because of her.

As long as you include reasons for your dislike, as in the list and in the paragraph, you can use them again in considering the story more fully, when you will surely also expand thoughts, include new details, pick new topics for development as paragraphs, and otherwise modify your journal entry. You might even change your mind. However, even if you do not, it is better to record your original responses and reasons honestly than to force yourself to say you like a story that you do not like.

Try to Put Dislikes into a Larger Context

Although it is important to be honest about disliking a work, it is more important to broaden your perspective and expand your taste. For example, a dislike based on the preference for only mystery or adventure stories, if generally applied, would cause a person to dislike most works of literature. This attitude seems unnecessarily self-limiting.

If negative responses are put in a larger context, it is possible to expand the capacity to like and appreciate good literature. For instance, some readers might be preoccupied with their own concerns and therefore be uninterested in remote or "irrelevant" literary figures. However, if by reading about literary characters, they can gain insight into general problems of life, and therefore their own concerns, they can find something to like in just about any work. Other readers might like sports and therefore not read anything but the daily sports pages. What probably interests them about sports is competition, however, so if they can follow the *competition* or *conflict* in a literary work, they will have discovered something to like in that work.

As an example, let us consider again the dislike based on a preference for adventure stories, and see whether this preference can be widened. Here are some reasons for liking adventures:

1. Adventure has fast action.
2. It has danger and tension, and therefore interest.
3. It has daring, active, and successful characters.
4. It has obstacles that the characters work hard to overcome.

No one could claim that the first three points apply to "The Necklace," but the fourth point is promising. Mathilde, the major character, works hard to overcome an obstacle: She pitches in to help her husband pay the large debt. If you like adventures because the characters try to gain worthy goals, then you can also like "The Necklace" for the same reason. The principle here is clear: If a reason for liking a favorite work or type of work can be found in another work, then there is reason to like that new work.

The following paragraph shows a possible application of this "bridging" process of extending preferences. (The sample essay [page 50] is also developed along these lines.)

> I usually like only adventure stories, and therefore I disliked "The Necklace" at first because it is not adventure. But one of my reasons for liking adventure is that the characters work hard to overcome difficult obstacles, like finding buried treasure or exploring new places. Mathilde, Maupassant's main character in "The Necklace," also works hard to overcome an obstacle—helping to pay back the money and interest for the borrowed 18,000 francs used as part of the payment for the replacement necklace. I like adventure characters because they stick to things and win out. I see the same toughness in Mathilde. Her problems get more interesting as the story moves on after a slow beginning. I came to like the story.

The principle of "bridging" from like to like is worth restating: *If a reason for liking a favorite work or type of work can be found in another work, then there is reason to like that new work.* A person who adapts to new reading in this open-minded way can redefine dislikes, no matter how slowly, and may consequently expand the ability to like and appreciate many kinds of literature.

An equally open-minded way to develop understanding and widen taste is to put dislikes in the following light: An author's creation of an *unlikable* character, situation, attitude, or expression may be deliberate. Your dislike might then result from the author's *intentions*. A first task of study, therefore, is to understand and explain the intention or plan. As you put the plan into your own words, you may find that you can like a work with unlikable things in it. Here is a paragraph that traces this pattern of thinking, based again on "The Necklace":

> Maupassant apparently wants the reader to dislike Mathilde, and I do. At first, he shows her being unrealistic and spoiled. She lies to everyone and nags her husband. Her rushing away from the party so that no one can see her shabby coat is a form of lying. But I like the story itself because Maupassant makes another kind of point. He does not hide her bad qualities, but makes it clear that she herself is the cause of her trouble. If people like Mathilde never face the truth, they will get into bad situations. This is a good point, and I like the way Maupassant makes it. The entire story is therefore worth liking even though I still do not like Mathilde.

Both of these "bridging" analyses are consistent with the original negative reactions. In the first paragraph, the writer applies one of his principles of liking to include "The Necklace." In the second, the writer considers her initial dislike in the context of the work, and discovers a basis for liking the story as a whole while still disliking the main character. The main concern in both responses is to keep an open mind despite initial dislike and then to see whether the unfavorable response can be more fully and broadly considered.

However, if you decide that your dislike overbalances any reasons you can find for liking, then you should explain your dislike. As long as you relate your response to the work accurately and measure it by a clear standard of judgment, your dislike of even a commonly liked work is not unacceptable. The important issue is not so much that you like or dislike a particular work *but that you develop your own abilities to analyze and express your ideas.*

₸ WRITING ABOUT YOUR RESPONSES OF LIKES OR DISLIKES

In writing about your responses, rely on your first informed reactions to the work you have read. Because at least a little time will have elapsed between your first reading and your gathering of materials to begin writing, you can use your journal observations to guide you in your prewriting as you reconstruct your initial informed reactions to the work. Develop your essay by stressing those characters, incidents, thoughts, and emotions that interest (or do not interest) you.

As with many essays, you will be challenged to connect details from the work to your central idea. That is, once you have begun by stating that you like (or dislike) the story, you might forget to highlight this response as you enumerate details. Therefore, you need to stress your involvement in the work. You can show your attitudes by indicating approval (or disapproval), by commenting favorably (or unfavorably) on the details, by indicating things that seem new (or shopworn) and particularly instructive (or wrong), and by giving assent to (or dissent from) ideas or expressions of feeling.

Organize Your Essay about Likes or Dislikes

INTRODUCTION.   Briefly describe the conditions that influence your response. Your central idea should be why you like or dislike the work. Your thesis sentence should include the major causes of your response, which are to be developed in the body.

BODY.   The most common approach is to consider specific details that you like or dislike. The list on page 45 may help you articulate your responses. For example, you admired a particular character, or you got so interested in a story that you could not put it down, or you liked a particular passage in a poem or play, or you felt thrilled as you finished reading the work. Also, you may wish to develop a major idea, a fresh insight, or a particular outcome, as in the sample paragraph on page 44, which shows a surprise ending as the cause of a favorable response.

A second approach is to explain any changes in your responses about the work (i.e., negative to positive and vice versa). This approach requires that you isolate the causes of the change, but it does *not* require you to retell the story from beginning to end.

1. One way to deal with such a change—the "bridge" method of transferring preference from one type of work to another—is shown in the sample essay (page 50).
2. Another way is to explain a change in terms of a new awareness or understanding that you did not have on a first reading. Thus, for example, your first response to Poe's "The Cask of Amontillado" (page 345) might be unfavorable or neutral because the story seems unnecessarily sensational and lurid. But further consideration might lead you to discover new insights that change your mind, such as the needs to overcome personal pride and to stop minor resentments from growing and festering. Your essay would then explain how these new insights have caused you to like the story.

CONCLUSION.   Here you might summarize the reasons for your major response. You might also face any issues brought up by a change or modification of your first reactions. For example, if you have always held certain assumptions about your taste but like the work despite these assumptions, you may wish to talk about your own change or development. This topic is personal, but in an essay about your personal responses, discovery about yourself is legitimate and worthy.

Sample Essay

Some Reasons for Liking Maupassant's "The Necklace"°

---

[1]
To me, the most likable kind of reading is adventure. There are many reasons for my preference, but an important one is that adventure characters work hard to overcome obstacles. Because Guy de Maupassant's "The Necklace" is not adventure, I did not like it at first. But in one respect the story is <u>like</u> adventure: The major character, Mathilde Loisel, works hard with her husband for ten years to overcome a difficult obstacle. <u>Thus, because Mathilde does what adventure characters also do, the story is likable.</u>* <u>Mathilde's appeal results from her hard work, strong character, and sad fate, and also from the way our view of her changes.</u>†

[2]
<u>Mathilde's hard work makes her seem good.</u> Once she and her husband are faced with the huge debt of 18,000 francs, she works like a slave to pay it back. She gives up her servant and moves to a cheaper place. She does the household drudgery, wears cheap clothes, and haggles with shopkeepers. Just like the characters in adventure stories who do hard and unpleasant things, she does what she has to, and this makes her admirable.

[3]
<u>Her strong character shows her endurance, a likable trait.</u> At first she is nagging and fussy, and she always dreams about wealth and tells lies, but she changes and gets better. She recognizes her blame in losing the necklace, and she has the toughness to help her husband redeem the debt. She sacrifices "heroically" (paragraph 98) by giving up her comfortable way of life, even though in the process she also loses her youth and beauty. Her jobs are not the exotic and glamorous ones of adventure stories, but her force of character makes her as likable as an adventure heroine.

[4]
<u>Her sad fate also makes her likable.</u> In adventure stories the characters often suffer as they do their jobs. Mathilde also suffers, but in a different way, because her suffering is permanent while the hardships of adventure characters are temporary. This fact makes her especially pitiable because all her sacrifices are not necessary. This unfairness invites the reader to take her side.

[5]
<u>The most important quality promoting admiration is the way in which Maupassant shifts our view of Mathilde.</u> As she goes deeper into her hard life, Maupassant stresses her work and not the innermost thoughts he reveals at the beginning. In other words, the view into her character at the start, when she dreams about wealth, invites dislike; but the focus at the end is on her achievements, with never a complaint—even though she still has golden memories, as the narrator tells us:

°See pages 5–12 for this story.
*Central idea.
†Thesis sentence.

[5]   But sometimes, when her husband was at work, she sat down near the window, and she dreamed of that evening so long ago, of that party, where she had been so beautiful and so admired. (paragraph 104)

A major quality of Maupassant's changed emphasis is that Mathilde's fond memories do not lead to anything unfortunate. His shift in focus, from Mathilde's dissatisfaction to her sharing of responsibility and sacrifice, encourages the reader to like her.

[6]   "The Necklace" is not an adventure story, but Mathilde has some of the good qualities of adventure characters. Also, the surprise revelation that the lost necklace was false is an unforgettable twist, and this makes her more deserving than she seems at first. Maupassant has arranged the story so that the reader finally admires Mathilde. "The Necklace" is a skillful and likable story.

❦ COMMENTARY ON THE ESSAY

This essay demonstrates how a reader may develop appreciation by transferring a preference for one type of work to a work that does not belong to the type. In the essay, the "bridge" is an already established taste for adventure stories, and the grounds for liking "The Necklace" are that Mathilde, the main character, shares the admirable qualities of adventure heroes and heroines.

In paragraph 1, the introduction, the grounds for transferring preferences are established. Paragraph 2 deals with Mathilde's capacity to work hard, and paragraph 3 considers the equally admirable quality of endurance. The fourth paragraph describes how Mathilde's condition evokes sympathy and pity. These paragraphs hence explain the story's appeal by asserting that the main character is similar to admirable characters from works of adventure.

The fifth paragraph shows that Maupassant, as the story unfolds, alters the reader's perceptions of Mathilde from bad to good. For this reason paragraph 5 marks a new direction from paragraphs 2, 3, and 4: It moves away from the topic material itself—Mathide's character—to Maupassant's *technique* in handling the topic material.

Paragraph 6, the conclusion, restates the comparison and also introduces the surprise ending as an additional reason for liking "The Necklace." With the body and conclusion together, therefore, the essay establishes five separate reasons for approval. Three of these, derived directly from the main character, constitute the major grounds for liking the story, and two are related to Maupassant's techniques as an author.

Throughout the essay, the central idea is brought out in words and expressions such as "likable," "Mathilde's appeal," "strong character," "she does what she has to," "pitiable," and "take her side." Many of these expressions were first made in the writer's journal; and, mixed as they are with details from the story, they make for continuity. It is this thematic development, together with details from the story as supporting evidence, that shows how an essay on the responses of liking and disliking may be both informed and informative.

👣 SPECIAL WRITING TOPICS FOR STUDYING PERSONAL RESPONSES (LIKES AND DISLIKES)

1. In the last six months, what literary works have you read that you liked or disliked? Write a brief essay explaining your reasons for your positive or negative responses. To illustrate your points, you may make liberal references to these works, and, in addition, you may refer to films or TV shows that you have recently seen.

2. Some readers dislike Poe's story "The Cask of Amontillado" because of the speaker's cruel act of revenge against Fortunato. Respond to this reaction to the work.

3. Consider the sample likes/dislikes essay on Maupassant's "The Necklace." Do you accept the arguments in the essay? What other details and arguments can you think of for either liking or disliking the story?

4. For what reasons should a reader like Shakespeare's Sonnet 116: "Let Me Not to the Marriage of True Minds"?

5. Explain why a negative response to Glaspell's *Trifles* is not justified by what happens in the play.

6. How can a person like Hawthorne's "Young Goodman Brown" even if that same person dislikes what happens to Brown's character and outlook?

7. Write contrasting paragraphs about a character (whom you know or about whom you have read). In the first paragraph, try to make your reader like the character. In the second, try to make your reader dislike the character. Explain how you tried to create these opposite responses. How fair would it be for a reader to dislike your negative paragraph even though your hostile portrait is successful?

chapter 3

Writing About Character:
The People in Literature

Writers of fiction create narratives that enhance and deepen our understanding of human character and human life. In our own day, under the influences of pioneers like Freud, Jung, and Skinner, the science of psychology has influenced both the creation and study of literature. It is well known that Freud buttressed some of his psychological conclusions by referring to literary works, especially plays by Shakespeare. Widely known films such as *Spellbound, The Snake Pit,* and *Final Analysis* have popularized the relationships between literary character and psychology. Without doubt, the presentation and understanding of character is a major aim of literature.

In literature, a **character** may be defined as a verbal representation of a human being. Through action, speech, description, and commentary, authors portray characters who are worth caring about, rooting for, and even loving, although there are also characters you may laugh at, dislike, or even hate.

In a story or play emphasizing a major character, you may expect that each action or speech, no matter how small, is part of a total presentation of that complex combination of both the inner and the outer self that constitutes a human being. Whereas in life things may "just happen," in literature all actions, interactions, speeches, and observations are deliberate. Thus, you read about important actions like a long period of work and sacrifice (Maupassant's "The Necklace"), the exciting discovery of a previously unknown literary work (Keats's "On First Looking Into Chapman's Homer"), an act of vengeance (Poe's "The Cask of Amontillado"), or a young man's fanciful but poignant dream of freedom (Bierce's "An Occurrence at Owl Creek Bridge"). By making such actions interesting, authors help you understand and appreciate not only their major characters but also life itself.

✤ CHARACTER TRAITS

In studying a literary character, try to determine the character's outstanding traits. A **trait** is a quality of mind or habitual mode of behavior, such as never repaying borrowed money, avoiding eye contact, or always thinking oneself the center of attention. Sometimes, of course, the traits we encounter are minor and therefore negligible, but often a trait may be a person's *primary* characteristic (not only in fiction but also in life). Thus, characters may be ambitious or lazy, serene or anxious, aggressive or fearful, thoughtful or inconsiderate, open or secretive, confident or self-doubting, kind or cruel, quiet or noisy, visionary or practical, careful or careless, impartial or biased, straightforward or underhanded, "winners" or "losers," and so on.

With this sort of list, to which you may add at will, you can analyze and develop conclusions about character. For example, Mathilde in Maupassant's "The Necklace" (pages 5–12) indulges in dreams of unattainable wealth and comfort, and is so swept up in her visions that she scorns her comparatively good life with her reliable but dull husband. It is fair to say that this aversion to reality is her major trait. It is also a major weakness, because Maupassant shows how her dream life harms her real life. By contrast, the speaker of Lowell's poem "Patterns" considers the destruction of her hopes for happiness because of the news that her fiancé has been killed in war. Because she faces her difficulties directly, she exhibits strength. By similarly analyzing the actions, speeches, and thoughts of the characters you encounter, you can also draw conclusions about their qualities and strengths.

Distinguish Between Circumstances and Character Traits

When you study a fictional person, distinguish between circumstances and character, for circumstances have value *only if they demonstrate important traits*. Thus, if our friend Sam wins a lottery, let us congratulate him on his luck; but the win does not say much about his *character*—not much, that is, unless we also learn that he has been spending hundreds of dollars each week for lottery tickets. In other words, making the effort to win a lottery *is* a character trait, but winning (or losing) *is not*.

Or, let us suppose that an author stresses the neatness of one character and the sloppiness of another. If you accept the premise that people care for their appearance according to choice—and that choices develop from character—you can use these details to draw conclusions about a person's self-esteem or the lack of it. In short, when reading about characters in literature, look beyond circumstances, actions, and appearances, and *determine what these things show about character*. Always try to get from the outside to the inside, for it is the *internal* quality that determines the *external* behavior.

☙ HOW AUTHORS DISCLOSE CHARACTER IN LITERATURE

Authors use five ways to make their characters live. Remember that you must use your own knowledge and experience to make judgments about the qualities of the characters being revealed.

1. *Actions by characters reveal their natures.* What characters *do* is our best clue to understanding what they *are*. For example, the character Farquhar in Bierce's "An Occurrence at Owl Creek Bridge" tries to sabotage the Union army's railway system near his country estate. This action shows both loyalty (to the Confederate cause) and personal bravery, despite the fact that he is caught. Actions may also signal qualities of character such as naiveté, weakness, deceit, and subterfuge, and they may also demonstrate a character's new awareness or the development of particular character strengths. Often characters are unaware of the meanings and implications of their actions. Smirnov in Chekhov's *The Bear*, for example, would be a fool to teach Mrs. Popov to use her dueling pistol, because she has threatened to kill him with it. His change is his sudden awareness that he loves her, and his cooperative and potentially self-destructive (and comic) action shows that his loving nature has overwhelmed his instinct for self-preservation. Similarly, a strong inner conflict is seen in the two women in Glaspell's *Trifles*. They have a theoretical obligation to the law, but they recognize a stronger personal obligation to the accused killer, Minnie. Hence their silence about the incriminating evidence that they uncover is an action showing their roundness and dynamism.

2. *The author's descriptions, both personal and environmental, tell us about characters.* Appearance and environment reveal much about a character's social and economic status, and they also tell us about character traits. Mathilde in Maupassant's "The Necklace" dreams about wealth and unlimited purchase power. Although her unrealizable desires ultimately destroy her way of life, they also cause her character strength to emerge. The descriptions of country folkways in Hardy's "The Three Strangers" are independently interesting and unique, but they also make plain the personal loyalty of the peasants and their social stability and solidity.

3. *What characters say—dramatic statements and thoughts—reveals what they are like.* Although the speeches of most characters are functional—essential to keep the action moving along—they provide material from which you may draw conclusions. When the second traveler of "Young Goodman Brown" speaks, for example, he reveals his devious and deceptive nature even though ostensibly he appears friendly. The lawmen in *Trifles* speak straightforwardly and directly, and these speeches suggest that their characters are similarly orderly. Their constant ridicule of the two women, however, indicates their limitations.

   Often, characters use speech to hide their motives, though we as readers should see through such a ploy. The narrator Montresor in Poe's "The Cask of Amontillado," for example, is a vengeful schemer, and we conclude this much from his indirect and manipulative language to the equally unpleasant but gullible Fortunato. To Fortunato, Montresor seems friendly and sociable, but to us, he is lurid and demonic.

4. *We learn about characters from what others say about them.* By studying what characters say about each other, you can often enhance your understanding of the character being discussed. In this regard, Glaspell's *Trifles* is unique because the main character, Minnie, is the center of attention and discussion even though she does not appear in the drama at all. Everything we learn about her is gained from the dialogue (and the actions) of those characters who are actually onstage.

   Ironically, speeches often indicate something other than what the speakers intend, perhaps because of prejudice, stupidity, or foolishness. Thus the sister in O'Connor's "First Confession" tells about her brother's violent outburst against their grandmother, but in effect she describes the boy's individuality just as she also discloses her own spitefulness.

5. *The author, speaking as a storyteller or an observer, may tell us about characters.* What the author, speaking as a work's authorial voice, says about a character is usually accurate, and the authorial voice can be accepted factually. However, when the authorial voice *interprets* actions and characteristics, as in Hawthorne's "Young Goodman Brown," the author himself or herself assumes the role of a reader or critic, and any opinions may be questioned. For this reason, authors frequently avoid interpretations and devote their skill to arranging events and speeches so that readers can draw their own conclusions.

☞ TYPES OF CHARACTERS: ROUND AND FLAT

No writer can present an entire life history of a protagonist, nor can each character in a story get "equal time" for development. Accordingly, some characters grow to be full and alive, while others remain shadowy. The British novelist and critic E. M. Forster, in his critical work *Aspects of the Novel*, calls the two major types "round" and "flat."

1. Round Characters Undergo Change

The basic trait of **round characters** is that authors present enough detail about them to render them full, lifelike, and memorable. Their roundness is characterized by both individuality and unpredictability. A complementary quality about round characters is therefore that they are **dynamic**. That is, they *recognize, change with,* or *adjust to* circumstances. Such changes may be shown in (1) an action or actions, (2) the realization of new strength and therefore the affirmation of previous decisions, (3) the acceptance of a new condition and the need for making changes, or (4) the discovery of unrecognized truths. For example, Minnie Wright, in Glaspell's *Trifles,* is dynamic. We learn that as a young woman, she was happy and musical, but that she has been deprived and blighted by her thirty-year marriage. Finally, however, a particularly cruel action by her husband so enrages her that she breaks out of her subservient role and commits an act of violence. In short, her action shows her as a dynamic character capable of radical change.

Because a round character usually plays a major role in a story, he or she is often called the **hero** or **heroine.** Some round characters are not particularly heroic, however, so it is preferable to use the more neutral word **protagonist** (the "first actor"). The protagonist is central to the action, moves against an **antagonist** (the "opposing actor"), and exhibits the ability to adapt to new circumstances.

2. Flat Characters Stay the Same

Unlike round characters, **flat characters** do not grow. They remain the same because they are stupid or insensitive or because they lack knowledge or insight. They end where they begin and thus are **static,** not dynamic. Flat characters are not worthless, however, for they highlight the development of the round characters, as with the lawmen in Glaspell's *Trifles.* Usually, flat characters are minor (e.g., relatives, acquaintances, functionaries), although not all minor characters are necessarily flat.

Sometimes flat characters are prominent in certain types of literature, such as cowboy, police, and detective stories, where the focus is less on character than on performance. Such characters might be lively and engaging, even though they do not develop or change. They must be strong, tough, and clever enough to perform recurring tasks such as solving a crime, overcoming a villain, or finding a treasure. The term **stock character** refers to characters in these repeating situations. To the degree that stock characters have many common traits, they are **representative** of their class or group. Such characters, with variations in names, ages, and sexes, have been constant in literature since the ancient Greeks. Some regular stock characters are the insensitive father, the interfering mother, the sassy younger sister or brother, the greedy politician, the resourceful cowboy or detective, the overbearing or henpecked husband, the submissive or nagging wife, the angry police captain, the lovable drunk, and the town do-gooder.

Stock characters stay flat as long as they do no more than perform their roles and exhibit conventional and unindividual traits. When they possess no attitudes except those of their class, they are called **stereotype** characters, because they all seem to have been cast in the same mold.

When authors bring characters into focus, however, no matter what roles they perform, the characters emerge from flatness and move into roundness. For example, at first the major character in Mansfield's "Miss Brill" seems quite dull. She almost literally has no life, and as a character she is flat. But the story demonstrates that she protects herself with remarkable imagination and creativity. She is, finally, a round character. Minnie Wright in *Trifles*, who has led an ordinary, dull, flat life during her thirty-year marriage, dynamically breaks out of that role. In sum, the ability to grow and develop and to be altered by circumstances makes characters round and dynamic; the absence of these traits makes characters flat and static.

ᵒ REALITY AND PROBABILITY: VERISIMILITUDE

Characters in fiction should be true to life. Therefore their actions, statements, and thoughts must all be what human beings are *likely* to do, say, and think under the conditions presented in the literary work. This is the standard of **verisimilitude, probability,** or **plausibility.** One may readily admit that there are people *in life* who perform tasks or exhibit characteristics that are difficult or seemingly impossible (such as always leading the team to victory, always getting A+'s on every test, always being cheerful and helpful, or always understanding the needs of others). However, such characters *in fiction* would not be true to life because they do not fit within *normal* or *usual* behavior.

You should therefore distinguish between what characters may *possibly* do and what they *most frequently* or *most usually* do. Thus, in "The Necklace," it is possible that Mathilde could be truthful and tell her friend Jeanne Forrestier about the lost necklace. In light of her pride and sense of self-respect, however, it is more in character for her and her husband to hide the loss, borrow money for a replacement, and endure the consequences for ten years. Granted the possibilities of the story (either self-sacrifice or the admission of a fault), the decision she makes with her husband is the more *probable* one.

Nevertheless, probability does not rule out surprise or even exaggeration. The sudden and seemingly impossible changes concluding *The Bear*, for example, are not improbable because Chekhov early in the play shows that both Mrs. Popov and Smirnov are emotional, somewhat foolish, and impulsive. Even in the face of their unpredictable embraces closing the play, these qualities of character dominate their lives. For such individuals, surprise may be accepted as a probable condition of life.

There are many ways of rendering probability in character. Works that attempt to mirror life—realistic, naturalistic, or "slice of life" stories like Hardy's "The Three Strangers"—set up a pattern of everyday probability. Less realistic conditions establish different frameworks of probability, in which characters are *expected* to be unusual. Such an example is Hawthorne's "Young Goodman Brown." Because a major way of explaining this story is that Brown is having a nightmarish psychotic trance, his bizarre and unnatural responses are probable. Equally probable is the way the doctors explain Louise Mallard's sudden death at the end of "The Story of an Hour," even though their smug analysis is totally (and comically) wrong.

You might also encounter works containing *supernatural* figures such as the second traveler in "Young Goodman Brown." You may wonder whether such characters are probable or improbable. Usually, gods and goddesses embody qualities of the best and most moral human beings, and devils like Hawthorne's guide take on attributes of the worst. However, you might remember that the devil is often given dashing and engaging qualities so that he can deceive gullible sinners and lead them into hell. The friendliness of Brown's guide is therefore not an improbable trait. In judging characters of this or any other type, your best criteria are probability, consistency, and believability.

☙ WRITING ABOUT CHARACTER

Usually your topic will be a major character in a story or drama, although you might also study one or more minor characters. After your customary overview, begin taking notes. List as many traits as you can, and also determine how the author presents details about the character through actions, appearance, speeches, comments by others, or authorial explanations. If you discover unusual traits, determine what they show. The following suggestions and questions will help you get started.

Raise Questions to Discover Ideas

- Who is the major character? What do you learn about this character from his or her own actions and speeches? From the speeches and actions of other characters? How else do you learn about the character?

- How important is the character to the work's principal action? Which characters oppose the major character? How do the major character and the opposing character(s) interact? What effects do these interactions create?
- What actions bring out important traits of the main character? To what degree is the character creating or just responding to events?
- Characterize the main character's actions: Are they good or bad, intelligent or stupid, deliberate or spontaneous? How do they help you understand the protagonist?
- Describe and explain the traits, both major and minor, of the character you plan to discuss. To what extent do the traits permit you to judge the character? What is your judgment?
- What descriptions (if any) of the character's appearance do you discover in the story? What does the appearance demonstrate about the character?
- In what ways is the character's major trait a strength—or a weakness? As the story progresses, to what degree does the trait become more (or less) prominent?
- Is the character round and dynamic? How does the character recognize, change with, or adjust to circumstances?
- If the character you are analyzing is flat or static, what function does he or she perform in the story (for example, by doing a task or by bringing out qualities of the major character)?
- If the character is a stereotype, to what type does he or she belong? To what degree does the character stay in the stereotypical role or rise above it? How?
- What do any of the other characters do, say, or think to give you insight into the character you are analyzing? What does the character say or think about himself or herself? What does the storyteller or narrator say? How valid are their comments and insights? How helpful in providing insights into the character?
- Is the character lifelike or unreal? Consistent or inconsistent? Believable or not believable?

Organize Your Essay About Character

INTRODUCTION. Identify the character you are studying, and refer to noteworthy problems in determining this character's qualities. Use your central idea and thesis sentence to create the form for the body of your essay.

BODY. Consider one of the following approaches to organize your ideas and form the basis for your essay:

1. **Plan to develop a central trait or major characteristic,** such as "a single-minded dedication to vengeance" (Montresor of "The Cask of Amontillado") or "the habit of seeing the world only on one's own terms" (Miss Brill of "Miss Brill"). This kind of structure shows how the work embodies the trait. For example, in one part a trait may be brought out through speeches that characters

make about the major character (as at the end of Mansfield's "Miss Brill"), and in another part through that character's own speeches and actions. Studying the trait thus enables you to focus on the differing ways in which the author presents the character, and it also enables you to focus on separate parts of the work.

2. **Plan to explain a character's growth or change.** This type of essay describes a character's traits at the work's beginning and then analyzes changes or developments. *It is important to stress the actual alterations as they emerge, but at the same time to avoid retelling the major actions in the work.* Additionally, you should not only describe the changing traits but also analyze how they are brought out within the work (such as the dream of Goodman Brown, or Minnie Wright's long ordeal).

3. **Plan to organize your essay around central actions, objects, or quotations that reveal primary characteristics.** Key incidents may stand out, along with objects closely associated with the character being analyzed. There may be important quotations spoken by the character or by someone else in the work. Show how such elements serve as signposts or guides to understanding the character. (See the sample essay for an illustration of this type of development.)

4. **Plan to develop qualities of a flat character or characters.** If the character is flat (such as the men in *Trifles* or the servants in *The Bear*), you might develop topics such as the function and relative significance of the character, the group that the character represents, the relationship of the flat character to the round ones, the importance of this relationship, and any additional qualities or traits. For a flat character, you should explain the circumstances or defects that keep the character from being round, and the importance of these shortcomings in the author's presentation of character.

CONCLUSION. In your conclusion, show how the character's traits are related to the work as a whole. If the person was good but came to a bad end, does this misfortune make him or her seem especially worthy? If the person suffers, does this fact suggest any attitudes about the class or type of which he or she is a part? Or does it illustrate the author's general view of human life? Or both? Do the characteristics explain why the person helps or hinders other characters? How does your essay help to clear up first-reading misunderstandings?

Sample Essay

The Character of Minnie Wright in Glaspell's Trifles°

[1]   Minnie Wright is Susan Glaspell's major character in <u>Trifles</u>. We learn about her, however, not from seeing and hearing her, for she is not a speaking or an acting character in the play, but rather from the secondhand evidence provided by the play's actual characters. Lewis Hale, a neighboring farmer, tells about Minnie's behavior after the body of her husband, John, was found strangled. Mrs. Hale, Hale's wife, tells about Minnie's young womanhood and about how she became alienated from her nearest neighbors because of John's stingy and unfriendly ways. Both Mrs. Hale and Mrs. Peters, the Sheriff's wife, make observations about Minnie based on the condition of her kitchen. <u>From this information we get a full portrait of Minnie, who has changed from passivity to destructive assertiveness.</u>* <u>Her change in character is indicated by her clothing, her dead canary, and her unfinished patchwork quilt.</u>†

[2]   <u>The clothes that Minnie has worn in the past and in the present indicate her character as a person of charm who has withered under neglect and contempt.</u> Martha mentions Minnie's attractive and colorful dresses as a young woman, even recalling a "white dress with blue ribbons" (speech 134). Martha also recalls that Minnie, when young, was "sweet and pretty, but kind of timid and—fluttery" (speech 107). In the light of these recollections, Martha observes that Minnie had changed, and changed for the worse, during her twenty years of marriage with John Wright, who is characterized as a "raw wind that gets to the bone" (speech 104). As more evidence for Minnie's acceptance of her drab life, Mrs. Peters says that Minnie asks for no more than an apron and shawl when under arrest in the sheriff's home. This modest clothing, as contrasted to the colorful dresses of her youth, suggests her suppression of spirit.

[3]   <u>The end of this suppression of spirit and also the emergence of Minnie's rage is shown by the discovery of her dead canary.</u> We learn that Minnie, who when young had been in love with music, has endured her cheerless farm home for thirty years. During this time her husband's contempt has made her life solitary, cheerless, unmusical, and depressingly impoverished. But her buying the canary (speech 87) suggests the reemergence of her love of song, just as it also suggests her growth toward self-assertion. That her husband wrings the bird's neck may thus be seen as the cause not only of her immediate sorrow (shown by the dead bird in a "pretty box" (speech 109) but also of the anger that marks her change from a stock, obedient wife to a person angry enough to kill.

[4]   <u>Like her love of song, her unfinished quilt indicates her creativity.</u> In thirty years on the farm, never having had children, she has nothing creative to do except for needlework like the quilt. Mrs. Hale comments on the beauty of

°See pages 375–85 for this play.
*Central idea.
†Thesis sentence.

[4] Minnie's log-cabin design (speech 72), and a stage direction draws attention to the pieces in the sewing basket (speech 71 S.D.). The inference is that even though Minnie's life has been bleak, she has been able to indulge her characteristic love of color and form—and also of warmth, granted the purpose of a quilt.

Ironically, the quilt also shows Minnie's creativity in the murder of her husband. Both Mrs. Hale and Mrs. Peters interpret the breakdown of her stitching on the quilt as signs of distress about the dead canary and also of her nervousness in planning revenge. Further, even though nowhere in the play is it said that John is strangled with a quilting knot, no other conclusion is possible. Both Mrs. Hale and Mrs. Peters agree that Minnie probably intended to knot the quilt rather than sew it in a quilt stitch, and Glaspell pointedly causes the men to learn this detail also, even though they scoff at it and ignore

[5] it. In other words, we learn that Minnie's only outlet for creativity—needlework—has enabled her to perform the murder in the only way she can, by strangling John with a slip-proof quilting knot. Even though her plan for the murder is deliberate (Mrs. Peters reports that the arrangement of the rope was "crafty" [speech 65]), Minnie is not cold or remorseless. Her passivity after the crime demonstrates that planning to evade guilt, beyond simple denial, is not in her character. She is not so diabolically creative that she plans or even understands the irony of strangling her husband (he killed the bird by wringing its neck). Glaspell, however, makes the irony plain.

It is important to emphasize again that we learn about Minnie from others. Nevertheless, Minnie is fully realized, round, and poignant. For the greater part of her adult life, she has patiently accepted her drab and colorless marriage even though it is so cruelly different from her youthful expectations. In the dreary surroundings of the Wright farm, she suppresses her grudges, just

[6] as she suppresses her prettiness, colorfulness, and creativity. In short, she had been nothing more than a flat character. The killing of the canary, however, causes her to change and to destroy her husband in an assertive rejection of her stock role as the suffering wife. She is a patient woman whose patience finally reaches the breaking point.

☞ COMMENTARY ON THE ESSAY

The strategy of this essay is to use details from the play to support the central idea that Minnie Wright is a round, developing character. Hence the essay illustrates one of the types in the third approach described on page 61. Other plans of organization could also have been chosen, such as the qualities of acquiescence, fortitude, and potential for anger (first approach); the change in Minnie from submission to vengefulness (second approach); or the reported actions of Minnie's singing, knotting quilts, and sitting in the kitchen on the morning after the murder (a type of the third approach).

Because Minnie does not appear in the play but is described only in the words of the major characters, the introductory paragraph of the sample essay deals with the way we learn about her. The essay thus highlights how Glaspell uses methods 2 and 4 (see pages 55–56) as the ways of rendering the story's main character, while omitting methods 1, 3, and 5.

The body is developed through inferences made from details in the play, namely Minnie's clothing (paragraph 2), her canary (paragraph 3), and her quilt (paragraphs 4 and 5). The last paragraph summarizes a number of these details, and it also considers how Minnie transcends the stock qualities of her role as a farm wife and gains roundness as a result of this outbreak.

As a study in composition, paragraph 3 demonstrates how a specific character trait, together with related details, may contribute to the essay's central idea. The trait is Minnie's love of music (shown by her canary). The connecting details, selected from study notes, are the loss of music in her life, her isolation, her lack of pretty clothing, the contemptibility of her husband, and her grief when putting the dead bird into the box. In short, the paragraph weaves together enough material to show the relationship between Minnie's trait of loving music and the crisis of her developing anger—a change that marks her as a round character.

☙ SPECIAL WRITING TOPICS
FOR STUDYING CHARACTER

1. Compare the ways in which actions and speeches are used to bring out the character traits of Farquhar of "An Occurrence at Owl Creek Bridge" and of Montresor of "The Cask of Amontillado."

2. Write a brief essay comparing the changes or developments of two major or *round* characters in stories or plays included in Appendix C. You might deal with issues such as what the characters are like at the beginning; what conflicts they confront, deal with, or avoid; or what qualities are brought out that signal the changes or developments.

3. Compare the qualities and functions of two or more *flat* characters (e.g., the men in *Trifles* or the secondary characters in "The Story of an Hour"). How do they bring out qualities of the major characters? What do you discover about their own character traits?

4. Using Miss Brill ("Miss Brill"), Minnie Wright (*Trifles*), and Farquhar ("An Occurrence at Owl Creek Bridge") as examples, describe the effects of circumstance on character. Under the rubric "circumstance" you may consider elements such as education, family, economic and social status, wartime conditions, and geographic isolation.

5. Write a brief story about an important decision you have made (e.g., picking a school, beginning or leaving a job, declaring a major, or ending a friendship). Show how your own qualities of character (to the extent that you understand them), together with your own experiences, have gone into the decision. You

may write more comfortably if you give yourself another name and describe your actions in the third person.

6. Topics for paragraphs or short essays:

   a. What characteristics of the speaker are brought out by Lowell in "Patterns"? Should the classifications "round" and "flat" even apply to her? Why or why not?

   b. Why does the speaker of "Dover Beach" philosophize about the darkness and the pounding surf nearby? What qualities of character do his thoughts reveal?

   c. Consider this proposition: *To friends who haven't seen us for a time, we are round, but to ourselves and most other people, we are flat.*

7. Using the card catalogue or computer catalogue in your library, find two critical studies of Nathaniel Hawthorne published by university presses. How fully do these studies describe and explain Hawthorne's depictions of character? Referring to these studies, write a short, research-based essay on selected characters in Hawthorne's fiction.

chapter 4

Writing About Setting:
The Background of Place, Objects, and Culture in Literature

Like all human beings, literary characters do not exist in isolation. Just as they become human by interacting with other characters, they gain identity because of their possessions, their jobs, their homes, and their cultural and political allegiances. Plays, stories, and narrative poems must therefore necessarily include descriptions of objects, places, and backgrounds—the **setting.**

☙ WHAT IS SETTING?

Setting is a work's natural, manufactured, political, cultural, and temporal environment, including everything that characters know and own. Characters may be either helped or hurt by their surroundings, and they may fight about possessions and goals. Further, as characters speak with each other, they reveal the degree to which they share the customs and ideas of their times.

Learn the Three Basic Types of Settings

1. NATURE AND THE OUTDOORS ARE IMPORTANT LOCATIONS FOR MANY WORKS. The natural world is an obvious location for the action of many stories, plays, and narrative poems. It is therefore important to note natural surroundings (hills, shorelines, valleys, mountains, meadows, fields, trees, lakes, streams); living creatures (birds, dogs, horses, snakes); and also the times, seasons, and conditions in which things happen (day or night, summer or winter, sunlight or darkness, wind or stillness, rain or snow, day or night, fogginess or clarity, heat or cold, dryness or humidity, storminess or calmness)—any or all of which may influence character and action.

2. OBJECTS OF HUMAN MANUFACTURE AND CONSTRUCTION ARE VI-TALLY IMPORTANT IN MANY WORKS. To reveal or highlight qualities of character, and also to make narratives lifelike, authors include many details about objects of human manufacture and construction. Houses, both interiors and exteriors, are common, as are possessions, such as walking sticks, kitchen tables, park benches, distant lights, necklaces, hair ribbons, and rocking chairs. In Maupassant's "The Necklace," the loss of a comfortable home brings out the best in a character by causing her to adjust to her economic reversal. The lugubrious vaults in Poe's "The Cask of Amontillado" reveal the similarly lugubrious and sinister nature of Poe's narrator.

Objects also enter directly into literary action and character. A broken birdcage reveals the pathetic husband-wife relationship in *Trifles*; a letter from abroad brings about the speaker's concluding indignation in "Patterns"; a telegram occasions the unfortunate circumstances in "The Story of an Hour"; gunnery practice at sea occasions the speaker's monologue in Hardy's poem "Channel Firing."

3. CULTURAL CONDITIONS AND ASSUMPTIONS FIGURE SIGNIFICANTLY IN WHAT CHARACTERS DO AND SAY. Just as physical setting influences characters, so do historical and cultural conditions and assumptions. O'Connor's "First Confession" assumes that readers will understand the role of the Catholic Church in early-twentieth-century life. In "Dover Beach," the speaker assumes an understanding of the religious skepticism that developed in the nineteenth century. In Chekhov's *The Bear*, the action takes place on a relatively isolated nineteenth-century Russian estate, and the characters therefore see life in ways that are vastly different from our own. The broad cultural setting of Layton's poem "Rhine Boat Trip" brings out the contrast between the beauty of German scenery and mythology, on the one hand, and the ugliness and insane depravity of German atrocities in World War II, on the other.

THE USES THAT WRITERS MAKE OF SETTING

Just as painters render ideas through the use of backgrounds and objects, authors manipulate setting to render ideas. Such a use of setting is seen in Hawthorne's "Young Goodman Brown," where major topographical features include many obstacles and ill-defined woodland paths. Although such difficulties are normal granted the location, time, and circumstances of the story, they succeed in conveying the idea that life is difficult and uncertain. Similarly, in Glaspell's *Trifles,* the fixtures and utensils in the kitchen of the Wright farm indicate the bleakness and oppressiveness of midwestern homesteads early in the twentieth century.

Setting Is Important in Many Ways

To study the setting in a narrative (or play), you need to discover the important details and then try to explain their function. Depending on the author's purpose, the amount of detail may vary. Poe provides many graphic and also impressionistic details in "The Cask of Amontillado," so that we can follow, almost visually, the bizarre action at the story's end. In some works, the setting is so intensely present, like the countryside in Hardy's "The Three Strangers," that it might be considered as an additional participant in the action.

1. A CREDIBLE SETTING HELPS ESTABLISH LITERARY CREDIBILITY.   One of the major purposes of literary setting is to establish **realism** or **verisimilitude.** As the description of location and objects becomes particular and detailed, the events of the work become more believable. In "The Story of an Hour," Chopin gives us details about the inside of the Mallard household, particularly Louise's room and the stairway landing at the front door. These are essential aspects of setting for the story's major scenes. Even futuristic, symbolic, and fantastic stories, as well as ghost stories, seem more believable if they include places and objects from the real world. Hawthorne's "Young Goodman Brown" and Poe's "The Cask of Amontillado" are such stories. Though they make no pretenses to everyday realism, their credibility is enhanced because their settings are so realistic.

2. SETTING MAY BE A STRONG GUIDE TO CHARACTER.   Setting may intersect with character as a means by which authors underscore the importance of place, circumstance, and time on human growth and change. Glaspell's setting in *Trifles* is the kitchen of the lonely, dreary Wright farm. The kitchen is a place of such hard work, oppression, and unrelieved joylessness that it explains the extinguishing of Minnie's early brightness and promise, and also helps us understand her angry act. (A blending of setting and character as seen in Maupassant's "The Necklace" is explored in the two drafts of the sample essay in Chapter 1).

The way characters respond and adjust to setting can reveal their strength or weakness. Peyton Farquhar's scheme to make an escape from his fate, even when it is almost literally hanging before him, suggests his character strength ("An Occurrence at Owl Creek Bridge"). In contrast,

Goodman Brown's Calvinistic religious conviction that human beings are totally depraved, which not reality but his nightmarish encounter confirms, indicates the weakness of his character because it alienates him from family and community ("Young Goodman Brown").

3. **AUTHORS MAY USE SETTING AS AN ORGANIZING ELEMENT IN MANY WORKS.** An author may often use setting to organize a work graphically, as in Maupassant's "The Necklace" where Mathilde and her husband move from a respectable apartment to a cheap attic flat. The story's final scene is believable because Mathilde takes a nostalgic walk on the Champs-Elysées, the most fashionable street in Paris. Without this shift of setting, she would not have encountered Jeanne Forrestier again, for their ways of life no longer bring them together.

Another organizational application of place, time, and object is the **framing** or **enclosing setting**, whereby a work begins and ends with descriptions of the same scene, thus forming a frame or an enclosure. An example is Hardy's "The Three Strangers," which both begins and ends with a description of the lonely English countryside containing a solitary cottage ("Higher Crowstairs"), where the main action takes place. The use of objects as a frame is seen in Mansfield's "Miss Brill," which opens and closes with references to the heroine's shabby fur piece. In such ways, framing creates a formal completeness, just as it may underscore the author's ideas about the human condition.

4. **SETTINGS MAY SERVE AS LITERARY SYMBOLS.** If the scenes and materials of setting are highlighted or emphasized, they also may be taken as symbols through which the author expresses ideas. The horse Toby in Chekhov's *The Bear* is such a symbol. Mrs. Popov has made caring for the horse, which was her dead husband's favorite, a major part of her memorial obligations. When Mrs. Popov tells the servants not to give oats to this horse, Chekhov is using this ordinary barnyard animal to indicate that new commitments replace old ones. In Arnold's poem "Dover Beach," the light that gleams from across the English Channel and that is soon "gone" may be read as a symbol of the extinguishing of intellectual and religious faith that Arnold believed had taken place in the nineteenth century.

5. **SETTING MAY BE USED TO ESTABLISH A WORK'S ATMOSPHERE.** Setting also helps to create **atmosphere** or **mood**, which refers to an enveloping or permeating emotional texture within a work. Most actions *require* no more than a functional description of setting. Thus, taking a walk in a forest needs just the statement that there are trees. However, if a story includes descriptions of shapes, light and shadow, animals, wind, and sounds, you can be sure that the author is creating an atmosphere or a mood for the action (as in Hawthorne's "Young Goodman Brown"). There are many ways to develop moods. Descriptions of bright colors (red, orange, yellow) may con-

tribute to a mood of happiness. The contrast of such bright colors with darkness and dark colors, as in Poe's "The Cask of Amontillado," may invoke gloom or augment hysteria. References to smells and sounds further bring the setting to life by asking additional sensory responses from the reader. The setting of a story in a small town or large city, in green or snow-covered fields, or in middle-class or lower-class residences may evoke responses to these places that contribute to the work's atmosphere.

6. SOME AUTHORS USE SETTING IRONICALLY.   Just as setting may reinforce character and theme, so also it may establish expectations that are the opposite of what occurs. The colorful and orderly garden described in Lowell's poem "Patterns," for example, is an ironic background for the speaker's deep anguish and grief. A bizarre irony is created by Hardy in "Channel Firing" when the noise of large guns being fired from ships at sea awakens the skeletons buried in an English churchyard. The irony is that those engaged in the gun practice, if "red war" gets still redder, will quickly join the skeletons. An equally ironic situation is created by Poe in "The Cask of Amontillado," when Montresor repeats Fortunato's appeal "For the love of God" as he puts in place the final bricks of Fortunato's living tomb.

℣ WRITING ABOUT SETTING

In preparing to write about setting, determine the number and importance of locations, artifacts, and customs. Ask questions such as those in the following section.

Raise Questions to Discover Ideas

- How fully are objects described? How vital are they to the action? How important are they in the development of the plot or idea? How are they connected to the mental states of the characters?
- What connections, if any, are apparent between locations and characters? Do the locations bring characters together, separate them, facilitate their privacy, make intimacy and conversation difficult?
- How well done are the visual descriptions? Does the author provide such vivid and carefully arranged details about surroundings that you might even be able draw a map or plan? Or is the scenery vague and difficult to imagine?
- How important to plot and character are shapes, colors, times of day, clouds, storms, light and sun, seasons of the year, and conditions of vegetation?
- Are the characters poor, moderately well-off, or rich? How does their economic lot determine what happens to them? How does their economic condition affect their actions and attitudes?

- What cultural, religious, and political conditions are displayed and acted upon in the story? How do the characters accept and adjust to these conditions? How do the conditions affect the characters' judgments and actions?
- What is the state of houses, furniture, and objects (e.g., new and polished, old and worn)? What connections can you find between this condition and the outlook and behavior of the characters?
- How important are sounds or silences? To what degree is music or other sound important in the development of character and action?
- Do characters respect or mistreat the environment? If there is an environmental connection, how central is it to the story?
- What conclusions do you think the author expects you to draw as a result of the neighborhood, culture, and larger world of the story?

Organize Your Essay About Setting

INTRODUCTION. Your introduction should contain a brief description of the setting or scenes of the work, specifying the amount and importance of detail.

BODY. Following are five possible approaches for the bodies of essays on setting. Choose one that seems appropriate, bearing in mind that some works invite one approach rather than others. As you develop your essay, however, you may find it necessary to introduce one or more of the other approaches. Whatever approach you use, be sure to consider setting not as an end in itself, but rather as illustration and evidence.

1. *Setting and action.* Explore the importance of setting in the work. How extensively is the setting described? Are locations essential or incidental to the actions? Does the setting serve as part of the action (e.g., places of flight or concealment; public places where people meet openly, or hidden places where they meet privately; natural or environmental conditions; seasonal conditions such as searing heat or numbing cold; customs and conventions)? Do any objects cause inspiration, difficulty, or conflict (e.g., a bridge, a cellar, a fur piece, a walking stick, a necklace, a box, a hair ribbon, a breadknife, a dead bird)? How directly do these objects influence the action?

2. *Setting and organization.* How is the setting connected to the various parts of the work? Does it undergo any changes as the action develops? Why are some parts of the setting more important than others? Is the setting used as a structural frame or an enclosure for the story? How do objects, such as money or property, affect the motivation of the characters? How do descriptions made at the start become important in the action later on?

3. *Setting and character.* (For examples of this approach, see the two drafts of the sample student essay in Chapter 1.) Analyze the degree to which setting influences and interacts with character. Are the characters happy or unhappy where they live? Do they get into discussions or arguments about their home environments? Do they want to stay or leave? Do the economic, philosophical,

religious, or ethnic aspects of the setting make the characters undergo changes? What jobs do the characters perform because of their ways of life? What freedoms or restraints do these jobs cause? How does the setting influence their decisions, transportation, speech habits, eating habits, attitudes about love and honor, and general behavior?

4. *Setting and atmosphere.* To what extent does setting contribute to the atmosphere of the story? Does the setting go beyond the minimum needed for action or character? How do descriptive words paint verbal pictures and evoke moods through references to colors, shapes, sounds, smells, or tastes? Does the setting establish a feeling, say, of joy or hopelessness, plenty or scarcity? Do events happen in daylight or at night? Do the movements and locations of the characters suggest permanence or impermanence (like the return to a darkened room, the creation of a brick wall, or the purchase of a fragile toy)? Are things warm and pleasant, or cold and harsh? What connection do you find between the story's atmosphere and the author's apparent thoughts about existence?

5. *Setting and other aspects.* Does setting reinforce the story's credibility and meaning? Does it establish irony about the circumstances and ideas in the story? If you choose this approach, consult the section earlier in this chapter titled "The Uses That Writers Make of Setting." If you want to write about the symbolic implications of a setting, consult the discussions of symbolism in Chapter 10.

CONCLUSION. To conclude, summarize your major points or write about related aspects of setting that you have not considered. Thus, if your essay treats the relationship of setting and action, your conclusion could mention connections of the setting with character or atmosphere. You might also point out whether your central idea about setting also applies to other major aspects of the story.

Sample Essay

Poe's Use of Setting to Create a Mood of Horror and Repulsion in "The Cask of Amontillado"°

---

[1]   In "The Cask of Amontillado," Edgar Allan Poe uses many details of setting to create a mood of horror and repulsion.* The story is a detailed narration of an act of premeditated and ghastly vengeance. Poe's character Montresor is both the narrator and the principal creator of the twisted act of murder. He believes that his vengeance must be known by the victim, Fortunato, and that

°See pages 345–50 for this story.
*Central idea.

[1] it must be threatening and irrevocable. At the end he is successful, and the reader is both fascinated and repulsed by the story's mood of ghastliness and heartlessness. The mood is established through Poe's descriptions of under-ground rooms, space, and sound.[†]

[2] The height of Poe's graphic description is the story's evocation of gloomy and threatening vaults. The journey into the hellish "catacombs of the Montresors" (paragraph 25), which are also the area for the storage of Montre-sor's wine collection, ends with a room "lined with human remains, piled to the vault overhead" (paragraph 68). The walls in the rooms leading to this last, horrible room are dark and damp, and they drip moisture from the river above; they also become increasingly airless and suffocating. The bones on the walls and floors are evidence of generations of death. In addition, Montresor uses the bones first to hide his bricks and mortar and then to disguise the wall within which he entombs Fortunato. The mood is further fixed by the narrator's ob-servations that each of the catacomb rooms is progressively more covered and shrouded by spiderlike white and ghostly films of nitre, which gloomily suggest increasing death and decay.

[3] The most disturbing of the catacomb rooms is the last one, the "interior recess" which is to be Fortunato's vertical grave. It is an inauspicious area, which Poe indicates was built "for no especial use within itself" (paragraph 68), but its dimensions are ominous. It is no accident that Poe gives us the mea-surements of the recess. It is four feet deep, three feet wide, and six or seven feet high—exactly the size of a large coffin standing on end. The failure of the faltering torches to illuminate the area suggests the ending of breath and light, and the beginning of death. What could be more appropriately sinister, dis-tressing, and ghostly?

[4] The rooms not only provoke horror but also are spatially arranged to complement Montresor's horrible act of vengeance. To reach these increas-ingly dark areas, the characters must walk downward. A circular staircase be-gins the descent, followed by a first and then a second set of stairs that end in the last deep crypt. The downward direction is like an inevitable journey to-ward the grave, and it also suggests a journey into a bleak, cold, dark, and damp hell.

[5] Within this interior of death, Poe adds the eeriness of fearsome sound. Fortunato has a terrible rasping cough, to which Poe devotes an entire para-graph (paragraph 32). The jingling of the bells on Fortunato's carnival cap ap-pears at first ordinary (paragraph 26), then bizarre (paragraph 40), and finally sepulchral (paragraph 89). Fortunato's attempt to get free of the chains results in desperate clanking (paragraph 76). He also moans (paragraph 76), laughs in fear and disbelief (paragraph 78), speaks weakly and sadly (paragraph 78), and at the end is silent (paragraph 89). Perhaps the most grisly sounds de-scribed by Poe are those of Fortunato's screams of protest, which Montresor cruelly stifles by screaming even louder and longer (paragraph 77)—an action that was duplicated by the insane man in the film *The Silence of the Lambs*. These described sounds, having their source in Montresor's diabolical action, create a mood of uneasiness, anxiety, repulsion, and horror.

[6] Thus Poe's setting within the eerie catacombs is both descriptive and evocative. The major action takes place in the last room, in the gravelike re-cess, leading to the climax of the story's movement into darkness and the very walls of death. In this way, Poe uses his setting to show the horror of how a

[†]Thesis sentence.

twisted and depraved person carries out a cruel and pitiless act of revenge.
[6]   The events of the story, the sustained mood, and the narrator's compulsion
with vengeance are all tied together by Poe's skillful control of setting.

❦ COMMENTARY ON THE ESSAY

Because it treats the relationship of setting to mood or atmosphere, this
essay illustrates the fourth approach described on page 72. The essay considers those aspects of setting needed for the story and then stresses how
Poe's descriptions create the story's dominant mood of horror and repulsion.

In the body, paragraphs 2 and 3 form a unit describing the physical
layout of the deathly catacombs, and also pointing out the exactness and
evocativeness of Poe's descriptions. Paragraph 4 concentrates on Poe's description of downward movement, suggesting that this use of space is a visual accompaniment of the story's conclusion in Fortunato's death.

Paragraph 5 treats Poe's use of sound as an accompaniment to the descriptions of the deadly catacombs. The paragraph's topic idea is that the
sounds move progressively toward silence, in keeping with Montresor's
creation of death. References to sound are therefore one of Poe's major
means of achieving an atmosphere complementary to the repulsive and horrible action.

The conclusion summarizes the central idea, stressing once again that
Poe goes beyond simple description to heighten the twisted, macabre mood
of his story.

❦ SPECIAL WRITING TOPICS
FOR STUDYING SETTING

1. Compare and contrast how details of setting are used to establish the qualities
   and traits of the following characters: Mrs. Popov of *The Bear*; Miss Brill of
   "Miss Brill"; the speakers of "Patterns," "Rhine Boat Trip," or "Dover Beach";
   or Montresor of "The Cask of Amontillado."

2. In what ways might we say that both "The Story of an Hour" and "The Cask
   of Amontillado" are inseparable from their settings? To answer this question,
   consider the relationship of character to place and circumstance. How could
   the actions of the stories happen without the locations in which they occur?

3. Choose a story included in Appendix C, and rewrite a page or two, taking the
   characters out of their setting and placing them in an entirely new setting, or
   in the setting of another story (you choose). Then write a brief analysis dealing

with these questions: How were your characters affected by their new settings? Did you make them change slowly or rapidly? Why? As a result of your rewriting, what can you conclude about the uses of setting in fiction?

4. Write a short narrative as though it is part of a story (which you may also wish to write for the assignment), using option a and/or b.

   a. Relate a natural setting or type of day to a mood—for example, a nice day to happiness and satisfaction, or a cold, cloudy, rainy day to sadness. Or create irony by relating the nice day to sadness or the rainy day to happiness.

   b. Indicate how an object or a circumstance becomes the cause of conflict or reconciliation (such as the lost necklace in "The Necklace," the dead canary in *Trifles*, the trip through the forest in "Young Goodman Brown," or the wine in "The Cask of Amontillado."

5. In your library locate two books on the career of Edgar Allan Poe. On the basis of the information you find in these sources, write a brief account of Poe's uses of setting and place to evoke atmosphere and to bring out qualities of human character.

chapter 5

Writing About Plot and Structure:

The Development and Organization of Narratives and Drama

Stories and plays are made up mostly of **actions** or **incidents** that follow one after another in chronological order. Finding a sequential or narrative order, however, is only the first step toward the more important consideration—the **plot,** or the controls governing the development of the actions.

ẽ PLOT: THE MOTIVATION AND CAUSATION OF FICTION AND DRAMA

The English novelist E. M. Forster, in *Aspects of the Novel*, presents a memorable illustration of plot. To show a bare set of actions, he uses the following: "The king died, and then the queen died." He points out, however, that this sequence does not form a plot because it lacks *motivation* and *causation*. These he introduces in his next example: "The king died, and then the queen died of grief." The phrase "of grief" shows that one thing (grief) controls or overcomes another (the normal desire to live), and motivation and causation enter the sequence to form a plot. In a well-plotted story or play, a thing precedes or follows another not simply because time ticks away, but more importantly because *effects* follow *causes*. In a good work, nothing is irrelevant or accidental; everything is related and causative.

Determine the Conflict in a Story or Play

The controlling impulse in a connected pattern of causes and effects is **conflict,** which refers to people or circumstances that a character must face and try to overcome. Conflict brings out the extremes of human energy, causing characters to engage in the decisions, actions, responses, and inter-actions that make up fictional and dramatic literature.

In its most elemental form, a conflict is the opposition of two people. Their conflict may take the shape of envy, hatred, anger, argument, avoid-ance, gossip, lies, fighting, and many other forms and actions. Conflicts may also exist between groups, although conflicts between individuals are more identifiable and therefore more suitable for stories. Conflicts may also be ab-stract, such as when an individual opposes larger forces like natural objects, ideas, modes of behavior, or public opinion. A difficult or even impossible *choice*—a **dilemma**—is a natural conflict for an individual person. A conflict may also be brought out in ideas and opinions that clash. In short, conflict shows itself in many ways.

CONFLICT IS DIRECTLY RELATED TO DOUBT, TENSION, AND INTEREST. Conflict is the major element of plot because opposing forces arouse *curios-ity*, cause *doubt*, create *tension*, and produce *interest*. The same responses are the lifeblood of athletic competition. Consider which kind of athletic event is more interesting: (1) One team gets so far ahead that the winner is no longer in doubt, or (2) both teams are so evenly matched that the winner is in doubt even in the final seconds. Obviously, games are uninteresting—as games—unless they are contests between teams of comparable strength. The same principle applies to conflicts in stories and dramas. There should be uncertainty about a protagonist's success: Unless there is doubt, there is no tension, and without tension there is no interest.

FIND THE CONFLICTS TO DETERMINE THE PLOT.   To see a plot in opera-tion, let us build on Forster's description. Here is a simple plot for a story of our own: "John and Jane meet, fall in love, and get married." This is a plot because it shows cause and effect (they get married *because* they fall in love), but with no conflict, the plot is not interesting. However, let us introduce conflicting elements in this common "boy meets girl" story:

> John and Jane meet at school and fall in love. They go together for two years and plan to marry, but a problem arises. Jane wants a career first, and after marriage she wants to be an equal contributor to the family. John understands Jane's wishes, but he wants to get married first and let her finish her studies and have her career after they have had children. Jane believes that John's plan is not for her because it constitutes a trap from which she will never es-cape. This conflict interrupts their plans, and they part in anger and regret.

Even though they still love each other, both marry other people and build separate lives and careers. Neither is happy even though they like and respect their spouses. The years pass, and, after children and grandchildren, Jane and John meet again. He is now divorced, and she is a widow. Because their earlier conflict is no longer a barrier, they marry and try to make up for the past. Even their new happiness, however, is tinged with regret and reproach because of their earlier conflict, their unhappy solution, their lost years, and their increasing age.

Here we have a true plot because our original "boy meets girl" story outline now contains a major conflict from which a number of related conflicts develop. These conflicts lead to attitudes, choices, and outcomes that make the story interesting. The situation is lifelike; the conflicts rise out of realistic aims and hopes; the outcome is true to life.

🌱 WRITING ABOUT THE PLOT OF A STORY OR PLAY

An essay about plot is an analysis of the conflict and its developments. The organization of the essay should not be modeled on sequential sections and principal events, however, because these invite only a retelling of the story. Instead, the organization is to be developed from the important elements of conflict. Ask yourself the following questions as you look for ideas about plot.

Raise Questions to Discover Ideas

- Who are the protagonist and antagonist, and how do their characteristics put them in conflict? How would you describe the conflict?
- How does the action develop from the conflict?
- If the conflict stems from contrasting ideas or values, what are these, and how are they brought out?
- What problems does the major character (or do the major characters) face? How does the character (characters) deal with these problems?
- How do the major characters achieve (or not achieve) their major goal(s)? What obstacles do they overcome? What obstacles overcome them or alter them?
- At the end, are the characters successful or unsuccessful, happy or unhappy, satisfied or dissatisfied, changed or unchanged, enlightened or ignorant? How has the resolution of the major conflict produced these results?

Organize Your Essay About Plot

INTRODUCTION. To keep your essay brief, be selective. After you refer briefly to the principal characters, circumstances, and issues of the plot, be sure that your thesis sentence includes the topics for fuller development.

BODY. Stress the major elements in the conflict or conflicts developed in the work. Rather than describing everything a major character does, for example, focus on his or her conflict. Thus, an essay on O'Connor's "First Confession" might emphasize Jackie as he deals with the obstacles either in his own home or else in his preparation for his impending confession. Similarly, an essay on Chopin's "The Story of an Hour" might emphasize how Louise develops a conflict between her grief over her supposedly dead husband and her relief at realizing that for the first time, she may be free to do as she pleases. When there is a conflict between two major characters, the obvious approach is to focus equally on both. For brevity, however, emphasis might be placed on just one. Thus, an essay on the plot of Poe's "The Cask of Amontillado" might stress the things we learn about the narrator, Montresor, that are important to his being the initiator of the action.

In addition, the plot may be analyzed more broadly in terms of impulses, goals, values, issues, and historical perspectives. Thus, you might emphasize the elements of chance working against Mathilde in Maupassant's "The Necklace" as a contrast to her dreams about wealth. A discussion of the plot of Mansfield's "Miss Brill" might stress the reclusiveness of Miss Brill, the major character, because the plot could not develop without the disclosure of her secret life. In a similar approach, an essay on the plot of "The Cask of Amontillado" might stress the diabolism of Montresor, because the plot depends on how this quality has produced his plan to bring Fortunato to destruction.

CONCLUSION. The conclusion may contain a brief summary of the points you have made. It is also a fitting location for a brief consideration of the effect or *impact* produced by the conflict. Additional ideas might focus on whether the author has arranged actions and dialogue to direct your favor toward one side or the other, or on whether the plot is possible or impossible, serious or comic, fair or unfair, or powerful or weak.

Sample Essay (on Plot)

Conflicting Values in Hardy's "The Three Strangers" °

[1] As one begins reading Thomas Hardy's "The Three Strangers," the nature of the plot is not immediately clear. There is no apparent protagonist, no single major character but rather a number of characters, and no apparent conflict. At first one thinks the major character may be Shepherd Fennel, but he stands out only as the cooperative host and opener of doors for the strangers entering his home during the stormy night. The first stranger might then seem to be the major character, and this possibility is strengthened because of the jarring and obnoxious second stranger. Here the story establishes the beginning of a conflict, but a puzzling one because it seems no more than a contrast of personalities. The third stranger to enter the cottage does not stay long enough to make him seem a protagonist, for he leaves as quickly as he enters. However, it becomes clear, once all the characters have been involved in the story, that Hardy's plot stems not so much from the conflict of individual characters as from a conflict between aspects of legality and the law. On one side is justice, and on the other injustice.* This opposition may be analyzed according to the characters on each side.†

[2] In the order in which Hardy interweaves the opposing parts of his plot, the unjust side—the side opposing the people at the Fennels—is represented by the second stranger, the Hangman. The cruelty of the Hangman's duties is underlined by his own personal selfishness, egotism, and arrogance. He drinks all the mead in the large common cup, never caring about the wants of anyone else. He sings a merry song about his grisly job as hangman. He is officious in ordering the guests to pursue the third stranger. He shows his contempt for the people by calling them "simple-minded souls, you know, stirred up to anything in a moment" (paragraph 125). To make clear just how obnoxious this Hangman is, Hardy compares him to the devil (paragraph 87). In short, the Hangman, because of these qualities, is the story's cruel and thoughtless antagonist, and for this reason he stands as the negative part of Hardy's plot.

[3] By far the most powerful aspect of the plot is the positive and just side, represented by the Fennels, their guests, and the first and third strangers. They are ordinary, good folks, no more and no less, and their feelings about life are perhaps best shown by their celebration of the christening of the daughter of the Fennels. With regard to law, the story makes clear that such people favor fairness and compassion above strict punishment. Thus, when one of the guests explains that Timothy Summers (the first stranger) has been sentenced to be hanged because he had stolen a sheep when his "family were astarving" (paragraph 80), the other guests become hushed. Further, when the Hangman starts pushing them to start a search, they are slow and unwilling,

°See pages 312–26 for this story.
*Central idea.
†Thesis sentence.

[3] and when they go out looking, they produce the wrong man. As we learn, the first stranger is really the fugitive Summers, whose crime is justifiable in the eyes of the people, and the third stranger is the fugitive's brother, who flees not because he is guilty but because he wants to deflect suspicion away from Summers. These are the characters toward whom Hardy directs our understanding, admiration, and sympathy. Any attempt to sentence anyone harshly, as the law has done with Summers, brings out their hesitation and resistance.

[4] An integral aspect of Hardy's plot is the countryside itself, which during the search becomes an almost active opponent of the legal capriciousness represented by the Hangman. The treacherous hill, containing the "flint slopes" of the hog's-back elevation near Higher Crowstairs, causes the searchers to stumble and tumble and make mistakes. After the initial search for Summers proves fruitless, the people and the countryside unite to foil the thoughtlessly harsh law. The "woods and fields and lanes," together with the "lofts and out-houses" (paragraph 160) furnish hiding places for Summers, so that this man, the first stranger, is "never recaptured" (paragraph 161).

[5] This side of rightness represented by the people is shown by Hardy as not just occasional, but rather eternal. He carefully sets the story in the framework of "the lapse of centuries" (paragraph 1), and he includes references to the ancient figures Timon and Nebuchadnezzar, as though the happenings at the party of the Fennels are as ageless as human history (paragraph 2). Beyond this, Hardy compares the activities of the shepherd folk to the movements of the universe itself, for the energetic dancing moves "in planet-like courses, direct and retrograde, from apogee to perigee" (paragraph 10). When the third stranger is discovered, he steps out from behind an ash tree that was "probably sown there by a passing bird some fifty years before" (paragraph 131). Hardy's concluding paragraph places the entire story in the fabric of virtual myth, thus stressing the continuum from the past to the present. In other words, people like the shepherds share a common humanity that is as old as time.

[6] This brief description of the major conflict making up the plot of "The Three Strangers" does not account for the story's power. Hardy skillfully paints a sympathetic picture of the shepherds and their way—a way of friendliness and good will in which the literal and harsh application of law has little place. His contrasting antagonist, the Hangman, personally violates the shepherd's home just as the law he represents violates the concept of justice felt by the people there. Admittedly, the complete intermeshing of the plot does not seem certain until the circumstances are explained by the brother of Timothy Summers—an explanation that makes clear the opposition between the people's justice and the Hangman's injustice. Hardy's plot in "The Three Strangers" is strong because it is so real, and because the people themselves are presented as a collective force for fairness and justice over an application of law that is unfair and unjust.

❦ COMMENTARY ON THE ESSAY

Because the subject is plot, this essay emphasizes the conflicting elements in Hardy's "The Three Strangers"—the forces of understanding and humanity, on the one hand, and of harshness and cruelty, on the other. The first paragraph demonstrates how this conflict emerges in the story after a somewhat hesitant opening. Throughout the body of the essay, the conflict is stressed as the major element of Hardy's plot.

Note that the essay assumes that readers know the story already. Hence the essay is not a plot "summary" but is instead an analysis of the elements making up the plot. As much summary as is included here occurs in paragraph 6, in which the explanations by the third stranger are cited to show how Hardy does not make all aspects of his plot clear until near the story's end.

In the body of the essay, paragraph 2 deals with the characteristics of the antagonist, the Hangman. Following this, the greater portion of the body considers the collective (not individual) protagonist arrayed against the Hangman and the harsh law he represents. Thus the human protagonists are the people and the first and third strangers (paragraph 3), the geographical protagonist is the countryside around Higher Crowstairs (paragraph 4), and the historical protagonist is time itself (paragraph 5).

The concluding paragraph summarizes the conflicts of the plot and concludes with a final reference to the central idea, that the story exalts fairness and justice and deplores unfairness and injustice.

❦ THE STRUCTURE OF NARRATIVES AND DRAMA

Structure refers to the ways in which writers arrange materials in accord with the general ideas and purposes of their works. Unlike plot, which is concerned with conflict or conflicts, structure defines the layouts of works—the ways the story, play, or poem is shaped. Structure is about matters such as placement, balance, recurring themes, true and misleading conclusions, suspense, and the imitation of models or forms like reports, letters, conversations, or confessions. A work might be divided into numbered sections or parts, or it might begin in a countryside (or one state) and conclude in a city (or in another state), or it might develop a relationship between two people from their first introduction to their falling in love. To study structure is to study such arrangements and the purposes for which they are made.

❦ FORMAL CATEGORIES OF STRUCTURE

Many aspects of structure are common to all genres of literature. Particularly for stories and plays, however, the following aspects form a skeleton, a pattern of development.

The *Exposition* Provides the Materials
Necessary to Put the Plot into Operation

Exposition is the laying out, the putting forth, of the materials in the story—the main characters, their backgrounds, their characteristics, interests, goals, limitations, potentials, and basic assumptions. It may not be limited to the beginning of the work, where it is most expected, but may be found anywhere. Thus, intricacies, twists, turns, false leads, blind alleys, surprises, and other quirks may be introduced to interest, perplex, intrigue, and otherwise please readers. Whenever something new arises, to the degree that it is new, it is a part of exposition.

The *Complication* Is the Beginning
and the Growth of the Conflict

The **complication** is the onset and development of the major conflict—the plot. The major participants are the protagonist and antagonist, together with whatever ideas and values they represent, such as good or evil, freedom or oppression, independence or dependence, love or hate, intelligence or stupidity, or knowledge or ignorance.

The *Crisis* Marks the Decisions Made
to End the Conflict

The **crisis** (Greek for *turning point*) marks that point where the conflict reaches its greatest tension. During the crisis, a decision or an action to resolve the conflict is undertaken, and therefore the crisis is the point at which curiosity, uncertainty, and tension are greatest. Usually the crisis is followed closely by the next stage, the *climax*. Often, in fact, the two are so close together that they are considered the same.

The *Climax* Is the Conclusion
of the Conflict

Because the **climax** (Greek for *ladder*) is a consequence of the crisis, it is the story's *high point* and may take the shape of a decision, an action, an affirmation or denial, or an illumination or a realization. It is the logical conclusion of the preceding actions; no new major developments follow it. In most stories, the climax occurs at the end or close to it. In Chekhov's *The Bear*, for example, the climax is that Smirnov, after touching and holding Mrs. Popov when instructing her in how to hold a pistol, impetuously declares that he loves her. This declaration brings their hostility to an unexpected height and also to a sudden reversal. In Lowell's "Patterns" the climax is the very last sentence, "Christ, what are patterns for?" This outburst summarizes the speaker's developing sorrow, frustration, and anger.

The *Resolution* or *Dénouement* Finishes the Work and Releases the Tension

The **resolution** (a releasing or an untying) or **dénouement** (untying) is the completing of the story or play after the climax, for once the climax has occurred, the work's tension and uncertainty are finished, and most authors conclude quickly to avoid losing their readers' interest. For instance, the dénouement of "Miss Brill" comprises a few short details about the major character's returning home, sitting down, and putting away her muff. Some authors provide even fewer details, as in Poe's "The Cask of Amontillado," which compresses fifty years into a single concluding sentence. In a similarly brief way, Chekhov ends *The Bear* with his two major characters kissing in front of their dumfounded servants.

❦ FORMAL AND ACTUAL STRUCTURE

The structure just described is a *formal* one, an ideal pattern that moves directly from beginning to end. Few narratives and dramas follow this pattern exactly, however. Thus a typical mystery story holds back crucial details of exposition (because the goal is to mystify); a suspense story keeps the protagonist ignorant but provides readers with abundant details in order to maximize concern and tension about the outcome.

More realistic, less "artificial" stories might also contain structural variations. For example, Hardy's "The Three Strangers" produces a *double take* because of unique structuring. Toward the story's end, Hardy raises the suspicion that the fugitive prisoner is the third stranger to enter the peasant household. At the end, however, Hardy makes clear that the fugitive is really the first stranger, who is already present when the third stranger enters and leaves. This complication introduces and emphasizes a new understanding of the position of the first stranger as both a righteous person and also a brave one. "The Three Strangers" is just one example of how a structural variation maximizes the impact of a work.

There are many other possible variants in structure. One of these is called **flashback,** or **selective recollection,** in which present circumstances are explained by the selective introduction of past events. The moment at which the flashback is introduced may be a part of the resolution of the plot, and the flashback might lead you into a moment of climax but then go from there to develop the details that are more properly part of the exposition.

Let us again consider our brief plot about John and Jane and use the flash-back method of structuring the story.

> Jane is now old, and a noise outside causes her to remember the argument that forced her to part with John many years before. They were deeply in love, but their disagreement about her wishes for a career split them apart. Then she pictures in her mind the years she and John have spent happily together after they married. She then contrasts her present happiness with her memory of her earlier, less happy, marriage, and from there she recalls her youthful years of courtship with John before their disastrous conflict developed. Then she looks over at John, reading in a chair, and smiles. John smiles back, and the two embrace. Even then, Jane has tears on her face.

In this structure the action begins and remains in the present. Important parts of the past flood the protagonist's memory in flashback, though not in the order in which they happened. Memory might be used structurally in other ways. An example is Shelly Wagner's "The Boxes," which is partially a narrative poem spoken by a mother to her dead son. The events of the poem are disclosed through the speaker's memories of the past, but the poem's conclusion depends on the speaker's temporary consideration that time has changed to a point before the death, so that she can speak to her son as though he is still living. The poem thus searingly illustrates the poignancy and finality of the situation. In short, a technique like selective recollection creates a unique narrative that departs significantly from a strictly formal and chronological structural pattern.

Each narrative or drama has its own particular structure. Some works can be structured according to geography or room arrangements, as in Irving Layton's poem "Rhine Boat Trip" (meditation upon castles observed by a tourist on the Rhine leading to thoughts of cattle cars during the Holocaust), or in Maupassant's "The Necklace" (movement from a modest apartment, to an attic flat, to a local street), or in Poe's "The Cask of Amontillado" (movement from local streets downward into a sequence of catacombs). A work can unfold in an apparently accidental way, with the characters drawing conclusions as they make discoveries about the major characters, as in Glaspell's *Trifles*. Parts or scenes can be carried on through a ceremony witnessed by a major character, as in "Young Goodman Brown." A play or story can unfold in an apparently accidental way, with the characters making vital discoveries about the major characters, as in Glaspell's *Trifles*. Additionally, parts of a work may be set out as fragments of conversation, as in "First Confession," or as a ceremony, as in "Young Goodman Brown," or as an announcement of a party, as in "The Necklace." The possible variations are extensive.

🦋 WRITING ABOUT STRUCTURE

Your essay should concern arrangement and shape. In form, the essay should not restate or summarize the part-by-part unfolding of the narrative or argument. Rather, it should explain why things are where they are: "Why is this here and not there?" is the fundamental question you need to answer. Thus it is possible to begin with a consideration of a work's crisis, and then to consider how the exposition and complication have built up to it. A vital piece of information, for example, might have been withheld in the earlier exposition (as in Bierce's "An Occurrence at Owl Creek Bridge" and Hardy's "The Three Strangers") and introduced only at or near the conclusion; therefore, the crisis might be heightened because there would have been less suspense if the detail had been introduced earlier. Consider the following questions as you examine the story's structure.

Raise Questions to Discover Ideas

- If spaces or numbers divide the story into sections or parts, what structural importance do these parts have?
- If there are no marked divisions, what major sections can you discover? (You might make divisions according to places where actions occur, to various times of day, to changing weather, or to increasingly important events.)
- If the story departs in major ways from the formal structure of exposition, complication, crisis, climax, and resolution, what purpose do these departures have?
- What variations in chronological order, if any, appear in the story (for example, gaps in the time sequence, flashbacks or selective recollection)? What effects are achieved by these variations?
- Does the story delay any crucial details of exposition? Why? What effect is achieved by the delay?
- Where does an important action or a major section (such as the climax) begin? End? How is it related to the other formal structural elements, such as the crisis? Is the climax an action, a realization, or a decision? To what degree does it relieve the work's tension? What is the effect of the climax on your understanding of the characters involved in it? How is this effect related to the arrangement of the climax?

Organize Your Essay About Structure

INTRODUCTION.   Your essay should discuss why an entire story is arranged the way it is—to reveal the nature of a character's situation, to create surprise, or to bring out maximum humor. You might also, however, discuss the structure of no more than a part of the story, such as the climax or the complication.

BODY.   The essay is best developed in concert or agreement with what the work contains. The location of scenes is an obvious organizing element. Thus, essays on the structure of Hawthorne's "Young Goodman Brown" and Mansfield's "Miss Brill" might be based on the fact that both take place outdoors (a dark forest for one and a sunny public park for the other). Similarly, an essay might explore the structure of Maupassant's "The Necklace" by contrasting the story's indoor and outdoor locations. In Glaspell's *Trifles*, much is made of the various parts of a kitchen in an Iowa farmhouse, and an essay might trace the structural importance of these.

Other ways to consider structure may be derived from a work's notable aspects, such as the growing suspense and horrible conclusion of Poe's "The Cask of Amontillado" or the revelations about the "sinfulness" of Goodman Brown's father and neighbors in Hawthorne's "Young Goodman Brown."

CONCLUSION.   The conclusion should highlight the main parts of your essay. You may also deal briefly with the relationship of structure to the plot. If the work you have analyzed departs from chronological order, you might stress the effects of this departure. Your aim should be to focus on the success of the work as it has been brought about by the author's choices in development.

Sample Essay (on Structure)

The Structure of Conflict and Suspense in Hardy's "The Three Strangers" °

---

[1]   Thomas Hardy's "The Three Strangers" is a finely woven story of conflict and suspense. The suspense is essential to the conflict, which is an opposition of right and wrong when applied to criminal justice. <u>Hardy controls the story's structure to develop this opposition, which embodies the idea that the letter of the law is insignificant when compared with the spirit.</u>* The application of strict legality in Hardy's story is shown as wrong, while understanding and forgiveness, even if in a nominally illegal context, is shown as to seem right. As the basis of this idea, Hardy builds the story toward a major incident which presents a conflict for his Wessex shepherds between (1) duty toward law, and (2) duty toward a human being who has been legally condemned but whose

°See pages 312–26 for this story.
*Central idea.

crime has been extenuated. <u>Hardy develops his conflict and brings out his idea by showing the lives of his country people positively, by portraying his hangman negatively, and by creating suspense about his first stranger, who is the legally condemned "criminal."</u>[†]

[2] <u>Although readers may not be aware of it during the early part of the story, Hardy arranges events to demonstrate a generous view of right and wrong.</u> The first one-sixth of the story is an exposition of the way of life of the natives of Higher Crowstairs, who are shown to be warm and human. But in the service of his idea, Hardy is actually building up one side of the conflict by demonstrating that his natives are such nice, ordinary peasant folk that their judgment on matters of life and death is to be trusted. This is the positive side of Hardy's narratively presented argument.

[3] <u>When Hardy does engage both sides of the conflict—a complication occurring about midway through the story—by introducing the second stranger (the Hangman), he has already established the grounds for his case, but he solidifies his argument by negatively presenting this ghoulish figure as brash, selfish, and obnoxious.</u> When the natives learn of the second stranger's identity as the Hangman, they are startled "with suppressed exclamations" (paragraph 79). The exclamations apparently take the form that if men like the hangman are associated with the letter of the law, the natives—along with the reader—will prefer the spirit even if the spirit may lead people to support actions that are strictly illegal. This reaction could not be sustained if the crime of the escaped criminal had been a violent one, but the "crime" was really the theft of a sheep to feed his starving family (paragraph 80). One may grant that Hardy is mitigating the crime here, but the conflict is not between right when it is right and wrong when it is wrong, but rather between legality when it is wrong and illegality when it is right. As Hardy structures the events in the story, it is not possible to disagree with the judgment of the natives at the end that the intended hanging of the thief "was cruelly disproportioned to the transgression" (paragraph 160), for even if a reader wanted to disagree with Hardy's argument on legal grounds, the emotional thrust of the story leads toward extenuation.

[4] <u>Critical to this extenuation is Hardy's creation of suspense about the identity of the first stranger as Timothy Summers, the escaped prisoner.</u> Because throughout the story readers have assented to the values and way of life of Shepherd Fennel and his guests, Hardy's crisis and climax forestall a purely legalistic reaction. Hardy puts Summers before the eyes of both country folk and readers as a brave and witty human being, not as a fugitive who has just escaped hanging. The revelation at the end therefore causes a second view of Summers. In retrospect, readers join the natives in admiring this first stranger's "marvellous coolness and daring in hob-and-nobbing with the hangman" (paragraph 160), and consequently would be indignant if such a person were actually to be hanged. As a result of Hardy's judicious withholding and disclosing of detail, he leads readers to deny the law when it is used unfairly.

[5] <u>Related to the major conflict are a number of lesser but still important conflicts that Hardy includes in the narrative.</u> At crucial points, for example, he establishes that the natives living marginally in the "country about Higher Crowstairs" (paragraph 162) are uneasy and fearful of the law. When they realize that the second Stranger is the Hangman, they "start back," and one of them begins trembling (paragraph 79). Hardy invites readers to conclude that

---

[†]Thesis sentence.

[5] the natives view the conviction of Summers as a threat also to themselves. In a comic vein, Hardy contrasts the law with the ineptness of the shepherds who are called upon to enforce it (paragraphs 106–34). He makes the law so remote from their lives that when they actually make an arrest—of the third stranger—they use words more appropriate to criminals or to priests (paragraphs 132–34). As an ironic dénouement of the story, Hardy tells us that the shepherds, resisting the legal but troubling Hangman and Magistrate, diligently search for Summers everywhere but where they know he can be found (paragraph 160).

[6] In addition, Hardy includes other little but human contrasts in order to develop sympathy for the folk and therefore to strengthen his argument. Although the Fennels have twenty guests in their home, Mrs. Fennel is alarmed about giving them too much food and drink, and she is disturbed when the Hangman singlehandedly depletes her store of mead. There is a small family disagreement on this score. Another minor and amusing conflict is set up by Hardy when Mrs. Fennel asks the musicians to stop playing, but they continue because they have been bribed by the amorous shepherd, Oliver Giles. There are also some noticeable contrasts in age among couples. Beyond these contrasts or opposites, which are vital to the story's structure, the technique of suspense is a conflict in itself, for it forces a readers to consider and evaluate elements of the story a second time. <u>These are all conflicts that Hardy employs in developing his major conflict between the right of the spirit and the wrong of the letter in "The Three Strangers."</u>

☙ COMMENTARY ON THE ESSAY

As expressed in paragraph 1, this essay focuses on how Hardy structures character and action in "The Three Strangers" to achieve a contrast between right and wrong. The discussion of all materials leading to the people's exoneration of the fugitive is seen not as narrative but as a contributing part of Hardy's argument. The essay thus explains that the parts of the story are placed where they are because they are aspects of Hardy's developing argument. To emphasize this aim, words and phrases are introduced, such as "arranges events," "engage both sides of the conflict," "structures the events," "creation of suspense," "establishes," and "in order to develop sympathy." All these expressions are intended as reminders that the subject of the essay is the way in which Hardy structures the story.

In the body, paragraph 2 describes how Hardy introduces the natives and their guests at the Fennels to illustrate their qualities of warmth and humanity. Paragraph 3 stresses the negative reaction of the country folk when they learn that the second stranger is the Hangman. Together, then, paragraphs 2 and 3 serve to explain the underlying causes of Hardy's arrangement of the narrative.

In paragraph 4 the essay explains Hardy's delay in identifying the fugitive as an aspect of his positive picture of the country folk and their values, and also in terms of persuading readers of the story to concur in the decision for justice that the natives make. Paragraph 5 states that other conflicts in the story show that the natives are uneasy with the law and fearful of it—attitudes that reinforce their decision to favor the first stranger. The concluding paragraph, 6, describes how additional "but human" contrasts are placed so as to augment Hardy's favorable portraits of the Fennels and their guests.

☘ SPECIAL WRITING TOPICS FOR STUDYING PLOT AND STRUCTURE

1. What kind of story might "The Three Strangers" be, structurally, if the first stranger were named and identified when he first enters the cottage, before the entrance of the other strangers?

2. Consider the surprises in "An Occurrence at Owl Creek Bridge," "The Story of an Hour," "The Necklace," *The Bear*, and "The Three Strangers." How much preparation is made for the surprises? In retrospect, to what degree are the surprises not surprises at all, but rather are necessary outcomes of the preceding parts of the works?

3. Compare the use and placement of interior scenes in "The Story of an Hour," "First Confession," and *Trifles*. How do these scenes bring out the various conflicts in the works? How do characters in the interiors contribute to plot developments? What is the relationship of these characters to the major themes of the works?

4. Compare "The Story of an Hour" and "Young Goodman Brown" as stories developing plots about clashing social or religious values. In what ways are the plots similar and different?

5. Compare the ways in which attitudes toward law are presented in Glaspell's *Trifles* and Hardy's "The Three Strangers." How do these works structure your responses toward the people representing the law? Toward the people who have violated the law?

6. Select a circumstance in your life that caused you doubt, difficulty, and conflict. Making yourself anonymous (give yourself a fictitious name and put yourself in a fictitious location), write a brief story about the occasion, stressing how your conflict began, how it affected you, and how you resolved it. You might describe the details in chronological order, or you might begin the story in the present tense and then introduce details in flashback.

chapter 6

Writing About Point of View:
The Position or Stance
of the Work's Narrator
or Speaker

The term **point of view** refers to the **speaker, narrator, persona,** or **voice** created by authors to tell stories, present arguments, and express attitudes and judgments. Point of view involves not only the speaker's physical position as an observer and recorder, but also the ways in which the speaker's social, political, and mental circumstances affect the narrative. For this reason, point of view is one of the most complex and subtle aspects of literary study.

Bear in mind that authors try not only to make their works vital and interesting but also to bring their *presentations* alive. The presentation is similar to a dramatic performance: In a play, the actors are always themselves, but in their roles they *impersonate* and temporarily *become* the characters whom they act. In fictional works, not only do authors impersonate or pretend to be characters who do the talking, but also they *create* these characters. One such character is Jackie, the narrator of O'Connor's "First Confession," who is telling about events that occurred when he was a child. Because he is the subject as well as the narrator, he has firsthand knowledge of the actions, even though he also says things indicating that he, as an adult, has not fully assimilated his childhood experience. Another such character is the unnamed speaker of Lowell's poem "Patterns." This speaker is visualized as a real woman telling about her despair after learning that her fiancé has been killed during a war. She is therefore the major participant, possessing her own identity, which is totally separate from that of the writer, Lowell. Still another speaking character is the unnamed narrator of Hawthorne's "Young Goodman Brown." This narrator is telling a story about someone else and is uninvolved and distant from the action. Because of this distance, the speaker is not easily separated from the author, even though the words we read may be different from those that Hawthorne himself might have chosen if speaking in his own person. In other words, the speaker is Hawthorne's authorial creation—his assumed voice that tells us the story of "Young Goodman Brown."

Because of the ramifications of creating a narrative voice, point of view may also be considered as the centralizing or guiding intelligence in a work—the mind that filters the fictional experience and presents only the most important details to create the maximum impact. Thus in Poe's "The Cask of Amontillado," we constantly hear the speaker's voice and are influenced not only by his narration but also by his attitudes.We are similarly affected by the unnamed narrator of Hardy's "The Three Strangers." This speaker obviously has strong opinions about the opposition between the people of Higher Crowstairs and the intrusive second stranger, and he arranges the narrative to make us sympathetic to his views. In other words, the way reality is presented in stories—the point of view or guiding intelligence created by the author—determines how we read, understand, and respond.

✾ AN EXERCISE IN POINT OF VIEW: REPORTING AN ACCIDENT

As an exercise to show that point of view is derived from lifelike situations, let us imagine that there has been an auto accident: Two cars, driven by Alice and Bill, have collided, and the scene is as we see it in the drawing. How might this accident be reported by a number of people? What would Alice say? What would Bill say?

Now assume that Frank, who is Bill's best friend, and Mary, who knows neither Bill nor Alice, were witnesses. What might Frank say about who was responsible? What might Mary say? Additionally, assume that you are a reporter for a local newspaper and are sent to report on the accident. You know none of the people involved. How will your report differ from the other reports? Finally, to what degree are all the statements designed to persuade listeners and readers of the correctness of the details and claims made in the respective reports?

The likely differences in the various reports may be explained by reference to point of view. Obviously, because both Alice and Bill are deeply involved—each of them is a major participant or what may be called a *major mover*—they will arrange their words to make themselves seem blameless. Frank, because he is Bill's best friend, will likely report things in Bill's favor.

Mary will favor neither Alice nor Bill, but let us assume that she did not look up to see the colliding cars until she heard the crash. Thus, she did not see the accident happening but only the immediate aftereffects. Amid all this mixture of partial and impartial views of the action, to whom should we attribute the greatest reliability?

It seems clear that each person's report will have the "hidden agenda" of making herself or himself seem honest, objective, intelligent, impartial, and thorough. Thus, although both Alice and Bill may be truthful in their own eyes, it is unlikely that their reports will be reliable because they both have something to gain from avoiding responsibility for the accident. Also, Frank may not be reliable because he is Bill's friend and may report things to Bill's advantage. Mary could be reliable, but she did not see everything; therefore, she is unreliable not because of motivation but rather because of her location as a witness. Most likely, *your* account as an impartial reporter will be the most reliable and objective of all, because your major interest is to learn all the details and to report the truth accurately, with no concern about the personal interests of either Alice or Bill.

As you can see, the ramifications of describing actions are far-reaching, and the consideration of the various interests and situations is subtle. Indeed, of all the aspects of literature, point of view is the most complex because it is so much like life itself. On the one hand, point of view is intertwined with the many interests and wishes of humanity at large; on the other hand, it is linked to the enormous difficulty of uncovering and determining truth.

❦ CONDITIONS THAT AFFECT POINT OF VIEW

As this exercise in observation and expression demonstrates, point of view depends on two major factors. The first factor is *the physical situation of the narrator, or speaker, as an observer.* How close to the action is the speaker? Is the speaker a major participant, or no more than a witness, either close or distant? How much is he or she privileged to know? How accurate and complete are his or her reports? How do the speaker's characteristics emerge from the narration? What are his or her qualifications or limitations as an observer? The second factor is the speaker's intellectual and emotional position: How might the speaker gain or lose from what takes place in the story? Are the speaker's observations and words colored by these interests? Does he or she have any persuasive purpose beyond being a straightforward recorder or observer? What values does the speaker impart to the action?

In a story, as in many poems using narrative, authors take into account all these subtleties. For example, Poe's narrator Montresor in "The Cask of Amontillado" is a man who describes the details of a murderous act of revenge that he carried out fifty years before the time of narration. O'Con-

> **DISTINGUISH POINT OF VIEW FROM OPINION**
>
> Sometimes people mistakenly equate point of view with *opinions* or *beliefs.* It must be stressed that point of view is not synonymous with ideas. Rather, point of view refers to a work's mode of narration, comprising narrator, language, audience, and perceptions of events and characters. Opinions and beliefs are thoughts and ideas that may have nothing to do with a narration. A discussion of point of view should therefore emphasize how the dramatic situation of a work actually *shapes* and *creates* the work. If ideas seem to be a particularly important matter in a story, your objective should not be to analyze and discuss the ideas *as ideas*, but rather to consider *if and how these ideas affect what the narrator concludes and says about the story's actions and situations.*

nor's speaker in "First Confession" tells about boyhood family problems and his first experience with the sacrament of confession, but he he has not yet fully separated himself from some of his youthful antagonisms. The speaker-narrator of Wagner's poem "The Boxes" is a mother describing the horror of searching for her lost son, who has drowned, and the anguish of her feelings in the years after the death. For all these reasons, the narrators reveal their involvement and concern in the events they describe. As readers, we need to determine how such differing modes of presentation determine the effects of these and all other stories and narrative poems.

☞ DETERMINING A WORK'S POINT OF VIEW

In your reading you will encounter a wide variety of points of view. To begin your analysis, first determine the work's grammatical voice. Then, study the ways in which the subject, characterization, dialogue, and form interact with the point of view.

In the First-Person Point of View, the Narrator Tells About Events He or She Has Personally Witnessed

If the voice of the work is an "I," the author is using the **first-person point of view**—the impersonation of a fictional narrator or speaker who may be named or unnamed. In our hypothetical accident reports, both Alice and Bill are first-person speakers who are named. Also named and clearly identified is the narrator of Poe's "The Cask of Amontillado."

First-person speakers might report events as though they have acquired their knowledge in a number of ways:

- What they themselves have done, said, heard, and thought (firsthand experience)
- What they have observed others doing and saying (firsthand witness)
- What others have said to them or otherwise communicated to them (secondhand testimony and hearsay)
- What they are able to infer or deduce from the information they have found (inferential information)
- What they are able to conjecture about how a character or characters might think and act, given their knowledge of a situation (conjectural, imaginative, or intuitive information)

Of all the points of view, that of the first person is the most independent of the author, because the first-person speaker may have a unique identity, with name, job, and economic and social position. Often, however, the author creates a more anonymous but still independent first-person speaker, as with the unnamed narrators of Arnold's "Dover Beach" and Lowell's "Patterns." There are also situations in which an "I" narrative is pluralized by "we" when the first person includes other characters. Such a first-person-plural point of view lends reliability to the narrative, as in Wagner's poem "The Boxes," because the characters included as "we," even if they are unidentified by the speaker, may be considered as additional witnesses.

DETERMINE THE DEGREE OF RELIABILITY OF THE SPEAKER.   When you encounter a first-person narrative (whether a story or poem), determine the narrator's position and ability, prejudices or self-interest, and judgment of his or her readers or listeners. Most first-person speakers describing their own experiences are to be accepted as **reliable** and authoritative. But sometimes first-person speakers are **unreliable** because they may have interests or limitations that lead them to mislead, distort, or even lie. There is reason to question that the narrator Montresor of Poe's "The Cask of Amontillado" is telling the complete truth about his enmity against Fortunato, for example, because his act of revenge against Fortunato is clearly less a matter of honor than a result of a psychopathic and demonic personality. Whether first-person speakers are reliable or unreliable, however, they are one of the means by which authors confer an authentic, lifelike aura to their works.

In the Second-Person Point of View, the Narrator Is Speaking to Someone Else Who Is Called "You" and Who May or May Not Be the Major Character in the Action

The **second-person point of view,** the least common of the points of view, offers the writer two major possibilities. In the first, a narrator (almost necessarily a first-person speaker) tells a present and involved listener what the listener himself or herself has done and said at a past time. The actions might be a simple retelling of events, as when a parent tells an older child about something the child did during infancy, or when a doctor tells a patient with amnesia about events before the causative injury. The actions might also be subject to dispute and interpretation, as when a prosecuting attorney describes a crime for which a defendant is on trial or when a spouse lists grievances against an alienated spouse in a custody or divorce case.

The second possibility is more complex. Some narrators seem to be addressing a "you" but are instead referring mainly to themselves—and to listeners only tangentially—in preference to an "I." In addition, some narrators follow the usage—common in colloquial speech—of the indefinite "you." In this kind of narration, speakers use "you" to refer not to a specific listener but rather to anyone at all—in this way avoiding the more formal use of words like "one," "a person," or "people." (Incidentally, the selection of "you" is non–gender specific, because it eliminates the need for pronouns such as "he," "she," or "he or she.")

In the Third-Person Point of View, the Speaker Is Usually Anonymous and Not Intrusive, and This Speaker Emphasizes the Actions and Speeches of Others

If events in the work are described in the third person (*he, she, it, they*), the author is using the **third-person point of view**. It is not always easy to characterize the voice in this point of view. Sometimes the speaker may use an "I" (as in Hughes's "Negro") and be seemingly identical with the author, but at other times the author may create a distinct **authorial voice**, as in Mansfield's "Miss Brill." There are three variants of the third-person point of view: *dramatic* or *objective, omniscient,* and *limited omniscient.*

THE DRAMATIC OR OBJECTIVE POINT OF VIEW IS THE MOST BASIC METHOD OF NARRATION. The most direct presentation of action and dialogue is the **dramatic** or **objective point of view** (also called **third-person objective**). It is the basic method of rendering action and speech that all the points of view share. The narrator of the dramatic point of view is an unidentified speaker who reports things in a way that is analogous to a hovering or tracking motion-picture camera or to what some critics have called "a fly on the wall (or tree)." Somehow, the narrator is always on the spot—within rooms, forests, village squares, moving vehicles, or even in outer space—to tell us what is happening and what is being said.

In drama, the presentation is limited *only* to what is said and what happens. There is no attempt to draw conclusions or make interpretations, because the premise of the dramatic point of view is that readers, like a jury, can form their own interpretations if they are given the right evidence. Thus, Masefield's "Cargoes" objectively describes three different types of ships from three different periods of history. From these descriptions, we the readers are *invited* to draw a number of conclusions about how civilization has changed in the last three thousand years, but because of the dramatic point of view, Masefield does not *state* any of these conclusions for us.

THE NARRATOR IN THE OMNISCIENT POINT OF VIEW CAN SEE ALL AND DISCLOSE ALL.   The third-person point of view is **omniscient** (all-knowing) when the speaker not only presents action and dialogue, but also is able to report what goes on in the minds of the characters. In our everyday real world, we can never know *absolutely* what other people are thinking. However, we always make assumptions about the thoughts of others, and these assumptions are the basis of the omniscient point of view. Authors use it freely but judiciously to explain responses, thoughts, feelings, and plans— an additional dimension that aids in the development of character. For example, in Maupassant's "The Necklace," the speaker assumes omniscience to explain the responses and thoughts of the major character and also, though to a lesser degree, of her husband.

THE NARRATOR IN THE LIMITED, OR LIMITED-OMNISCIENT, POINT OF VIEW FOCUSES ON THOUGHTS AND DEEDS OF A MAJOR CHARACTER.   More common than the omniscient point of view is the *limited third person*, or **limited-omniscient third-person point of view,** in which the author confines or *limits* the narration to the actions and thoughts of a major character. In our accident case, Frank, being Bill's friend, would be sympathetic to Bill; thus, his report of the collision would likely be third-person limited, with Bill as the center of interest. Depending on whether a narration focuses on action or motivation, the narrative may explore the mentalities of the characters either lightly or in depth. The name given to the central figure on whom the third-person omniscient point of view is focused is the **point-of-view character.** Thus, Miss Brill in "Miss Brill," Peyton Farquhar in "An Occurrence at Owl Creek Bridge," and Goodman Brown in "Young Goodman Brown" are all point-of-view characters. Virtually everything in these stories is there because the point-of-view characters see it, hear it, respond to it, think about it, imagine it entirely, do it or share in it, try to control it, or are controlled by it.

☙ THE MINGLING OF POINTS OF VIEW

In many works, authors mingle points of view in order to imitate reality. For example, many first-person narrators use various types of the third-person point of view during much of their narration. Authors may also vary points of view to sustain interest, create suspense, or put the burden of response entirely upon readers. For example, Mansfield in "Miss Brill" inter-

---

CONSIDER VERB TENSES AS AN ASPECT OF POINT OF VIEW

Usually *point of view* refers to the ways narrators and speakers perceive and report actions and speeches, but in the broadest sense, point of view may be considered as a total way of rendering truth, and for this reason the *tense* chosen by the narrators is important. Most narratives rely on the past tense: The actions happened in the past, and they are now over. The introduction of dialogue, however, even in a past-tense narration, is a dramatic means of bringing the story into the present. The dialogue concluding Maupassant's "The Necklace," for example, emphasizes the immediacy of Mathilde's problems. In addition, the narrator of a past-tense narrative may introduce present-tense commentary during the narration—a strong means of signifying the importance of past events. Such narrators occur in Hardy's "The Three Strangers," in which the narrator begins and ends in the present, and Arnold's "Dover Beach," in which the speaker shifts past tense to present tense both to express past action and also to make general comments. In addition, as noted in Chapter 10, the narrators of *parables* and *fables* use past-tense narratives as vehicles for teaching current lessons in philosophy and religion.

In recent years, many writers have used the present tense as their principal time reference. With the present tense, the narrative story or poem is rendered as a virtual drama that is unfolded moment by moment. In Wagner's "The Boxes," for instance, the speaker employs the present tense to emphasize the immediate experiences of her sorrow. Some writers intermingle tenses to show how time itself may be merged with the human consciousness and to show the fusion of past, present, and future within a character's mind. For example, at the end of Bierce's "An Occurrence at Owl Creek Bridge," the past-tense narration shifts into the present tense to demonstrate the vividness of the main character's perceptions just before his death (paragraph 36).

---

rupts the limited omniscient focus on Miss Brill's thoughts and reactions immediately after she has been insulted by the young couple on the bench. The last paragraphs are objective until the last sentence, when the limited omniscient point of view is resumed. The result is that Miss Brill is made totally alone in her grief, cut off; readers can no longer share her sorrow as they earlier shared her observations about the characters in the park. A similar shift occurs at the end of Hawthorne's "Young Goodman Brown," where the narrator objectively and almost brutally summarizes Brown's morose and loveless life after his nightmare about evil.

👕 GUIDELINES FOR POINTS OF VIEW

The following guidelines summarize and further classify the types of points of view. Use them to distinguish differences and shades of variation in stories and poems.

1. **First person (*I, my, me,* and [sometimes] *we, our,* and *us*).** First-person speakers are involved to at least some degree in the actions of the work. Such narrators may have (1) complete understanding, (2) partial or incorrect understanding, (3) no understanding at all, or (4) complete understanding with the motive to mislead or lie. Although the narrators described in 2 through 4 usually are *reliable* and tell the truth, they may also sometimes be *unreliable.*

   a. *Major participant,*
      i. Who tells his or her own story and thoughts as a **major mover.**
      ii. Who tells a story about others and also about herself or himself as one of the major movers.
      iii. Who tells a story mainly about others, and about himself or herself only tangentially.
   b. *Minor participant,* who tells a story about events experienced and witnessed.
   c. *Nonparticipating but identifiable speaker,* who learns about events in other ways (e.g., listening to participants, examining documents, hearing news reports, imagining what might have occurred). The narrative of such a speaker is a combination of fact and conjectural reconstruction.

2. **Second person (*you*).** This use occurs (1) when the speaker (e.g., parent, psychologist) knows more about a character's actions than the character himself or herself; or (2) when the speaker (e.g., lawyer, spouse, friend, sports umpire) is explaining to another person (the "you") that person's disputable actions and statements. The speaker may also use "you" to mean (3) himself or herself or (4) anyone at all.

3. **Third person (*she, he, it, they*).** The speaker is outside the action and is mainly a reporter of actions and speeches. Some speakers may have unique and distinguishing traits even though no separate identity is claimed for them ("the unnamed third-person narrator"). Other third-person speakers who are not separately identifiable may represent the words and views of the authors themselves ("the authorial voice").

   a. *Dramatic or third-person objective.* The narrator reports only what can be seen and heard. The thoughts of characters are included only if they are spoken or written (dialogue, reported or overheard conversation, letters, reports, etc.).
   b. *Omniscient.* The omniscient speaker sees all, reports all, knows all, and explains the inner workings of the minds of any or all characters (when necessary).
   c. *Limited, or limited omniscient.* The focus is on the actions, responses, thoughts, and feelings of a single major character. The narration may involve primarily what the character does, and it may also probe deeply within the consciousness of the character.

☙ WRITING ABOUT POINT OF VIEW

Your goal is to explain how point of view contributes to making the work exactly as it is. In prewriting, therefore, consider language, authority and opportunity for observation, the involvement or detachment of the speaker, the selection of detail, interpretive commentaries, and narrative development. The following questions will help you get started.

Raise Questions to Discover Ideas

- How is the narration made to seem real or probable? Are the actions and speeches reported authentically, as they might be seen and reported in life? Is the narrator identifiable? What are the narrator's qualifications as an observer? How much of the story seems to result from the imaginative or creative powers of the narrator?
- How does the narrator perceive the time of the actions? If the predominant tense is the past, what relationship, if any, does the speaker establish between the past and the present (e.g., drawing lessons, providing explanations). If the tense is present, what effect does this tense have on your understanding of the story?
- To what extent does the point of view make the work interesting and effective, or uninteresting and ineffective?

First-Person Point of View

- What is the speaker's background? What situation prompts her to tell the story?
- Is the speaker talking to the reader, a listener, or himself? How does his audience affect what he says? Is the level of language appropriate to him and the situation? How much does he tell about himself?
- To what degree is the narrator involved in the action (i.e., as a major participant, minor participant, or nonparticipating observer)? Does she make herself the center of humor or admiration? How? Does she seem aware of changes that she undergoes?
- Does the speaker criticize other characters? Why? Does he seem to report fairly and accurately what others have told him?
- How reliable is the speaker? Does the speaker seem to have anything to hide? Does it seem that she may be using the story for self-justification or exoneration? What effect does this complexity have on the story?

Second-Person Point of View

- What is the situation that prompts the use of the second person? How does the speaker acquire the authority to explain things to the listener? How directly involved is the listener? If the listeners are indefinite, why does the speaker choose to use the "you" as the basis of the narration?

Third-Person Point of View

- Does the author seem to be speaking in an authorial voice, or has the author adopted a special but unnamed voice for the work?
- What is the speaker's level of language? Are actions, speeches, and explanations made fully or sparsely?
- From what apparent vantage point does the speaker report action and speeches? Does this vantage point make the characters seem distant or close? How much sympathy does the speaker express for the characters?

- To what degree is your interest centered on a particular character? Does the speaker give you the thoughts and responses of this character (limited third person)?
- If the work is third-person omniscient, how extensive is this omniscience (e.g., for all the characters or just a few)? Generally, what limitations or freedoms can be attributed to this point of view?
- What special kinds of knowledge does the narrator assume that the listeners or readers possess (e.g., art, religion, history, navigation, music)?

Organize Your Essay About Point of View

Throughout your essay, your object should be to develop your analysis of how the point of view determines such aspects as situation, form, general content, and language. The questions in the preceding section will help you decide how the point of view interacts with these other elements.

INTRODUCTION.   Begin by briefly stating the major influence of the point of view on the work. (Examples: "The omniscient point of view permits many insights into the major character," or "The first-person point of view permits the work to resemble an exposé of backroom political deals.") How does the point of view make the work interesting and effective? How will your analysis support your central idea?

BODY.   An excellent way to build your argument is to explore how some other point of view might affect the work you are considering. Hardy's poem "Channel Firing," for example, uses a first-person speaker— a skeleton long buried in a churchyard cemetery near the ocean. This speaker is awakened by the noise of nearby naval guns, a bizarre situation prompting ironic humor that could not be duplicated with a third-person point of view. Hardy's first-person point of view is essential because we learn, firsthand, about the narrator's feelings. Indeed, the poem is totally dependent on this narrator. Conversely, Mansfield's "Miss Brill" employs the third-person limited point of view, with the speaker presenting an intimate portrait of the major character but also preserving an objective and ironic distance. If Miss Brill herself were the narrator, we would get the intimacy that encourages us to sympathize with her, but we would lose the distance that permits us to see her objectively.

You can see that this approach requires creative imagination, for you must speculate about a point of view that is not present. Considering alternative points of view deeply, however, will greatly enhance your analytical and critical abilities.

CONCLUSION.   In your conclusion, evaluate the success of the point of view: Is it consistent, effective, truthful? What does the writer gain or lose (if anything) by the selection of point of view?

Sample Essay

Bierce's Control over Point of View in "An Occurrence at Owl Creek Bridge"°

[1]
Ambrose Bierce's control over point of view in "An Occurrence at Owl Creek Bridge" is essential to his success in showing the human mental capacity to register an immense length of perceived time and action in no more than an instant of real time.* The story is based on the idea that it is an individual's mind, not the actual passage of time, that governs time perception. Ordinarily, time seems steady and unvarying, like the ticking of a clock (see paragraph 5 of the story); but at certain heightened instances of perception—in the story, the moment just before death—a person may fully imagine experiences that take much longer than the measurable, real time. Bierce brings this idea to life by using a narrative in the dramatic point of view as the frame of a narrative in the third-person limited omniscient point of view.†

[2]
The story is framed, at both the opening and closing, by materials narrated from the dramatic point of view. The opening is an objective account of the story's basic circumstances: During the Civil War, Peyton Farquhar, a Southern loyalist, is about to be hanged by the Union army, apparently for the attempted sabotage of the railroad bridge spanning Owl Creek, a stream in northern Alabama. Bierce changes from the objective point of view in the fourth paragraph, and he then centers on Farquhar through the limited omniscient point of view. The second section of the story, which views Farquhar objectively, explains how Farquhar got to the point of hanging. Almost the entire third section—twenty descriptive paragraphs—focuses exclusively on Farquhar's last moments of life. Beginning with the reality of his drop, he perceives that the rope breaks and that he falls into the water, avoids the rifle and cannon fire of the Union soldiers, swims to shore, walks home, and is greeted by his wife. This dream of happiness is ended in paragraph 37, the last, which marks an abrupt and brutal return to the dramatic point of view with which the story opens:

> Peyton Farquhar was dead; his body, with a broken neck, swung gently from side to side beneath the timbers of the Owl Creek bridge.

[3]
The best part of the story, the "framed" part, is Bierce's use of a limited third-person narration to render Farquhar's mental perceptions. We first encounter this method in the narrator's ironic statement about Farquhar: "The arrangement [i.e., the apparatus for hanging] commended itself to his judgment as simple and effective" (paragraph 4). Bierce carefully explains how the rest of the story is to be told. First, he states that Farquhar's "thoughts, which have here to be set down in words, were flashed into the doomed man's brain"

°See pages 304–10 for this story.
*Central idea.
†Thesis sentence.

[3]
(paragraph 7). He also states that the hanging man's agony heightens his understanding: "Something in the awful disturbance of his organic system" exalts and refines his physical senses so that they record things "never before perceived" (paragraph 20, underlining added). On this principle of narration, Bierce's narrator plumbs the depths of Farquhar's dying consciousness—an entire narrative of escape that flashes through Farquhar's mind during his last moments.

[4]
The escape, which forms the narrative of the third section, seems to be happening plausibly and realistically in just the way that the reader, naturally sympathetic to Farquhar, wants it to happen. The power of the story results from this tension between desire and actuality. Bierce's limited omniscient narrator is careful in the very second sentence of the third section to fuse together the two elements of time and perception so vital to the story's development: "ages later, it seemed to him" (paragraph 18). All the details about Farquhar's dreams of escape stem out of the words ages and seemed. Under special circumstances, in other words, human perception can fit almost a lifetime of detail into no more than fractions of a second.

[5]
Therefore the dying man's perception of detail is the story's major emphasis. At first, the narrator's descriptions indicate that Farquhar's imagination is sharp enough even to record the eye color of one of the Union soldiers. Farquhar's mind soon gets weaker, however, and his perceptions become more dreamlike and impressionistic. By describing the road bordered by "black bodies" of trees forming "a straight wall on both sides, terminating on the horizon in a point," Bierce's narrator demonstrates Farquhar's dimming consciousness and increasing distortion of reality (paragraph 34). Paragraph 36, which changes the narrative from the past to the present tense, contains Farquhar's vision during the last split second of his life. His final mental image is that his wife "steps down from the verandah to meet him," and "stands waiting" for him (present tenses underlined). It is then that his life is ended forever by the very realistic "blow upon the back of the neck."

[6]
Even though the events are told through Farquhar's hopeful vision of escape, however, this realistic blow reminds us that the narrative constantly reveals his physical agony. A number of times we are told that Farquhar is feeling "pain," that he is "suffocating," that he feels a "sharp pain in his wrist," and that "his neck ached horribly; his brain was on fire" (paragraphs 18, 19, 35). We may take as equally real Farquhar's sensation that his "visible world" seems to be wheeling "slowly round" (paragraph 21), for this perception is consistent with the sensations of a hanging, dying man. In other words, just as the narrative concentrates on Farquhar's understanding of reality, it also demonstrates the true reality of his final death pangs.

[7]
Without doubt, the merging of Bierce's narrative voice with the consciousness of the dying man makes the story unique. No other method could give the story its credibility and power, which depend on the disclosure of what is happening in the protagonist's mind. For example, the use of the dramatic point of view, with which the story opens and closes, does not permit access to the internal thoughts of a character. In much the same way, the first-person point of view—focusing on an unconscious and dying man—does not permit any recording of what is happening. It is therefore clear that Bierce's limited omniscient point of view is absolutely right. The method permits him to make the events seem both realistic and convincing and also to create sympathy for Farquhar because of his poignant hopes and dreams.

[8]
Such masterly control over point of view is a major cause of Bierce's success in "An Occurrence at Owl Creek Bridge." His narrative method is to establish a frame of normal reality and normal time, and then to render con-

[8] trasting interior perceptions of perceived reality and perceived time. He is so successful that a casual reader might at first conclude that Farquhar's escape is real. The reality is not in the events, however, but in the perceptions. Without Bierce's mingling of the dramatic and the limited points of view, it would not be possible to claim such success for the story.

❦ COMMENTARY ON THE ESSAY

The strategy of this essay is to explain how Bierce's use of the limited omniscient point of view is fundamental to his success in demonstrating how time may be compressed in heightened moments of awareness. Words of tribute throughout the essay are "success," "control," "dominating," "right," and "masterly."

The introductory paragraph sets out two major areas of investigation for the essay: first, the use of the dramatic point of view as a frame, and, second, the limited omniscient point of view as the center of concentration.

The first part of the essay (paragraph 2) is relatively brief. Only enough is brought out about the dramatic point of view to establish that Bierce uses it as a beginning and an ending frame for the deep examination of the narration happening in the protagonist's mind.

The second part of the body (paragraphs 3 to 7) emphasizes how Bierce delves into the dying protagonist's mind. The goal of paragraphs 3 to 5 is to show how the narrator's point of view virtually merges with that of Farquhar. Paragraph 6 is designed as a defense of the narrative method because throughout the narration, Bierce always reports the immense pain that Farquhar is feeling. In other words, the story faithfully and truthfully renders the perception of both agony and extended time. Continuing the thread of the argument, paragraph 7 examines other narrative possibilities for presenting Farquhar's vision and concludes that Bierce's actual choices are the best that could have been made.

The concluding paragraph (8) emphasizes again how Bierce's success is attributable to his use of both the dramatic and the limited omniscient points of view.

❦ SPECIAL WRITING TOPICS FOR STUDYING POINT OF VIEW

1. Write a short narrative from the point of view of one of these characters:
   a. Mathilde Loisel in "The Necklace": How I ruined ten years of my life by not telling the truth.
   b. The baker in "Miss Brill": My favorite customer.

   c. Fortunato in "The Cask of Amontillado": Now, why did he do this to me?

   d. Faith in "Young Goodman Brown": What could possibly have gotten into my husband?

   e. Nora in "First Confession": My terrible younger brother.

2. How would the story "Young Goodman Brown" be affected if told by a narrator with a different point of view (different knowledge, different interests, different purposes for telling the story), such as the narrators of "The Three Strangers" or "An Occurrence at Owl Creek Bridge"?

3. Recall a childhood occasion on which you were punished. Write an explanation of the punishment as though you were the adult who was in the position of punishing you. Be sure to consider your childhood self objectively, in the third person. Present things from the viewpoint of the adult, and try to determine how the adult would have learned about your action, judged it, and decided on your punishment.

4. Write an essay about the proposition that people often have something to gain when they speak and that therefore we need to be critical about what others tell us. Are they trying to change our judgments and opinions? Are they telling the truth? Are they leaving out any important details? Are they trying to sell us something? In your discussion, you may strengthen your ideas by referring to stories that you have been reading.

5. In the reference section of your library, find two books on literary terms and concepts. How completely and clearly do these works explain the concept of point of view? With the aid of these books, together with the materials in this chapter, describe the interests and views of the narrators in "First Confession," "An Occurrence at Owl Creek Bridge," "Echo," "On First Looking Into Chapman's Homer," or another work of your choice.

chapter 7

Writing About an Idea or a Theme:

The Meaning and the Message in Literature

The word **idea** refers to the result or results, of general, particular, and abstract thinking. Synonymous words are *concept, thought, opinion,* and *principle.* In literary study, the consideration of ideas relates to *meaning, interpretation, explanation,* and *significance.* Although ideas are usually extensive and complex, separate ideas may be named by single words, such as *right, good, love, piety, causation, wilderness,* and, not unsurprisingly, *idea* itself.

✻ IDEAS AND ASSERTIONS

Although single words alone may thus name ideas, we must put these words into operation in *sentences* or *assertions* before they can advance our understanding. Good operational sentences about ideas are not the same as ordinary conversational statements such as "It's a nice day." An observation of this sort may be true (depending on the weather), but it gives us no ideas and does not stimulate our minds. Rather, a sentence asserting an idea should initiate *thought* about the day's quality, such as "A nice day requires light breezes, blue sky, a warm sun, and relaxation." Because this sentence makes an assertion about "nice," it allows us to consider and develop the idea of a nice day.

In studying literature, always express ideas as assertions. For example, you might state that an idea in Chekhov's *The Bear* is "love," but it would be difficult to discuss anything more unless you make an assertion such as "*The Bear* demonstrates the idea that love is irresistible and irrational." This assertion would lead you to explain the unlikely love that bursts out in the story. Similarly, for Shakespeare's Sonnet 73 ("That Time of Year Thou Mayest in Me Behold"), an assertion like the following would help advance further thinking: "The speaker's explanation of his increasing age embodies the idea that love can take place only within a narrow span of time."

Although we have noted only one idea in these two works, most stories contain many ideas. When one of the ideas seems to be the major one, it is called the **theme.** In practice, the words *theme* and *major idea* are the same.

🗝 IDEAS AND VALUES

Literature embodies **values** along with ideas. *Value,* of course, commonly refers to the price of something, but in the realm of ideas and principles, it is a standard of what is desired, sought, esteemed, and treasured. For example, *democracy* refers to our political system, but it is also a complex idea of representative government that we esteem most highly, and so also do we esteem concepts like honor, cooperation, generosity, and love. A vital idea/value is *justice,* which, put most simply, involves equality before the law and also the fair evaluation of conduct that is deemed unacceptable or illegal. Such an idea of justice is a major topic of Glaspell's play *Trifles.* Glaspell dramatizes the story of a farm wife who, for thirty years, endures her husband's intimidation and her abject circumstances of life, but who finally rises up to strangle her husband in his sleep. By a rigid concept of justice as guilt-conviction-punishment, the wife, Minnie Wright, is guilty and should be convicted. But justice as an idea also involves a full and fair consideration of the circumstances and motivation of wrongdoing, and it is such a consideration that the two women on stage make during their examination of Minnie's kitchen. Many of their speeches showing their sympathy to Minnie are equivalent to a jurylike deliberation. Their final decision is like a verdict, and their final covering up of Minnie's crime is evidence for their idea that justice, to be most highly valued, should be tempered with understanding—even if they never use these exact words in their discussions of Minnie's situation. In short, the idea of justice underlying Glaspell's *Trifles* also involves a deeply felt value.

🗝 THE PLACE OF IDEAS IN LITERATURE

Because writers of poems, plays, and stories are usually not systematic philosophers, it would be a mistake to go "message hunting" as though their works contained nothing but ideas. Indeed, there is great benefit and pleasure to be derived from just savoring a work—following the patterns of narrative and conflict, getting to like the characters, understanding the work's implications and suggestions, and listening to the sounds of the author's words—to name only a few of the reasons for which literature is treasured.

Nevertheless, ideas are vital to understanding and appreciating literature: Writers have ideas and want to communicate them. For example, in *The Bear,* Chekhov directs laughter at two unlikely people suddenly and unpredictably falling in love. The play is funny, however, not only because it is preposterous but also because it is based on the *idea* that love takes precedence over other resolutions that people might make. Blake in "The Tyger" describes the "fearful symmetry" of a wild tiger in "the forests of the night," but the poem also embodies *ideas* about the inexplicability of evil, the mystery of life, and the unsearchability of divine purpose in the universe.

Distinguish Between Ideas and Actions

As you analyze works for ideas, it is important to avoid the trap of confusing ideas and actions. Such a trap is contained in the following sentence about O'Connor's "First Confession": "The major character, Jackie, misbehaves at home and tries to stab his grandmother with a bread knife." This sentence successfully describes a major action in the story, but it does not express an *idea* that connects characters and events, and for this reason it obstructs understanding. Some possible connections might be achieved with sentences like these: "'First Confession' illustrates the idea that family life sometimes produces anger and potential violence"; or "'First Confession' shows that compelling children to accept authority may produce effects that are the opposite of adult intentions." A study based on these connecting formulations could be focused on ideas and would not be sidetracked into doing no more than retelling O'Connor's story.

Distinguish Between Ideas and Situations

You should also distinguish between ideas and situations. For example, in Lowell's "Patterns," the narrator describes what is happening to her as a result of her fiancé's death. Her plight is a situation, but it is not any of the ideas brought out by the situation. For example, one of the poem's major ideas is that future plans may be destroyed by uncontrollable circumstances. In such ways, if you are able to distinguish a work's various situations from the writer's major idea or ideas, as we have done here, you will be able to focus on ideas and therefore sharpen your own thinking.

❦ HOW TO FIND IDEAS

Ideas are not as obvious as characters or setting. To determine an idea, you need to consider the meaning of what you read and then to develop explanatory and comprehensive assertions. Your assertions need not be the same as those that others might make. People notice different things, and individual formulations vary. In Chopin's "The Story of an Hour," for example, an initial expression of some of the story's ideas might take any of the following forms: (1) Partners in even a good marriage may have ambiguous ideas about their married life. (2) An accident may bring out negative but previously unrecognized thoughts in a woman. (3) Even those closest to a person may never realize that person's innermost feelings. Although any one of these choices could be a basic idea for studying "The Story of an Hour," they all have in common the main character's surprising feelings of release when she is told that her husband has been killed. In discovering ideas, you should follow a similar process—making a number of formulations for an idea and then selecting one for further development.

As you read, be alert to the different ways in which authors convey ideas. One author might prefer an indirect way through a character's speeches, whereas another may prefer direct statement. In practice, authors may employ any or all the following methods.

1. **Study the words of the authorial voice.** Although authors mainly render action, dialogue, and situation, they sometimes state ideas to guide us and deepen our understanding. In the second paragraph of "The Necklace," for example, Maupassant's authorial voice presents the idea that women have only charm and beauty to get on in the world. Ironically, Maupassant uses the story to show that for the major character Mathilde, nothing is effective, for her charm cannot prevent disaster. Hawthorne, in "Young Goodman Brown," expresses a powerful idea that "The fiend in his own shape is less hideous than when he rages in the breast of man" (paragraph 53). This statement is made as authorial commentary just when the major character, Goodman Brown, is speeding through the "benighted wilderness" on his way to the satanic meeting. Although the idea is complex and will bear extensive discussion, its essential aspect is that the causes of evil originate within human beings themselves, with the implication that we alone are responsible for all our actions, whether good or evil.

2. **Study the words and thoughts of the first-person speaker.** First-person narrators or speakers frequently express ideas along with their depiction of actions and situations, and they also make statements from which you can make inferences about ideas. (See also Chapter 6.) Because what they say is part of a dramatic presentation, they may be right or wrong, well-considered or thoughtless, good or bad, or brilliant or half-baked, depending on the speaker. The speaker in Arnold's "Dover Beach," for example, laments the diminution of vital ideas from the past, concluding that this loss is accompanied by in-

creasing ignorance, uncertainty, and violence in the world. In Hardy's "Channel Firing," the speaker—a skeleton suddenly awakened by the noise of nearby naval gunfire—implies that warfare has been a constant menace to humanity from ancient days to the present. If the speaker possesses a dubious character, such as the narrator Montresor of Poe's "The Cask of Amontillado," you may nevertheless still study and evaluate such a speaker's ideas. Montresor, for example, begins his narrative by describing his idea of personal revenge—an unpleasant idea, but an idea just the same.

3. **Study the dramatic statements made by characters.** In stories, poems, and plays, characters often express their own views, which may be right or wrong, thought-provoking or negligible. When you consider such dramatic speeches, you must do considerable interpreting and evaluating yourself. For example, In Chekhov's *The Bear*, both Smirnov and Mrs. Popov express many silly ideas as they begin speaking to each other, and it is their sudden love that reveals to them how wrongheaded their ideas have been. The men in Glaspell's *Trifles* express conventional masculine ideas about the need for men to control women ("a sheriff's wife is married to the law" [speech 143]). The play itself, however, demonstrates the shortcomings and pomposity of their thought.

4. **Study the work's figurative language.** One of the major components of poetry is figurative language. (See also Chapter 9.) In the sonnet "Bright Star," for example, Keats symbolizes the idea of constancy with his references to a fixed star, presumably the North Star. In addition, figurative language is to be found liberally in fiction and drama. Thus at the opening of Mansfield's "Miss Brill," the narrator likens a sunny day to gold and white wine—a lovely comparison conveying the idea that the world is a place of beauty and happiness. This idea contrasts ironically with the indifference and cruelty that Miss Brill experiences. In Glaspell's *Trifles*, a character compares John Wright, the murdered husband, with "a raw wind that gets to the bone" (speech 103). With this figurative language, Glaspell conveys the idea that bluntness, indifference, and cruelty create great personal damage.

5. **Observe the degree to which characters may stand for ideas.** Characters and their actions may often be equated with certain ideas and values. The power of Mathilde's story in "The Necklace," for example, enables us to explain that she represents the idea that unrealizable dreams may invade and damage the real world. Two diverse or opposed characters may embody contrasting ideas, as with Louise and Josephine of Chopin's "The Story of an Hour"; each woman may be taken to represent differing views about the role of women in marriage.

    In effect, characters who stand for ideas may assume symbolic status, as in Hawthorne's "Young Goodman Brown," where the protagonist symbolizes the alienation accompanying zealousness. The speaker of Frost's "Desert Places" invites identification as a symbol of the frightening qualities of emptiness and unconcern within human beings. Such characters may be equated directly with particular ideas, and to talk about them is a shorthand way of talking about the ideas.

6. **Consider the work itself as an embodiment of ideas.** One of the most important ways in which authors express ideas is to interlock them within all parts

and aspects of the work. The art of painting is instructive here, for a painting may be taken in with a single view that comprehends all the aspects of color, form, action, and expression, which may also be considered separately. In the same way, when a work is considered in its totality, the various parts collectively may embody major ideas. For example, Christina Rossetti builds the poem "Echo" (Chapter 14, page 205) on the idea that the loss of time does not diminish the significance of memory and love. The third section of Bierce's "An Occurrence at Owl Creek Bridge" is based on the idea that under stressful conditions, the human mind operates with lightning speed. Most works represent ideas in a similar way. Even "escape literature," which ostensibly enables readers to forget immediate problems, contains conflicts between good and evil, love and hate, good spies and bad, earthlings and aliens, and so on. Thereby, such works *do* embody ideas, even though their avowed intention is not to make readers think but rather to help them forget.

☌ WRITING ABOUT A MAJOR IDEA IN LITERATURE

Most likely you will write about a major idea or theme, but you may also get interested in one of your story's other ideas. As you begin brainstorming and developing your first drafts, consider questions such as the following.

Raise Questions to Discover Ideas

General Ideas

- What ideas do you discover in the work? How do you discover them (through action, character depiction, scenes, language)?
- To what do the ideas pertain? To the individuals themselves? To individuals and society? To religion? To social, political, or economic justice?
- How balanced are the ideas? If a particular idea is strongly presented, what conditions and qualifications are also presented (if any)? What contradictory ideas are presented?
- Are the ideas limited to members of any groups represented by the characters (age, race, nationality, personal status)? Or are the ideas applicable to general conditions of life? Explain.
- Which characters in their own right represent or embody ideas? How do their actions and speeches bring these ideas out?
- If characters state ideas directly, how persuasive is their expression, how intelligent and well-considered? How germane are the ideas to the work? How germane to more general conditions?
- With children, young adults, or the old, how do the circumstances express or embody an idea?

A Specific Idea

- What idea seems particularly important in the work? Why? Is it asserted directly, indirectly, dramatically, ironically? Does any one method predominate? Why?
- How pervasive in the work is the idea (throughout or intermittent)? To what degree is it associated with a major character or action? How does the structure of the work affect or shape your understanding of the idea?
- What value or values are embodied in the idea? Of what importance are the values to the work's meaning?
- How compelling is the idea? How could the work be appreciated without reference to any idea at all?

Organize Your Essay on a Major Idea or Theme

Remember that in well-written stories, poems, and plays, narrative and dramatic elements have a strong bearing on ideas. In this sense, an idea is like a key in music or like a continuous thread tying together actions, characters, statements, symbols, and dialogue. As readers, you can trace such threads throughout the entire fabric of the work.

As you write about ideas, you may find yourself relying most heavily on the direct statements of the author's voice, or on a combination of these and your interpretation of characters and action; or you might focus exclusively on a first-person speaker, and use his or her ideas to develop your analysis. Always make clear the sources of your details, and distinguish the sources from your own commentary.

INTRODUCTION. In your introduction, state your general goal of describing an idea and of showing its importance in the work. Your statement of the idea will be your central idea for your essay.

BODY. Each separate work will invite its own approach, but here are a number of strategies you might use to organize your essay.

1. **Analyze the idea as it applies to character.** Example: "Minnie Wright embodies the idea that living with cruelty and insensitivity leads to alienation, unhappiness, despair, and sometimes to violence" (Glaspell's *Trifles*).

2. **Show how actions bring out the idea.** Example: "That Mrs. Popov and Smirnov fall in love rather than go their separate ways indicates Chekhov's idea that love literally rescues human lives" (*The Bear*).

3. **Show how dialogue and separate speeches bring out the idea.** Example: "The priest's responses to Jackie's confession embody the idea that kindness and understanding are the best means to encourage religious and philosophical commitment" (O'Connor's "First Confession").

4. **Show how the work's structure is determined by the idea.** Example: "The idea that horror may infect a nation's beauty and tradition leads Layton to introduce and conclude the poem by referring to elements of the Holocaust" ("Rhine Boat Trip").

5. **Treat variations or differing manifestations of the idea.** Example: "The idea that zealousness leads to harm is shown in Brown's nightmarish distortion of reality, his rejection of others, and his dying gloom" (Hawthorne's "Young Goodman Brown").

6. **Deal with a combination of these (together with any other significant aspect).** Example: "Chekhov's idea in *The Bear* that love is complex and contradictory is shown in Smirnov's initial scorn of Mrs. Popov, his self-declared independence of character, and his concluding embrace." (Here the idea is traced through speech, character, and action.)

CONCLUSION. Your conclusion might begin with a summary, together with your evaluation of the validity or force of the idea. If you have been convinced by the author's ideas, you might say that the author has expressed the idea forcefully and convincingly, or else you might show the relevance of the idea to current conditions. If you are not persuaded by the idea, you should demonstrate the idea's shortcomings or limitations. If you wish to mention a related idea, whether in the story you have studied or in some other story, you might introduce that idea here, but be sure to stress the connections.

Sample Essay

The Idea of Love's Power in Chekhov's The Bear °

---

[1]   In the one-act farce *The Bear,* Anton Chekhov presents a previously unacquainted man and woman, twenty minutes after they first meet, falling passionately in love. With such an unlikely main action, ideas may seem unimportant, but the play does contain a number of ideas. Some of these are that responsibility to life is stronger than to death, that people may justify even the most stupid and contradictory actions, that love makes people do foolish things, and that lifelong commitments may be made with hardly any thought at all. One of the play's major ideas is that love and desire are powerful enough to overcome even the strongest obstacles.* This idea is shown as the force of love conquers commitment to the dead, renunciation of womankind, unfamiliarity, and anger.†

°See pages 366–75 for this play.
*Central idea.
†Thesis sentence.

[2]

<u>Commitment to her dead husband is Mrs. Popov's obstacle to love</u>. She states that she has made a vow never to see daylight because of her mourning (speech 4), and she wallows in her own self-righteousness. Her devotion is so intense that she claims to be almost dead herself out of sympathy for her husband:

> My life is already ended. He lies in his grave; I have buried myself in these four walls . . . we are both dead. (speech 2)

In her, Chekhov has created a strong obstacle so that he might show the power of all-conquering love. By the play's end, Mrs. Popov's embracing Smirnov is a visual example of the idea (speech 151, S.D.).

[3]

<u>Renunciation of women is Smirnov's obstacle</u>. He tells Mrs. Popov that women have made him bitter and that he no longer gives "a good goddamn" about them (speech 69). These words seem to make him an impossible candidate for love; but, in keeping with Chekhov's idea, Smirnov soon confesses his sudden and uncontrollable love at the peak of his anger against Mrs. Popov. Within him, the force of love operates so strongly that he would even claim happiness at being shot by Mrs. Popov's "little velvet hands" (speech 140).

[4]

<u>As if these personal causes were not enough to stop love, a genuine obstacle is that the two people are strangers</u>. Not only have they never met, but also they have never even heard of each other. According to the main idea, however, this unfamiliarity is no major problem. Chekhov is dramatizing the power of love, and shows that it is strong enough to overcome even the lack of familiarity or previous friendship.

[5]

<u>Anger and the threat of violence, however, make the greatest obstacle</u>. The two characters get so irritated about Smirnov's demand that Mrs. Popov pay her dead husband's debt that, as an improbable climax of their heated words, Smirnov challenges Mrs. Popov, a woman, to a duel! He shouts,

> And do you think just because you're one of those romantic creations, that you have the right to insult me with impunity? Yes? I challenge you! (speech 105)

[6]

Along with their own personal barriers against loving, it would seem that the threat of shooting each other, even if poor Luka could stop them, would cause lifelong hatred. Yet love knocks down all these obstacles, in line with Chekhov's idea that love's power is as irresistible as a flood.

The idea of love's power is not new or unusual. It is the subject of popular songs, stories, other plays, movies, and T.V. shows. What is surprising about Chekhov's use of the idea is that love in *The Bear* overcomes such unlikely conditions and wins so suddenly. These conditions bring up an interesting and closely related idea: Chekhov is showing that intensely negative feeling may lead not to hatred but rather to love. The speeches of Smirnov and Mrs. Popov contain disappointment, regret, frustration, annoyance, anger, rage, and potential destructiveness. Yet at the high point of these negative feelings, love takes over. It is as though hostility finally collapses because it is the nature of people to prefer loving to hating. <u>*The Bear* is an uproarious dramatization of the power of love, and it is made better because it is founded on a truthful judgment of the way people really are.</u>

⚘ COMMENTARY ON THE ESSAY

This essay follows the sixth strategy (page 114) by showing how separate components from the play exhibit the pervasiveness of the idea. Throughout, dialogue, situations, soliloquies, and actions are evidence for the various conclusions. Transitions between paragraphs are effected by phrases like "these personal causes" (paragraph 4), "greatest obstacle" (paragraph 5), and "the idea" (paragraph 6), all of which emphasize the continuity of the topic.

Paragraph 1 notes that the play contains a number of ideas, the major one being that love has the power to surmount great obstacles. The thesis sentence lists the four obstacles to be explored in the body.

As the operative aspects of Chekhov's idea, paragraphs 2 through 5 detail the nature of each of the obstacles. The obstacle of paragraph 2, Mrs. Popov's commitment to her husband's memory, is "strong." The one in paragraph 3, Smirnov's dislike of women, is seemingly "impossible." The one in paragraph 4, their being total strangers, is a "genuinely real" difficulty. In paragraph 5, the obstacle of anger is more likely to produce "hatred" than love.

Paragraph 6, beyond providing a brief summary, suggests another related and important idea, namely that people cannot long sustain destructive anger. Obviously this second idea is a broad generalization and could bear extensive treatment in its own right. Even though the topic would require greater development if it came at the beginning, it is effective as a part of the conclusion. The final sentence blends the two ideas, thereby looking both inward into the theme and outward toward the consideration of new ideas.

⚘ SPECIAL WRITING TOPICS
FOR STUDYING IDEAS

1. Compare two works containing similar events and themes. (Examples: "Dover Beach" and "Channel Firing"; "Bright Star" and "Let Me Not to the Marriage of True Minds"; "Desert Places" and "Young Goodman Brown"; "Rhine Boat Trip" and "The Cask of Amontillado"; "The Story of an Hour" and *The Bear*; "Echo" and "The Boxes.") For help in developing your essay, consult Chapter 13 on the technique of comparison-contrast.

2. Consider "The Necklace" in terms of the idea of economic determinism (see also Appendix A). That is, to what degree are the circumstances and traits of the characters, particularly Mathilde, controlled and limited by their economic status? According to the idea, how likely is it that the characters can ever rise above their circumstances?

3. Write an essay criticizing the ideas in a work in this anthology which you dislike or to which you are indifferent. With what statements in the work do you disagree? What actions? What characters? How do your own beliefs and values cause you to dislike the work's ideas? How might the work be changed to illustrate ideas with which you would agree? (See also Chapter 2.)

4. Select an idea that particularly interests you, and write a story showing how characters may or may not live up to the idea. If you have difficulty getting started, try one of these possible ideas:

   a. Interest and enthusiasm are hard to maintain.
   b. People always want more than they have or need.
   c. The concerns of adults are different from those of children.
   d. It is awkward to confront another person about a grievance.
   e. Making a decision is hard because it requires a complete change in life's direction.

5. Using books that you discover in the card or computer catalogue in your college or local library, search for discussions of only one of the following topics, and write a brief report on what you find.

   a. John Keats on the significance of intuition and imagination as creative power
   b. Nathaniel Hawthorne on the significance of religion, both good and bad
   c. Thomas Hardy on the power of the people and the working classes
   d. The ideas underlying Edgar Allan Poe's concept of the short story as a form

chapter 8

Writing About Imagery:
The Literary Work's Link to the Senses

In literature, **imagery** refers to words that trigger your imagination to recall and recombine **images**—memories or mental pictures of sights, sounds, tastes, smells, sensations of touch, and motions. The process is active and even vigorous, for when words or descriptions produce images, you are using your personal experiences with life and language to help you understand the works you are reading. In effect, you are re-creating the work *in your own way* through the controlled stimulation produced by the writer's words. Imagery is therefore one of the strongest modes of literary expression because it provides a channel to your active imagination, and along this channel, writers bring their works directly to you and into your consciousness.

For example, reading the word *lake* may bring to your mind your literal memory of a particular lake. Your mental picture—or image—may be a distant view of calm waters reflecting blue sky, a nearby view of gentle waves rippling in the wind, a close-up view of the sandy lake bottom from a boat, or an overhead view of a sun-drenched shoreline. Similarly, the words *rose, apple, hot dog, malted milk,* and *pizza* all cause you to recollect these objects, and, in addition, may cause you to recall their smells and tastes. Active and graphic words like *row, swim,* and *dive* stimulate you to picture moving images of someone performing these actions.

∜ RESPONSES AND THE WRITER'S USE
OF DETAIL

In studying imagery, we try to comprehend and explain our imaginative re-construction of the pictures and impressions evoked by the work's images. We let the poet's words simmer and percolate in our minds. To get our imaginations stirring, we might follow Coleridge in this description from "Kubla Khan":

> A damsel with a dulcimer
> In a vision once I saw:
> It was an Abyssinian maid,
> And on her dulcimer she played
> Singing of Mount Abora. (lines 37–41)

We do not read about the color of the young woman's clothing, or anything else about her appearance except that she is playing a stringed instrument, a dulcimer, and that she is singing a song about a mountain in a foreign, re-mote land. But Coleridge's image is enough. From it we can imagine a vivid, exotic picture of a young woman from a distant land singing, to-gether with the loveliness of her song (even though we never hear it or un-derstand it). The image lives.

∜ THE RELATIONSHIP OF IMAGERY
TO IDEAS AND ATTITUDES

Images do more than elicit impressions. By the *authenticating* effects of the vision and perceptions underlying them, they give you new ways of seeing the world and of strengthening your old ways of seeing it. Shakespeare, in "Let Me Not to the Marriage of True Minds," for example, develops the idea that love provides people with consistency of purpose in their lives. Rather than stating the idea directly, he uses images of a landmark or lighthouse and also of a fixed star—sights with which his readers are totally familiar:

> . . . it is an ever fixèd mark
> That looks on tempests and is never shaken;
> It is the star to every wandering bark
> Whose worth's unknown, although his height be taken.

These images form a link with readers that is clear and also verifiable by ob-servation. Such uses of imagery comprise one of the strongest means by which literature reinforces ideas.

ᛦ CLASSIFICATION OF IMAGERY

1. Visual Imagery Is the Language of Sight

Sight is the most significant of our senses, for it is the key to our remembrance of other impressions. Therefore, the most frequently occurring literary imagery is to things we can visualize either exactly or approximately—**visual images**. In "Cargoes" (the subject of the sample student essay on pages 124–25), Masefield asks us to re-create mental pictures or images of ocean-going merchant vessels from three periods of human history. He refers to a large sailing vessel, a quinquereme, from the ancient Near East, associated with the Biblical King Solomon. Then he turns to a "stately Spanish galleon," and finally refers to a modern British ship caked with salt, carrying grubby and cheap freight over the English Channel. His images are vivid as they stand and need no further amplification. For us to reconstruct them imaginatively, we do not need ever to have seen the ancient biblical lands or waters, or ever to have seen or handled the cheap commodities on a modern merchant ship. We have seen enough in our lives both in reality and in pictures to *imagine* places and objects like these, and hence Masefield is successful in fixing his visual images in our minds.

2. Auditory Imagery Is the Language of Sound

Auditory images trigger our experiences with sound. For such images, let us consider Wilfred Owen's "Anthem for Doomed Youth," which is about the death of soldiers in warfare and the sorrow of their loved ones. The poem begins with the question of "what passing-bells" may be tolled for "those who die as cattle." Owen's speaker is referring to the traditional tolling of a parish church bell to announce the burial of a parishioner. Reference to the sounds of such a ceremony suggests a period of peace and order, when there is time to pay respect to the dead. But the poem then points out that the only sound for those who have fallen in battle is the "rapid rattle" of "stuttering" rifles—in other words, not the solemn, dignified sounds of peace, but the horrifying noises of war. Owen's auditory images evoke corresponding sounds in our imaginations, and they help us to experience the poem and to hate the uncivilized depravity of war.

3, 4, 5. Olfactory, Gustatory, and Tactile Imagery Refers to Smell, Taste, and Touch

In addition to sight and sound, you will also find images from the other senses. An **olfactory image** refers to smell, a **gustatory image** to taste, and a **tactile image** to touch. A great deal of love poetry, for example, includes *olfactory images* about the fragrances of flowers.

Images derived from and referring to taste—*gustatory images*—are also common, though less frequent than those referring to sight and sound. Lines 5 and 10 of Masefield's "Cargoes," for example, includes references to "sweet white wine" and "cinnamon." Although the poem refers to these commodities as cargoes, the words themselves also register in our minds as gustatory images because they evoke our sense of taste.

Tactile images of touch and texture are not as common because touch is difficult to render except in terms of effects. The speaker of Lowell's "Patterns," for example (page 358), uses tactile imagery when imagining a never-to-happen embrace with her fiancé, who we learn has been killed on a wartime battlefield. Her imagery records the effect of the embrace ("bruised"), whereas her internalized feelings are expressed in metaphors ("aching, melting"):

> And the buttons of his waistcoat bruised my body as he clasped me
> Aching, melting, unafraid. (lines 51–52)

Tactile images are not uncommon in love poetry, where references to touch and feeling are natural. Usually, however, love poetry deals with yearning and hope rather than sexual fulfillment (as in Keats's "Bright Star").

6. Kinetic and Kinesthetic Imagery Refers to Motion

References to movement are also images. Images of general motion are **kinetic** (remember that *motion pictures* are called "cinema"; note the closeness of *kine* and *cine*), whereas the term **kinesthetic** is applied to human or animal movement. Imagery of motion is closely related to visual images, for motion is most often seen. Masefield's "British coaster," for example, is a visual image, but when it goes "Butting through the channel," the motion makes it also kinetic. When Hardy's skeletons sit upright at the beginning of "Channel Firing," the image is kinesthetic, as is the action of Amy Lowell's speaker walking in the garden after hearing about her fiancé's death.

The areas from which kinetic and kinesthetic imagery can be derived are too varied and unpredictable to describe. Occupations, trades, professions, businesses, recreational activities—all these might furnish images. One poet introduces references from gardening, another from money and banking, another from modern real estate developments, another from the falling of leaves in autumn, another from life in the jungle. The freshness, newness, and surprise of much poetry result from the many and varied areas from which writers draw their images.

☝ WRITING ABOUT IMAGERY

Raise Questions to Discover Ideas

In preparing to write, you should develop a set of thoughtful notes dealing with issues such as the following:

- What type or types of images prevail in the work? Visual (shapes, colors)? Auditory (sounds)? Olfactory (smells)? Tactile (touch and texture)? Gustatory (taste)? Kinetic or kinesthetic (motion)? Or is the imagery a combination of these?
- To what degree do the images reflect the writer's actual observation or the writer's reading and knowledge of fields such as science or history?
- How well do the images stand out? How vivid are they? How is this vividness achieved?
- Within a group of images, say visual or auditory, do the images pertain to one location or area rather than another (e.g., natural scenes rather than interiors, snowy scenes rather than grassy ones, loud and harsh sounds rather than quiet and civilized ones)?
- What explanation is needed for the images? (Images might be derived from the classics or the Bible, the Revolutionary War or World War II, the behaviors of four-footed creatures or birds, and so on.)
- What effect do the circumstances described in the work (e.g., conditions of brightness or darkness, warmth or cold, etc.) have upon your responses to the images? What poetic purpose do you think the poet achieves by controlling these responses?
- How well are the images integrated within the poem's argument or development?

Answering questions like these should provide you with a sizable body of ready-made material that you can convert directly to the body of your essay.

Organize Your Essay About Imagery

INTRODUCTION.   Connect a brief overview of the poem to your plan of development, such as that the writer uses images to strengthen ideas about war, character, or love, or that the writer relies predominantly on images of sight, sound, and action.

BODY.   You might deal exclusively with one of the following aspects, or, equally likely, you may combine your approaches, as you wish.

1. *Images suggesting ideas and/or moods.* Such an essay should emphasize the effects of the imagery. What ideas or moods are evoked by the images? (The au-

ditory images beginning Owen's "Anthem for Doomed Youth," for example, all point toward a condemnation of war's brutal cruelty.) Do the images promote approval or disapproval? Cheerfulness? Melancholy? Are the images drab, exciting, vivid? How? Why? Are they conducive to humor or surprise? How does the writer achieve these effects? Are the images consistent, or are they ambiguous? (For example, the images in Masefield's "Cargoes" first indicate approval and then disapproval, with no ambiguity.)

2. *The types of images.* Here the emphasis is on the categories of images themselves. Is there a predominance of a particular type of image (e.g., visual or auditory images), or is there a blending? Is there a bunching of types at particular points in the poem or story? If so, why? Is there any shifting as the work develops (as, for example, in Owen's "Anthem for Doomed Youth" (page 362) where the auditory images first describe loudness and harshness, but later images describe quietness and sorrow)? Are the images appropriate, granting the nature and apparent intent of the work? Do they assist in making the ideas seem convincing? If there seems to be any inappropriateness, what is its effect?

3. *Systems of images.* Here the emphasis should be on the areas from which the images are drawn. This is another way of considering the appropriateness of the imagery. Is there a pattern of similar or consistent images, such as darkness and dinginess (Poe's "The Cask of Amontillado") or brightness changing to darkness (Mansfield's "Miss Brill")? Do all the images adhere consistently to a particular frame of reference, such as a sunlit garden (Lowell's "Patterns"), an extensive recreational forest and garden (Coleridge's "Kubla Khan"), a church graveyard (Hardy's "Channel Firing"), the sea in various stages of light (Masefield's "Cargoes"), or a darkened forest (Blake's "The Tyger")? What is unusual or unique about the set of images? What unexpected or new responses do they produce?

CONCLUSION.   Your conclusion, in addition to recapitulating your major points, is the place for additional insights. It would not be proper to go too far in new directions here, but you might briefly take up one or more of the ideas that you have not developed in the body. In short, what have you learned from your study of imagery in the work?

Sample Essay

The Images of Masefield's "Cargoes"°

[1]
In the three-stanza poem "Cargoes," John Masefield uses imagery skillfully to create a negative impression of modern commercial life.* There is a
contrast between the first two stanzas and the third, with the first two idealizing
the romantic, distant past and the third demeaning the modern, gritty, grimy
present. Masefield's images are thus both positive and lush, on the one hand,
and negative and stark, on the other.†

[2]
The most evocative and pleasant images in the poem are in the first
stanza. The speaker asks that we imagine a "Quinquereme of Nineveh from
distant Ophir" (line 1), an ocean-going, many-oared vessel loaded with treasure for the biblical King Solomon. As Masefield identifies the cargo, the visual
images are rich and romantic (lines 3 to 5):

> With a cargo of ivory,
> And apes and peacocks,
> Sandalwood, cedarwood, and sweet white wine.

Ivory suggests richness, which is augmented by the exotic "apes and peacocks" in all their spectacular strangeness. The "sandalwood, cedarwood, and
sweet white wine" evoke pungent smells and tastes. The "sunny" light of ancient Palestine (line 2) not only illuminates the imaginative scene (visual), but
invites readers to imagine the sun's warming touch (tactile). The references to
animals and birds also suggest the sounds that these creatures would make
(auditory). Thus, in this lush first stanza, images derived from all the senses
are introduced to create impressions of a glorious past.

[3]
Almost equally lush are the images of the second stanza, which completes the poem's first part. Here the visual imagery evokes the royal splendor
of a tall-masted, full-sailed galleon (line 6) at the height of Spain's commercial
power in the sixteenth century. The galleon's cargo suggests wealth, with
sparkling diamonds and amethysts, and Portuguese "gold moidores" gleaming
in open chests (line 10). With cinnamon in the second stanza's bill of lading
(line 10), Masefield includes the image of a pleasant-tasting spice.

[4]
The negative imagery of the third stanza is in stark contrast to the first
two stanzas. The visual image is a modern "Dirty British coaster" (line 11),
which draws attention to the griminess and suffocation of modern civilization.
This spray-swept ship, caked in sea-salt, is loaded with materials that pollute
the earth with noise and smoke. The smoke-stack of the coaster (line 11) and
the firewood it is carrying suggest choking smog. The Tyne Coal (line 13) and
road rails (line 14) suggest the noise and smoke of puffing railroad engines. As
if this were not enough, the "pig-lead" (line 14) to be used in various industrial
processes indicates not just more unpleasantness, but also something poiso-

°See page 361 for this poem.
*Central idea.
†Thesis sentence.

[4]

nous and deadly. In contrast to the lush and stately imagery of the first two stanzas, the images in the third stanza invite the conclusion that people now, when the "Dirty British coaster" butts through the English Channel, are surrounded and threatened by visual, olfactory, and auditory pollution.

[5]

The poem thus establishes a romantic past and ugly present through images of sight, smell, and sound. The images of motion also emphasize this view: In the first two stanzas, the quinquereme is "rowing" and the galleon is "dipping." These kinetic images suggest dignity and lightness. The British coaster, however, is "butting," an image indicating bull-like hostility and stupid force. <u>These, together with all the other images, focus the poem's negative views of modern life.</u> The facts that existence for both the ancient Palestinians and the Renaissance Spaniards included slavery (of those men rowing the quinquereme) and piracy (by those Spanish "explorers" who robbed and killed the natives of the Isthmus) should probably not be emphasized as a protest against Masefield's otherwise valid contrasts in images. His final commentary may hence be thought of as the banging of his "cheap tin trays" (line 15), which makes a percussive climax of the oppressive images filling too large a portion of modern lives.

ᶳ COMMENTARY ON THE ESSAY

This essay illustrates the first strategy for writing about imagery (page 122), using images to develop ideas and moods. All the examples—derived directly from the poem—emphasize the qualities of Masefield's images. This method permits the introduction of imagery drawn from all the senses in order to demonstrate Masefield's ideas about the past and the present. Other approaches might have concentrated exclusively on Masefield's visual images, or upon his images drawn from trade and commerce. Because Masefield uses auditory and gustatory images, but does not develop them extensively, sound or taste might be appropriately treated in short, paragraph-length essays.

The introductory paragraph of the sample essay presents the central idea that Masefield uses his images climactically to lead to his negative view of modern commercialism. The thesis sentence indicates that the topics to be developed are those of (1) lushness and (2) starkness.

Paragraphs 2 and 3 form a unit stressing the lushness and exoticism of the first stanza and the wealth and colorfulness of the second stanza. In particular, paragraph 2 uses words like "lush," "evocative," "rich," "exotic," "pungent," and "romantic" to characterize the pleasing mental pictures that the images invoke. Although the paragraph indicates enthusiastic responses to the images, it does not go beyond the limits of the images themselves.

Paragraph 4 stresses the contrast of Masefield's images in the third stanza with those of the first two stanzas. To this end, the paragraph illustrates the imaginative reconstruction needed to develop an understanding of this contrast. The unpleasantness, annoyance, and even the danger of the cargoes mentioned in the third stanza are therefore emphasized as the qualities evoked by the images.

The last paragraph demonstrates that the imagery of motion—not much stressed in the poem—is in agreement with the rest of Masefield's imagery. As a demonstration of the need for fair, impartial judgment, the conclusion introduces the possible objection that Masefield may be slanting his images by including not a full but rather a partial view of their respective historical periods. Thus the concluding paragraph adds balance to the analysis illustrated in paragraphs 2, 3, and 4.

❦ SPECIAL WRITING TOPICS FOR STUDYING LITERARY IMAGERY

1. Compare the images of home in "Anthem for Doomed Youth" (page 362) and "An Occurrence at Owl Creek Bridge" (page 304). Describe the differing effects of the images. How are the images used? How effectively do these images aid in the development of the attitudes toward war expressed in each poem? How is your reading of the poems affected by the knowledge that both Owen and Bierce were killed in war?

2. On the basis of the poems in Appendix C by Arnold, Blake, Coleridge, Frost, and Layton, write an essay discussing the poetic use of images drawn from the natural world. What sorts of references do the poets make? What attitudes do they express about the details they select? What is the relationship between the images and religious views? What judgments about God and nature do the poets show by their images?

3. Considering the imagery of Hardy's "Channel Firing," Shakespeare's Sonnet 73: "That Time of Year Thou Mayst in Me Behold," or Blake's "The Tyger," write an essay explaining the power of imagery. As you develop your thoughts, be sure to consider the dramatic nature of the images in the poem you choose and to account for the impressions and ideas that they create. You may also wish to introduce references to images from other poems that are relevant to your points.

4. Write a poem describing one of the following:

    a. Athletes who have just completed an exhausting run
    b. Children getting out of school for the day
    c. The antics of your dog, cat, horse, turtle, or other pet
    d. A cat that always sits down on your schoolwork
    e. A particularly good meal you had recently
    f. The best concert that you ever attended
    g. Driving to work/school on a rainy/snowy day

Then, write an analysis of the images you selected for your poem, and explain your choices. What details stand out in your mind? What do you recall best—sight, smell, sound, action? What is the relationship between your images and the ideas you express in your poem?

5. Write an essay considering the graphic or pictorial nature of the imagery in Coleridge's "Kubla Khan," Keats's "On First Looking Into Chapman's Homer," and Rossetti's "Echo," along with other works that you may wish to include. What similarities and differences do you find in subject matter, treatment, arrangement, and general idea? On the basis of your comparison, what relationships do you perceive between sight and literary imagery?

6. Use the retrieval system (computer or card catalogue) in your library to research the topic of imagery in Shakespeare (see *imagery* or *style and imagery*). How many titles do you find? Over how many years have these works been published? Take one of the books out, and write a brief report on one of the chapters. What topics are discussed? What types of imagery are introduced? What relationship does the author make between imagery and content?

chapter 9

Writing About Metaphor and Simile:

A Source of Depth and Range in Literature

Metaphor and simile are patterns of comparison that illuminate, broaden, extend, and deepen meaning. When people speak of **figurative language**, **figures of speech**, **rhetorical figures**, or simply **figures**, they are likely speaking of metaphors and similes. These important modes of comparison may be expressed in single words, phrases, clauses, or entire structures. Metaphors *equate* (e.g., "Your words are music to my ears," "Waves of luck came to him," "I'm in a squirrel cage") and similes *compare* (e.g., "Your words are like music to me," "Luck came to him as though in waves," "I feel like a squirrel in a cage"). The equation or comparison not only explains the thing but also offers distinctive and original ways of seeing it and thinking about it. Metaphors and similes therefore enable writers to magnify their ideas while still employing a relatively small number of words.

❦ METAPHOR AND SIMILE: THE MAJOR RHETORICAL FIGURES

Although metaphorical language is sometimes called "ornate," as though it were unnecessarily decorative, it is not uncommon in ordinary conversational speech, and it is essential in literary thought and expression. Unlike the writing of the social and "hard" sciences, imaginative literature does not purport to be direct and absolute, offering a one-to-one relationship of words to things. Yes, literature does offer descriptions and explanations, but equally important, it also offers implications and suggestions through the use of metaphors and similes. Such language is a sine qua non in imaginative literature, particularly poetry, but it would be difficult to find any good writing that does not at least occasionally use figurative language.

A Metaphor Makes an Equation

A **metaphor** (a "carrying out a change") equates an object or action directly with something else. For example, in a heavy storm, trees may be said to *bow* in the wind. *Bow* is a metaphor because the word more usually refers to performers' acknowledging applause by bending forward. One of Shakespeare's best-known metaphors is "All the world's a stage, / And all the men and women merely players," in which Shakespeare's character Jacques (JAY-queez) from Act II, scene 7, of *As You Like It*, explains human life in terms of stage life: All the things that are said and done by stage actors are also said and done by living people in real life. It is important to recognize that Shakespeare's metaphor does not state that the world is *like* a stage, but that it literally *is* a stage.

A Simile Shows That Things Are Similar

Whereas a metaphor merges identities, a **simile** (the "showing of similarity or oneness") utilizes *similarity* to carry out the explanation. A simile is distinguishable from a metaphor because it is introduced by *like* with nouns and *as* (also *as if* and *as though*) with clauses. Consider the famous poem "A Valediction: Forbidding Mourning" by the early-seventeenth-century poet John Donne. This is a dramatic poem spoken by a lover about to go on a trip; his loved one is sorrowful, and he attempts to console her by claiming that even when he is gone, he will be together with her in spirit. The following stanza contains a famous simile to this effect:

> Our two souls therefore, which are one,
>   Though I must go, endure not yet
> A breach, but an expansion
>   Like gold to airy thinness beat.

The simile compares the souls of the speaker and his loved one to gold, which is extremely malleable. By the simile, the speaker asserts that the impending departure will not be a separation but rather a thinning out, so that the lovers will remain connected even though the distance between them expands. Because the simile is introduced by *like*, the emphasis of the figure is on the *similarity* of the lovers' love to gold hammered out to "airy thinness," not on the *identification* of the two. Similarly, the sentence "Come with . . . eyes as bright / As sunlight on a stream," from Rossetti's "Echo," compares the listener's eyes to a bright and gleaming natural scene.

☜ CHARACTERISTICS OF METAPHORICAL LANGUAGE

In Chapter 8, we saw how imagery stimulates the imagination and recalls memories (*images*) of sights, sounds, tastes, smells, sensations of touch, and motions. Metaphors and similes go beyond literal imagery to introduce perceptions and comparisons that can be unusual, unpredictable, and surprising, as in Donne's simile comparing the lovers' relationship to gold. How many people have ever perceived such a metaphorical connection—between the thinning out of metal and the constancy of lovers? The comparison emphasizes the bond between two lovers; the reference to gold shows how valuable the bond is.

In this way, metaphorical language extends knowledge and awareness by introducing perceptions that otherwise would not come to light. Such perceptions as these connect the thing or things to be communicated—such as qualities of love, the fear of advancing age, the need for psychological assurance, or the excitement of unexpected discovery—with a new insight that is made objective through the comparison of a simile or the equation of a metaphor. First and foremost, the use of metaphors and similes is one of the ways in which great literature leads us to see the world in fresh and original ways.

To see metaphorical language in operation, let us take a commonly expressed idea—happiness. In everyday speech, we might use the sentence "She was happy" to state that a particular character was experiencing joy and excitement. The sentence is of course accurate, but it is not interesting. A more

---

VEHICLE AND TENOR

To describe the relationship between a writer's ideas and the metaphors and similes chosen to objectify them, two useful terms have been coined by I. A. Richards (in *The Philosophy of Rhetoric*). First is the **tenor**, which is the totality of ideas and attitudes not only of the literary speaker but also of the author. Second is the **vehicle**, or the specific words of the metaphor or simile. For example, the tenor of Donne's simile in "A Valediction: Forbidding Mourning" is the inseparable love and unbreakable connection of the two lovers; the vehicle is the beating of gold "to airy thinness." Similarly, the tenor of the similes in the sestet of Keats's sonnet (next page) is awe and wonder; the vehicle is the description of astronomical and geographical discovery.

vivid way of saying the same thing is to use an image of action, such as "She jumped for joy." This image gives us a literal picture of a person demonstrating happiness. But an even better way of communicating joy is the following simile: "She felt as if she had just won a hundred million dollars in the lottery." Because readers easily understand the disbelief, excitement, exhilaration, and delight that such an event would bring, they also understand—and feel—the character's happiness. It is the *simile* that evokes this perception and enables each reader to personalize the experience, for no simple description could help a reader comprehend the same degree of emotion.

As a parallel poetic example, let us refer to Keats's sonnet "On First Looking into Chapman's Homer," which Keats wrote soon after reading the translation of Homer's *Iliad* and *Odyssey* by the Renaissance poet George Chapman. Keats's idea is that Chapman not only translated Homer's words but also transmitted his greatness:

John Keats (1795–1821)

On First Looking Into Chapman's Homer°   1816

Much have I travell'd in the realms of gold,
   And many goodly states and kingdoms seen:
   Round many western islands have I been
Which bards in fealty to Apollo° hold.
Oft of one wide expanse had I been told   5
   That deep-brow'd Homer ruled as his demesne;°   *realm, estate*
   Yet did I never breathe its pure serene°
Till I heard Chapman speak out loud and bold:
Then felt I like some watcher of the skies
   When a new planet swims into his ken;°   *range of vision*   10
Or like stout Cortez° when with eagle eyes
   He star'd at the Pacific—and all his men
Look'd at each other with a wild surmise°—   *conjecture, supposition*
   Silent, upon a peak in Darien.

Chapman's Homer: George Chapman (c. 1560–1634) published his translations of Homer's *Iliad* in 1612 and *Odyssey* in 1614–1615.
   4. *bards . . . Apollo:* writers who are sworn subjects of Apollo, the Greek god of light, music, poetry, prophecy, and the sun.
   7. *serene:* a clear expanse of air; also grandeur, clarity; rulers were also sometimes called "serene majesty."
   11. *Cortez:* Hernando Cortés (1485–1547), a Spanish general and the conqueror of Mexico. Keats confuses him with Vasco de Balboa (c. 1475–1519), the first European to see the Pacific Ocean (in 1510) from Darien, an early name for the Isthmus of Panama.

As a first step in understanding the power of metaphorical language, we may briefly paraphrase the sonnet's content:

> I have enjoyed much art and read much European literature and have been told that Homer is the best writer of all. However, I could not really appreciate his works (because I do not know Greek) until I discovered them in Chapman's "loud and bold" translation. This experience was exciting and awe-inspiring.

If all Keats had written were a paragraph like this one, we would pay no attention to it, for it carries no sense of excitement or stimulation. But the last six lines of the sonnet contain two memorable similes ("like some watcher" and "like stout Cortez") that stand out and demand a special effort of imagination. When we mull over these similes, we might suppose that we actually *are* astronomers just discovering a new and previously unknown planet, and that we actually *are* the first explorers to see the Pacific Ocean. As we imagine ourselves in these roles, we can also comprehend the amazement, wonder, excitement, exhilaration, anticipation, and joy that would accompany such a discovery. With that discovery comes the realization that the world—the universe—is far bigger and more wonderful than we had ever dreamed.

Metaphorical language therefore makes strong demands on our creative imagination. It bears repeating that as we create our own mental pictures prompted by metaphors and similes, we also respond with our own accompanying attitudes and feelings. Let us consider once more Keats's metaphor "realms of gold," which invites us to think of brilliant and shining kingdoms and also stimulates us to join Keats in valuing and loving not just poetry but all literature. If we respond sensitively to metaphorical language in this way—by allowing our feelings to augment and reinforce our understandings—the works of writers like Keats produce both mental and emotional experiences that were previously hidden to us. They constantly give us something new and increase our power to think and know. They enlarge us.

WRITING ABOUT METAPHORS AND SIMILES

Begin by determining the use, line by line, of metaphors or similes. Obviously, similes are the easiest figures to recognize, because they introduce comparisons with the words "like" or "as." Metaphors may be recognized because the topics are discussed not as themselves but as other topics. If the poems speak of falling leaves or law courts, for example, but the subjects are memory or increasing age, you are looking at metaphors.

Raise Questions to Discover Ideas

- What figures does the work contain? Where do they occur? Under what circumstances? How extensive are they?
- How do you recognize them? Are they signaled by a single word or phrase, such as "desert places" in Frost's "Desert Places" (page 354), or are they more extensively detailed, as in Shakespeare's Sonnet 30: "When to the Sessions of Sweet Silent Thought" (page 135)?
- How vivid are the figures? How obvious? How unusual? What kind of effort is needed to understand them in context?
- Structurally, how are the figures developed? How do they rise out of the situation? To what degree are the figures integrated into the work's development of ideas? How do they relate to other aspects of the work?
- Is one type of figure used in a particular section, while another predominates in another? Why?
- If you have discovered a number of figures, what relationships can you find among them (such as the judicial and financial connections in Shakespeare's "When to the Sessions")?
- How do they broaden, deepen, or otherwise assist in making the ideas in the work forceful?
- In short, how appropriate and meaningful are the figures in the work? What effect do the figures have on your understanding and appreciation of the work?

Organize Your Essay About Metaphor and Simile

INTRODUCTION. Relate the quality of the figures to the nature of the work. Thus, metaphors and similes of suffering might be appropriate to a religious, redemptive work, whereas those of sunshine and cheer might be right for a romantic one. If there is a contrast between the metaphorical language and the topic, you might take that contrast for a central idea, for it would clearly indicate the writer's ironic perspective. Suppose that the topic of the poem is love, but the metaphorical language puts you in mind of darkness and cold: What would the writer be saying about the quality of love? You should also try to justify any claims that you make about the figures. Your introduction is the place to establish ideas and justifications of this sort.

BODY. The following approaches for discussing rhetorical figures are not mutually exclusive, and you may combine them as you wish. Most likely, your essay will bring in most of the following classifications.

1. **Interpret the meaning and effect of the figures.** Here you explain how the figures enable you to make an interpretation. In lines 17 to 19 of "Kubla Khan," for example, Coleridge introduces the following simile:

And from this chasm, with ceaseless turmoil seething,
As if this earth in fast thick pants were breathing,
A mighty fountain momently was forced:

Coleridge's simile of "fast thick pants" almost literally animates the earth as a moving, working power, panting as it forces the fountain out of the chasm. The idea is that the phenomena of nature are not dead, but vigorously alive. Such a direct, interpretive approach requires that metaphors, similes, or other figures be expanded and interpreted, including the explanation of necessary references and allusions.

2. **Analyze the frames of reference and their appropriateness to the subject matter**. Here you classify and locate the sources and types of the references and determine the appropriateness of these to the poem's subject matter. Ask questions similar to those you might ask in a study of imagery: Does the writer refer extensively to nature, science, warfare, politics, business, reading (e.g., Shakespeare's metaphor equating personal reverie with courtroom proceedings)? How appropriate is the metaphor? Does it seem right in the poem's development? How?

3. **Focus on the interests and sensibilities of the writer.** In a way, this approach is like the second one, but the emphasis here is on what the selectivity of the writer might show about his or her vision and interests. You might begin by listing the figures in the poem and then determining the sources, just as you would do in discussing the sources of images. But then you should raise questions such as the following: Does the writer use figures derived from one sense rather than another (i.e., sight, hearing, taste, smell, touch)? Does he or she record color, brightness, shadow, shape, depth, height, number, size, slowness, speed, emptiness, fullness, richness, drabness? Has the writer relied on the associations of figures of sense? Do metaphors and similes referring to green plants and trees, to red roses, or to rich fabrics, for example, suggest that life is full and beautiful; or do references to touch suggest amorous warmth? This approach is designed to help you to draw whatever conclusions you can about the author's—or the speaker's—taste or sensibility.

4. **Examine the effect of one figure on the other figures and ideas of the poem.** The assumption of this approach is that literary works are unified and organically whole, so that each part is closely related and inseparable from everything else. Usually it is best to choose a figure that occurs at the beginning of the work and then to determine how this figure influences your perception of what follows. Your aim is to consider the relationship of part to parts, and part to whole. The beginning of Frost's "Desert Places," for example, describes "snow falling and night falling." What is the effect of this opening upon the poem's metaphor of human "desert places"? To help you in approaching such a question, you might substitute a different detail, such as, here, a rising sun on a beautiful day or playing with a kitten, rather than the onset of cold and night. Such suppositions, which would clearly be out of place and inappropriate, may help you to understand and then explain the writer's metaphorical language.

CONCLUSION.   In your conclusion, summarize your main points, describe your general impressions, try to describe the impact of the figurative language, indicate your personal responses, or show what might further be done along the lines you have been developing. If you know other works by the same writer or works by other writers who use comparable or contrasting figures, you might explain the relationship of the other work or works to your present analysis.

Sample Essay

A Study of Shakespeare's Metaphors in Sonnet 30: "When to the Sessions of Sweet Silent Thought"

When to the sessions of sweet silent thought,
I summon up remembrance of things past,
I sigh the lack of many a thing I sought,
And with old woes new wail my dear time's waste:
Then can I drown an eye (un-used to flow)   *5*
For precious friends hid in death's dateless night,
And weep afresh love's long since cancelled woe,
And moan th' expense of many a vanished sight.
Then can I grieve at grievances foregone,
And heavily from woe to woe tell o'er   *10*
The sad account of fore-bemoaned moan,
Which I new pay, as if not paid before.
    But if the while I think on thee (dear friend)
    All losses are restored, and sorrows end.

[1]   In this sonnet Shakespeare's speaker stresses the sadness and regret of remembered experience, but he states that a person with these feelings may be cheered by the thought of a friend. His metaphors, cleverly used, create new and fresh ways of seeing personal life in this perspective.* He presents metaphors drawn from the public and business world of law courts, money, and banking or money-handling.†

[2]   The courtroom metaphor of the first four lines shows that memories of past experience are constantly present and influential. Like a judge commanding defendants to appear in court, the speaker "summon[s]" his memory of "things past" to appear on trial before him. This metaphor suggests that people are their own judges and that their ideals and morals are like laws by which they measure themselves. The speaker finds himself guilty of wasting his time in the past. Removing himself, however, from the strict punishment that a real judge might require, he does not condemn himself for his "dear time's waste" but instead laments it (line 4). The metaphor is thus used to indicate that a person's consciousness is made up just as much of self-doubt and reproach as of more positive qualities.

*Central idea.
†Thesis sentence.

[3]
With the closely related reference of money in the next four lines, Shakespeare shows that living is a lifelong investment and is valuable for this reason. According to the money metaphor, living requires the spending of emotions and commitment to others. When friends move away and loved ones die, it is as though this expenditure has been lost. Thus, the speaker's dead friends are "precious" because he invested time and love in them, and the "sights" that have "vanished" from his eyes make him "moan" because he went to great "expense" for them (line 8).

[4]
Like the money metaphor, the metaphor of banking or money-handling in the next four lines emphasizes that memory is a bank in which life's experiences are deposited. The full emotions surrounding experience are recorded there, and may be withdrawn in moments of "sweet silent thought" just as a depositor may withdraw money. Thus the speaker states that he counts out the sad parts of his experience—his woe—just as a merchant or banker counts money: "And heavily from woe to woe tell o'er" (line 10). Because strong emotions still accompany his memories of past mistakes, the metaphor extends to borrowing and the payment of interest. The speaker thus says that he pays again with "new" woe the accounts that he had already paid with old woe. The metaphor suggests that the past is so much a part of the present that a person never stops feeling pain and regret.

[5]
The legal, financial, and money-handling metaphors combine in the last two lines to show how a healthy present life may overcome past regrets. The "dear friend" being addressed in these lines has the resources (financial) to settle all the emotional judgments that the speaker as a self-judge has made against himself (legal). It is as though the friend is a rich patron who rescues him from emotional bankruptcy (legal and financial) and the possible doom resulting from the potential sentence of emotional misery and depression (legal).

[6]
In these metaphors, therefore, Shakespeare's references are drawn from everyday public and business actions, but his use of them is creative and unusual. In particular, the idea of line 8 ("And moan th' expense of many a vanished sight") stresses that people spend much emotional energy on others. Without such personal commitment, one cannot have precious friends and loved ones. In keeping with this metaphor of money and investment, one could measure life not in months or years, but in the spending of emotion and involvement in personal relationships. Shakespeare, by inviting readers to explore the values brought out by his metaphors, gives new insights into the nature and value of life.

❦ COMMENTARY ON THE ESSAY

This essay treats the three classes of metaphors that Shakespeare introduces in Sonnet 30. It thus illustrates the second approach (page 134); but the aim of the discussion is not to explore the extent and nature of the comparison between the metaphors and the personal situations described in the sonnet. Instead, the goal is to explain how the metaphors develop Shakespeare's meaning. This method therefore also illustrates the first approach (page 133).

The objective of the introductory paragraph is to include a brief general description of the work together with a brief specific description of the essay's topic. Of particular note is that Shakespeare's metaphors are introduced in relation to the issue of their possibly being overly clever and far-fetched, and, as a result, inappropriate. This issue is raised as a concession to be argued against. From it, the assertion is presented that the metaphors, because they lead to new and fresh insights, do just what metaphors are supposed to do, and thus they are appropriate. Once this argument is established, the central idea and thesis sentence follow logically. The introductory paragraph hence brings out all the necessary topics and issues to be considered in the body.

Paragraph 2 deals with the meaning of Shakespeare's courtroom metaphor. His money metaphor is explained in paragraph 3. Paragraph 4 considers the banking, or money-handling, figure. The fifth paragraph shows how Shakespeare's last two lines bring together the three strands of metaphor. The conclusion comments generally on the creativity of Shakespeare's metaphors, and it also amplifies the way in which the money metaphor leads toward an increased understanding of life.

Throughout the essay, transitions are made by the linking words in the topic sentences. In paragraph 3, for example, the words "closely related" and "next group" move the reader from paragraph 2 to the new content. In paragraph 4, the words effecting the transition are "like the money metaphor" and "the next four lines." The opening sentence of paragraph 5 refers collectively to the subjects of paragraphs 2, 3, and 4, thereby focusing them on the new topic of paragraph 5.

🐝 SPECIAL WRITING TOPICS FOR STUDYING METAPHOR AND SIMILE

1. Consider some of the metaphors and similes in the works (poems, stories, plays) included in Appendix C. Write an essay that answers the following questions: How effective are the figures you select? What insights do the figures provide within the contexts of their respective poems? How appropriate are they? Might they be expanded more fully, and if they were, what would be the effect? You might choose any of the following topics:

   - The "darkling plain" simile in Arnold's "Dover Beach"
   - The metaphors of constancy in Shakespeare's "Let Me Not to the Marriage of True Minds," or of autumn in his "That Time of Year Thou Mayest in Me Behold"
   - The metaphorical significance of the knot in Glaspell's *Trifles*
   - Metaphor in Blake's "The Tyger"
   - The metaphor of the Rhine in Layton's "Rhine Boat Trip"

- Similes in Owen's "Anthem for Doomed Youth" or Coleridge's "Kubla Khan"
- The metaphor of "red war" in Hardy's "Channel Firing"
- Metaphor and simile in Keats's "On First Looking Into Chapman's Homer"
- The use of similes in Hughes's "Negro"
- The title of Poe's "The Cask of Amontillado" as a metaphor
- The horse Toby as a metaphor in Chekhov's *The Bear*

2. Write a poem in which you create a governing metaphor or simile. An example might be: My girlfriend/boyfriend is like (a) an opening flower, (b) a difficult book, (c) an insoluble mathematical problem, (d) a bill that cannot be paid, (e) a slow-moving chess game. Another example: Teaching a person how to do a particular job is like (a) shoveling heavy snow, (b) climbing a mountain during a landslide, (c) having someone force you underwater when you're gasping for breath. When you finish, describe the relationship between your comparison and the development and structure of your poem.

3. In your library's reference section, find the third edition of J. A. Cuddon's *A Dictionary of Literary Terms and Literary Theory* (1991) or some other dictionary of literary terms. Study the entries for *metaphor* and *simile*, and write a brief report on these sections.

chapter 10

Writing About Symbolism and Allegory:
Keys to Extended Meaning

Like metaphors and similes, symbolism and allegory are modes that expand meaning. They are literary devices developed from the connections that real-life people make between their own existence and particular objects, places, or occurrences—either through experience or reading. A young man might remember making a vital realization about his moral being during a rowboat ride. A bereaved mother might associate personal grief with ordinary packing boxes. The significance of details like these can be meaningful not just at the time they occur, but throughout an entire lifetime. Merely bringing them to mind or speaking about them unlocks all their meanings, implications, and consequences. It is as though the reference alone can be the same as pages of explanation and analysis.

It is from this principle that both symbolism and allegory are derived. By highlighting details as *symbols,* and stories or parts of stories as *allegories,* writers expand their meaning while keeping their works within reasonable lengths.

🐞 SYMBOLISM

The words **symbol** and **symbolism** are derived from the Greek word meaning "to throw together" (*syn,* together, and *ballein,* to throw). A symbol creates a direct meaningful equation between (1) a specific object, scene, character, or action, and (2) ideas, values, persons, or ways of life. In effect, a symbol is a *substitute* for the elements being signified, much as the flag stands for the ideals of the nation.

When we first encounter a symbol in a poem, play, or story, it may seem to carry no more weight than its surface or obvious meaning. It may be a description of a character, an object, a place, an action, or a situation, and may function perfectly well in this capacity. What makes a symbol symbolic, however, is its capacity to signify additional levels of meaning—major ideas, simple or complex emotions, or philosophical or religious qualities or values. There are two types of symbols—*cultural* and *contextual.*

Cultural Symbols Are Parts of Cultural and Historical Heritage

Many symbols are *generally* or *universally* recognized, and are therefore **cultural** (also called **universal**). They embody ideas and emotions that writers and readers share as heirs of the same historical and cultural tradition. When using cultural symbols, a writer assumes that readers already know what the symbols represent. An example is the character Sisyphus of ancient Greek myth. As a punishment for trying to overcome death not just once but twice, Sisyphus is doomed by the underworld gods to roll a large boulder up a high hill forever. Just as he gets the boulder to the top, it rolls down, and then he is fated to roll it up again—and again—and again—because the boulder always rolls back. The plight of Sisyphus has been interpreted as a symbol of the human condition: In spite of constant struggle, a person rarely if ever completes anything. Work must always be done over and over from day to day and from generation to generation, and the same problems confront humanity throughout all time. Because of such fruitless effort, life seems to have little or no meaning. Nevertheless, there is hope: People who confront their tasks, as Sisyphus does, stay involved and active, and their work makes their lives meaningful. A writer referring to Sisyphus would expect us to understand that this ancient mythological figure symbolizes these conditions.

Similarly, ordinary water, because living creatures cannot live without it, is recognized as a symbol of life. It has this meaning in the ceremony of baptism, and it may convey this meaning and dimension in a variety of literary contexts. Thus, a spouting fountain may symbolize optimism (as upwelling, bubbling life), and a stagnant pool may symbolize the pollution and diminution of life. Water is also a universal symbol of sexuality, and its condition or state may symbolize various romantic relationships. For instance, stories in which lovers meet near a turbulent stream, a roaring waterfall, a beach with high breakers, a wide river, a stormy sea, a mud puddle, or a calm lake symbolically represent love relationships that range from uncertainty to serenity.

Contextual Symbols Are Symbolic Only in Individual Works

Objects and descriptions that are not universal symbols can be symbols *only if they are made so within individual works.* These are **contextual, private,** or **authorial** symbols. Unlike cultural symbols, it is the context and circumstances of individual works that make contextual symbols symbolic. For example, the word *pattern* is an ordinary word, but in Amy Lowell's "Patterns," it takes on powerful symbolic value. Things conforming to patterns come to symbolize not only confining and stultifying cultural expectations, but also the organized destructiveness of warfare. It is the *context* of the poem that creates this symbolism. Similarly, Arnold uses the ebbing surf in "Dover Beach" to symbolize his speaker's sadness at the loss of religious and philosophical certainty. Like Lowell's patterns, then, Arnold's surf is a major *contextual* symbol.

However, there is no carryover of contextual symbolism. In other works, pounding surf or formal patterns are not symbolic unless the writers deliberately invest them with symbolic meaning. Further, if they are symbolic in other works, they may represent very different qualities than in the poems by Lowell and Arnold.

Determine What Is Symbolic (and Not Symbolic)

In determining whether a particular object, action, or character is a symbol, you need to judge the importance that the author gives to it. If the element is prominent and also maintains a constancy of meaning, you may justify interpreting it as a symbol. For example, Miss Brill's fur piece in Mansfield's "Miss Brill" is shabby and moth-eaten. It has no value; but because Mansfield makes it especially important at both the beginning and ending of the story, it contextually symbolizes Miss Brill's poverty and isolation. At the beginning of Wagner's "The Boxes," the speaker refers to "boxes in the house," including footlockers, hampers, and a trunk. Readers will note that such large containers would easily conceal a small boy. At the story's end, however, the speaker states that she still visits the cemetery where her son is buried. The box she mentions at the end is thus a coffin, and for this reason the "Boxes" of the poem's title may be construed as a contextual symbol of death.

❦ ALLEGORY

An **allegory** is like a symbol because it transfers and broadens meaning. The term is derived from the Greek word *allegorein,* which means "to speak so as to imply other than what is said." Allegory, however, is more sustained than symbolism. An allegory is to a symbol as a motion picture is to a still picture. In form, an allegory is a complete and self-sufficient narrative, but it also signifies another series of events or conditions. Although some stories are allegories from beginning to end, many stories that are not allegories may nevertheless contain brief sections or episodes that are *allegorical.*

Understand the Applications and Meaning of Allegory

Allegories and the allegorical method are more than literary exercises. Without question, readers and listeners learn and memorize stories and tales more easily than moral lessons, and therefore allegory is a favorite method of teaching morality. In addition, thought and expression have not always been free. The threat of censorship and the danger of reprisal have sometimes caused authors to express their views indirectly in the form of allegory rather than to write openly, name names, and risk political reprisal or accusations of libel. Hence, the double meaning of many allegories is based in both need and reality.

In studying allegory, determine whether all or part of a work may have an extended, allegorical meaning. The popularity of George Lucas's film *Star Wars* and its sequels, for example (in videotape and newly refurbished rereleases), is attributable at least partly to its being an allegory about the conflict between good and evil. Obi Wan Kenobi (intelligence) enlists the aid of Luke Skywalker (heroism, boldness), and instructs him in "the force" (moral or religious faith). Thus armed and guided, Skywalker opposes the powers of Darth Vader (evil) to rescue the Princess Leia (purity and goodness) with the aid of the latest spaceships and weaponry (technology). The story is an exciting adventure film, accompanied by dramatic music and ingenious visual and sound effects. With the obvious allegorical overtones, however, it stands for any person's quest for self-fulfillment.

To apply a part of the allegory more specifically, consider that for a time the evil Vader imprisons Skywalker and that Skywalker must exert all his skill and strength to get free and overcome Vader. In the allegorical application of the episode, this temporary imprisonment signifies those moments of doubt, discouragement, and depression that people experience while trying to better themselves through education, work, self-improvement, friendship, marriage, and so on.

Almost from the beginning of recorded literature, similar heroic deeds have been represented in allegorical forms. From ancient Greece, the allegorical hero Jason sails on the *Argo* to distant lands to gain the Golden Fleece (those who take risks are rewarded). From Anglo-Saxon England, the hero Beowulf saves King Hrothgar's throne by killing Grendel and his monstrous mother (victory comes to those who rely on the forces of good). From seventeenth-century England, Bunyan's *The Pilgrim's Progress* tells how the hero Christian overcomes difficulties and temptations while traveling from this world to the next (belief, perseverance, and resistance to temptation save the faithful). As long as the parallel connections are close and consistent, such as those mentioned here, an allegorical interpretation is valid.

ｉ FABLE, PARABLE, AND MYTH

Closely related to symbolism and allegory in the ability to extend and expand meaning are three additional forms—*fable, parable,* and *myth.*

FABLE. The **fable** (from Latin *fabula,* a story or narration) is an old, brief, and popular form. Often but not always, fables are about animals who possess human traits (such fables are called **beast fables**). Past collectors and editors of fables have attached "morals" or explanations to the brief stories, as is the case with Aesop, the most enduringly popular of fable writers. Tradition has it that Aesop was a slave who composed fables in ancient Greece. His fable "The Fox and the Grapes" signifies the trait of belittling things we cannot have. More recent contributions to the fable tradition include Walt Disney's "Mickey Mouse," Walt Kelly's "Pogo," and Berke Breathed's "Bloom County." The adjective *fabulous* refers to the collective body of fables of all sorts, even though the word is often used as little more than a vague term of approval.

PARABLE. A **parable** (from Greek *parabolé,* a "setting beside" or comparison) is a short, simple allegory with a moral or religious bent. Parables are most often associated with Jesus, who used them to embody unique religious insights and truths. His parables "The Good Samaritan" and "The Prodigal Son," for example, are interpreted to show God's love, concern, understanding, and forgiveness.

MYTH. A **myth** (from Greek *muthos,* a story or plot) is a traditional story that embodies and codifies the religious, philosophical, and cultural values of the civilization in which it is composed. Usually the central figures of mythical stories are heroes, gods, and demigods, such as Zeus, Hera, Prometheus, Athena, Sisyphus, Oedipus, and Atalanta from ancient Greece. Most myths are of course fictional, but some have a basis in historical truth. They are by no means confined to the past, for the word *myth* may also refer to abstractions and ideas that people today hold collectively, such as the concept of never-ending economic growth, or the idea that problems may be solved by science. Sometimes the words *myth* and *mythical* are used with the meaning "fanciful" or "untrue." Such disparagement is misleading because the truths of mythology are not to be found literally in the myths themselves but rather in their symbolic and allegorical interpretations.

ALLUSION IN SYMBOLISM AND ALLEGORY

Cultural or universal symbols and allegories often allude to other works from our cultural heritage, such as the Bible, ancient history and literature, and works of the British and American traditions. Sometimes understanding a story may require knowledge of politics and current events.

If the meaning of a symbol is not immediately clear to you, you will need a dictionary or other reference work. The scope of your college dictionary will surprise you. If you cannot find an entry there, however, try one of the major encyclopedias, or ask your reference librarian, who can direct you to shelves loaded with helpful books. A few excellent guides are *The Oxford Companion to Classical Literature* (ed. M. C. Howatson and Io Chilvers), *The Oxford Companion to English Literature* (ed. Margaret Drabble), William Rose Benét's *The Reader's Encyclopedia*, Timothy Gantz's *Early Greek Myth: A Guide to Literary and Artistic Sources*, and Richmond Y. Hathorn's *Greek Mythology*. Useful aids in finding biblical references are *Cruden's Complete Concordance*, which in various editions has been used since 1737, and *Strong's Exhaustive Concordance*, which has been revised and expanded regularly since it first appeared in the nineteenth century. These concordances list all the major words used in the Bible, so that you can easily locate the chapter and verse of any and all biblical passages. If you still have trouble after using sources like these, see your instructor.

WRITING ABOUT SYMBOLISM OR ALLEGORY

To discover possible parallels that determine the presence of symbolism or allegory, consider the following questions:

Raise Questions to Discover Ideas

a. Symbolism
- What cultural or universal symbols can you discover in names, objects, places, situations, or actions in a work (e.g., the character Faith and the walking stick

in "Young Goodman Brown," the funeral bells in "Anthem for Doomed Youth," the snow in "Desert Places," or the woods in "Young Goodman Brown")?

- What contextual symbolism can be found in a work? What makes you think it is symbolic? What is being symbolized? How definite or direct is the symbolism? How systematically is it used? How necessary to the work is it? To what degree does it strengthen the work? How strongly does the work stand on its own without the reading for symbolism?

- Is it possible to make parallel lists to show how qualities of a particular symbol match the qualities of a character or an action? Here is such a list for the shepherd's home and the shepherds in Hardy's "The Three Strangers":

Circumstances of the Shepherd's Home	Comparable Qualities in the Shepherds and Their Lives
1. Remote	1. Unfamiliar with the outside world and the law
2. Solitary	2. Individualistic, and resentful of outside interference
3. Weatherbeaten	3. Adaptable and self-reliant
4. Humble	4. Poor
5. Providing an assembling place for guests	5. Hospitable

b. Allegory

- How clearly does the author point you toward an allegorical reading (i.e., through names and allusions, consistency of narrative, literary context)?
- How consistent is the allegorical application? Does the entire work, or only a part, embody the allegory? On what basis do you draw these conclusions?
- How complete is the allegorical reading? How might the allegory yield to a diagram such as the one on Hawthorne's "Young Goodman Brown," on p. 146 which shows how characters, actions, objects, or ideas correspond allegorically?

c. Other Forms

- What enables you to identify the story as a parable or fable? What lesson or moral is either clearly stated or implicit?
- What mythological identification is established in the work? What do you find in the story (names, situations, etc.) that enables you to determine its mythological significance? How is the myth to be understood? What symbolic value does the myth have? What current and timeless application does it have?

Organize Your Essay on Symbolism and Allegory

INTRODUCTION.   Relate the central idea of your essay to the meaning of the major symbols or allegorical thrust of the story. An idea about "Young Goodman Brown," for example, is that fanaticism darkens and lim-

YOUNG GOODMAN BROWN	Brown Himself	The Citizens of the Village	The Forest Figure (Father), the Devil	Faith	The Forest Meeting	Retreat into a Life of Suspicion and Distrust.
Allegorical Application to Morality and Faith	Potential for good	Culture and religious reinforcement	Forces of evil and deceit	Salvation and love, ideals to be rescued and preserved	Attack upon ideals; incentive to disillusionment	Destruction of faith; doubt, spiritual negligence, loss of certainty, increase of gloom and suspicion
Allegorical Application to Personal and General Concerns	Individual in pursuit of goals	External support for personal strength and growth	Obstacles to overcome, or by which to be overcome	Personal involvement, steadiness, happiness, religious conviction	Susceptibility to deceit, lack of conviction, misunderstanding, misinterpretation of others	Failure, depression, discouragement, disappointment, bitterness

its the human soul. An early incident in the story provides symbolic support for this idea. Specifically, when Goodman Brown enters the woods, he resolves "to stand firm against the devil," and he then looks up toward "Heaven above him." As he looks, a "black mass of cloud" appears to hide the "brightening stars" (paragraph 45). Within the limits of our central idea, the cloud can be seen as a symbol, just like the widening path or the night walk itself. Look for ways to make solid connections like this in your symbolic ascriptions.

Also, your essay will need to include justifications for your symbols or allegorical parallels. If you treat Montresor's vaults in Poe's "The Cask of Amontillado" as a symbol of deterioration and death, for example, it is important to draw attention to its skeletons and the increasingly unnourishing air. These defects justify treating the vaults symbolically. In the same way, in describing the allegorical elements in "Young Goodman Brown," you need to establish a comprehensive statement such as the following: People lose ideals and forsake principles not because they are evil, but because they misunderstand the people around them.

BODY.   There are a number of strategies for discussing symbolism and allegory. You might use one exclusively, or a combination. If you want to write about symbolism, you might consider the following:

Symbolism

1. *The meaning of a major symbol.* Identify the symbol and what it stands for. Then answer questions such as these: Is the symbol cultural or contextual? How do you decide? How do you derive your interpretation of the symbolic meaning? What is the extent of the meaning? Does the symbol undergo modification or new applications if it reappears? How does the symbol affect your understanding of the story? Does the symbol bring out any ironies? How does the symbol add strength and depth to the story?

2. *The development and relationship of symbols.* For two or more symbols, consider issues such as these: How do the symbols connect with each other (like night and the cloud in "Young Goodman Brown" as symbols of a darkening mind)? What additional meanings do the symbols provide? Are they complementary, contradictory, or ironic (such as the boxes in Wagner's "The Boxes")? Do the symbols control the form of the work? How? (For example, in "The Cask of Amontillado" the descent into the catacombs of the Montresors begins at dusk, and the time lapse of the story suggests that the conclusion takes place in total darkness. A similar movement may be seen in "Miss Brill," in the progression from the sunlit outdoors to the protagonist's small and dark room.) Can these comparable objects and conditions be viewed symbolically in relationship to the development of the two stories? Other issues are whether the symbols fit naturally or artificially into the context of the story, or whether and how the writer's symbols create unique qualities or excellences.

Allegory

When writing about allegory, you might use one of the following approaches:

1. *The application and meaning of the allegory.* What is the subject of the story (allegory, fable, parable, myth)? How may it be more generally applied to ideas or to qualities of human character, not only of its own time but also of our own? What other versions of the story do you know, if any? Does it illustrate, either closely or loosely, particular philosophies or religious views? If so, what are these? How do you know?

2. *The consistency of the allegory.* Is the allegory used consistently throughout the story, or is it used intermittently? Explain and illustrate this use. Would it be correct to call your story *allegorical* rather than an *allegory*? Can you determine

how parts of the story are introduced for their allegorical importance? Examples are the increasingly dark pathway in "An Occurrence at Owl Creek Bridge" and the frozen preserves in *Trifles,* which are allegorical equivalents of life's destructive difficulties, and the Parisian street in "The Necklace," which corresponds to the temptation to live beyond one's means.

CONCLUSION. In concluding, you might summarize main points, describe general impressions, explain the impact of the symbolic or allegorical methods, indicate personal responses, or suggest further lines of thought and application. You might also assess the quality and appropriateness of the symbolism or allegory (such as the opening of "Young Goodman Brown" being in darkness, with the closing in gloom).

Sample Essay

Allegory and Symbolism in Hawthorne's "Young Goodman Brown"°

---

[1] It is hard to read beyond the third paragraph of Nathaniel Hawthorne's "Young Goodman Brown" without recognizing the story's allegory and symbolism. The opening at first seems realistic. Goodman Brown, a young Puritan, leaves his home in colonial Salem to take an overnight trip. His wife's name, "Faith," however, suggests a symbolic reading, and as soon as Brown goes into the forest, his ordinary walk changes into an allegorical trip into evil. The idea that Hawthorne shows by this trip is that rigid belief destroys even the best human qualities.* He develops this thought in the allegory and in many symbols, particularly the sunset, the walking stick, and the path.†

[2] The allegory of the story concerns the ways in which people develop destructive ideas. Most of the story is dreamlike and unreal, and the ideas that Brown gains are also unreal. At the weird "witch meeting," he concludes that everyone he knows is sinful, and he then permits mistrust and loathing to distort his previous love for his wife and neighbors. As a result, he becomes harsh and gloomy for the rest of his life. The location of the story in colonial Salem indicates that Hawthorne's allegorical target is the zealous pursuit of religious principles that exclude love while dwelling on sinfulness. However, modern readers may also apply the allegory to the ways in which people uncritically accept any ideal (most often political loyalties or racial or national prejudices), and thereby reject the integrity and rights of others. If people like Brown apply a rigid standard and if they never try to understand those they condemn, they can condemn anyone. In this way, Hawthorne's allegory ap-

---

°See pages 327–36 for this story.
*Central idea.
†Thesis sentence.

plies to any narrow-minded acceptance of ideals or systems that exclude the importance of love, understanding, and tolerance.

[3]   Hawthorne's attack on such dehumanizing belief is found not just in the allegory but also in his many symbols. For example, the seventh word in the story, "sunset," may be taken as a symbol. In reality, sunset merely indicates the end of day. Coming at the beginning of the story, however, it suggests that Goodman Brown is beginning his long night of hatred, his spiritual death. For him the night will never end because his final days are shrouded in "gloom" (paragraph 72).

[4]   The next symbol, the guide's walking stick or staff, suggests the arbitrariness of the standard by which Brown judges his neighbors. Hawthorne's description indicates the symbolic nature of this staff:

> . . . the only thing about him [the guide] that could be fixed upon as remarkable, was his staff, which bore the likeness of a great black snake, so curiously wrought, that it might almost be seen to twist and wriggle itself like a living serpent. This, of course, must have been an ocular deception, assisted by the uncertain light. (paragraph 13)

The serpent symbolically suggests Satan, who in Genesis (3:1–7) is the originator of all evil, but the phrase "ocular deception" creates an interesting and realistic ambiguity about the symbol. Since the perception of the snake may depend on nothing more than the "uncertain" light, the staff may be less symbolic of evil than of the tendency to find evil where it does not exist (and could the uncertain light symbolize the uncertainty of human understanding?).

[5]   In the same vein, the path through the forest is a major symbol of the destructive mental confusion that overcomes Brown. As he walks, the path grows "wilder and drearier, and more faintly traced," and "at length" it vanishes (paragraph 51). This is like the biblical description of the "broad" way that leads "to Destruction" (Matthew 7:13). As a symbol, the path shows that most human acts are bad, and a small number, like the "narrow" way to life (Matthew 7:14), are good. Goodman Brown's path is at first clear, as though sin is at first unique and unusual. Soon, however, it is so indistinct that he can see only sin wherever he turns. The symbol suggests that, when people follow evil, their moral vision becomes blurred and they soon fall prey to "the instinct that guides mortal man to evil" (paragraph 51).

[6]   Through Hawthorne's allegory and symbols, "Young Goodman Brown" presents the paradox of how noble beliefs can backfire. Goodman Brown dies in gloom because he believes that his wrong vision is true. This form of evil is the hardest to stop, because wrongdoers who are convinced of their own goodness are beyond reach. In view of such self-righteous evil, whether cloaked in the apparent virtues of Puritanism or of some other blindly rigorous doctrine (political as well as religious), Hawthorne writes that "the fiend in his own shape is less hideous, than when he rages in the breast of man" (paragraph 53). Young Goodman Brown thus is the central symbol of the story. He is one of those who think they walk in light but who really create their own darkness.

❦ COMMENTARY ON THE ESSAY

The introduction justifies the treatment of allegory and symbolism on the grounds that Hawthorne early in the story invites such a reading. The central idea relates Hawthorne's method to the idea that rigid belief destroys the best human qualities.

Paragraph 2 considers the allegory as a criticism of rigid Puritan morality. The major thread running through the paragraph is the hurtful effect of monomaniacal views like those of Brown. Paragraphs 3, 4, and 5 deal with three major symbols: sunset, the staff, and the path. The aim of this discussion is to show how the symbols apply to Hawthorne's attack on unquestioning belief. Throughout these three paragraphs the central idea—the relationship of rigidity to destructiveness—is stressed. Hawthorne's allusions to both the Old and New Testaments are pointed out in paragraphs 4 and 5. The last paragraph builds to the conclusion that Brown symbolizes the idea that the primary cause of evil is the inability to separate reality from unreality.

If you write exclusively about allegory, use paragraph 2 of the sample essay as a guide either for a single paragraph or, when expanded, for an entire essay. If the allegory of "Young Goodman Brown," for example, were to be expanded, additional topics might be Brown's gullibility, the meaning of faith and the requirements for maintaining it, and the causes for preferring to think evil rather than good of other people. Such points are sufficiently important to sustain an entire essay on the topic of allegory.

❦ SPECIAL WRITING TOPICS FOR STUDYING SYMBOLISM AND ALLEGORY

1. Write an essay on the allegorical method of one or more of the allegories included in the Gospel of St. Luke, such as "The Bridegroom" (5:34–35), "The Garments and the Wineskins" (5:36–39), "The Sower" (8:4–15), "The Good Samaritan" (10:25–37), "The Prodigal Son" (15:11–32), "The Ox in the Well" (14:5–6), "The Watering of Animals on the Sabbath" (13:15–17), "The Rich Fool" (12:16–21), "Lazarus" (16:19–31), "The Widow and the Judge" (18:1–8), and "The Pharisee and the Publican" (18:9–14).

2. Why do writers who are interested in morality, philosophy, or religion utilize symbolism or allegory? In discussing this question, you might introduce references from "Young Goodman Brown," "Desert Places," "The Tyger," "Channel Firing," and "Dover Beach."

3. Compare and contrast the symbolism in Chopin's "The Story of an Hour," Shakespeare's Sonnet 116: "Let Me Not to the Marriage of True Minds," and Hughes's "Negro." To what degree do the works rely on contextual symbols? On universal symbols?

4. Consider the symbolism in "Miss Brill," *The Bear*, and "The Story of an Hour" as it pertains to the role of single and married women.

5. Write a poem using a widely recognized cultural symbol such as the flag (patriotism, love of country, a certain type of politics), water (life, sexuality, regeneration), or the population explosion (the end of life on earth). By arranging the sequence of your ideas, make clear the issues conveyed by your symbol, and also try to resolve the conflicts that the symbol might raise among supporters and detractors.

6. Write a brief story in which you develop your own contextual symbol. You might, for example, demonstrate how holding a job brings out character strengths that are not at first apparent, or how neglecting to care for the inside or outside of a house indicates a character's decline. The principle is to take something that may at first seem normal and ordinary, and then to make that thing symbolic as you develop your story.

7. Using the card or computer catalogue of your library, discover a recent critical-biographical book or books about Hawthorne. Explain what the book says about Hawthorne's uses of symbolism. To what extent does the book relate Hawthorne's symbolism to his religious and family heritage?

chapter 11

Writing About Tone:

The Writer's Control
over Attitudes and Feeling

Tone refers to the methods by which writers and speakers reveal attitudes or feelings. It is an aspect of all spoken and written statements, whether earnest declarations of love, requests to pass a dinner dish, letters from students asking parents for money, or official government notices threatening penalties if taxes and fines are not paid. Because tone is often equated with *attitude*, it is important to realize that tone refers not so much to attitude itself but instead to those techniques and modes of presentation that reveal or create attitude.

As a literary concept, *tone* is adapted from the phrase *tone of voice* in speech. Tone of voice reflects attitudes toward a particular object or situation, and also toward listeners. Let us suppose that Mary has a difficult assignment, on which she expects to work all day. Things go well, and she finishes quickly. She happily tells her friend Anne, "I'm so pleased. I needed only two hours for that." Then she decides to buy tickets for a popular play and must wait through a long and slow line. After getting her tickets, she tells the people at the end of the line, "I'm so pleased. I needed only two hours for that." The sentences are exactly the same, but by changing her emphasis and vocal inflection, Mary indicates her disgust and impatience with her long wait and also shows her sympathy with the people still in line. By controlling the *tone* of her statements, in other words, Mary conveys attitudes of satisfaction at one time, and indignation and also sympathy at another.

As this example indicates, an attitude itself may be summarized with a word or phrase (satisfaction or indignation, love or contempt, deference or command, and so on), but the study of tone examines those aspects of situation, language, action, and background that *bring out* the attitude. In the last two lines of Owen's "Anthem for Doomed Youth," for example, the speaker refers to the reactions of those at home for the young men who die in battle:

> Their flowers [shall be] the tenderness of patient minds,
> And each slow dusk a drawing-down of blinds.

These words suggest that the anguish of immediate sorrow is past, and those left at home must endure a more enduring, lifelong, quiet sorrow, indicated by the "drawing down of blinds," which by shutting out light also symbolizes the elimination of at least one aspect of life.

❦ TONE AND ATTITUDES

In most literary works, attitudes point in a number of directions, so that tone becomes a highly complex matter. The following things to look for, however, should help you in understanding and describing literary tone.

Determine the Writer's Attitude Toward the Material

By reading a work carefully, we may deduce the author's attitude or attitudes toward the subject matter. In "The Story of an Hour," for example, Chopin sympathetically portrays a young wife's secret wishes for freedom, just as she also humorously reveals the unwitting smugness that often pervades men's relationships with women. In "Echo," Rossetti's speaker addresses a lover who is long dead, and by this means Rossetti renders attitudes of yearning and sorrow. In a broader perspective, authors may view human beings with amused affection, as in Chekhov's *The Bear*, or with amused resignation, as in Hardy's "Channel Firing." All these works exhibit various degrees of irony, which is one of the most significant aspects of authorial tone.

Discover the Writer's Attitude Toward Readers

Authors recognize that readers participate in the creative act and that all elements of a story—word choice, characterization, allusions, levels of reality—must take readers' responses into account (note the discussion of

"Reader Response" criticism in Appendix A). When Hawthorne's woodland guide in "Young Goodman Brown" refers to "King Philip's War," for
example, Hawthorne assumes that his readers know that this war was inhu-
mane, greedy, and cruel. By allowing this assumption to stand, he indicates
respect for the knowledge of his readers, and he also assumes their agreement with his interpretation. Chekhov in *The Bear* assumes that readers understand that Smirnov's speeches reveal him as irascible and petulant, but
they also show him as both generous and funny. Authors always make such
considerations about readers by implicitly complimenting them on their
knowledge and also by satisfying their curiosity and desire to be interested,
stimulated, and pleased.

Determine Other Dominant Attitudes

Beyond general authorial tone, there are many internal and dramatically rendered expressions of attitude. For example, the speaker of Lowell's
"Patterns" is a decent and proper upper-class young woman. Yet at the
news of her fiancé's death, her sorrowful meditation brings out that she had
made a promise to him to make love outside, on a "shady seat" in the garden (lines 86 to 89). This personal confession reveals the inner warmth that
her external appearance does not suggest, and it also makes the poem pa-
thetically poignant.

In addition, as characters interact, their tone dramatically shows their
judgments about other characters and situations. The brusque young
woman in Mansfield's "Miss Brill" compares Miss Brill's fur muff with a
"fried whiting" (paragraph 14). Her speech indicates contempt, indifference, and cruelty. A complicated control of tone occurs in Glaspell's *Trifles*,
where the two major characters, Mrs. Hale and Mrs. Peters, decide to cover
up incriminating evidence about Minnie Wright. When Mrs. Peters agrees
to this obstruction of justice, however, she speaks not about illegality, but
rather about the possible embarrassment of the action:

> MRS. PETERS. (*Takes the bottle, looks about for something to wrap it in; takes petticoat
> from the clothes brought from the other room, very nervously begins winding this
> around the bottle. In a false voice.*) "My! it's a good thing the men couldn't hear
> us. Wouldn't they just laugh! Getting all stirred up over a little thing like a—
> dead canary. As if that could have anything to do with—with—wouldn't they
> *laugh*! (speech 137)

Notice that her words reveal her knowledge that men scoff at feminine concerns, like Minnie's quilting knots, and therefore she openly anticipates the
men's amusement. The reader, however, knows that she is joining Mrs.
Hale in covering up the evidence about Minnie.

❦ TONE AND HUMOR

A major aspect of tone is humor. Everyone likes to laugh, and shared laughter is part of good human relationships; but not everyone can explain why things are funny. Laughter resists close analysis; it is unplanned, personal, idiosyncratic, and usually unpredictable. Nonetheless, there are a number of common elements:

1. *There must be an object to laugh at.* There must be something to laugh at—a person, a thing, a situation, a custom, a habit of speech or a dialect, or an arrangement of words.

2. *Laughter usually stems out of a disproportion called* **incongruity.** People normally know what to expect under given conditions, and anything contrary to these expectations is *incongruous* and may therefore generate laughter. When the temperature is 100°F, for example, you expect people to dress lightly, but if you were to see a man wearing a heavy overcoat, a warm hat, a muffler, and large gloves, and waving his arms and stamping his feet to keep warm, he would violate your expectations. Because his garments and behavior are *inappropriate* or *incongruous,* you would think he was funny. A student in a language class once wrote about a *"congregation* of verbs" and also about parts of speech as "nouns, verbs, and *proverbs."* The student meant the *conjugation* of verbs, of course, and also (maybe) either *adverbs* or *pronouns,* but somehow his understanding slipped, and he created a comic incongruity. Such inadvertent verbal errors are called **malapropisms**, after Mrs. Malaprop, a character in Sheridan's eighteenth-century play *The Rivals.* In the literary creation of malapropisms, the tone is directed against the speaker, for the amusement of both readers and author alike.

3. *Safety and/or goodwill prevents harm and insures laughter.* Seeing a person slip on a banana peel and hurtle through the air may cause laughter, but only if we ourselves are not that person, for laughter depends on insulation from danger and pain. In comic situations that involve physical abuse—falling down stairs or being hit in the face by cream pies—the abuse never harms the participants. The incongruity of such situations causes laughter, and the immunity from pain and injury prevents responses of horror. Goodwill enters into humor in romantic comedy or in any other work where we are drawn into general sympathy with the major figures, such as Smirnov and Mrs. Popov in Chekhov's *The Bear.* As the author leads the characters toward their unexpected outburst of love, our involvement produces happiness, smiles, and even sympathetic laughter.

4. *Unfamiliarity, newness, and uniqueness are needed to produce the spontaneity of laughter.* Laughter depends on seeing something new or unique, or on experiencing something familiar in a new light. Because laughter is prompted by flashes of insight or sudden revelations, it is always spontaneous, even when readers already know what they are laughing at. Indeed, the task of the comic writer is to develop ordinary materials to that point when spontaneity frees readers to laugh. Thus you can read and reread Frank O'Connor's "First

Confession" and laugh each time because, even though you know what will happen, the story shapes your acceptance of how reconciliation penetrates a wall of anger and guilt. Young Jackie's experience is and always will be comic because it is so spontaneous and incongruous.

⚱ TONE AND IRONY

The capacity to have more than one attitude toward someone or something is a uniquely human trait. We know that people are not perfect, but we love a number of them anyway. Therefore, we speak to them not only with love and praise, but also with banter and criticism. On occasion, you may have given mildly insulting greeting cards to your loved ones, not to affront them but to amuse them. You share smiles and laughs, and at the same time you also remind them of your affection.

The word **irony** describes such contradictory statements or situations. Irony is natural to human beings who are aware of life's ambiguities and complexities. It develops from the realization that life does not always measure up to promise, that friends and loved ones are sometimes angry at each other, that the universe contains incomprehensible mysteries, that the social and political structure is often oppressive rather than liberating, that doubt exists even in the certainty of knowledge and faith, and that human character is built through chagrin, regret, and pain as much as through emulation and praise. In expressing an idea ironically, writers pay the greatest compliment to their audience, for they assume that readers have sufficient intelligence and skill to discover the real meaning of quizzical or ambiguous statements and situations.

Understand the Four Major Kinds of Irony: Verbal, Situational, Cosmic, and Dramatic

VERBAL IRONY DEPENDS ON THE INTERPLAY OF WORDS. In **verbal irony,** one thing is said, but the opposite is meant. In the example opening this chapter, Mary's ironic expression of pleasure after her two-hour wait for tickets really means that she is disgusted. There are important types of verbal irony. In **understatement,** the expression does not fully describe the importance of a situation, and therefore makes its point by implication. For example, in Bierce's "An Occurrence at Owl Creek Bridge," the condemned man contemplates the apparatus designed by the soldiers to hang him. After considering the method, the man's response is described by the narrator: "The arrangement commended itself to his judgment as simple and effective" (paragraph 4). These words would be appropriate for the appraisal of ordinary machinery, perhaps, but because the apparatus will cause the man's death, the understated observation is ironic.

By contrast, in **overstatement,** or **hyperbole,** the words are far in excess of the situation, and readers or listeners therefore understand that the true meaning is considerably less than what is said. An example is the priest's exaggerated dialogue with Jackie in "First Confession" (paragraphs 38 to 50). Though the priest makes incongruously hyperbolic comments on Jackie's plans for slaughtering his grandmother, readers automatically know he means no such thing. The gulf between what is said and what is meant creates smiles and chuckles.

Often verbal irony is ambiguous, having double meaning or **double entendre.** Midway through "Young Goodman Brown," for example, the woodland guide leaves Brown alone while stating, "when you feel like moving again, there is my staff to help you along" (paragraph 40). The word "staff" is ambiguous, for it refers to the staff that resembles a serpent (paragraph 13). The word therefore suggests that the devilish guide is leaving Brown not only with a real staff but also with the spirit of evil (unlike the divine "staff" of Psalm 23 that gives comfort). Ambiguity, of course, may be used in relation to any topic. Quite often *double entendre* is used in statements about sexuality, usually for the amusement of listeners or readers.

SITUATIONAL IRONY FILLS THE GAP BETWEEN HOPE AND REALITY. **Situational irony,** or **irony of situation,** refers to the chasm between what we hope for or expect and what actually happens. It is often pessimistic because it emphasizes that human beings usually have little or no control over their lives or anything else. The forces of opposition may be psychological, social, cultural, political, or environmental. The situation is not temporary, one might add, but permanent and universal, as in Hardy's "Channel Firing," in which the topic is the omnipresence of war in the past, present, and future. Although situational irony often involves disaster, it need not always do so. For example, a happier occurrence of situational irony is in Chekhov's play *The Bear*, for the two characters shift from anger to love as they fall into the grips of emotions that are "bigger than both of them."

COSMIC IRONY STEMS FROM THE POWER OF CHANCE AND FATE. A special kind of situational irony that emphasizes the pessimistic and fatalistic side of life is **cosmic irony,** or **irony of fate.** By the standard of cosmic irony, the universe is indifferent to individuals, who are subject to blind chance, accident, uncontrollable emotions, perpetual misfortune, and misery. Even if things temporarily go well, people's lives end badly, and their best efforts do not rescue them or make them happy. A work illustrating cosmic irony is Glaspell's *Trifles*, which develops out of the stultifying conditions of farm life experienced by Minnie Wright. She has no profession, no other hope, no other life except the lonely, dreary farm—nothing. After thirty years of wretchedness, she buys a canary that warbles for her to make her life pleasant. Within a year, her boorish husband wrings the bird's neck, and she in turn gains revenge against him. Her situation is cosmically ironic, for the implication of *Trifles* is that human beings are caught in a web of adverse circumstances from which there is no escape.

DRAMATIC IRONY RESULTS FROM MISUNDERSTANDING AND LACK OF KNOWLEDGE. Like cosmic irony, **dramatic irony** is a special kind of situational irony. It happens when a character either has no information about a situation or else misjudges it, but readers (and often some of the other characters) see everything completely and correctly. The model of dramatic irony is found in Sophocles' ancient Greek play *Oedipus the King*. In this play, everyone—other characters and readers alike—knows the truth long before Oedipus knows it. Writers of nondramatic works also make use of dramatic irony. For instance, the doctors in Chopin's "The Story of an Hour" do not know Louise's true responses to the reports about her husband's death, but we readers do, and therefore we understand their vanity.

☙ WRITING ABOUT TONE

Begin with a careful reading, noting those elements of the work that convey attitudes. Consider whether the work genuinely creates the attitudes it is designed to evoke. In "The Cask of Amontillado," for example, do the gloomy catacombs evoke emotions of fear, or do they seem exaggerated? In Masefield's "Cargoes," how adequately does the British coaster convey disapproval of modern industry? Depending on the work, your devising and answering such questions will help you understand an author's control over tone. Similar questions apply when you study internal qualities such as style and characterization.

Raise Questions to Discover Ideas

- How strongly do you respond to the work? What attitudes can you identify and characterize? What elements in the story elicit your concern, indignation, fearfulness, anguish, amusement, or sense of affirmation?
- What causes you to sympathize or not to sympathize with characters, situations, or ideas? What makes the circumstances in the work admirable or understandable (or deplorable)?
- In fiction and drama, what does the dialogue suggest about the author's attitudes toward the characters? How does it influence your attitudes? What qualities of diction permit and encourage your responses?
- To what degree, if any, does the work supersede any previous ideas you might have had about the same or similar subject matter? What do you think changed your attitude?

- What role does the narrator/speaker play in your attitudes toward the dramatic or fictional material? Does the speaker seem intelligent/stupid, friendly/unfriendly, sane/insane, or idealistic/pragmatic?
- In an amusing or comic story, what elements of plot, character, and diction are particularly comic? How strongly do you respond to humor-producing situations? Why?
- What ironies do you find in the work (verbal, situational, cosmic)? How is the irony connected to philosophies of marriage, family, society, politics, religion, or morality?
- To what extent are characters controlled by fate, social or racial discrimination, limitations of intelligence, economic and political inequality, and limited opportunity?
- Do any words seem unusual or noteworthy, such as words in dialect, polysyllabic words, or foreign words or phrases that the author assumes you know? Are there any especially connotative or emotive words? What do these words suggest about the author's apparent assumptions about the readers?

Organize Your Essay on Tone

INTRODUCTION. Your introduction should describe the general situation of the work and its dominant moods or impressions, such as that the work leads to cynicism, as in "Channel Firing," or to laughter and delight, as in *The Bear*. Problems connected with describing the work's tone should also be introduced here.

BODY. Your goal is to show how the author establishes the dominant moods of the work, such as the poignancy of "Miss Brill" or the hilarity of *The Bear*. Some possibilities are the use or misuse of language, the exposé of a pretentious speaker, the use of exact and specific descriptions, the isolation of a major character, the failure of plans, and the continuance of naiveté in a disillusioned world. You might find a convenient approach in one of these:

1. *Audience, situation, and characters.* Is any person or group directly addressed by the speaker? What attitude is expressed (love, respect, condescension, confidentiality, confidence, etc.)? What is the basic situation in the work? Do you find irony? If so, what kind is it? What does the irony show (optimism or pessimism, for example)? How is the situation controlled to shape your responses? That is, can actions, situations, or characters be seen as expressions of attitude, or as embodiments of certain favorable or unfavorable ideas or positions? What is the nature of the speaker or persona? Why does the persona speak exactly as he or she does? How is the persona's character manipulated to show apparent authorial attitude and to elicit reader response? Does the work promote respect, admiration, dislike, or other feelings about character or situation? How?

2. *Descriptions, diction.* Descriptions or diction in the work should not be analyzed for themselves alone but should be related to attitude. *For descriptions:* To what degree do descriptions of natural scenery and conditions (snowstorms, cold, rain, ice, intense sunlight) convey an attitude that complements or opposes the circumstances of the characters? Are there any systematic references to colors, sounds, or noises that collectively reflect an attitude? *For diction:* Do connotative meanings of words control response in any way? To what degree does the diction require readers to have a large or technical vocabulary? Do speech patterns or the use of dialect evoke attitudes about speakers or their condition of life? Is the level of diction normal, slang, standard, or substandard? What is the effect of such a level? Are there unusual or particularly noteworthy expressions? If so, what attitudes do these show? Does the author use verbal irony? To what effect?

3. *Humor.* Is the work funny? How funny, how intense? How is the humor achieved? Does the humor develop out of incongruous situations or language, or both? Is there an underlying basis of attack in the humor, or are the objects of laughter still respected or even loved even though they cause amusement?

4. *Ideas.* Are any ideas advocated, defended mildly, or attacked? How does the author clarify his or her attitude toward these ideas—directly, by statement, or indirectly, through understatement, overstatement, or a character's speeches? In what ways does the work assume a common ground of assent between author and reader? That is, what common assumptions do you find about history, religion, politics, morality, behavioral standards, and so on? Is it easy to give assent (temporary or permanent) to these ideas, or is any concession needed by the reader to approach the work? (For example, a major subject of *Trifles* is the negative effects on a farm wife caused by the isolation and bleakness of life on an early twentieth-century farm. Things have changed since the time of the play, and the life of such women is certainly better, but sympathetic modern readers can readily understand the psychological situation of the play and can find Minnie Wright's situation important because of a common desire to learn as much as possible about human beings.)

5. *Unique characteristics of the work.* Each work has unique properties that contribute to the tone. Rossetti's "Echo," for example, considers the speaker's memory of her dead lover and presents details suggesting her despair and the hopelessness of her situation. Hardy's "Channel Firing" develops from the comic idea that guns being fired at sea are so loud they waken the dead in their coffins. In other works, there might be some recurring word or phrase that seems special. For example, Hughes in "Negro" introduces stanzas with phrases beginning "I am" and "I've been"; thereby, Hughes gives great weight and power to the assertions of the strong and self-aware speaker.

CONCLUSION.   In your conclusion, first summarize your main points and then go on to redefinitions, explanations, or afterthoughts, together with ideas reinforcing earlier points. You might also mention some other major aspect of the story's tone that you did not develop in the body.

Sample Essay

Chopin's Use of Irony in "The Story of an Hour"°

[1] "The Story of an Hour" is a remarkably short short-story that exhibits Kate Chopin's complex control over tone. <u>There are many ironies in the story, which grow out of error, misunderstanding, incorrect expectation, and a certain degree of pompous pride.</u>* In addition, the story raises an ironic question about the nature of marriage as an institution. All this is a great deal for so brief a story, yet it is all there. <u>The story contains a rich mixture of situational, cosmic, and dramatic irony.</u>†

[2] <u>The center of the story's situational irony is Louise Mallard, the central character.</u> Not much is disclosed about her character, her major circumstances being that she seems to be a faithful and dedicated housewife and that she suffers from heart disease. Her situation reaches a crisis when she is given the information that her husband has died. As a loving wife, she weeps convulsively at the news and then retreats to her room, presumably to grieve in solitude. Previously unknown and unsuspected feelings then come upon her—feelings that she is now "free." In other words, she realizes that her marriage has put her in bondage, even though at the same time she recognizes that her husband "had never looked save with love upon her" (paragraph 13). For the first time she recognizes the gap between her life and her hidden hopes and expectations, virtually a definition of situational irony.

[3] <u>Both situational and cosmic ironies are focused on the people closest to Louise, namely her sister Josephine and Brently Mallard's friend Richards.</u> They are kindly and have the best intentions toward her. Richards verifies the truth of the train wreck before coming to the Mallard household with the news, and then tells Josephine. In turn, Josephine breaks the news gently to Louise, in "veiled hints that revealed in half concealing" (paragraph 2), so as to forestall the shock that would bring on a fatal heart attack. Josephine is successful, and her concern causes her to beg Louise to come out of her room, for Josephine believes that Louise will make herself ill with grief (paragraph 17). With these best intentions, of course, Josephine becomes the inadvertent cause of bringing Louise in sight of the front door just as Brently Mallard enters it, and the shock of seeing him brings about the fatal heart attack. Thus, through no fault of her own, Josephine brings about the blow of fate that she and Richards have tried to avoid.

[4] <u>Another major cosmic irony in the story results from the inaccuracy and unreliability of information.</u> At the time of the story (1894), the best and most modern method of sending information over distances was by telegraph. Richards is in the newspaper office "when intelligence of the railroad disaster was received, with Brently Mallard's name leading the list of 'killed'" (paragraph 2). Since the news could never have come so rapidly in the days before

°See pages 310–312 for this story.
*Central idea.

[4] telegraphy was common, we may suppose that Louise would never have had the news of the death in the days before telegraphy, and therefore would never have experienced the emotional crisis brought about by the inaccurate news. The error of information may be caused by human mistake, but the consequences are cosmic for Louise—and, one might add, for her unsuspecting husband, who enters the house only to witness his wife's sudden death.

[5] This irony-filled story also contains dramatic irony that may be found in two details. None of the characters understands what Louise begins feeling as she sits upstairs. Their experience and their imagination simply make it impossible to comprehend her feelings. This failure of understanding is particularly sad with regard to Josephine and Richards, for these two are the closest ones to her. Thus in effect, Louise dies alone even though she is surrounded by the people who love her most. In the case of the doctors who diagnose the cause of Louise's death, the lack of understanding is bitterly ironic:

> When the doctors came they said she had died of heart disease—of joy that kills. (paragraph 23)

The somewhat pompous doctors find it impossible to imagine the true reason for Louise's shock, for, they obviously think, what other reason than joy at seeing her restored husband could bring about such a powerful assault on her system? "The Story of an Hour," of course, ends on this grim but also somewhat comic note.

[6] The story's crowning situational irony is the discrepancy between normal and conventional ideas of marriage as ideal and the reality of marriage as fact. One senses the authorial voice insisting strongly on uncomfortable reality when Louise contemplates a future life free of the need for satisfying anyone else:

> There would be no powerful will bending hers in that blind persistence with which men and women believe they have a right to impose a private will upon a fellow-creature. (paragraph 14)

Louise's marriage has not been bad, but the story at this point straightforwardly goes to the heart of the conflict between personal freedom and marital obligation. Chopin's words "blind persistence" are particularly effective here in establishing an attitude of disapproval if not of protest.

[7] Even though "The Story of an Hour" may thus be considered as a tract against marriage, it is above all a superbly crafted story. In just twenty-three paragraphs, it introduces a complex number of ironies revolving about the crisis created by the mistakes and misunderstandings of a single hour. It is the sudden coming together of all the ironies that crash in on Louise Mallard and destroy her. In her case, these ironies come into full play only when she believes that her husband has been killed and then quickly discovers that he is alive. In life, for most people, such crises may never come into play. As a general principle, the story's major irony is that even the best and most enviable circumstances of life contain inherent imperfections, unarticulated frustration, and potential unhappiness.

COMMENTARY ON THE ESSAY

The topic of this essay on tone is Chopin's complex use of irony in "The Story of an Hour." Throughout the essay, a good deal of the story's action is used to exemplify the sorts of irony being discussed. Links and connections within the essay are brought out by phrases like "even though," "also," "the crowning situational irony," "another," and "both."

Paragraph 1, the introduction, contains the central idea that announces the causes producing irony. The thesis sentence indicates that the combination of situational, cosmic, and dramatic irony will be explored in the body. Paragraph 2 demonstrates how situational irony applies to the circumstances of the major character, Louise. Paragraph 3 shows how both situational and cosmic irony enter into the story through Louise's sister Josephine and Brently's friend Richards.

An additional element of cosmic irony is discussed in paragraph 4. This irony is made to seem particularly unfortunate because the telegraphic errors are totally modern and could never have occurred in a pretechnological age.

In paragraph 5, the story's dramatic irony is introduced. This irony results from the lack of understanding by those closest to Louise and from the pompous intellectual blindness of the examining physicians. Paragraph 6 introduces Chopin's major idea criticizing marriage as an institution. Connected to the thematic purpose of the essay, however, this idea is shown to be integrated with the story's major situational irony. The final paragraph, 7, pays tribute to the story as a story, and speculates about how Chopin deals truthfully with difficult issues of life and marriage.

SPECIAL WRITING TOPICS
FOR STUDYING TONE

1. In "First Confession," the adult narrator, Jackie, is describing events that happened to him as a child. What are your attitudes toward Jackie? What do you think are O'Connor's attitudes toward him? To what degree has Jackie separated himself from his childish emotions? What does he say that might be considered residual childhood responses? What effect, if any, do such comments create?

2. Consider a story or poem in which the speaker is the central character (for example, "The Cask of Amontillado," "First Confession," "Dover Beach," "Desert Places," "Bright Star," "Echo," and "The Boxes." Write an essay showing how the language of the speaker affects your attitudes toward him or her (that is, your sympathy for the speaker, your interest in the story or the situation).

3. Write an essay comparing and contrasting attitudes toward two or more of the following female characters: Louise in "The Story of an Hour," Mathilde in "The Necklace," Mrs. Popov in *The Bear,* Minnie Wright in *Trifles,* and Miss Brill in "Miss Brill." How does the author's presentation control your understanding of them? What details of tone are important in a feminist approach to these works (see Appendix A)?

4. Write a fragment of a story of your own about, for example, a student, a supervisor, or a politician. Treat your main character with dramatic irony; that is, your character thinks he or she knows all the details about a situation but really does not (e.g., a male student declares interest in a female student without realizing that she is already engaged; a supervisor expresses distrust of one of the best workers in the firm; a politician accuses an opponent of actions that were done not by the opponent but by a supporter). What action, words, and situations do you choose to make your irony clear?

5. Write either (a) two character sketches, or (b) two descriptions of an action, as though you were planning to include them as part of a story. For either your sketches or your descriptions, make the first favorable, and the second negative. Analyze your word choices in the contrasting accounts: What kinds of words do you select, and on what principles? What words might you select to create a neutral account? On the basis of your answers, what can you conclude about the development of a fiction writer's style?

6. In your school library, consult the most recent copy of the *MLA International Bibliography of Books and Articles on the Modern Languages and Literatures,* and make a short list of books and articles on Bierce, Chopin, Hardy, Mansfield, or O'Connor. Consult at least three of the works, and with these, together with your own insights, write a short description of the writer's irony (comic or serious).

chapter 12

Writing About a Problem:
Challenges to Overcome
in Reading

A **problem** is any question that you cannot answer easily and correctly about a body of material that you know. The question "Who is the major character in Shakespeare's tragedy *Hamlet*?" is not a problem, because the obvious answer is Hamlet.

Let us, however, ask another question: "Why is it *correct* to say that Hamlet is the major character?" This question is not as easy as the first, and for this reason it is a problem. It requires that we think about our answer, even though we do not need to search very far. Hamlet is the title character. He is involved in most of the actions of the play. He is so much the center of our interest, concern, and liking that his death causes sadness and regret. To "solve" this problem has required a set of responses, all of which provide answers to the question "why?"

More complex, however, and more typical of most problems, are questions such as these: "Why does Hamlet talk of suicide in his first soliloquy?" "Why does he treat Ophelia so coarsely in the 'nunnery' scene?" "Why does he delay in avenging his father's death?" Essays on a problem are normally concerned with such questions, because they require a good deal of thought, together with a number of interpretations knitted together into a whole essay. More broadly, dealing with problems is one of the major tasks of the intellectual, scientific, social, and political disciplines. Being able to advance and then explain solutions is therefore one of the most important techniques that you can acquire.

☞ STRATEGIES FOR DEVELOPING AN ESSAY ABOUT A PROBLEM

Your first purpose is to convince your reader that your solution is a good one. This you do by using evidence correctly in making sound conclusions. In nonscientific subjects like literature you rarely find absolute proofs, so your conclusions will not be *proved* in the way you prove triangles congruent in geometry. But your organization, your use of facts from the text, your interpretations, and your application of general or specific knowledge should all make your conclusions convincing. Thus, your basic strategy is *persuasion*.

Strategy 1: Demonstrate That Conditions for a Solution Are Fulfilled

Suppose that you are writing on the problem of why Hamlet delays revenge against his stepfather, King Claudius. Suppose also that you make the point that Hamlet delays because he is never sure that Claudius is guilty. This is your "solution" to the problem. In your essay, you support your answer by challenging the credibility of the information that Hamlet receives about the crime (i.e., the two visits from the Ghost and Claudius's distress at the play within the play). Once you have "attacked" these sources of data on the grounds that they are unreliable, you have succeeded because your solution is consistent with the details of the play.

Strategy 2: Analyze Significant Words in the Phrasing of the Problem

Your object in this approach is to clarify important words in the statement of the problem, and then to decide how applicable they are. This kind of attention to words, in fact, might give you enough material for all or part of your essay. Thus, an essay on the problem of Hamlet's delay might focus in part on a treatment of the word *delay:* What, really, does *delay* mean? For Hamlet, is there a difference between delay that is reasonable and delay that is unreasonable? Does Hamlet delay unreasonably? Is his delay the result of a psychological fault? Would speedy revenge be more or less reasonable than the delay? By the time you have answered such pointed questions, you will also have sufficient material for your full essay.

Strategy 3: Refer to Literary Conventions or Expectations

The theory of this aspect of argument is that literary problems can be solved by reference either to the literary mode or conventions of a work, or to the limitations of the work itself. In other words, what appears to be a problem is really no more than a normal characteristic. For example, a question might be raised about why Mathilde in "The Necklace" does not tell her friend Jeanne Forrestier about the loss of the necklace. A plausible answer is that, all motivation aside, the story builds up to a surprise (at least for first-time readers), which could be spoiled by an early disclosure. To solve the problem, in other words, one has recourse to the structure of the story—to the literary convention that Maupassant observes in "The Necklace." Similarly, a student once raised a problem about the impossibility of skeletons speaking in Hardy's "Channel Firing." The answer to this problem is that Hardy is playing with the idea that the noise of naval gunnery blasting away at sea is loud enough to waken the dead. Once this given circumstance is accepted, there is no problem at all.

Strategy 4: Argue Against Possible Objections

With this strategy, you raise your own objections and then argue against them. Called **procatalepsis** or **anticipation,** this approach helps you sharpen your arguments, because *anticipating* and dealing with objections forces you to make analyses and to use facts that you might otherwise overlook. Although procatalepsis can be used point by point throughout your essay, you may find it most useful at the end.

The situation to imagine is that someone is raising objections to your solution to the problem. It is then your task to show that the objections (1) are not accurate or valid, (2) are not strong or convincing, or (3) are based on unusual rather than usual conditions (on an exception and not the rule). Here are some examples of these approaches.

A. THE OBJECTION IS NOT ACCURATE OR VALID. You reject this objection by showing that either the interpretation or the conclusions are wrong and also by emphasizing that the evidence supports your solution.

Although Hamlet's delay is reasonable, the claim might be made that his duty is to kill Claudius in revenge immediately after the Ghost's accusations. This claim is not persuasive because it assumes that Hamlet knows everything the audience knows. The audience accepts the Ghost's word that Claudius is guilty, but Hamlet has no certain reasons to believe the Ghost. Would it not seem insane for Hamlet to kill Claudius, who reigns legally, and then to claim he did it because of the Ghost's words? The argument for speedy revenge is not good because it is based on an incorrect view of Hamlet's situation.

B. THE OBJECTION IS NOT STRONG OR CONVINCING. You *concede* that the objection has some truth or validity, but you then try to show that it is weak and that your own solution is stronger.

> One might claim that Claudius's distress at the play within the play is evidence for his guilt and that therefore Hamlet should carry out his revenge right away. This argument has merit, and Hamlet's speech after Claudius has fled the scene ("I'll take the Ghost's word for a thousand pound") shows that the "conscience of the king" has been caught. But the king's guilty behavior is not a strong cause for killing him. Hamlet could justifiably ask for an investigation of his father's death on these grounds, but he could not justify a revenge killing. Claudius could not be convicted in any court on the testimony that he was disturbed at seeing "the Murder of Gonzago." Even after the play within the play, the reasons for delay are stronger than for action.

C. THE OBJECTION DEPENDS ON UNUSUAL RATHER THAN USUAL CONDITIONS. You reject the objection on the grounds that it could be valid only if normal conditions were suspended. The objection depends on an exception, not a rule.

> The case for quick action is simple: Hamlet should kill Claudius right after seeing the Ghost (I.3), or else after seeing the King's reaction to the stage murder of Gonzago (III.2) or else after seeing the Ghost again (III.4). Redress under these circumstances, goes the argument, must be both personal and extralegal. This argument wrongly assumes that due process does not exist in the Denmark of Hamlet and Claudius. Nothing in the play indicates that the Danes, even though they carouse a bit, do not value legality and the rules of evidence. Thus Hamlet cannot rush out to kill Claudius, because he knows that the King has not had anything close to due process. The argument for quick action is poor because it rests on an exception being made from civilized law.

WRITING ABOUT A PROBLEM

Remember that writing an essay on a problem requires you to argue in favor of a position: Either there is a solution, or there is not. To develop your position requires that you show the steps to your conclusion. Your general thematic form is thus (1) to describe the conditions that need to be met for the solution you propose, and then (2) to demonstrate that these conditions exist. If you assert that there is no solution, then your form would be the same for the first part, but your second part—the development—would show that these conditions have *not* been met.

Organize Your Essay About a Problem

INTRODUCTION.   Begin with a statement of the problem, and refer to the conditions that must be established for a solution. Your central idea is your answer to the question, and your thesis sentence indicates the main heads of your development.

BODY.   In developing your essay, use one or more of the strategies described in this chapter. These are, again: (1) to demonstrate that conditions for a solution are fulfilled; (2) to analyze the words in the phrasing of the problem; (3) to refer to literary expectations or limitations; and (4) to argue against possible objections. You might combine these. Thus, if we assume that your argument is that Hamlet's delay is reasonable, you might first consider the word *delay* (strategy 2); then you might use strategy 1 to explain the reasons for Hamlet's delay. Finally, to answer objections to your argument, you might show that he acts promptly when he believes he is justified (strategy 4). Whatever your topic, the important thing is to use the method or methods that best help you make a good argument for your solution.

CONCLUSION.   In your conclusion, try to affirm the validity of your solution in view of the supporting evidence. You might do this by reemphasizing your strongest points by simply presenting a brief summary, or by thinking of your argument as still continuing and thus using the strategy of procatalepsis to raise and answer possible objections to your solution, as is done in the last paragraph of the following sample essay.

Sample Essay

The Problem of Frost's Use of the Term "Desert Places" in the Poem "Desert Places"°

---

[1]   In the last line of "Desert Places," the meaning suggested by the title undergoes a sudden shift. At the beginning, it clearly refers to the snowy setting described in the first stanza, but in the last line it refers to a negative state of soul. The problem is this: Does the change happen too late to be effective? That is, does the new meaning come out of nowhere, or does it really work as a closing thought? To answer these questions, one must grant that the change cannot be effective if there is no preparation for it before the last line of the poem. If there is preparation—that is, if Frost does provide hints that the

°See page 354 for this poem.

[1] speaker feels an emptiness like that of the bleak, snowy natural world—then the shift is both understandable and effective even though it comes at the very end. It is clear that Frost makes the preparation and therefore that the change is effective.* The preparation may be traced in Frost's references, word choices, and concluding sentences.†

[2] In the first two stanzas, Frost includes the speaker in his reference to living things being overcome. His opening scene is one of snow that covers "weeds and stubble" (line 4) and that almost literally smothers hibernating animals "in their lairs" (line 6). The speaker then focuses on his own mental state, saying that he is "too absent-spirited to count," and that the "loneliness" of the scene "includes" him "unawares" (lines 7 and 8). This movement—from vegetable, to animal, to human—shows that everything alive is changed by the snow. Obviously, the speaker will not die like the grass or hibernate like the animals, but he indicates that the "loneliness" overcomes him. These first eight lines thus connect the natural bleakness with the speaker.

[3] In addition, a number of words in the third stanza are preparatory because they may be applied to human beings. The words "lonely" and "loneliness" (line 9), "more lonely" (line 10), "blanker" and "benighted" (line 11), and "no expression, nothing to express" (line 12) may all refer equally to human or to natural conditions. The word "benighted" is most important, because it suggests not only the darkness of night but also intellectual or moral ignorance. Since these words invite the reader to think of negative mental and emotional states, they provide a context in which the final shift of meaning is both logical and natural.

[4] The climax of Frost's preparation for the last two words is in the sentences of the fourth stanza. All along, the speaker claims to feel an inner void that is similar to the bleakness of the cold, snowy field. This idea emerges as the major focus in the last stanza, where in two sentences the speaker talks about his feelings of emptiness or insensitivity:

> They cannot scare me with their empty spaces
> Between stars—on stars where no human race is.
> I have it in me so much nearer home
> To scare myself with my own desert places. (lines 13–16)

[5] In the context of the poem, therefore, the shift in these last two words is not sudden or illogical. It rather pulls together the two parts of the comparison that Frost has been building from the first line. Just as "desert places" refers to the snowy field, it also suggests human coldness, blankness, unconcern, insensitivity, and cruelty. The phrase does not spring out of nowhere but is the strong climax of the poem.

[6] Although Frost's conclusion is effective, a critic might still claim that it is weak because Frost does not develop the thought about the negative soul. He simply mentions "desert places" and stops; the poem is not a long psychological study. To ask for more than Frost gives would be to expect more than sixteen lines can provide. A better claim against the effectiveness of the concluding shift of meaning is that the phrase "desert places" is both vague and

*Central idea.
†Thesis sentence.

[6] perhaps boastfully humble. If the phrase were taken away from the poem, this criticism might be acceptable. The fact is that the phrase is in the poem, and that it must be judged only in the poem. There, it takes on the connotations of the previous fifteen lines, and does so with freshness and surprise. <u>Thus the shift of meaning is a major reason for Frost's success in "Desert Places."</u>

☕ COMMENTARY ON THE ESSAY

The development of this essay illustrates strategy 1 described earlier in this chapter (page 166). The attention to the word *effective* in paragraph 1 briefly illustrates the second strategy (page 166). The concluding paragraph shows two approaches to the fourth strategy (page 167), using the arguments that the objections are not good because they (4a) are not accurate or valid (here the inaccuracy is related to strategy 3), and (4c) are based on the need for an exception, namely that the phrase in question be removed from the context in the poem.

After introducing the problem, paragraph 1 emphasizes that a solution is available only if the poem prepares the reader for the problematic shift of meaning. The central idea is that the poem satisfies this requirement and that the shift is effective. The thesis sentence indicates three subjects for development.

Paragraph 2 asserts that there is preparation even early in the poem. (A discussion of paragraph 3 follows.) Paragraph 4 asserts that the concluding sentences build toward a climax of Frost's pattern or development.

The argument of paragraph 3, like that of paragraph 2, is that the texture of the poem, right from the start, demonstrates the central idea (stated in the introductory paragraph) that the conditions for a solution to the problem are met. The method in this paragraph is to show how particular words and expressions, because they are applicable to both nature and human beings, connect the bleak opening scene with the speaker's professed spiritual numbness. The word "benighted" (line 11) is the most illustrative, because it particularly refers to cultural and intellectual bleakness. The paragraph hence demonstrates how the careful selection and analysis of key words can be part of a total argument.

Paragraphs 5 and 6 form a two-part conclusion to the essay. Paragraph 5 summarizes the arguments and offers an interpretation of the phrase. Paragraph 6 raises and answers two objections. The essay thus shows that a careful reading of the poem eliminates the grounds for claiming that there is any problem about the last line.

❦ SPECIAL WRITING TOPICS FOR STUDYING PROBLEMS

1. In "Dover Beach," the lines "Ah, love, let us be true / To one another!" have been read to refer not so much to the need for love as for the need for fidelity in all relationships. Which choice seems more correct? Explain.

2. Coleridge was planning a much longer poem when he began writing "Kubla Khan," but he was interrupted and could write no more. Some critics, however, are satisfied that the poem is complete as it stands. Defend the judgment that the poem may be considered finished.

3. Montresor, the narrator of Poe's "The Cask of Amontillado," believes that he is justified in making a victim out of Fortunato. Should his justification be accepted? Why is he not more specific about what Fortunato has done to him?

4. To what degree would more details opposing war make "Anthem for Doomed Youth" a more or less effective poem?

5. Some readers claim that the speaker's reactions to her fiancé's death in "Patterns" are too reserved, not sufficiently angry or passionate. What is your response to this view of the poem?

chapter 13

Writing an Essay
of Comparison and Contrast:

Learning by Seeing
Literary Works Together

A comparison-contrast essay is used to compare and contrast different authors, or two or more works by the same author; different drafts of the same work; or characters, incidents, techniques, and ideas in the same work or in different works. The virtue of comparison-contrast is that it enables the study of works in perspective. No matter what works you consider together, the method helps you isolate and highlight individual characteristics, for the quickest way to get at the essence of one thing is to compare it with another. Similarities are brought out by comparison; differences, by contrast. In other words, you can enhance your understanding of what a thing *is* by using comparison-contrast to determine what it *is not*.

For example, our understanding of Shakespeare's Sonnet 30: "When to the Sessions of Sweet Silent Thought," may be enhanced if we compare it with Christina Rossetti's poem "Echo." Both poems treat personal recollections of past experiences, told by a speaker to a listener who is not intended to be the reader. Both also refer to persons, now dead, with whom the speakers were closely involved. In these respects, the poems are comparable.

In addition to these similarities, there are important differences. Shakespeare's speaker numbers the dead persons as friends whom he laments generally, whereas Rossetti refers specifically to one person with whom the speaker was in love. Rossetti's topic is the sorrow of dead love, the irrevocability of the past, and the present loneliness of the speaker.

Shakespeare includes the references to dead friends as a way of accounting for present sorrows, but then his speaker turns to the present and asserts that thinking about the "dear friend" being addressed enables him to restore past "losses" and end all "sorrows." In Rossetti's poem, there is no reconciliation of past and present; instead, the speaker focuses entirely upon the sadness of the present moment. Though both poems are retrospective, Shakespeare's poem looks toward the present, and Rossetti's looks to the past. These differences show how the poems may be contrasted.

ꙮ GUIDELINES FOR THE COMPARISON-CONTRAST METHOD

The preceding example, although brief, shows how the comparison-contrast method makes it possible to identify leading similarities and distinguishing differences in two works. Frequently you can overcome difficulty with one work by comparing and contrasting it with another work on a comparable subject. A few guidelines will help direct your efforts in writing comparison-contrast essays.

Clarify Your Intention

When planning a comparison-contrast essay, first decide on your goal, for you can use the method in a number of ways. One objective may be the *equal and mutual illumination of two (or more) works.* For example, an essay comparing Hardy's "The Three Strangers" with Hawthorne's "Young Goodman Brown" might be designed to (1) compare ideas, characters, or methods in these stories equally, without stressing or favoring either. You might also (2) emphasize "Young Goodman Brown," and therefore you would use "The Three Strangers" as material for highlighting Hawthorne's story. Or, instead, you could (3) show your liking of one story at the expense of another, or (4) emphasize a method or idea that you think is especially noteworthy or appropriate.

A first task, therefore, is to decide what to emphasize. The sample essay on pages 179–80 gives "equal time" to both works being considered, without claiming the superiority of either. Unless you have a different rhetorical goal, this essay is a suitable model for most comparisons.

Find Common Grounds for Comparison

The second stage in prewriting for a comparison-contrast essay is to select a common ground for discussion. It is pointless to compare dissimilar things, for the resulting conclusions will not have much value. Instead, compare like with like: idea with idea, characterization with characterization, imagery with imagery, point of view with point of view, tone with tone, problem with problem. Nothing much can be learned from a comparison of O'Connor's view of individuality with Chekhov's view of love; but a comparison of the relationship of individuality with identity and character in O'Connor and Chekhov suggests common ground, with the promise of significant ideas to be developed through the examination of similarities and differences.

In seeking common ground, you will need to be inventive and creative. For instance, if you compare Maupassant's "The Necklace" and Chekhov's *The Bear*, these two works at first seem dissimilar. Yet common ground can be discovered, such as the treatment of self-deceit, the effects of chance on human affairs, and the authors' views of women. Although other works may seem even more dissimilar than these, it is usually possible to find a common ground for comparison and contrast. Much of your success in an essay of this type depends on your finding a workable basis—a common denominator—for comparison.

Integrate the Bases of Comparison

Let us assume that you have decided on your rhetorical purpose and on the basis or bases of your comparison. You have done your reading and taken notes, and you have a rough idea of what to say. The remaining problem is the treatment of your material.

One method is to make your points first about one work and then about the other. Unfortunately, such a comparison makes your paper seem like two separate lumps. ("Work 1" takes up one-half of your paper, and "Work 2" takes up the other half.) Also, the method involves repetition because you must repeat many points when you treat the second subject.

Therefore, *a better method* is to treat the major aspects of your main idea and to refer to the two (or more) works as they support your arguments. Thus you refer constantly to *both* works, sometimes within the same sentence, and remind your reader of the point of your discussion. There are reasons for the superiority of this method: (1) You do not repeat your points needlessly, for you develop them as you raise them. (2) By constantly referring to the two works, you make your points without requiring a reader with a poor memory to reread previous sections.

As a model, here is a paragraph on "Natural References as a Basis of Comparison in Frost's 'Desert Places' and Shakespeare's Sonnet 73: 'That Time of Year Thou Mayest in Me Behold.'"[1] The virtue of the paragraph is that it uses material from both poems simultaneously (as nearly as the time

[1]These poems are on pages 354 and 362.

sequence of sentences allows) as the substance for the development of the ideas:

> (1) Both writers link their ideas to events occurring in the natural world. (2) Night as a parallel with death is common to both poems, with Frost speaking about it in his first line, and Shakespeare introducing it in his seventh. (3) Along with night, Frost emphasizes the onset of winter and snow as a time of death and desolation. (4) With this natural description, Frost also symbolically refers to empty, secret, dead places in the inner spirit—crannies of the soul where bleak winter snowfalls correspond to selfishness and indifference. (5) By contrast, Shakespeare uses the fall season, with yellowing and dropping of leaves and migrating birds, to stress the closeness of real death and therefore the need to love fully during the time remaining. (6) Both poems therefore share a sense of gloom, because both present death as inevitable and final, just like the emptiness of winter. (7) Because Shakespeare's sonnet is addressed to a listener who is also a loved one, however, it is more outgoing than the more introspective poem of Frost. (8) Frost turns the snow, the night, and the emptiness of the universe inwardly in order to show the speaker's inner bleakness, and by extension, the bleakness of many human spirits. (9) Shakespeare instead uses the bleakness of seasons, night, and dying fires to state the need for loving "well." (10) The poems thus use common and similar references for different purposes and effects.

The paragraph links Shakespeare's references to nature to those of Frost. Five sentences speak of both authors together; three speak of Frost alone, and two of Shakespeare alone, but all the sentences are unified topically. This interweaving of references indicates that the writer has learned both poems well enough to think of them at the same time, and it also enables the writing to be more pointed and succinct than if the works were separately treated.

You can learn from this example: If you develop your essay by putting your two subjects constantly together, you will write economically and pointedly (not only for essays but also for tests). Beyond that, if you digest the material as successfully as this method indicates, you demonstrate that you are fulfilling a major educational goal—the assimilation and *use* of material. Too often, because you learn things separately (in separate works and courses, at separate times), you tend also to compartmentalize them. Instead, you should always try to relate them, to *synthesize* them. Comparison and contrast help in this process of putting together, of seeing things not as fragments but as parts of wholes.

Avoid the "Tennis-Ball" Method

As you make your comparison, do not confuse an interlocking method with a "tennis-ball" method, in which you bounce your subject back and forth constantly and repetitively, almost as though you were hitting observations back and forth over a net. The tennis-ball method is shown in the

following example from a comparison of the characters Mathilde (Maupassant's "The Necklace") and Mrs. Popov (Chekhov's *The Bear*):

> Mathilde is a young married woman; Mrs. Popov is also young but a widow.
> Mathilde has at least some kind of social life, even though she doesn't have
> more than one friend; but Mrs. Popov chooses to lead a life of solitude.
> Mathilde's daydreams about wealth are responsible for her misfortune, and
> Mrs. Popov's dedication to the memory of her husband could ruin her also.
> Mathilde is therefore made unhappy because of her own shortcomings, but
> Mrs. Popov is rescued despite her shortcomings. In Mathilde's case the focus
> is on adversity not only causing trouble but also strengthening character. Simi-
> larly, in Mrs. Popov's case the focus is on a strong person realizing her
> strength regardless of her conscious decision to weaken herself.

Imagine the effect of an entire essay written in this boring "1, 2, 1, 2, 1, 2"
order. Aside from the repetition and unvaried patterning of subjects, the
tennis-ball method does not permit much illustrative development. You
should not feel so constrained that you cannot take two or more sentences
to develop a point about one writer or subject before you include comparative references to another. If you remember to interlock the two subjects of
comparison, however, as in the paragraph about Frost and Shakespeare,
your method will give you the freedom to develop your topics fully.

₮ WRITING A COMPARISON-CONTRAST
ESSAY

In planning your essay, you must first narrow and simplify your topic so
that you can handle it conveniently. Should your subject be a comparison of
two poets (as in the comparison-contrast of Lowell and Owen on pages
179–80), choose one or two of each poet's poems on the same or a similar
topic, and write your essay about these.

    Once you have found an organizing principle, along with the relevant
works, begin to refine and to focus the direction of your essay. As you study
each work, note common or contrasting elements, and use these to form
your central idea. At the same time, you can select the most illustrative
works and classify them according to your topic, such as war, love, work,
faithfulness, or self-analysis.

Organize Your Comparison-Contrast Essay

    INTRODUCTION. Begin by stating the works, authors, characters, or
ideas that you are considering; then show how you have narrowed the
topic. Your central idea should briefly highlight the principal grounds of

comparison and contrast, such as that both works treat a common topic, exhibit a similar idea, use a similar form, or develop an identical attitude, and also that major or minor differences help make the works unique. You may also assert that one work is superior to the other, if you wish to make this judgment and defend it.

BODY. The body of your essay is governed by the works and your basis of comparison (ideas and themes, depictions of character, uses of setting, qualities of style, uses of point of view, and so on). For a comparison-contrast treatment on such a basis, your goal should be to shed light on both (or more) of the works you are treating. For example, you might examine a number of stories written in the first-person point of view (see Chapter 6). An essay on this topic might compare the ways that each author uses the point of view to achieve similar or distinct effects; or you might compare a group of poems that employ similar images, symbols, or ironic methods. Sometimes, the process can be as simple as identifying female or male protagonists and comparing the ways in which their characters are developed. Another approach is to compare the *subjects,* as opposed to the *idea.* You might identify works dealing with general subjects such as love, death, youth, race, or war. Such groupings provide a basis for excellent comparisons and contrasts.

As you develop your essay, remember to keep comparison-contrast foremost. That is, your discussions of point of view, metaphorical language, or whatever should not so much explain these topics *as topics* but rather explore *similarities and differences* of the works you are comparing. If your topic is an idea, for example, you need to explain the idea, but only enough to establish points of similarity or difference. As you develop such an essay, you might illustrate your arguments by referring to related uses of elements such as setting, characterization, rhythm or rhyme, symbolism, point of view, or metaphor. When you introduce these new subjects, you will be on target as long as you use them comparatively.

CONCLUSION. In concluding, you may reflect on other ideas or techniques in the works you have compared, make observations about similar qualities, or summarize briefly the grounds of your comparison. If there is a point that you have considered especially important, you might stress that point again in your conclusion. Also, your comparison might have led you to conclude that one work—or group of works—is superior to another. Stressing that point again would make an effective conclusion.

Sample Essay

The Treatment of Responses to War in Lowell's "Patterns" and Owen's "Anthem for Doomed Youth"°

[1] "Patterns" and "Anthem for Doomed Youth" are both powerful and unique condemnations of war.* Owen's short poem speaks broadly and generally about the ugliness of war and also about large groups of sorrowful people; Lowell's longer poem focuses on the personal grief of just one person. In a sense, Lowell's poem begins where Owen's ends, a fact that accounts for both the similarities and differences between the two works. The antiwar themes may be compared on the basis of their subjects, their lengths, their concreteness, and their use of a common metaphor.†

[2] "Anthem for Doomed Youth" attacks war more directly than "Patterns." Owen's opening line, "What passing-bells for those who die as cattle?" suggests that in war human beings are depersonalized before they are slaughtered, like so much meat, while his observations about the "monstrous" guns and the "shrill, demented" shells unambiguously condemn the horrors of war. By contrast, in "Patterns," warfare is far away, on another continent, intruding only when the messenger delivers the letter stating that the speaker's fiancé has been killed (lines 63 to 64). A comparable situation governs the last six lines of Owen's poem, quietly describing how those at home respond to the news that their loved ones have died in war. Thus the antiwar focus in "Patterns" is the contrast between the calm, peaceful life of the speaker's garden and the anguish of her responses. In "Anthem for Doomed Youth," the stress is more the external horrors of war that bring about the need for ceremonies honoring the dead.

[3] Another difference is that Owen's poem is less than one-seventh as long as Lowell's. "Patterns" is an interior monologue or meditation of 107 lines, but it could not be shorter and still be convincing. In the poem, the speaker thinks of the past and contemplates her future loneliness. Her final outburst, "Christ! What are patterns for?" could make no sense if she did not explain her situation as extensively as she does. On the other hand, "Anthem for Doomed Youth" is brief—a fourteen-line sonnet—because it is more general and less personal than "Patterns." Although Owen's speaker shows great sympathy, he or she views the sorrows of others distantly, unlike Lowell, who goes right into the mind and spirit of the grieving woman. Owen's use, in his last six lines, of phrases such as "tenderness of patient minds" and "drawing down of blinds" is a powerful representation of deep grief. He gives no further detail even though thousands of individual stories might be told. In contrast, Lowell tells one of these stories as she focuses on her solitary speaker's lost hopes and dreams. Thus the contrasting lengths of the poems are governed by each poet's treatment of the topic.

°See pages 358 and 362 for these poems.
*Central idea.
†Thesis sentence.

[4] Despite these differences of approach and length, both poems are similarly concrete and real. Owen moves from the real scenes and sounds of far-off battlefields to the homes of the many soldiers who have been killed in battle, but Lowell's scene is a single place—the garden of her speaker's estate. The speaker walks on real gravel along garden paths that contain daffodils, squills, a fountain, and a lime tree. She thinks of her clothing and her ribboned shoes, and also of her fiancé's boots, sword hilts, and buttons. The images in Owen's poem are equally real but are not associated with individuals as in "Patterns." Thus Owen's images are those of cattle, bells, rifle shots, shells, bugles, candles, and window blinds. Although both poems reflect reality, Owen's details are more general and public; Lowell's are more personal and intimate.

[5] Along with this concreteness, the poems share a major metaphor: that cultural patterns both control and frustrate human wishes and hopes. In "Patterns," this metaphor is shown in warfare itself (line 106), which is the pinnacle of organized human patterns of destruction. Further examples of the metaphor are found in details about clothing (particularly the speaker's stiff, confining gown in lines 5, 18, 21, 73, and 101, and also the lover's military boots in lines 46 and 49); the orderly, formal garden paths in which the speaker is walking (lines 1, 93); her external restraint at hearing about her lover's death; and her courtesy, despite her grief, in ordering refreshment for the messenger (line 69). Within such rigid patterns, her hopes for happiness have vanished, along with the sensuous spontaneity symbolized by her lover's plans to make love with her on a "shady seat" in the garden (lines 85 to 89). The metaphor of the constricting pattern is also seen in "Anthem for Doomed Youth," except that in this poem the pattern is the funeral, not love or marriage. Owen's speaker contrasts the calm, peaceful tolling of "passing-bells" (line 1) to the frightening sounds of war represented by the "monstrous anger of the guns," "the stuttering rifles' rapid rattle," and "the demented choirs of wailing shells" (lines 2 to 8). Thus, while Lowell uses the metaphor to reveal the irony of hope and desire being destroyed by war, Owen uses it to reveal the irony of war's negation of peaceful ceremonies.

[6] Though the poems, in these ways, share topics and some aspects of treatment, they are distinct and individual. "Patterns" includes many references to visible things, whereas "Anthem for Doomed Youth" emphasizes sound (and silence). Both poems conclude on powerfully emotional although different notes. Owen's poem dwells on the pathos and sadness that war brings to many unnamed people, and Lowell's expresses the most intimate thoughts of a woman who is alone in the agony of sorrow. Although neither poem attacks the usual platitudes and justifications for war (the needs to mobilize, to sacrifice, to achieve peace through fighting, and so on), the attack is there by implication, for both poems make their appeal by stressing how war destroys the relationships that make life worth living. For this reason, despite their differences, both "Patterns" and "Anthem for Doomed Youth" are parallel antiwar poems, and both are strong expressions of feeling.

❦ COMMENTARY ON THE ESSAY

This sample essay shows how approximately equal attention can be given to the two works being studied. Words stressing similarity are *common, share, equally, parallel, both, similar,* and *also.* Contrasts are stressed by *while, whereas, different, dissimilar, contrast, although,* and *except.* Transitions from paragraph to paragraph are not different in this type of essay from those in other essays. Thus, the phrases *despite, along with this,* and *in these ways,* which are used here, could be used anywhere for the same transitional purpose.

The central idea—that the poems mutually condemn war—is brought out in paragraph 1, together with the supporting idea that the poems blend into each other because both show responses to news of battle casualties.

Paragraph 2, the first in the body, discusses how each poem brings out its attack on warfare. Paragraph 3 explains the differing lengths of the poems as a function of differences in perspective. Because Owen's sonnet views war and its effects at a distance, it is brief; but Lowell's interior monologue views death intimately, needing more detail and greater length.

Paragraph 4, on the topic of concreteness and reality, shows that the two works can receive equal attention without the bouncing back and forth of the tennis-ball method. Three of the sentences in this paragraph (3, 4, and 6) are devoted exclusively to details in one poem or the other; but sentences 1, 2, 5, and 7 refer to both works, stressing points of broad or specific comparison. The scheme demonstrates that the two works are, in effect, interlocked within the paragraph.

Paragraph 5, the last in the body, considers the similar and dissimilar ways in which the poems treat the common metaphor of cultural patterns.

The conclusion, paragraph 6, summarizes the central idea, and it also stresses the ways in which both poems, although similar, are distinct and unique.

❦ SPECIAL WRITING TOPICS FOR STUDYING COMPARISON AND CONTRAST

1. The use of the speaker in Arnold's "Dover Beach" and Hughes's "Negro"
2. The description of fidelity to love in Keats's "Bright Star" and Shakespeare's Sonnet 73: "That Time of Year Thou Mayest in Me Behold," Arnold's "Dover Beach," or Lowell's "Patterns"
3. The view of women in Chekhov's *The Bear* and Maupassant's "The Necklace," or in Glaspell's *Trifles* and Rossetti's "Echo"

4. The use of descriptive scenery in Hawthorne's "Young Goodman Brown" and Lowell's "Patterns," or in Poe's "The Cask of Amontillado" and Bierce's "An Occurrence at Owl Creek Bridge"

5. Symbols of disapproval in Hardy's "Channel Firing" and Frost's "Desert Places"

6. The treatment of loss in Rossetti's "Echo" and Wagner's "The Boxes"

chapter 14

Writing About Prosody:
Sound, Rhythm, and Rhyme
in Poetry

Prosody (the pronunciation of a song or poem) is the general word describing the study of poetic sounds and rhythms. Common alternative words are **metrics, versification, mechanics of verse**, and the **music of poetry**. Most readers, when reading poetry aloud, interpret the lines and develop an appropriate speed and expressiveness of delivery—a proper *rhythm*. Indeed, some people think that rhythm and sound are the *music* of poetry because they convey musical rhythms and tempos. Like music, poetry often requires a regular beat. The tempo and loudness may vary freely, however, and a reader may stop at any time to repeat the sounds and to think about the words and ideas.

It is important to recognize that poets, being especially attuned to language, blend words and ideas together so that "the sound" becomes "an echo to the sense" (Pope). Readers may therefore accept as a rule that *prosodic technique cannot be separated from a poem's content*. For this reason, the study of prosody determines how poets have controlled their words so that the sound of a poem complements its expression of emotions and ideas.

☞ IMPORTANT DEFINITIONS
FOR STUDYING PROSODY

To study prosody, you need a few basic linguistic facts. Individual sounds in combination make up syllables and words, and separate words in combination make up lines of poetry. Syllables and words are made up of **segments**, or individually meaningful sounds (*segmental phonemes*). In the word *top*, there are three segments: *t*, *o*, and *p*. When you hear these three sounds in order, you recognize the word *top*. It takes three alphabetical letters—*t*, *o*, and *p*—to spell (or *graph*) *top*, because each letter is identical with a segment. Sometimes, however, it takes more than one letter to spell a segment. For example, in the word *enough*, there are four segments (*e*, *n*, *u*, *f*), although six letters are required for the correct spelling: *e*, *n*, *ou*, and *gh*. The last two segments (*u* and *f*) require two letters each (two letters forming one segment are called a *digraph*). In the word *through*, there are three segments but *seven* letters. To be spelled correctly in this word, the $\overline{oo}$ segment must have four letters (*ough*). Note, however, that in the word *flute*, the $\overline{oo}$ segment requires only one letter, *u*. When we study the effects of various segments in relationship to the poetic rhythm, we deal with sound; usually our concern is with prosodic devices such as **alliteration, assonance,** and **rhyme.**

When segments are meaningfully combined, they make up syllables and words. A **syllable,** in both prose and poetry, consists of a single meaningful strand of sound such as the article *a* in "*a* table," *lin* in "*lin*en," and *flounce* in "the little girls *flounce* into the room." (The article *a*, which is both a syllable and a word, has only one segment; *lin*, the first syllable of a two-syllable word (*lin* never occurs alone—it is always used in combinations such as *lingerie* and *linoleum*), contains three segments; *flounce* is a word of one syllable consisting of six segments: *f*, *l*, *ow*, *n*, *t*, and *s*). The understanding of what constitutes syllables is important because the rhythm of most poetry is determined by the measured relationship of heavily stressed to less heavily stressed syllables.

☞ SOUND AND SPELLING

It is important—vital—to distinguish between spelling, or **graphics,** and pronunciation, or **phonetics.** Not all English sounds are spelled and pronounced in the same way, as with *top*. Thus the letter *s* has three very different sounds in the words *sweet, sugar,* and *flows: s, sh* (as in "sharp"), and *z*. On the other hand, the words *shape, ocean, nation, sure, fissure, Eschscholtzia,* and *machine* use different letters or combinations of letters to spell the same *sh* sound.

Vowel sounds may also be spelled in different ways. The *ē* sound, for example, can be spelled *i* in *machine, ee* in *speed, ea* in *eat, e* in *even*, and *y* in *funny*, yet the vowel sounds in *eat, break*, and *bear* are not the same even though they are spelled the same. Remember this: With both consonants and vowel sounds, *do not confuse spellings with sounds.*

⁇ RHYTHM

Rhythm in speech is a combination of vocal speeds, rises and falls, starts and stops, vigor and slackness, and relaxation and tension. In ordinary speech and in prose, rhythm is not as important as the flow of ideas. In poetry, rhythm is significant because poetry is so emotionally charged, compact, and intense. Poets invite us to change speeds while reading—to slow down and linger over some words and sounds, and to pass rapidly over others. They also invite us to give more-than-ordinary vocal stress or emphasis to certain syllables, and less stress to others. The more intense syllables are called **heavy stress** syllables, and it is the heavy stresses that determine the **accent** or **beat** of a poetic line. The less intense syllables receive **light stress**. In traditional verse, poets select patterns called **feet,** which consist of a regularized relationship of heavy stresses to light stresses.

Scansion Is the Systematic Study of Poetic Rhythm

To study the patterns of versification in any poem, you **scan** the poem. The act of scanning—**scansion**—enables you to discover how the poem establishes a prevailing metrical pattern, and also how and why there are variations in the pattern.

DETERMINE STRESSES, OR BEATS.   In scansion, it is important to use a commonly recognized notational system to record stresses or accents. A *heavy* or *primary* stress (also called an **accented syllable**) is usually indicated by a prime mark or acute accent (´). A *light* stress (also called an **unaccented syllable**) is indicated by a bowl-like half circle called a **breve** (˘) or sometimes by a raised circle or degree sign (°). To separate one foot from another, a **virgule** or slash (/) is used. Thus, the following line, from Coleridge's "The Rime of the Ancient Mariner," is schematized formally in this way:

Wa - ter, / wa - ter, / ev - ery where,

Here the virgules show that the line contains two two-syllable feet followed by a three-syllable foot.

DETERMINE THE METER OR MEASURE. Another important part of scansion is the determination of a poem's **meter,** or the number of feet in its lines. Lines containing five feet are **pentameter,** four are **tetrameter,** three are **trimeter,** two are **dimeter,** and one is **monometer.** (To these may be added the less common line lengths **hexameter,** a six-foot line; **heptameter** or **the septenary,** seven feet; and **octameter,** eight feet.) In terms of accent or beat, a trimeter line has three beats (heavy stresses), a pentameter line five beats, and so on.

Metrical Feet Measure Syllables and Stresses

Equipped with this knowledge, you are ready to scan poems and to determine the rhythmical patterns of feet. The most important ones, the specific names of which are derived from Greek poetry, are the two-syllable foot, the three-syllable foot, and the one-syllable (or imperfect) foot.

THE TWO-SYLLABLE FOOT

(a) The Iamb: Light/Heavy. The most important two-syllable foot in English is the iamb, which contains a light stress followed by a heavy stress:

˘ ´
the winds

The iamb is the most common foot in English poetry because it most nearly duplicates natural speech while also elevating speech to poetry. It is the most versatile of English poetic feet, and it is capable of great variation. Even within the same line, iambic feet vary in intensity, so that they may support or undergird the shades of meaning designed by the poet. For example, in this line of iambic pentameter from Wordsworth's sonnet "The World Is Too Much with Us," each foot is unique:

˘ ´ ˘ ´ ˘ ´ ˘ ´ ˘ ´
The winds / that will / be howl- / ing at / all hours.

Even though "will" and "at" receive the heavy stress in their individual iambic feet, they are not as strongly emphasized as "winds," "howl-," and "hours" (indeed, they are also less strong than *all*, which is in the light-stress position in the concluding iamb). Such variability, approximating the stresses and rhythms of actual speech, makes the iamb suitable for both serious and light verse, and it therefore helps poets to focus attention on ideas and emotions. If they use it with skill, it never becomes monotonous, for it does not distract readers by drawing attention to its own rhythm.

(b) The Trochee: Heavy/Light. The trochee consists of a heavy accent followed by a light:

    ´   ᴗ
flow - er

Rhythmically, most English words are trochaic, as may be seen in words like *water, snowfall, author, willow, morning, early, follow, singing, window,* and *something.* A major exception is seen in two-syllable words beginning with prefixes, such as *sublime, because,* and *impel.* Another exception is found in two-syllable words that are borrowed from another language but are still pronounced as in the original language, as with *machine, technique, garage,* and *chemise,* all of which are French importations. To see the strength of the trochaic tendency in English, some French words borrowed six hundred or more years ago have lost their original iambic structure and have become trochaic, as with *language, very, nation,* and *cherry.*

Because trochaic rhythm has often been called *falling, dying, light,* or *anticlimactic,* whereas iambic rhythm is *rising, elevating, serious,* and *climactic,* poets have preferred the iambic foot. They therefore have arranged various placements of single- and multiple-syllable words, and have also used a variety of other means, so that the heavy-stress syllable is at the end of the foot, as in this line from Shakespeare:

ᴗ ´   ᴗ   ´   ᴗ ´   ᴗ   ´   ᴗ   ´
With - in / his bend - / ing sick - / le's com - / pass come, /

in which three successive trochaic words are arranged to match the iambic meter.

(c) The Spondee: Heavy/Heavy. The **spondee**—also called a **hovering accent**—consists of two successive, equally heavy accents, as in "men's eyes" in Shakespeare's line:

´ ᴗ   ᴗ ´   ᴗ ´   ᴗ ᴗ   ⋀⋀
When, in / dis -grace / with For - / tune and / men's eyes.

The spondee is mainly a substitute foot in English verse because successive spondees usually become iambs or trochees. An entire poem written in spondees would be unlikely within traditional metrical patterns and ordinary English syntax. As a substitute, however, the spondee creates emphasis. The usual way to indicate the spondaic foot is to link the two syllables together with chevronlike marks (⋀⋀), like this:

men's eyes

(d) The Pyrrhic: Light/Light.   The **pyrrhic** consists of two unstressed syllables (even though one of them may be in a normally stressed position), as in *on their* in Pope's line:

Now sleep - / ing flocks / on their / soft flee - / ces lie.

The pyrrhic is made up of weakly accented words such as prepositions (e.g., *on, to*) and articles (*the, a*). Like the spondee, it is usually substituted for an iamb or a trochee, and therefore a complete poem cannot be in pyrrhics. As a substitute foot, however, the pyrrhic acts as a rhythmic catapult to move the reader swiftly to the next heavy-stress syllable, and therefore it undergirds the ideas conveyed by more important words.

THE THREE-SYLLABLE FOOT

(a) The Anapest: Light/Light/Heavy.   The anapest consists of two light accents followed by a heavy accent:

by the dawn's / ear - ly light. (Key)

(b) The Dactyl: Heavy/Light/Light.   The dactylic foot has a heavy stress followed by two lights:

green as our / hope in it, / white as our / faith in it. (Swinburne)

THE IMPERFECT FOOT

Either a single stressed syllable (´) by itself or an unstressed syllable (˘) by itself creates an **imperfect foot**. This foot is a variant or substitute occurring in a poem in which one of the major feet forms the metrical pattern. The second line of Key's "The Star-Spangled Banner," for example, is anapestic, but it contains an imperfect foot at the end:

What so proud -/ ly we hailed/ at the twi-/ light's last gleam-/ing./

A Pause in a Poetic Line Is a *Caesura*

Whenever we speak, we run our words together rapidly, without pause. We do, however, stop briefly and almost unnoticeably between significant units or phrases. These significant units, both grammatically and rhythmically, are **cadence groups.** In poetry that emphasizes a regular meter, the cadence groups operate just as they do in prose to make the ideas intelligible. Although we are following the poetic rhythm, we also pause briefly at the ends of phrases and make longer pauses at the ends of sentences. In scansion, the name of these pauses, which linguists call *junctures*, is **caesura** (plural **caesurae**). When scanning a line, we note a caesura with two diagonal lines or virgules (//), so that the caesura can be distinguished from the single virgule separating feet. Sometimes the caesura coincides with the end of a foot, as at the end of the second iamb in this line by William Blake:

⏑　　／　⏑　／　　⏑　／　　⏑　／　⏑　／
With hands / di - vine // he mov'd / the gen - / tle Sod. /

The caesura, however, may fall within a foot, and there may be more than one in a line, as within the second and third iambs in this line by Ben Jonson:

　⏑　／　⏑　　　／　　⏑　　　／　⏑　／　⏑　／
Thou art / not, //Pens - / hurst, // built / to en - / vious show./

SPECIAL METERS

Many poems contain meters other than those described in the text. Poets like Browning, Tennyson, Poe, and Swinburne introduce special or unusual meters. Other poets manipulate pauses or **caesurae** to create the effects of unusual meters. For these reasons, you should know about metrical feet such as the following:

1. **The amphibrach.** Light/heavy/light:
⏑　／　⏑　　⏑　／　⏑　　⏑　／　　　　⏑
Ah feed me / and fill me / with pleas - sure. / (Swinburne)

2. **The amphimacer or cretic.** Heavy/light/heavy:
／　⏑　／
Love is best. / (Browning)

3. **The bacchius or bacchic.** Light/heavy/heavy:
⏑　／　／　　／　⏑
Some late lark / [sing - ing]. / (Henley)

4. **Dipodic measure, or syzygy.** Two ordinary feet making one: Dipodic measure (literally, two feet making one) develops in longer lines when a poet submerges two regular feet under a stronger beat, so that a "galloping" or "rollicking" rhythm results. The following line from Masefield's "Cargoes," for example, may be scanned as trochaic hexameter, with the concluding foot being an iamb:
／　⏑　　／　⏑　　／⏑　／　⏑　　／⏑　　⏑／
Quin-que / reme of / Nin-e- / veh from / dis-tant / O-phir, /

In reading, however, a stronger beat is superimposed, which makes one foot out of two—dipodic measure, or syzygy:
／　　　　　　／　　　　　　／
Quin - quer - eme of / Nin - e - veh from / dis - tant O -phir, /

When a caesura ends a line, usually marked by a comma, semicolon, or period, that line is **end-stopped,** as in this line which opens Keats's "Endymion" :

$$\breve{~}~\acute{~}~~\breve{~}~\acute{~}~~~~\breve{~}~~\acute{~}~\breve{~}~\acute{~}~~\breve{~}~\acute{~}~\breve{~}$$
A thing / of beau - / ty // is / a joy / for - ev -er. /

If a line has no punctuation at the end and runs over to the next line, it is called **run-on**. A term also used to indicate run-on lines is **enjambement**. The following passage, a continuation of the line from Keats, contains three run-on lines:

> Its loveliness increases; // it will never
> Pass into nothingness; // but still will keep
> A bower quiet for us, // and a sleep
> Full of sweet dreams, // . . .

Substitution is the Displacement of a Dominant Foot by a Variant Foot

There are two types of rhythmical substitution: formal and rhetorical.

1. FORMAL SUBSTITUTION IS THE INSERTION OF A DIFFERENT FOOT WITHIN A REGULAR PATTERN. Most regular poems follow a formal pattern that may be analyzed according to the feet we have been describing here. For interest and emphasis, however (and also perhaps because of the natural rhythms of English speech), poets may **substitute** other feet for the regular feet of the poem. For example, the following line is from the "January" Eclogue of Edmund Spenser's *Shepherd's Calendar*. Although the pattern of the poem is iambic pentameter (i.e., five iambs per line), Spenser includes two substitute feet in this line:

$$\acute{~}~\breve{~}~\breve{~}~\acute{~}~~~~~~~~~~~\breve{~}~\acute{~}~~\breve{~}~\acute{~}$$
All in / a sun - / shine day, / as did / be - fall./

In the first foot, *All in* is a trochee, and *shine day* is a spondee. These are *formal substitutions;* that is, Spenser uses separate, formally structured feet in place of the normal iambic feet. The effect is to move rapidly from *All* to *sunshine day* in order to allow the reader to delight in the sound of the words and also to savor the idea of unexpectedly nice weather during the middle of winter.

2. RHETORICAL SUBSTITUTION IS THE CREATION OF APPARENTLY VARIANT RHYTHMS THROUGH THE MANIPULATION OF CAESURAE. By manipulating the caesura, poets may achieve the effects that are provided by formal substitution. If the pauses are placed within feet, they may cause us actually to *hear* trochees, amphibrachs, and other variant feet even though the line may scan regularly in the established meter. This type of *de facto* variation is **rhetorical substitution**. A noteworthy example in an iambic pentameter line is this one from Pope's *Essay on Man:*

$$\breve{\text{His}}\ \acute{\text{ac-}}/\breve{\text{tions}}',//\acute{\text{pas-}}/\breve{\text{sions}}',//\acute{\text{be-}}/\breve{\text{ing's}},//\acute{\text{use}}/\breve{\text{and}}\ \acute{\text{end}}./$$

The theory of this type of line is that there should be a caesura after the fourth syllable, but in this one, Pope has made three, each producing a strong pause. The line is regularly iambic, but the effect is different in actual reading or speaking. Because of the caesurae after the third, fifth, and seventh syllables, the rhythm produces an amphibrach, a trochee, another trochee, and an amphimacer, thus:

$$\breve{\text{His}}\ \acute{\text{ac-}}\breve{\text{tions}}',//\acute{\text{pas-}}\breve{\text{sions}}',//\acute{\text{be-}}\breve{\text{ing's}},//\acute{\text{use}}\ \breve{\text{and}}\ \acute{\text{end}}./$$

AMPHIBRACH   TROCHEE TROCHEE   AMPHIMACER

The spoken substitutions produced by the caesurae in this regular line create the effect of substitution and therefore cause tension and interest.

When studying rhythm, your main concern in noting substitutions is to determine the formal metrical pattern and then to analyze the formal and rhetorical variations on this pattern and their principal techniques and effects. Always try to show how these variations have enabled the poet to get points across and to achieve emphasis.

⚜ SEGMENTAL POETIC DEVICES

Once you have completed your analysis of rhythms, you may go on to consider the segmental poetic devices in the poem. Usually these devices are used to create emphasis, but sometimes in context they may echo or imitate actions and objects. The segmental devices most common in poetry are *assonance, alliteration, onomatopoeia,* and *euphony and cacophony.*

Identical Vowel Sounds Create *Assonance*

Assonance is the repetition of identical *vowel* sounds in different words—for example, the short *ĭ* in "swift Camílla skims." It is a strong means of emphasis, as in the following line, where the *ŭ* sound connects the two words *lull* and *slumber,* and the short *ĭ* connects *him, in,* and *his:*

And more, to lull him in his slumber soft. (Spenser)

Identical Consonant Sounds
Create *Alliteration*

Like assonance, **alliteration** is a means of highlighting ideas by words containing the same **consonant** sound—for example, the repeated *m* in Spenser's "Mixed with a *m*urmuring wind," or the *s* sound in Waller's praise of Cromwell, "Your never-failing *s*word made war to *c*ease," which emphasizes the connection between the words "sword" and "cease."

There are two kinds of alliteration. Most commonly, alliteration is regarded as the repetition of identical consonant sounds that begin syllables in close patterns—for example, in Pope's lines "Laborious, heavy, busy, bold, and blind," and "While pensive poets painful vigils keep." Used judiciously, alliteration gives strength to ideas by emphasizing key words, but too much can cause comic and catastrophic consequences.

The second form of alliteration occurs when a poet repeats identical or similar consonant sounds that do not begin syllables but nevertheless create a pattern—for example, the z segment in the line "In these places freezing breezes easily cause sneezes," or the *m*, *b*, and *p* segments (all of which are made *bilabially*; that is, with both lips) in "The *m*iserably *m*u*mb*ling and *m*o*m*entously *m*ur*m*uring *b*eggar *p*ropels *p*egs and *p*e*bb*les in the *bub*bling *p*ool." Such clearly designed patterns are hard to overlook.

Verbal Imitation of Real Sounds Is
Onomatopoeia, Sometimes Called
"Poetic Sound Effects"

Onomatopoeia is a blend of consonant and vowel sounds designed to *imitate* or *suggest* a situation or an action. It is made possible in poetry because many English words are **echoic** in origin; that is, they are verbal echoes of the actions they describe, such as *buzz, bump, slap,* and so on. In his well-known poem "The Bells," Edgar Allan Poe used such words to create onomatopoeia. There, through the combined use of assonance and alliteration, he imitates the kinds of bells that he celebrates. Thus, wedding bells sound softly with "*mo*lten *go*lden *no*tes" (*o*), while alarm bells "*cl*ang and *cl*ash and roar" (*kl*).

Pleasing Sounds Create *Euphony*
and Harsh Sounds Create *Cacophony*

Words describing smooth or jarring sounds, particularly those resulting from consonants, are **euphony** and **cacophony.** Euphony ("good sound") refers to words containing consonants that permit an easy and smooth flow of spoken sound. Although there is no rule that some consonants are inherently more pleasant than others, students of poetry often cite sounds like *m, n, ng, l, v,* and *z,* together with *w* and *y,* as being especially easy on the ears. The opposite of euphony is cacophony ("bad sound"), in which percussive and choppy sounds make for vigorous and noisy pronunciation, as in tongue twisters like "black bug's blood" and "shuffling shellfish fashioned by a selfish sushi chef." Obviously, unintentional cacophony is a mark of imperfect control. When a poet deliberately creates it for effect, however, as in Tennyson's line "The bare black cliff clang'd round him," in Pope's "The hoarse, rough verse should like the torrent roar" (*An Essay on Criticism*), and in Coleridge's "Huge fragments vaulted like rebounding hail, / Or chaffy grain beneath the thresher's flail" ("Kubla Khan"), cacophony is a mark of poetic skill. Although poets generally aim at easily flowing, euphonious lines, cacophony does have a place, always depending on the poet's intention and subject matter.

✌ RHYME: THE DUPLICATION AND SIMILARITY OF SOUNDS

Rhyme refers to words containing identical final syllables. One type of rhyme involves words with identical concluding vowel sounds, or assonance, as in *day, weigh, grey, bouquet, fiancé,* and *matinee.* A second type of rhyme is created by assonance combined with identical consonant sounds, as in *ache, bake, break,* and *opaque,* or *turn, yearn, fern, spurn,* and *adjourn,* or *apple* and *dapple,* or *slippery* and *frippery.* Rhymes like these, because their rhyming sounds are identical, are called **exact rhymes**. It is important to note that rhymes result from *sound* rather than from spelling; words do not have to be spelled the same way or look alike to rhyme. All the words rhyming with *day,* for example, are spelled differently, but because they all contain the same *ā* sound, they rhyme.

Rhyme, above all, gives delight. It also strengthens a poem's psychological impact. Through its network of similar sounds that echo and resonate in our minds, rhyme promotes memory by clinching feelings and ideas. It has been an important aspect of poetry for hundreds of years, and, although many poets have shunned it because they find it restrictive and artificial, it is closely connected with how well particular poems move us or leave us flat.

Most often, rhymes are placed at the ends of lines. Two successive lines may rhyme, for example, or rhymes may appear in alternating lines. It is also possible to introduce rhyming words at intervals of four, five, or more lines. A problem, however, is that if rhyming sounds are too far away from each other, they lose their immediacy and therefore their effectiveness.

There are few restrictions on English rhymes. Poets may rhyme nouns with other nouns, or with verbs and adjectives, or with any other rhyming word, regardless of part of speech. Of course, exact rhymes are to be preferred, but the shortage of exact rhymes in English has enabled poets to be creative, rhyming words that almost rhyme but don't exactly (*slant rhyme*) or words that look alike but sound different (*eye rhyme*). Some poets use the same words to complete a rhyming pattern (*identical rhyme*), although this repetition eliminates some of the surprise and interest that good rhymes should produce.

The System of Rhyming Is a Rhyme Scheme

A **rhyme scheme** refers to a poem's pattern of rhyming sounds, which are indicated by alphabetical letters. The first rhyming sounds, such as *love* and *dove*, are marked with an *a*; the next rhyming sounds, such as *swell* and *fell*, receive a *b*; the next sounds, such as *first* and *burst*, receive a *c*, and so on. Thus, a pattern of lines ending with the words *love, moon, thicket; dove, June, picket;* and *above, croon, wicket,* may be schematized as *a b c; a b c; a b c*.

To formulate a rhyme scheme or pattern, you include the meter and the number of feet in each line as well as the letters indicating rhymes. Here is such a formulation:

Iambic pentameter: *a b a b, c d c d, e f e f*

This scheme shows that all the lines in the poem are iambic, with five feet in each. Commas separating the units indicate a stanzaic pattern of three 4-line units, or **quatrains**, with the rhymes falling on the first and third, and the second and fourth, lines of each quatrain.

Should the number of feet in the lines of a poem or **stanza** vary, you show this fact by using a number in front of each letter:

Iambic: *4a 3b 4a 3b 5a 5a 4b*

This formulation shows an intricate pattern of rhymes and line-lengths in a stanza of seven lines. The first, third, fifth, and sixth lines rhyme, and vary from four to five feet. The second, fourth, and seventh lines also rhyme, and vary from three to four feet.

The absence of a rhyme sound is indicated by an *x*. Thus, you formulate the rhyme scheme of **ballad measure** like this:

Iambic: *4x 3a 4x 3a*

The formulation shows that the quatrain alternates iambic tetrameter with trimeter. In this ballad quatrain, only lines 2 and 4 rhyme; there is no end rhyme in lines 1 and 3.

WRITING ABOUT PROSODY

Because studying prosody requires a good deal of specific detail and description, it is best to limit your study to a short poem or to a short passage from a long poem. A sonnet, a stanza of a lyric poem, or a fragment from a long poem will usually be sufficient. If you choose a fragment, it should be self-contained, such as an entire speech or a short episode or scene (as in the example from Tennyson chosen for the sample essay on pages 198–204).

The analysis of even a short poem, however, can grow long because of the need to describe word positions and stresses and also to determine the various effects. For this reason you do not have to exhaust your topic. Try to make your discussion representative of the prosody of your poem or passage.

Your first reading in preparation for your essay should be for comprehension. On second and third readings, make notes of sounds, accents, and rhymes by reading the poem aloud. To perceive sounds, one student helped herself by reading aloud in an exaggerated way in front of a mirror. If you have privacy or are not self-conscious, you might do the same. Let yourself go a bit. As you dramatize your reading (maybe even in front of fellow students), you will find that heightened levels of reading also accompany the poet's expression of important ideas. Mark these spots for later analysis, so that you will be able to make strong assertions about the relationship of sound to sense.

In planning, it is vital to prepare study sheets so that your observations will be correct, for if your factual analysis is wrong, your writing will also be wrong. Experience has shown that it is best to make four triple-spaced copies of the poem or passage (with photocopy or, if necessary, carbon paper). These will be for the separate analyses of rhythm, assonance, alliteration, and rhyme. If you have been assigned just one of these, of course, only one copy will be necessary. Leave spaces between syllables and words for marking out the various feet of the poem. Ultimately, this duplication of the passage, with your markings, should be included as a first page, as in the sample student essays in this chapter.

Carry out your study of the passage in the following way:

- Number each line of the passage, regardless of length, beginning with 1, so that you may use these numbers as location references in your essay.

- Determine the formal pattern of feet, using the short acute accent or stress mark for heavily stressed syllables (✔), and the breve for unaccented or lightly stressed syllables (◡). Use chevrons to mark spondees (⋀).
- Indicate the separate feet by a diagonal slash, or virgule (/). Indicate caesurae and end-of-line pauses by double virgules (//).
- Use colored pencils to underline, circle, make boxes, or otherwise mark the formal and rhetorical substitutions that you discover. Because such substitutions may occur throughout the poem, develop a numbering system for each type (e.g., 1 = anapest, 6 = trochee, etc., as in the sample work sheet on page 199). Provide a key to your numbers at the bottom of the page.
- Do the same for alliteration, assonance, onomatopoeia, and rhyme. It has proved particularly effective to draw lines to connect the repeating sounds, for these effects will be close together in the poem, and your connections will dramatize this closeness. The use of a separate color for each separate effect is helpful, for different colors make prosodic distinctions stand out clearly.
- Use your work sheets as a reference for your reader's benefit. In writing your essay, however, make your examples specific by including brief illustrative quotations, as in the examples (i.e., words, phrases, and entire lines, with proper marks and accents). Do not rely on line numbers alone.

Once you have analyzed the various effects in your poem and have recorded these on your work sheets and in your notes, you will be ready to formulate a central idea and organization. The focus of your essay should reflect the most significant features of prosody in relationship to some other element of the poem, such as speaker, tone, or ideas.

Organize Your Essay on Prosody

Depending on your assignment, you might wish to discuss all aspects of rhythm or sound, or perhaps just one, such as the poet's use of regular meter, a particular substitution, alliteration, or assonance. It is possible, for example, to devote an entire essay to (1) regular meter; (2) one particular variation in meter, such as the anapest or spondee; (3) the caesura; (4) assonance; (5) alliteration; (6) onomatopoeia; or (7) rhyme. For brevity, rhythm and segmental effects are treated together here in one essay, and rhyme is considered alone in a separate essay.

INTRODUCTION.   After a brief description of the poem (such as that it is a sonnet, a two-stanza lyric, a dipodic burlesque poem, and so on), establish the scope of your essay. Your central idea will outline the thought that you wish to carry out through your prosodic analysis, such as that regularity of meter is consistent with a happy, firm vision of love or life, or that frequent spondees emphasize the solidity of the speaker's wish to love, or that particular sounds echo some of the poem's actions.

BODY. The body may include all the following elements, or just one, depending on your instructor's assignment.

1. *Rhythm.* Establish the formal metrical pattern. What is the dominant metrical foot and line length? Are some lines shorter than the pattern? What relationship do the variable lengths have with the subject matter? If the poem is a lyric or a sonnet, are important words and syllables successfully placed in stressed positions in order to achieve emphasis? Try to relate line lengths to exposition, development of ideas, and rising or falling emotions. It is also important to look for either repeating or varying metrical patterns as the subject matter reaches peaks or climaxes. Generally, deal with the relationship between the formal rhythmical pattern and the poet's ideas and attitudes.

   When noting substitutions, analyze the formal variations and the principal effects of these. If you concentrate on only one substitution, describe any apparent pattern in its use, that is, its locations, recurrences, and effects on meaning.

   For caesurae, treat the effectiveness of the poet's control. Can you see any pattern of use? Are the pauses regular or random? Describe noticeable principles of placement, such as (1) the creation of rhythmical similarities in various parts of the poem, (2) the development of particular rhetorical effects, or (3) the creation of interest through rhythmical variety. Do the caesurae lead to important ideas and attitudes? Are the lines all end-stopped, or do you discover enjambement? How do these rhythmical characteristics aid in descriptions and in the expressions of ideas?

2. *Segmental effects.* Here you might be discussing, collectively or separately, the use and effects of assonance, alliteration, onomatopoeia, and cacophony and euphony. Be sure to establish that the instances you choose have really occurred systematically enough within the poem to form a pattern. Illustrate sounds by including relevant words within parentheses. You might make separate paragraphs on alliteration, assonance, and any other seemingly important pattern. Also, because space is always at a premium, you might concentrate on only one noteworthy effect, like a certain pattern of assonance, rather than on everything. Throughout your discussion, always keep foremost the relationship between content and sound.

   > Note: To make illustrations clear, emphasize the sounds to which you are calling attention. If you use an entire word to illustrate a sound, underline or italicize only the sound, not the entire word, and put the word within quotation marks (for example, "The poet uses a *t* [' *t*ip,' '*t*op,' and '*t*errific']"). When you refer to entire words containing particular segments, however, underline these words (for example, "The poet uses a *t* in *tip*, *top*, and *terrific*").

3. *Rhyme.* An essay on rhyme should describe the major features of the poem's rhymes, specifically the scheme and variants, the lengths and rhythms of the rhyming words, and noteworthy segmental characteristics. In discussing the grammar of the rhymes, note the kinds of words (i.e., verbs, nouns, etc.) used

for rhymes: Are they all the same? Does one form predominate? Is there variety? Can you determine the grammatical positions of the rhyming words? How may these characteristics be related to the idea or theme of the poem?

You might also discuss the qualities of the rhyming words. Are the words specific? Concrete? Abstract? Are there any striking rhymes? Any surprises? Any rhymes that are particularly clever and witty? Do any rhymes give unique comparisons or contrasts? How?

Generally, note any striking or unique rhyming effects. Without becoming overly subtle or far-fetched, you can make valid and interesting conclusions. Do any sounds in the rhyming words appear in patterns of assonance or alliteration elsewhere in the poem? Do the rhymes enter into any onomatopoeic effects? Broadly, what aspects of rhyme are uniquely effective because they blend so fully with the poem's thought and mood?

CONCLUSION.   In your conclusion, try to develop a short evaluation of the poet's prosodic performance. If we accept the premise that poetry is designed not only to stimulate emotions but also to provide information and transfer attitudes, to what degree do the prosodic techniques of your poem contribute to these goals? Without going into excessive detail (and writing another essay), what more can you say here? What has been the value of your study to your understanding and appreciating the poem? If you think your analysis has helped you to develop new awareness of the poet's craft, it would be appropriate to state what you have learned.

First Sample Essay

A Study of Tennyson's Rhythm and Segments in "The Passing of Arthur," Lines 349–360

Note: For illustration, this essay analyzes a passage from Tennyson's "The Passing of Arthur," which is part of *Idylls of the King*. Containing 469 lines, "The Passing of Arthur" describes the last battle and the death of Arthur, legendary king of early Britain. After the fight, in which Arthur has been mortally wounded by the traitor Mordred, only Arthur and his follower Sir Bedivere remain alive. Arthur commands Bedivere to throw the royal sword Excalibur into the lake from which Arthur had originally received it. After great hesitation and some false claims, Bedivere does throw the sword into the lake, and a hand rises out of the water to catch it. Bedivere then carries Arthur to the lake shore, where the dying king is taken aboard a mysterious funeral barge. In the passage selected for discussion (lines 349–360), Tennyson describes Bedivere's carrying Arthur down the hills and cliffs from the battlefield to the lake below.

1. *RHYTHMICAL ANALYSIS*

But the o- / ther swift- /ly strode // from ridge / to ridge, //   1

Clothed with / his breath, // and look- / ing, // as / he walk'd, //   2

Lar-ger / than hu- / man // on / the fro- / zen hills. //   3

He heard / the deep / be-hind/ him, // and / a cry   4

Be-fore. // His own / thought drove / him // like / a goad. //   5

Dry clash'd / his har- / ness // in / the i /cy caves   6

And bar-ren / chasms, // and all / to left / and right   7

The bare / black cliff / clang'd round / him, // as / he based   8

His feet / on juts / of slip- / pe-ry crag // that rang   9

Sharp- smit- / ten// with / the / dint / of ar- / med heels— //   10

And on / a sud- / den, // lo! // the lev- / el lake, //   11

And the / long glor- / ies // of / the win- / ter moon. //   12

1 = Anapaest, or effect of anapaest.   4 = Effect of imperfect foot.

2 = Amphibrach, or the effect   5 = Pyrrhic.
     of amphibrach.   6 = Trochee, or the effect

3 = Spondee.   of trochee.

2. ALLITERATION

But the other ⓢ wiftly ⓢ trode from ridge to ridge,   1

Clothed with his breath, and looking, as ⓗ e walked,   2

Larger than ⓗ uman on the frozen ⓗ ills.   3

Ⓗ e ⓗ eard the deep be ⓗ ind ⓗ im, and a cry   4

Before. Ⓗ is own thought drove him like a goad.   5

Dry ⓒ lashed ⓗ is ⓗ arness in the icy ⓒ aves   6

And ⓑ arren ⓒⓗ asms, and all to left and right   7

The ⓑ are ⓑ ⓛ ack ⓒ ⓛ iff ⓒ ⓛ anged round him, as he ⓑ ased   8

His feet on juts of s ⓛ ippery ⓒ rag that rang   9

Sharp-smitten with the dint of armed heels—   10

And on a sudden, ⓛ o! the ⓛ evel ⓛ ake,   11

And the ⓛ ong g ⓛ ories of the winter moon.   12

〰〰〰〰 = s   ——— = b

- - - - - - = h   ‿‿‿‿‿ = l as second consonant sound in words

· · · · · · · · = k   -—·-—·-— = l

3. ASSONANCE

But the other sw ⓘ ftly str ⓞ de from r ⓘ dge to r ⓘ dge, 1

Cl ⓞ thed w ⓘ th h ⓘ s breath, and looking, as he walked, 2

Larger than human on the fr ⓞ zen hills. 3

He heard the deep beh ⓘ nd him, and a cr ⓨ 4

Before. His ⓞⓦ n thought dr ⓞ ve him l ⓘ ke a g ⓞⓐ d. 5

Dr ⓨ clashed his harness in the ⓘ cy caves 6

And barren ch ⓐ sms, and all to left and r ⓘ ght 7

The bare bl ⓐ ck cliff cl ⓐ nged round him, as he based 8

H ⓘ s feet on juts of sl ⓘ ppery cr ⓐ g that r ⓐ ng 9

Sh ⓐⓡ p-sm ⓘ tten w ⓘ th the d ⓘ nt of ⓐⓡ med heels— 10

And on a sudden, lo, the level lake, 11

And the long glories of the winter moon! 12

―――――――― = ō*   ·―·―·―· = ä

------------ = ī   〜〜〜〜〜 = i

············ = ă

*Pronunciation symbols as in *Webster's New World Dictionary*, 2nd ed.

[1]   In these twelve lines, Tennyson describes the ordeal of Sir Bedivere as he carries King Arthur, who is dying, from the mountainous heights, where he was wounded, down to the lake, where he will be sent to his final rest. Tennyson emphasizes the bleakness and hostility of this ghostly and deserted landscape. The metrical pattern he uses is unrhymed iambic pentameter—blank verse—which is suitable for descriptions of actions and scenes. Appropriately, the verse augments the natural descriptions and echoes first Bedivere's tenseness and then his relaxation.* Tennyson's control enables a true blending of sound and sense, as may be seen in his use of rhythm and in his manipulation of segmental devices, including onomatopoeia.†

[2]   Tennyson controls his meter to emphasize exertions and moods. In line 1 the meter is regular, except for an anapest in the first foot. This regularity may be interpreted as emphasizing the swiftness and surefootedness of Bedivere. But he is about to undergo a severe test, and the rhythm quickly becomes irregular, as though to strain the pentameter verse in illustration of Bedivere's exertions. Tennyson therefore uses variations to highlight key words. For example, he uses the effect of anapests in a number of lines. In line 2 he emphasizes the chill air and Bedivere's vitality in the following way:

Clothed with / his breath,//

The image is one of being surrounded by one's own breath that vaporizes on hitting the cold air, and the rhythmical variation—a trochaic substitution in the first foot—enables the voice to build up to the word "breath," a most effective internal climax.

[3]   Tennyson uses the same kind of rhythmical effect in line 3. He emphasizes the frozen hills by creating a caesura in the middle of the third foot, and then by making the heavy stress of the third foot fall on the preposition on, which with the creates effect of an anapest consisting of two unstressed syllables leading up to the first, stressed, syllable of frozen. The effect is that the voice builds up to the word and thus emphasizes the extreme conditions in which Bedivere is walking:

// on / the fro - / zen hills.//

Tennyson uses this rhythmical effect twelve times in the passage. It is one of his major means of rhetorical emphasis.

[4]   Tennyson's most effective metrical variation is the spondee, which appears in lines 5, 6, 8 (twice), 10, and 12. These substitutions, occurring mainly in the section describing how Bedivere forces his way down the frozen hills, permits the descriptive lines to ring out, as in

The bare / black cliff / clanged round /

and

Dry clashed / his har - / ness//

*Central idea.
†Thesis sentence.

These substitutions are so strong that they are almost literally like the actual sounds of Bedivere's exertions. In addition to this use of the spondee as a sound effect, a remarkable use of the spondee for psychological effect occurs in line 5. Here, the stresses internalize Bedivere's distress, reaching a climax on the word drove:

His own / thought drove / him //

There is other substitution, too, both formal and rhetorical, and the tension these variations create keeps the responsive reader aware of Bedivere's tasks. One type of variation is the appearance of amphibrachic rhythm, which [5] is produced in lines 2, 3, 4, 6, 7, and 11. The effect is achieved by a pattern that complements the rhetorical anapests. A caesura in the middle of a foot leaves the three preceding syllables as a light, heavy, and light, the rhythmical form of the amphibrach. In line 2, for example, it appears thus:

// and look - / ing //

In line 6 it takes this form:

/ his har - / ness //

Still another related variation is that of the apparently imperfect feet in [6] lines 5, 8, 11, and 12. These imperfect feet are produced by a caesura, which isolates the syllable, as him is in line 8:

The bare / black cliff / clang'd round / him. //

In line 11 the syllable (on the word lo!) is surrounded by two caesurae, and is therefore thrust into a position of great stress:

And on / a sud - / den // lo! // the lev - / el lake //

Other, less significant substitutions are the trochees in lines 3 and 7 and the pyrrhic in line 12. All the described variations suggest the energy that Bedivere expends during his heroic action.

Many of the variations are produced by Tennyson's sentence structure, which results in a free placement of the caesurae and in a free use of end-stopping and enjambement. Four of the first five lines are end-stopped (two by commas, two by periods). Bedivere is exerting himself during these lines, and he is making short tests to gather strength. His dangerous descent is de-scribed during the next four lines, and none of these lines is end-stopped. Be- [7] divere is disturbed (being goaded by "his own thought"), but he must keep going, and the free sentence structure and free metrical variation underscore his physical and mental difficulties. But in the last two lines, when he has reached the lake, the lines "relax" with falling caesurae exactly at the fifth sylla-ble. In other words, the sentence structure of the last two lines is regular, an effect suggesting the return to order and beauty after the previous, rugged chaos.

This rhythmical virtuosity is accompanied by a similarly brilliant control over segmental devices. Alliteration is the most obvious, permitting Tennyson to tie key words and their signifying actions together, as in the s's in swiftly strode in line 1, or the b's in barren, bare, black, and based in lines 7 and 8. Other notable examples are the aspirated h's in lines 2 to 6 (he, human, hills, heard, behind, him, his, harness); the k's in lines 6 to 9 (clashed, caves, chasms, cliff, clanged, crag); and the l's in lines 11 and 12 (lo, level, lake, long, glories). One might compare these l's with the l's in the more anguished context of lines 8 and 9, where the sounds appear as the second segment in the heavy, ringing words there (black, cliff, clanged, slippery). The sounds are the same, and the emphasis is similar, but the effects are different.

[8]

Assonance is also present throughout the passage. In the first five lines, for example, the ō appears in six words. The first three ō's are in descriptive or metaphoric words (strode, clothed, frozen), while the last three are in words describing Bedivere's pain and anguish (own, drove, goad). The ō therefore ties the physical to the psychological. Other patterns of assonance are the ă in lines 7, 8, and 9 (chasms, clang'd, black, crag, rang); the ä of line 10 (shärp, ärmed); the ī of lines 4 to 7 (behind, cry, like, dry, icy, right); and the short ĭ of lines 1 and 2, and 9 and 10 (swiftly, ridge, with, his, slippery, smitten, with, dint). One might remark also that in the last two lines, which describe the level lake and the moon, Tennyson introduces a number of relaxed o and oo and similar vowel sounds:

[9]

> And on a sudden, lo! the level lake,
> And the long glories of the winter moon.

The last two lines are, in fact, onomatopoeic, since the liquid l sounds suggest the gentle lapping of waves on a lake shore. There are other examples of onomatopoeia, too. In line 2 Tennyson describes Bedivere in the cold air as being "Clothed with his breath," and in the following five lines Tennyson employs many words with the aspirate h (e.g., his harness). In the context, these sounds enable readers to see and hear sights and sounds just like those of Bedivere as he carries his royal burden. Similarly, the explosive stops b and k, and d, and t in lines 6 to 10 imitate the sounds of Sir Bedivere's feet on the "juts of slippery crag."

[10]

This short passage is filled with many examples of poetic excellence. Tennyson's sounds and rhythms actually speak along with the meaning. They emphasize the grandeur of Arthur and his faithful follower, and for one brief moment they bear out the magic that Tennyson associated with the fading past.

[11]

☕ COMMENTARY ON THE ESSAY ON RHYTHM AND SEGMENTAL EFFECTS

This essay presents a full treatment of the prosody of the passage from Tennyson. Paragraphs 2 through 7 deal with the relationship of the rhythm to the content. Note that prosody is not discussed in isolation, but as it augments Tennyson's descriptions of action and scenes. Thus, paragraph 4 refers to the use of the spondee as a substitute foot to reinforce ideas. Also in this paragraph, there is a short comparison of alternative ways of saying what Tennyson says so well. While such a speculative comparison should not be attempted often, it is effective here in bringing out the quality of Tennyson's use of the spondee as a means of emphasis.

Paragraphs 8 and 9 present a discussion of the alliteration and assonance of the passage, and paragraph 10 considers onomatopoeia.

Of greatest importance for the clarity of the essay, there are many supporting examples, spaced, centered, and accurately marked, and numbered by line. In any essay about prosody, readers are likely to be unsure of the validity of the writer's observation unless such examples are provided and are located within the poem.

Second Sample Essay

The Rhymes in Christina Rossetti's "Echo"

1	Come to me in the silence of the *n* night;	5a
2	Come in the speaking silence of a *n* dream;	5b
3	Come with soft rounded cheeks and eyes as *adj* bright	5a
4	As sunlight on a *n* stream;	3b
5	Come back in *n* tears,	2c
6	O memory, hope, love of finished *n* years.	5c
7	O dream how *adj* sweet, too sweet, too bitter sweet,	5d
8	Whose wakening should have been in *n* Paradise,	5e
9	Where souls brimful of love abide and *v* meet;	5d
10	Where thirsty longing *n* eyes	3e
11	Watch the slow *n* door	2f
12	That opening, letting in, lets out no *adv* more.	5f

13   Yet come to me in dreams, that I may *live*   5g

14   My very life again though cold in death: 5h

15   Come back to me in dreams, that I may *give*   5g

16   Pulse for pulse, breath for breath: 3h

17   Speak low, lean low,   2i

18   As long ago, my love, how long ago!   5i

Repeated words: n = noun
~~~~~ dream, dreams   v = verb
———— sweet   adj = adjective
—·—·— breath   adv = adverb
·············· low
- - - - - long ago
∿∿∿∿∿ come

[1]   In the three-stanza lyric poem "Echo," Christina Rossetti uses rhyme as a way of saying that one might regain in dreams a love that is lost in reality.* As the real love is to the dream of love, so is an original sound to an echo. This connection underlies the poem's title and also Rossetti's unique use of rhyme. Aspects of her rhyme are the lyric pattern, the forms and qualities of the rhyming words, and the special use of repetition.†

[2]   The rhyme pattern is simple, and, like rhyme generally, it may be thought of as a pattern of echoes. Each stanza contains four lines of alternating rhymes concluded by a couplet, as follows:

Iambic: 5a, 5b, 5a, 3b, 2c, 5c.

There are nine separate rhymes throughout the poem, three in each stanza. Only two words are used for each rhyme, and no rhyme is used twice. Of the eighteen rhyming words, sixteen are one syllable long—almost all the rhymes. The remaining two words consist of two and three syllables. With such a great number of single-syllable words, the rhymes are all rising ones, on the accented halves of iambic feet, and the end-of-line emphasis is on simple words.

[3]   The grammatical forms and positions of the rhyming words lend support to the introspective subject matter. Although there is variety, more than half the rhyming words are nouns. There are ten in all, and eight are placed as the objects of prepositions (e.g., of a dream, on a stream, of finished years). The nouns that are not the objects of prepositions are the subject and object of the same subordinate clause (lines 10 and 11). It seems clear that much of the poem's verbal energy occurs in the first parts of the lines, leaving the rhymes to occur in modifying elements, as in these lines:

*Central idea.
†Thesis sentence.

Come to me <u>in the silence of the night</u>; (1)

Yet come to me in dreams, <u>that I may live</u> (13)

My very life again <u>though cold in death</u>: (14)

Most of the other rhymes are also in such internalized positions. This careful arrangement is consistent with the speaker's emphasis on her yearning to re-live her love within dreams.

[4] <u>The qualities of the words are also consistent with the poem's emphasis on the speaker's internal life</u>. Most of the rhyming words are impressionistic. Even the specific words—<u>stream, tears, eyes, door</u>, and <u>breath</u>—reflect the speaker's mental condition. In this regard, the rhyming words of lines 1 and 3 are effective. These are <u>night</u> and <u>bright</u>, which contrast the bleakness of the speaker's solitary condition with the vitality of her inner life. Another effective contrast is in lines 14 and 16, where <u>death</u> and <u>breath</u> are rhymed. This rhyme underscores the sad fact that even though the speaker's love has vanished, it lives in present memory just as an echo continues after the original sound is gone.

[5] <u>It is in emphasizing how memory echoes experience that Rossetti creates her special use of rhyming words</u>. She creates an ingenious repetition of a number of words; these are the poem's echoes. The major echoing word is the verb <u>come</u>, which appears six times at the beginnings of lines in stanzas 1 and 3. But some of the rhyming words are also repeated. The most notable is <u>dream</u>, the rhyming word in line 2. Rossetti repeats the word in line 7 and uses the plural, <u>dreams</u>, in lines 13 and 15. In line 7 the rhyming word <u>sweet</u> is the third use of that word, a climax of "how sweet, too <u>sweet</u>, too bitter <u>sweet</u>." Concluding the poem, Rossetti repeats <u>breath</u> (16), <u>low</u> (17), and the phrase <u>long ago</u> (18). These repeating words justify the title "Echo," and they also stress the major idea that it is only in memory that experience has reality, even if dreams are no more than echoes.

[6] Thus rhyme is not just ornamental in "Echo," but integral. The ease of Rossetti's rhymes, like the poem's diction generally, keeps the focus on regret and yearning rather than self-indulgence. As in all rhyming poems, Rossetti's rhymes emphasize the line-endings. The rhymes go beyond this effect, however, because of the internal repetition—echoes—of the rhyming words. <u>"Echo" is a poem in which rhyme is inseparable from meaning</u>.

❦ COMMENTARY ON THE ESSAY ON RHYME

Throughout, illustrative words are highlighted, and numbers are used to indicate the lines from which the illustrations are drawn. The introductory paragraph asserts that rhyme is vital in Rossetti's poem. It also attempts to explain the title "Echo." The thesis statement indicates the four topics to be developed in the body.

Paragraph 2 deals with the mechanical, mathematical aspects of the poem's rhymes. The high number of monosyllabic rhyming words is used to explain the rising, heavy-stress rhyme.

Paragraph 3 treats the grammar of the rhymes. For example, an analysis and count reveal that there are ten rhyming nouns and three rhyming verbs. The verb of command *come* is mentioned to show that most of the rhyming words exist within groups modifying this word. The grammatical analysis is thus related to the internalized nature of the poem's subject.

Paragraph 4 emphasizes the impressionistic nature of the rhyming words and also points out two instances in which rhymes stress the contrast between real life and the speaker's introspective life. Paragraph 5 deals with how Rossetti repeats five of the poem's rhyming words. This repetition creates a pattern of echoes, in keeping with the poem's title.

The concluding paragraph summarizes that Rossetti uses rhyme integrally within "Echo," not ornamentally. In addition, the point is emphasized that the internal rhymes or echoes are an additional facet of Rossetti's rhyming skill.

☝ SPECIAL WRITING TOPICS FOR STUDYING PROSODY AND RHYME

1. For Shakespeare's Sonnet 73, "That Time of Year Thou Mayst in Me Behold," analyze the ways in which Shakespeare creates his iambics. That is, what is the relationship of lightly accented syllables to the heavily accented ones? Where does Shakespeare use articles (*the*), pronouns (*this, his*), prepositions (*upon, against, of*), relative clause markers (*which, that*), and adverb clause markers (*as, when*) in relation to syllables of heavy stress? On the basis of this study, how would you characterize Shakespeare's control of the iambic foot?

2. Analyze the rhymes in one of the Shakespeare sonnets, or else the rhymes in Coleridge's "Kubla Khan" or Arnold's "Dover Beach," or another poem of your choice. What is interesting or unique about the various rhyming words? What relationships can you discover between the rhymes and the topics of the poems?

3. Compare one of the rhyming poems with one of the nonrhyming poems included in this book. What differences in reading and sound can you discover as a result of the use or nonuse of rhyme? What benefits does rhyme give to the poem? What benefits does nonrhyme give?

4. Analyze Hardy's use of rhymes in "Channel Firing" (page 335). What effects does he create by rhyming words with trochaic rhythm, like *hatters* and *matters,* and also by rhyming three-syllable words (dactylic rhythms) *saner be* and *century*? What is the relationship of such rhymes to the rhymes that fall on heavy stresses in the poem?

5. Write a short poem of your own, using rhymes with trochaic words or dactylic words such as *computer, emetic, scholastic, remarkable, along with me, inedible, moron, anxiously, emotion, fishing,* and so on. If you have trouble with exact rhymes, see what you can do with slant rhymes and eye rhymes. The idea is to use your ingenuity.

6. Using the topical index in your library, take out a book on prosody, such as Harvey Gross's *Sound and Form in Modern Poetry* (1968) or *The Structure of Verse* (1966), or Gay Wilson Allen's *American Prosody* (1935, reprinted 1966). Select a topic (e.g., formal or experimental prosody) or a poet (e.g., Frost, Arnold, Shakespeare, Blake), and write a summary of the ideas and observations that the writers make on your subject. What relationship do the writers make about prosody and the poet's ideas? How does prosody enter into the writer's thought? Into the ways in which the poets emphasize ideas and images?

chapter 15

Writing an Essay Based on the Close Reading of a Poem or Short Prose Passage

An essay on a close reading is a detailed study of an entire short work or else a passage of prose or verse that is part of a longer work. This type of essay is specific because it focuses on the selected passage. It is also general because you do not consider only a single topic (such as *character, setting,* or *theme*), but rather deal with *all* the elements to be found in the passage. If the passage describes a person, for example, you must discuss character, but your emphasis should be on what the passage itself brings out about the character. You would also stress action, setting, and ideas, or even make comparisons, if you find that these matters are important. In other words, the content of a close-reading essay is variable; your passage dictates your content.

THE PURPOSE AND REQUIREMENTS OF A CLOSE-READING ESSAY

The general purpose of a close-reading essay is clear: If you can read a paragraph in a book, you can read the entire book; if you can read a speech, you can read the entire play or story; if you can read one poem by a poet, you can read other poems by the same poet or other poets. This is not to say that writing a close-reading essay automatically means you can immediately understand every work by the same author. Few people would insist that reading a passage from Joyce's *Dubliners* makes it possible to understand *Finnegans Wake*. What a close-reading essay gives you is a skill upon which you can build, an approach to any other text that you will encounter.

The essay is designed as an explanation of what is in the assigned passage. General content is the objective, together with anything else that is noteworthy. To write the essay, you do not need to undertake a detailed analysis of diction, grammar, or style. Instead, you should get at what you consider the most important aspects of the passage. Although you are free to discuss special words and phrases, and should do so if you find them important, your aim is primarily to get at the content of your passage.

☞ THE LOCATION OF THE PASSAGE IN THE WORK

Close-reading essays about portions of a work should demonstrate how the passage is connected to the rest of the work. The principle is that all parts are equally important and essential. Analyzing an individual part, therefore, should bring out not only the meaning of the part but also the function of the part within the larger structure of the work.

Expect an Early Passage to Get Things Going

If your passage occurs early in the play, poem, or story, you may conclude that the author is setting things in motion (exposition, complication). Thus, you should determine how themes, characterizations, and arguments in the passage are related to later developments. Always assume that everything is there for a purpose, and then find and explain that purpose.

Expect a Midpoint Passage to Include Anticipations of the Work's Conclusion

In a passage at the work's midpoint, the story or idea usually takes a particular turn—either expected or unexpected. If the change is unexpected, you should explain how the passage focuses the various themes or ideas and then propels them toward the forthcoming crisis or climax (the turning point or high point). It may be that the work features surprises, and the passage thus acquires a different meaning on second reading. It may be that the speaker has one set of assumptions while the readers have others, and that the passage marks the speaker's increasing self-awareness. In short, your task is to determine the extent to which the passage (a) builds on what has happened previously and (b) prepares the way for the outcome.

Expect Things to Come Together
in a Passage at or Near the Conclusion

A passage at or near the work's end is designed to solve problems or be a focal point or climax for all the cumulative situations and ideas. You will thus need to show how the passage brings together all details, ideas, and themes. What is happening? Is any action described in the passage a major action or a step leading to the major action? Has everything in the passage been prepared for earlier, or are there any surprises?

☃ WRITING ABOUT THE CLOSE READING
OF THE GENERAL CONTENT OF A PASSAGE

Focus on the general meaning and impact of the passage or poem. By raising and answering a number of specific questions, you can gather materials for shaping your essay. Once you create answers, write them into a form that you can adapt in your essay. Try to reach specific and focused conclusions.

Raise Questions to Discover Ideas

- Does the passage (1) describe a scene, (2) develop a character, (3) present an action, (4) reveal a character's thoughts, (5) advance an argument, or (6) introduce an idea?
- What is the situation in the work? Who is the speaker? Who is being addressed? What does the speaker want? What ideas are contained in the work?
- What is the thematic content of the passage? How representative is it of the work as a whole? How does the passage relate to earlier and later parts of the whole text? (To deal with this question, you may assume that your reader is familiar with the entire work.)
- What noticeable aspects of diction and ideas are present in the passage? Do speeches or descriptions seem particularly related to any characterizations or ideas that appear elsewhere in the work?

Organize Your Essay on a Close Reading

INTRODUCTION.   Because the close-reading essay is concerned with details, you might have a problem developing a thematic structure. You can overcome this difficulty if you begin to work with either a generalization about the passage or a thesis based on the relationship of the passage to the work. Suppose, for example, that the passage is factually descriptive or that it introduces a major character or raises a major idea. Any one of these observations may serve as a thesis.

NUMBER THE PASSAGE FOR EASY REFERENCE

In preparing your essay, prepare a copy of the entire passage just as it appears in the text. Include the copy at the beginning, as in the sample essay. For your reader's convenience, number the lines in poetry and the sentences in prose.

BODY.   Develop the body of the essay according to what you find in the passage. For a passage of character description, analyze what is disclosed about the character together with your analysis of what bearing this information has on the story or play as a whole. For a passage presenting an idea or ideas, analyze the idea, and also demonstrate how the idea is important for the rest of the work. In short, your aim in this kind of essay is double: First, discuss the passage itself; and second, show how the passage functions within the entire play, poem, or story.

CONCLUSION.   To conclude, stress the important details of your analysis. In addition, you may want to deal with secondary issues that arise in the passage but do not merit full consideration. The passage may contain specific phrases or underlying assumptions that you have not considered in the body of your essay. The conclusion is the place to mention these matters, without developing them fully.

Sample Essay

An Analysis of a Paragraph from O'Connor's "First Confession"°

---

[1] Nora's turn came, and I heard the sound of something slamming, and then her voice as if butter wouldn't melt in her mouth, and then another slam, and out she came. [2] God, the hypocrisy of women! [3] Her eyes were lowered, her head was bowed, and her hands were joined very low down on her stomach, and she walked up the aisle to the side altar looking like a saint. [4] You never saw such an exhibition of devotion, and I remembered the devilish malice with which she had tormented me all the way from our door, and wondered were all religious people like that, really. [5] It was my turn now. [6] With the fear of damnation in my soul I went in, and the confessional door closed of itself behind me.

°See pages 339–45 for this story.

[1]
This paragraph from Frank O'Connor's "First Confession" appears midway in the story. It is transitional, coming between Jackie's "heartscalded" memories of family troubles and his happier memory of the confession itself. Though mainly narrative, the passage is punctuated by Jackie's recollections of disgust with his sister and fear of eternal punishment for his childhood "sins." It reflects geniality and good nature.* This mood is apparent in the comments of the narrator, his diction, the comic situation, and the narrator's apparent lack of self-awareness.†

[2]
More impressionistic than descriptive, the paragraph concentrates in a good-humored way on the direct but somewhat exaggerated responses of the narrator, Jackie. The first four sentences convey Jackie's reactions to Nora's confession. Sentence 1 describes his recollections of her voice in the confessional, and sentence 3 makes his judgment clear about the hypocrisy of her pious appearance when she leaves for the altar. Each of these descriptive sentences is followed by Jackie's angry reactions, at which readers smile if not laugh. This depth of feeling is transformed to "fear of damnation" at the beginning of sentence 6, which describes Jackie's own entry into the confessional, with the closing door suggesting that he is being shut off from the world and thrown into hell. In other words, the paragraph succinctly presents Jackie's sights and reactions, and also his confusion about the scene itself, all of which are part of the story's brief and comic family drama.

[3]
The humorous action of the passage is augmented by Jackie's simple diction, which enables readers to concentrate fully on his responses. As an adult telling the story, Jackie is recalling unpleasant childhood memories, and his direct and descriptive choice of words enables readers to be both amused and sympathetic, at the same time. His words are neither unusual nor difficult. What could be more ordinary, for example, than *butter, slam, out, hands, joined, low, people,* and *closed*? Even Jackie's moral and religious words fall within the vocabulary of ordinary discussions about sin and punishment: *hypocrisy, exhibition, devilish malice, tormented,* and *damnation.* In the passage, therefore, the diction accurately conveys Jackie's vision of the oppressive religious forces which he dislikes and fears, and which he also exaggerates. Readers follow these words easily and with amusement.

[4]
It is from Jackie's remarks that the comedy of the passage develops. Much of the humor rests on the inconsistency between Nora's sisterly badgering and her saintly behavior at the confessional. Since Jackie is careful here to stress her "devilish malice" against him (sentence 4), readers might smile at the description of her worshipful pose. But readers surely know that Nora is not unusual; she has been behaving like any typical older sister or brother. So there is also a comic contrast between her normal actions and Jackie's negative opinions. The humor is thus directed more toward the narrator than the sister.

[5]
In fact, it may be that the narrator's lack of self-awareness is the major cause of humor in the passage. Jackie is an adult telling a story about his experience as a seven-year-old. Readers might expect him to be mature and therefore to be amused and perhaps regretful about his childhood annoyances and anger. But his child's-eye view seems still to be controlling his responses. Comments about Nora such as "looking like a saint" and "You never saw such an exhibition of devotion" are not consistent with a person who has put child-

*Central idea.
†Thesis sentence.

[5] hood in perspective. Hence readers may smile not only at the obvious comedy of Nora's hypocrisy, but also at the narrator's lack of self-awareness. As he comments on his sister with his still jaundiced attitude, he shows his own limitations and for this reason directs amusement against himself.

[6] Readers are more likely to smile at Jackie's remarks, however, than to object to his adult character. The thrust of the paragraph from "First Confession" is therefore on the good-natured comedy of the situation. For this reason the paragraph is a successful turning point between Jackie's disturbing experiences with his sister, grandmother, and father, on the one hand, and the joyful confession with the kind and genial priest on the other. The child goes into the confession with the fear of damnation in his thoughts, but after the following farce, he finds the assurances that his fears are not justified and that his anger is normal and can be forgiven. Therefore, in retrospect, Jackie's anger and disgust were unnecessary, but they were important to him as a child—so much so that his exaggerations make him the center of the story's comedy. Jackie's bittersweet memories are successfully rendered and made comic in this exemplary passage from O'Connor's story.

COMMENTARY ON THE ESSAY

A number of central ideas might have been made about the passage chosen for analysis: that it is dramatic, that it centers on the religious hypocrisy of Jackie's sister, that it brings together the major themes of the story, or that it creates a problem in the character of the narrator. The idea of the sample essay as brought out in paragraph 1, however, is that the passage reflects geniality and good nature. The essay does in fact deal with the sister's hypocrisy and also with the problem in the narrator's character, but these points are made in connection with the central idea.

In the body of the essay, paragraph 2 shows that the narrator's comments about his sister and his own spiritual condition add to the good nature of the passage. Paragraph 3 deals with the level of diction, noting that the words are appropriate both to the action and to Jackie's anger when recollecting it. Paragraph 4 explains the relationship between Jackie's remarks and the comedy being played out in the narration. In paragraph 5 the adult narrator's unwitting revelation of his own shortcomings is related to the good humor and comedy. The final paragraph connects the passage to the latter half of the story, suggesting that the comedy that shines through the passage is, comparatively, like the forgiveness that is believed to follow the act of confession.

Because the essay is based on a close reading, its major feature is the use of many specific details. Thus, the second paragraph stresses the actions and some of Jackie's comments upon it, while the third paragraph provides many examples of his word choices. The fourth paragraph stresses the details about Nora's posturing and Jackie's comments about her. Paragraph 5 provides details of more of Jackie's comments and the limitations of character that they show. Finally, the concluding paragraph includes the detail about Jackie's entering the confessional.

❦ SPECIAL WRITING TOPICS FOR DEVELOPING ANALYSES BASED ON CLOSE READING

For an Entire Poem

- Blake's "The Tiger" or Frost's "Desert Places." Try to establish how the poems bring out the speaker's sense of evil or spiritual blankness.
- Keats's "On First Looking Into Chapman's Homer." How does Keats convey his sense of intellectual excitement and discovery?

For a Paragraph from a Story (You Choose)

- Bierce's "An Occurrence at Owl Creek Bridge." Try to show how the passage connects the main character's imagination with his real death agony.
- Hardy's "The Three Strangers." Emphasize the connections between the details and the work's admiration of the shepherds living in the vicinity of Higher Crowstairs.

For a Speech from a Play (You Choose)

- Glaspell's *Trifles*. Demonstrate how the speech (or speeches) shows the relationship between men and women.
- Chekhov's *The Bear*. How does the speech create character as it also conveys the play's humor?

chapter 16

Writing About Film:
Drama on the Silver
and Color Screens

Film is the word most often used for motion pictures, although other common words are "picture," "cinema," and "movie." It is a specialized type of drama, utilizing, like drama, the techniques of dialogue, monologue, and action. Also like drama, it employs movement and spectacle. For these reasons, film can be studied for aspects such as character, structure, tone, theme, and symbolism. Unlike drama, however, film embodies techniques from photography, film chemistry, sound, and editing. These techniques are so specialized that they require special consideration.

❦ A THUMBNAIL HISTORY OF FILM

Film arose out of technologies developed in the late nineteenth century. The first of these was the creation of a flexible substance—celluloid—that could accept the chemical emulsions that in the early years of photography could be applied only to glass. Other significant inventions were the motion picture camera and projector, together with the screens, which were coated with reflective silver iodide and on which the pictures were projected. Once these were in place, and once producers and directors decided to use the medium for full-length dramas, movies as we know them came into existence.

Although the earliest filmmakers thought of motion pictures as private entertainment, it soon became apparent that the development of large

filmmaking studios, national distribution, and a system of local movie theaters could become extremely lucrative. The history of film is hence just as
much a history of the film business as of the art and development of film
dramas and film acting. The enormous potential of the movie business was
first realized with the production in 1915 of D. W. Griffith's landmark film
Birth of a Nation, which realized an enormous profit on a small investment.

The first motion pictures were black and white and were silent. Producers realized that large profits required easily recognized actors with "big
names," and so the "star system" made national figures out of actors such
as Mary Pickford, Charlie Chaplin, and Rudolph Valentino. In 1928 the first
talking picture, *Lights of New York,* was made. Film as we know it today was
substantially established in 1932 with the first technicolor film, *La Cucaracha,*
even though the use of color has undergone intense refinement and perfection since then.

For a time after the end of World War II, the growth of television in-
hibited the power of the large studios. Soon, however, many films were developed specifically for television viewing, and popular pictures were released for television use. In the last decade, with the advent of videotape
and laser technology, home viewing has become a normal feature of American life. Today, film rental outlets can be found in shopping districts everywhere, with the result that most of the movies ever made are within the
reach of anyone with a VCR and a television set.[1] Early dramatists dreamed
of filling their theaters for a number of consecutive performances, thus
reaching perhaps several thousand persons. Film writers today, however,
reach millions in first-run movie houses and many millions more on television reruns and videocassettes.

☘ STAGE PLAYS AND FILM

Although film is a form of drama, there are a number of important differences
between film and stage productions. Plays can be produced many times, in
many different places, with many different people. In bringing a play to life,
the producer and director use not only actors but also artists, scene designers,
carpenters, painters, lighting technicians, costume makers, choreographers,

---

[1]The technology of CD-ROM (*Compact Disk—Read Only Memory*) has provided additional materials for people seriously interested in film. Many films have now been released in
this medium. For example, *A Hard Day's Night,* starring the Beatles, includes the film itself
(which can be stopped, moved forward, or moved backward at any point), together with explanations, commentary, the original script, notes on the songs, and other materials. A new technology called DVD (*Digital Video Disk*) will augment and perhaps supplant CD-ROMs for film
study, although costs are still high. The DVD technology, which includes the features of CD-
ROM, promises improved video resolution superior to tape technology and current laser disks.
The implications that all the new technologies have for film study are overwhelming, particularly if disks can be made available for inexpensive rental.

music directors, and musicians. For the actual performance of a play, however, the stage itself limits what can be done. In each theater production, the actors, setting, and effects are all physically confined to the stage.

The stage for makers of film, however, is virtually infinite, and the absence of restrictions permits the inclusion of any detail whatever—car chases, underwater adventures, flying geese, wartime combat, legislative debates, executive discussions; scenes in living rooms, courtrooms, boxing rings, hotel rooms, football stadiums, kitchens; and locations in cities and countrysides anywhere—domestic or foreign, modern or ancient. If the setting is a desert island, the filmmaker can travel to such an island and film it in all its reality, complete with beach, palm trees, huts, and authentic natives-turned-actors. If the scene is a distant planet, the filmmaker can create an exotic planet location in the studio, with appropriate scenery, props, effects, lighting, and costumes for the space travelers. An additional freedom, sometimes too freely indulged, is offered by modern computerized special effects, which permit film scenes that were unimaginable for the greatest part of theater history. The freedom enjoyed by the filmmaker, in short, almost limitlessly exceeds the freedom of the play producer. Nothing is left to the audience's imagination. The two types of dramatic productions—drama and film—are therefore greatly different. Each new production of a play is different from every other production, because not only the actors but also the appurtenances of the staging are unique. Shakespeare's play *Hamlet*, for example, has been produced innumerable times since Shakespeare's actors at the Globe Theatre first performed it at the beginning of the seventeenth century, and each subsequent production, including the various filmed versions, has been different from all the rest.

Paradoxically, this same variety cannot occur with films. Although the filmmaker has great freedom in producing each individual movie, this freedom also imposes its own limitations. Because of extremely high production costs and also because films reach a mass audience through wide distribution, films are generally released in only one version, perhaps with "remakes" and dubbed versions for foreign audiences. Thus Orson Welles's *Citizen Kane* (1941) is in only one form, and although it was restored and reedited in 1991, it remains in this form even though it is frequently shown and seen. Interestingly, no person can ever claim to have seen all the productions of plays like *Hamlet*, but everyone who sees a film like *Citizen Kane* can claim to have seen it in its entirety.

❦ THE AESTHETICS OF FILM

To the degree that film is confined to a screen, it can be compared visually with the art of the painter and the still photographer. It uses the language of visual art. One object in a painting can take on special relationships to others as the artist directs the eyes of the observer. A color used in one part can be balanced with the same color, or its complement, in another part. Painters and photographers can introduce certain colors and details as symbols and can suggest allegorical interpretations through the inclusion of mythical figures or universally recognized objects. Particular effects can be achieved with the use of the textures of paint or with control over shutter speed, focus, and various techniques of development. The techniques and effects are extensive.

The filmmaker is able to utilize most of the resources of the still photographer and many of those of the painter, and can augment these with special effects. Artistically, the most confining aspect of film is the rectangular screen, but aside from that, film is unrestricted. Based in a dramatic text called a filmscript or shooting script, the film uses words and their effects, but it also employs the language of visual art and especially the particular vividness and power of moving pictures. When considering film, then, you should realize that film communicates not only with words but also by using various visual techniques. The visual presentation is inseparable from the medium of film itself.

✿ THE TECHNIQUES OF FILM

There are many techniques of film, and a full description and documentation of them can be—and has become—extensive.[2] In evaluating film, however, you need to familiarize yourself only with those aspects of technique that have an immediate bearing on your responses and interpretations.

Editing or Montage Is the Assembling of a Film out of Separate Parts

A finished film is a composite, not a continuous work filmed from start to end. The putting together of the film is the process of *editing*, or **montage** (assemblage, mounting, construction), which is, technically, a cutting and gluing. Depending on the flexibility of the filmscript, the various

[2]See, for example, Louis D. Giannetti, *Understanding Movies*, 7th ed. (Upper Saddle River, NJ: Prentice Hall, 1996); Ephraim Katz *The Film Encyclopedia*, 3rd ed., revised by Fred Klein and Ronald Dean Nolan (New York: HarperCollins, 1998); *Halliwell's Film and Video Guide 1998*, John Walker ed. (New York: HarperCollins, 1997); James Monaco et al., *The Encyclopedia of Film* (New York: Perigee, 1991); James Monaco, *How to Read a Film*, rev. ed. (New York: Oxford UP, 1981); Roger Ebert, *Roger Ebert's Video Companion, 1998* (1997, published annually in the fall, for the next year, by Andrews and McMeel of Kansas City); Daniel Talbot, ed., *Film: An Anthology* (Berkeley: U of California P, 1969); and John Wyver, *The Moving Image* (Oxford: Basil Blackwell, 1989).

scenes of the film are planned before shooting begins, but the major task of montage is accomplished in a studio by editing specialists.

If we again compare film with a stage play, we note that a theatrical production moves continuously, with pauses only for intermissions and scene changes. Your perception of the action is caused by your distance from the stage (perhaps aided by opera glasses or binoculars). Also, even as you move your eyes from one character to another, you still perceive the entire stage. In a film, however, the directors and editors *create* these continuous perceptions for you by piecing together different parts. The editors begin with many "takes" (separately filmed scenes, including many versions of the same scenes). What they select, or mount, will be the film, and we never see the discarded scenes. Thus, it is editing that puts everything together.

MONTAGE CREATES NARRATIVE CONTINUITY.   The first use of montage, already suggested, is narrative continuity. For example, a climb up a steep cliff can be shown at the bottom, middle, and top (with backward slips and falls to show the danger of the climb and to make viewers catch their breath). All such narrative sequences result from the assembling of individual pieces, each one representing phases of the activity. A classic example of a large number of separate parts forming a narrative unit is the well-known shower murder in Alfred Hitchcock's *Psycho* (1959), where a forty-five-second sequence is made up of seventy-eight different shots (the woman in the shower, the murderer behind the curtain, the attack, the slumping figure, the running water, the dead woman's eye, the bathtub drain, etc.).

MONTAGE HELPS THE EXPLANATION OF CHARACTER AND MOTIVATION. Montage is used in "flashbacks" to explain present, ongoing actions or characteristics, or in illustration of a character's thoughts and memories, or in brief examples from the unremembered past of a character suffering from amnesia. It also supplies direct visual explanation of character. A famous example occurs in Welles's *Citizen Kane* (the subject of the sample essay). The concluding scene shows overhead views of Kane's vast collection of statuary and mementos. At the very end, the camera focuses on a raging furnace, into which workmen have thrown his boyhood sled, which bears the brand name "Rosebud" (we have fleetingly seen Kane playing with the sled as a boy). Because "Rosebud" is Kane's last word, and everyone in the film is trying to decipher its meaning, this final scene reveals that Kane's dying thoughts were of his lost boyhood, before he was taken away from his parents, and that his unhappy life has resulted from his early rejection and personal pain.

MONTAGE FACILITATES DIRECTORIAL COMMENTARY.   In addition, montage is used symbolically as commentary, as in an early sequence in Charlie Chaplin's *Modern Times* (1936) that shows a large group of workers rushing to their factory jobs. Immediately following this scene is a view of a large, milling herd of sheep. By this symbolic montage, Chaplin suggests that the men are being herded and dehumanized by modern industry. Thus, montage and editorial statement go hand in hand.

MONTAGE IS USED IN MANY OTHER WAYS.   Montage can also produce other characteristics through camera work, development, and special effects. For example, filmmakers can reverse an action to emphasize its illogicality or ridiculousness. Editing can also speed up action (which makes even the most serious things funny) or slow things down. It can also blend one scene with another or juxtapose two or more actions in quick succession to show what people are doing while they are separated. The possibilities for creativity and innovation are extensive.

Film Utilizes Many Visual Techniques

THE CAMERA IS THE BASIC TOOL OF FILM.   Whereas editing or montage is a finishing technique, the work of film begins with the camera, which permits great freedom in the presentation of characters and actions. In a film, the visual viewpoint can shift. Thus, a film can begin with a distant shot of the actors—a "long shot"—much like the view of actors onstage. Then the camera can zoom in to show a close-up or zoom out to present a wide and complete panorama. Usually a speaking actor will be the subject of a close-up, but the camera can also capture other actors' reactions in close-up. You must interpret the effects of close-ups and long shots yourself, but it should be plain that the frequent use of either—or of middle-distance views—is a means by which film directors control the perceptions of their characters and situations.

The camera can also move from character to character or from character to object. In this way, film can mark a series of reactions, concentrate your attention on a character's attitude, or comment visually on a character's actions. If a man and woman are in love, for example, the camera can shift, either directly or through montage, from the couple to flowers and trees, thus associating their love visually with objects of beauty and growth. Should the flowers be wilted and the trees leafless, however, the visual commentary might be that their love is doomed and hopeless.

The camera can also create unique effects. Slow motion, for example, can focus on a certain aspect of a person's character. The concentrated focus on a child running happily in a meadow (as in *The Color Purple* [1985] by Steven Spielberg) suggests the joy inherent in such movement. Surprisingly, speed is sometimes indicated by slow motion, which emphasizes strong muscular effort (as in the running scenes in Hugh Hudson's *Chariots of Fire* [1981]).

Many other camera techniques bear on action and character. The focus can be sharp at one point, indistinct at another. Moving a speaking character out of focus can suggest that listeners are bored. Sharp or blurred focus can also show that a character has seen things exactly or inexactly. In action sequences, the camera can be mounted in a moving vehicle to "track" or follow running human beings or horses, speeding bicycles and cars (as in Woody Allen's *Annie Hall*), or moving sailboats, canoes, speedboats, or rowboats. A camera operator on foot can also be the tracker, or the camera may track ground movement from an aircraft. Movement can also be captured by a rotating camera that follows a moving object or character. Alternatively, the camera can be fixed while a character or object moves from one side to the other.

THE PICTURES IN FILM INVOLVE LIGHT, SHADOW, AND COLOR.   As in the theater, the filmmaker uses light, shadow, and color to reinforce ideas and to create realistic and symbolic effects. A scene in sunshine, which brings out colors, and the same scene in rain and clouds or in twilight, all of which mute colors, create different moods. Characters in bright light are presumably open and frank, whereas characters in shadow may be hiding something, particularly in black-and-white films. Flashing or strobe lights might indicate a changeable or sinister character or situation.

Colors, of course, have much the same meaning that they have in any other artistic medium. Blue sky and clear light suggest happiness, while greenish light can indicate something ghoulish. A memorable control of color occurs midway through David O. Selznick's *Gone with the Wind* (1939), when Scarlett O'Hara reflects upon the devastation of her plantation home, Tara. She resolves never to be hungry again, and as she speaks she is silhouetted against a darkened orange sky—a background that suggests how totally the way of life she knew as a young woman has been burned away. As in this example, you may expect colors to complement the story of the film. Thus, lovers may wear clothing with the same or complementary colors, whereas people who are not "right" for each other may wear clashing colors.

Action Is the Essence of Film

The strength of film is direct action. Actions of all sorts—running, swimming, driving a car, fighting, embracing and kissing, or even just sitting; chases, trick effects, ambushes—all these and more create a sense of immediate reality, and all are tied (or should be) to narrative development. Scenes of action can run on for several minutes, with little or no accompanying dialogue, to carry on the story or to convey ideas about the interests and abilities of the characters.

Film Presents Many Views of the Bodies, Heads, and Movements of Actors

Closely related to the portrayal of action is the way in which film shows the human body (and animal bodies), together with bodily motion and gesture (or body language). The view or perspective that the filmmaker presents is particularly important. A torso shot of a character may stress no more than the content of that character's speech. A close-up shot, however, with the character's head filling the screen, may emphasize motives as well as content. The camera can also distort ordinary expectations of reality. Using wide-angle lenses and close-ups, for example, human subjects can be made to seem bizarre or grotesque, as are the faces in the crowd in Woody Allen's *Stardust Memories* (1980). Sometimes the camera creates other bodily distortions—for example, enlarging the limbs of the forest dweller in Ingmar Bergman's *Virgin Spring* (1959) or throwing into unnatural prominence a scolding mouth or a suspicious eye. Distortion invites interpretation: The filmmaker may be asserting that certain human beings, even supposedly normal ones, are odd, sinister, intimidating, or psychotic.

Film Employs Many Techniques of Sound

DIALOGUE AND MUSIC ARE VITAL TO FILM DRAMATIZATIONS. The first business of the sound track is the spoken dialogue, which is "mixed" in editing to be synchronized with the action. There are also many other elements in the sound track. Music, the most important, creates and augments moods. A melody in a major or minor key, or in a slow or fast tempo, can affect our perception of actions. If a character is thinking deeply, a complementary sound may be muted strings. But if the character is going insane, the music may become discordant and percussive.

Sometimes, music gives a film a special identity. Hudson's *Chariots of Fire,* for example, includes music by Vangelis Papathanassiou. Although this music is independently popular, it is always associated with the film. In addition, musical accompaniments can directly render dramatic statement, without dialogue. An example occurs in Welles's *Citizen Kane.* Beginning that portion of the narrative derived from the autobiography of a character who is now dead (the scene first focuses on his statue), the musical sound track by Bernard Herrmann quotes the *Dies Irae* theme from the Catholic mass for the dead. The instrumentation, however, makes the music funny, and we smile rather than grieve. Herrmann, incidentally, varies this theme elsewhere in the film, usually for comic effect.

FILM USES SPECIAL AND OFTEN INGENIOUS SOUND EFFECTS. Special sound effects can also augment a film's action. The sound of a blow, for example, can be enhanced electronically to cause an impact similar to the force of the blow itself (as in the boxing scenes from the many *Rocky* films). At times some sounds, such as the noises of wailing people, squeaking or slamming doors, marching feet, or moving vehicles, are filtered electronically to create weird or ghostly effects. Often a character's words echo rapidly and sickeningly to show dismay or anguish. In a word, sound is a vital part of film.

☝ WRITING ABOUT A FILM

Obviously the first requirement is to see the film, either in a theater or on videocassette. No matter how you see it, you should go through it at least twice, making notes, because your discussion takes on value the more thoroughly you know the material. Include the names of the scriptwriter, director, composer, special effects editor, chief photographer, and major actresses and actors. If particular speeches are worth quoting, remember the general circumstances of the quotation and also, if possible, key words. Take notes on costume and color, or (if the film is in black and white) on light and shade. You will need to rely on memory, but if you have videotape, you can easily check important details.

Raise Questions to Discover Ideas

Action
- How important is action? Is there much repetition of action, say, in slow motion, or from different angles? Are actors (and animals) viewed closely or distantly? Why?
- What actions are stressed (chases, concealment, gun battles, lovemaking, etc.)? What does the type of action contribute to the film?
- What do close-ups show about character and motivation (smiles and laughter, frowns, leers, anxious looks, etc.)?
- What actions indicate seasonal conditions (cold by a character's stamping of feet, warmth by the character's removing a coat or shirt)? What connection do these actions have to the film's general ideas?
- Does the action show any changing of mood, say, from sadness to happiness or from indecision to decision?

Cinematographic Techniques
- What notable techniques are used (colors, lighting, etc.)? What is their relationship to the film's characterizations and themes?
- What characterizes the use of the camera (tracking, close-ups, distant shots, camera angles, etc.)? How do the camera perspectives reinforce or detract from the film's theme and plot?

- How does the editing (the sequencing of scenes) reinforce or detract from story and theme?
- What scene or scenes best exemplify how the cinematographic techniques interact with the theme, plot, characters, setting, and so on? Why?

Acting

- How well do the actors adapt to the medium of film? How convincing are their performances?
- How well do the actors control their facial expressions and body movement? Are they graceful? Awkward?
- What does their appearance lend to your understanding of their characters?
- Does it seem that the actors are genuinely creating their roles, or are they just reading through the parts?

Organize Your Essay on Film

INTRODUCTION.   State your central idea and thesis sentence. You should include the background necessary to support points you make in the body of the essay and should also name the major creative and performing persons of the film.

BODY.   Any of the organizing strategies on topics discussed elsewhere in this book, like plot, structure, character, ideas, or setting, are equally valid for an essay on a film, except that you will need to consider them in a visual context. For example, if you choose to discuss the effects of a character on the plot, you need to develop your argument using the evidence of camera techniques, montage, sound effect, and the like.

When discussing film techniques, be sure to have good notes so that your supporting details are accurate. A good method is to concentrate on technique in only a few scenes. If you analyze the effects of montage, for example, you can use a videocassette recorder to go over the scene a number of times.

CONCLUSION.   In the conclusion of your essay, you might evaluate the effectiveness of the cinematic form to story and idea. Are all the devices of film used in the best possible way? Is anything overdone? Is anything underplayed? Is the film good, bad, or indifferent up to a point, and then does it change? How? Why?

Sample Essay

Welles's Citizen Kane: *Whittling a Giant Down to Size"*°

[1] Citizen Kane (1941) is a superbly crafted film in black and white. The script is by Herman Mankiewicz and Orson Welles, with photography by Gregg Toland, music by Bernard Herrmann, direction and production by Welles, and the leading role by Welles. It is the story of a wealthy and powerful man, Charles Foster Kane, who exemplifies the American Dream of economic self-sufficiency, self-determination, and self, period. The film does not explore the "greatness" of the hero, however, but rather exposes him as a misguided, unhappy person who tries to buy love and remake reality.* All aspects of the picture—characterization, structure, and technique—are directed to this goal.†

[2] At the film's heart is the deterioration of Kane, the newly deceased newspaper magnate and millionaire. He is not all bad, for he begins well before going tragically downward. For example, the view we see of him as a child, being taken away from home, invites sympathy. When we next see him as a young man, he idealistically takes over a daily newspaper, the *Inquirer.* This idealism makes him admirable but also makes his deterioration tragic. As he says to Thatcher in a moment of insight, he could have been a great person if he had not been wealthy. His corruption begins when he tries to alter the world to suit himself, such as his demented attempt to make an opera star out of his second wife, Susan, and his related attempt to shape critical praise for her. Even though he builds an opera house for her and also sponsors many performances, he cannot change reality. This tampering with truth indicates how completely he loses his youthful integrity.

[3] The structure is progressively arranged to bring out such weaknesses. The film flows out of the opening obituary newsreel, from which we learn that Kane's dying word was the name "Rosebud" (the brand name of his boyhood sled, which is spoken at the beginning by a person [Kane] whose mouth is shown in close-up). The newsreel director, wanting to get the inside story, assigns a reporter named Thompson to learn about "Rosebud." Thompson's search unifies the rest of the film; he goes from place to place and person to person to collect materials and conduct interviews that disclose Kane's increasing strangeness and alienation. At the end, although the camera leaves Thompson to focus on the burning sled, he has been successful in uncovering the story of Kane's deterioration (even though he himself never learns what "Rosebud" means). Both the sled and the reporter therefore tie together the many aspects of the film.

[4] It is through Thompson's searches that the film presents the flashback accounts of Kane's deterioration. The separate persons being interviewed (in-

---

°The fiftieth anniversary reedited version (1991) of *Citizen Kane* is available from Turner Home Entertainment (© 1941 RKO Radio Pictures, Inc. Renewed © 1961 RKO General, Inc. All Rights Reserved. Package Design © 1991 Turner Entertainment Co.).
*Central idea.
†Thesis sentence.

[4] cluding Thatcher's handwritten account) each contribute something different to the narrative because their experiences with Kane have all been unique. As a result of these individual points of view, the story is quite intricate. For example, we learn in the Bernstein section that Jedediah proudly saves a copy of Kane's declaration about truth in reporting. We do not learn in Jedediah's interview, however, that he, Jedediah, sends the copy back to Kane as an indictment of Kane's betrayal of principle. Rather, it is in Susan's account that we learn about the return, even though she herself understands nothing about it. This subtlety, so typical of the film, marks the ways in which the biography of Kane is perceptively revealed.

[5] Thus, the major importance of these narrating characters is to reveal and reflect Kane's disintegration. Jedediah (Joseph Cotten) is a man of principle who works closely with Kane, but after the lost election he rebels when he understands the falseness of Kane's personal life. He is totally alienated after Kane completes the unfinished attack on Susan's performance. Jedediah's change, or perhaps his assertion of principle, thus reveals Kane's increasing corruption. Susan, Kane's second wife (Dorothy Comingore), is naive, sincere, and warm, but her drinking, her attempted suicide, and her final separation show the harm of Kane's warped visions. Bernstein (Everett Sloane), the first person Thompson interviews, is a solitary figure who is uncritical of Kane, but it is he who first touches the theme about the mystery of Kane's motivations. Bernstein also takes on life when he speaks poignantly of his forty-five year memory of the girl in white. Even though this revelation is brief, it suggests layers of feeling and longing.

[6] In addition to these perceptive structural characterizations, *Citizen Kane* is a masterpiece of film technique. The camera images are sharp, with clear depth of field. In keeping with Kane's disintegration and mysteriousness, the screen is rarely bright. Instead, the film makes strong use of darkness and contrasts, almost to the point at times of blurring distinctions between people. Unique in Gregg Toland's camera work are the many shots taken from waist height or below, distorting the bodies of the characters by distancing their heads—suggesting that the characters are preoccupied with their own concerns and oblivious to normal perspectives. Nowhere is this distortion better exemplified than in the scene between Kane and Jedediah in the empty rooms after the lost election, when Jedediah asks permission to leave for Chicago.

[7] As might be expected in a film so dominated by its central figure, the many symbols create strong statements about character. The most obvious is the sled, "Rosebud," the dominating symbol of the need for love and acceptance in childhood. Another notable symbol is glass and, in one scene, ice. In the party scene, two ice statues are in the foreground of the employees of the *Inquirer*. In another scene, a bottle looms large in front of Jedediah, who is drunk. In another, a pill bottle and drinking glass are in front of Susan, who has just used them in her suicide attempt. The suggestion of these carefully photographed symbols is that life is brittle and temporary. Particularly symbolic is the bizarre entertainment in the party scene. Because Kane joins the dancing and singing, the action suggests that he is doing no more than taking a role in life, never being himself or knowing himself. Symbols that frame the film are the wire fence and the "No Trespassing" sign at both beginning and end. These symbols suggest that even if we understand a little about Kane, or anyone else, there are boundaries we cannot pass, depths we can never reach.

[8] There are also amusing symbols that suggest the diminution not only of Kane, but also of the other characters. An example is Bernstein's high-backed

chair, which makes him look like a small child. Similarly, the gigantic fireplace at Xanadu makes both Kane and Susan seem like pygmies—a symbol that great wealth dwarfs and dehumanizes people. Especially comic is Kane's picnic at Xanadu. In going into the country, Kane and his friends do not walk, but ride in a long line of cars—more like a funeral procession than a picnic—and [8] they stay overnight in a massive tent. Quite funny is the increasing distance between Kane and Emily, his first wife, in the rapid-fire shots that portray their developing separation. Even more comic is the vast distance at Xanadu between Kane and Susan when they discuss their life together. They are so far apart that they must shout to be heard. Amusing as these symbols of diminution and alienation are, however, they are also pathetic, because at first Kane finds closeness with both his wives.

In all respects, *Citizen Kane* is a superb film. This is not to say that the characters are likable, or that the amusing parts make it a comedy. Instead, the film pursues truth, suggesting that greatness and wealth cannot give happiness. <u>It is relentless in whittling away at its major figure</u>. Kane is likable at times, and he is enormously generous (as shown when he sends Jedediah [9] $25,000 in severance pay). But these high moments show the contrasting depths to which Kane falls, with the general point being that people who are powerful and great may deteriorate even at their height. The goal of the newsreel director at the beginning is to get at the "real story" behind the public man. There is more to any person than a two-hour film can reveal, but within its limits, *Citizen Kane* gets at the real story, and the real story is both sad and disturbing.

☙ COMMENTARY ON THE ESSAY

The major point of the essay is that the film diminishes the major figure, Kane. In this respect the essay illustrates the analysis of *character* (Chapter 3), and it therefore emphasizes how film can be considered as a form of literature. Also shown in the essay are other methods of literary analysis: *structure* (Chapter 5) and *symbolism* (Chapter 10). Of these topics, only the use of symbols, because they are visually presented in the film, is unique to the medium of film as opposed to the medium of words.

Any one of the topics might be developed as a separate essay. There is more than enough about the character of Susan, for example, to sustain a complete essay, and the film's structure could be extensively explored. *Citizen Kane* itself as a repository of film techniques is rich enough for an exhaustive, book-length account.

Because the essay is about a film, the unique aspect of paragraph 1 is the opening brief description (stressing the medium of black and white) and the credits to the scriptwriters, principal photographer, composer, and director. Unlike works written by a single author, film is a collaborative medium, and therefore it is appropriate to recognize the separate efforts of the principal contributors.

Paragraph 2 begins the body and carries out a brief analysis of the major character. Paragraphs 3 to 5 discuss various aspects of the film's structure (the second topic announced in the thesis sentence) as they bear on Kane. In paragraph 3 the unifying importance of the sled and the reporter, Thompson, is explained. Paragraph 4 focuses on the film's use of flashback as a structural technique, while paragraph 5 discusses three of the flashback characters as they either intentionally or unintentionally reveal Kane's flaws. In paragraphs 6 to 8, the topic is film technique, the third and last topic of the thesis sentence. Paragraph 6 focuses on light, camera angles, and distortion; paragraph 7 treats visual symbols; paragraph 8 continues the topic of symbols but extends it to amusing ones. The final paragraph restates the central idea and also relates the theme of deterioration to the larger issue of how great wealth and power affect character. Thus, as a conclusion, this paragraph not only presents a summary but also notes the film's general ideas.

❦ SPECIAL WRITING TOPICS FOR STUDYING FILM

1. Select a single film technique, such as the use of color, the control of light, or the photographing of action, and write an essay describing how it is used in a film. For best results, use a videocassette for your study. As much as possible, try to explain how the technique is used throughout the film. Determine constant and contrasting features, the relationship of the technique to the development of story and character, and so on.

2. Write an essay explaining how all the film techniques of a particular part or section are employed (i.e., camera angles, close-ups or long shots, tracking, on-camera and off-camera speeches, lighting, depth of field). For your study, you will have to rerun the section a number of times, trying to notice elements for the first time and also reinforcing your first observations. To add a research element to this question, you might consult the works by Giannetti, Halliwell, Katz, Monaco, Ebert, Talbot, and Wyver listed in the footnote on page 220.

3. Pick out a news story and write a dramatic scene about it. Next, consider how to write the scene for a film, providing directions for actors and camera operators (e.g., "As Character A speaks, his face shows that he is lying; the camera zooms slowly in on his face, with a loss of focus," or "As Character A speaks, the camera focuses on Character B exchanging looks with Character C"). When you are done, write an explanation of how you intend your directions to bring out details about your story and characters.

chapter 17

Writing a Review Essay:
Developing Ideas for General or Particular Audiences

The review is a general essay on a literary work. It may also be thought of as a "critique," a "critical review," or simply an "essay." It is a free form, for in a review virtually everything is relevant—subject matter, technique, social and intellectual background, biographical facts, relationship to other works by the same author or by different authors, historical importance, and everything else. Unless you become a professional writer in the future, a review is the most likely kind of writing about literature that you may ever be called upon to do. Many businesses, associations, guilds, and other organizations issue regular newsletters or have meetings in which members are asked to discuss various subjects. Often, members of such groups are interested in learning about recent publications, and hence there is a need for good reviews.

A major aim of review writing is to provide a general overview of the work, including an evaluation of the author's performance together with other elements of the work that you should mention, special difficulties that you explain, and special features that you note.

Since the review provides for freedom of topics and development, it is also a challenge to the skills you have acquired thus far as a disciplined reader. Much of your experience has been *assimilation*—acquiring information and applying skills. Your tasks have been mainly doing assignments that you are given in your classes. But with a review, you are left to your own devices; you must decide what to write about as well as what to say.

Freedom of choice should be a constant goal, and it is important to realize that your experience is equipping you more and more to know what to do with this freedom. You should not only know how to answer questions but should also decide on the questions to be asked. You should be able to synthesize the knowledge you are acquiring.

☕ WRITING A REVIEW ESSAY

Because reviews can be personal as well as objective, you may experiment with form and development. If you choose to write about only a single topic, be sure to emphasize the various aspects with clear transitions. The third sample essay, for example, shows how the subject of faith or trust may be pursued throughout a review. Should you be writing a general review and select a number of topics, as in the first sample essay, be sure that your thesis sentence lists these topics.

Raise Questions to Discover Ideas

- Who are the people for whom you intend your review? Are they a general audience or part of a particular group? What are the special interests of the group? What general interests do people in the group have in common?
- How much detail, special or general, do you think you should include about the work itself? How much knowledge does your audience expect you to demonstrate in your review? Should you introduce references to comparable works by the same author or by different authors?
- Have the people who make up your audience read the work? Should you design your review to be a substitute for their reading the work? Should your review be designed to interest people in reading the work themselves?
- When was the work written? Just recently, or a long time ago? What is the nationality of the author (if he or she is of another nationality)? What kind of background knowledge is needed for an understanding of the work, or what kind, and how much, is supplied by the author (for example, a knowledge of military circumstances, of "old time" religion, of conditions in rural England or rural America)?
- To what genre does the work belong? What general issues need explaining before you begin your discussion of the work?
- What parts of the work are significant enough to warrant discussion in your review? What issues does the work bring out? What are the author's thoughts about these issues? How important are these thoughts? How timely is the work for today's readers?
- Do any particular characters, situations, or ideas stand out in the work you are reviewing? What are these? Why are they significant?

- What aspects of the writer's style and presentation are worthy of mention? How fully do you think you can refer to these without losing your audience's interest?

Organize Your Review Essay

INTRODUCTION. In your introduction, you should place the work in perspective. Although most frequently you will be asked to review a play or novel, it is good to bear in mind that you may also be writing a review about acting techniques or play production. If you are reviewing a new edition of an old work, you may be judging the relevance of the past to the present, and you may also be judging the apparatus supplied by the editor. Always try to show that your work has relevance to the present group of readers.

BODY. In the body, you should try either to arouse interest in the work or to discourage readers from reading it if it seems to dictate this conclusion.

Beyond providing introductory information, your principal objective is to describe the strengths and weaknesses of the work. To write such a description, you must call into play just about everything you have learned about analyzing literature for ideas, form, and style. In a sense, the review can be as specific as you wish to make it, because the greatest part of the body should be given to analysis. In this analysis, you should try to bring out your own strengths and interests as a critical reader. It may be, for example, that you have become proficient in discussing ideas. Suppose that you observe intricately developed ideas in the work. You might choose to discuss that element in the body of your review, thereby appealing to your reader's interest in thought and ideas. You should always recognize, however, that your discussion should be of limited extent. There is no need for a detailed, word-by-word analysis. It is not an essay on ideas, style, or artistic qualities that you want, but a review emphasizing such elements.

For specialized reviews you might call into play those disciplines that have interested you thus far in your college career. For example, you may feel competent in handling ideas connected with sociology. Hence, in your review of a novel you might bring your sociological awareness to bear on the work. Or you may have developed an interest in psychology and might treat the characters in a work according to your understanding of psychological problems.

Whatever your personal interests and specialties may be, however, your best guide for subject matter is the work itself, which might well channel your thinking along definite lines. For example, the second sample essay relates the obvious character flaw of the hero of "Young Goodman Brown" to religious concerns (for an audience of people interested in religion). The third sample essay adopts the position that the same story literally compels readers to consider the psychological importance of personal certainty and security. In the work you are assigned, you may similarly find that certain features will point you in a specific direction (the humor, a connection with existential philosophy, reflections on economic or social conditions, the nature of life on the frontier, and so on).

CONCLUSION.   Your conclusion should be an attempt to evaluate the work, certainly not extensively, but at least you should give an outline of your responses and a suggestion to your readers of how they might respond—assuming that you have shown that your interests coincide approximately with theirs. If the body of your review has emphasized evaluation, you should close your essay with a simple resumé of your points. If you are ever asked to review a work in, say no more than 150 words, the greatest part of the review should be devoted to evaluation.

First Sample Essay (A General Review)
Hawthorne's "Young Goodman Brown"°

[1]
"Young Goodman Brown" is an allegorical story by Nathaniel Hawthorne (1804–1864), the major American writer who probed deeply into the relationships between religion and guilt. Hawthorne's story is set in colonial Salem during the days of religious Puritanism. His major aim is to expose the weakness in the religious view that stresses the shortcomings and sins of human life.* Although this concern may seem narrow, the story itself is timely, presenting a dreamlike narrative, a realistic analysis of the growth of intolerance, and a number of questions of permanent importance.†

[2]
On the surface, the apparent vagueness and dreamlike nature of Hawthorne's details may leave some readers a little baffled. The action is a nighttime trip by Young Goodman Brown to a mysterious satanic gathering in a deep forest just outside the village of Salem. Brown begins his walk as a friendly youth, just three months married to a young woman named Faith. The cult-gathering disillusions and embitters him, however. He loses his faith, and he spends the rest of his life in pessimism and gloom. This much is clear, but the precise nature of Brown's experience is not. Does he really make a trip into the woods? It would seem so, but by the story's end, Hawthorne states that the whole episode may have been no more than a dream or nightmare, and he speaks about it as such. Yet when the morning comes, Brown walks back into town as though he is returning from an overnight trip, and he recoils

°See pages 327–36 for this story.
*Central idea.
†Thesis sentence.

[2] in horror from a number of his fellow villagers, including his wife. Just as uncertain is the identity of the stranger whom Brown encounters on the path. The man resembles Brown's father, but his serpentlike walking stick suggests the devil, who later presides at the satanic ritual deep within the forest.

[3] The fact is, however, that Hawthorne was clearly not interested in producing a realistic imitation of life in detail. Rather he wanted to get at the inward, psychological reality of persons like Goodman Brown, who build a wall of anger and bitterness between themselves and the people around them. From this perspective, Brown's walk into the forest is a symbol of one of the ways in which people may turn sour. In Brown's case, he falls under the control of his will to condemn evil. So strong is his view that he rejects anyone not measuring up, even if he must live the rest of his life spiritually alone as a result. Although he is at the extreme edge, he is like many who cannot forgive and get along with anyone who is different.

[4] Brown is thus anything but heroic, even if he is the story's major character. Nevertheless, the story is provocative and compelling, and it raises many timely questions. For example, how can something that is designed for human salvation, like the religious system that Brown inherited, become so damaging to its followers? Does the failure result from the people who misunderstand the basic message of the system, or from the system itself? To what degree can the religious structure of the story be related to political and social institutions? Should any religious or political philosophy be given greater importance than the goodwill that is the cornerstone of society? Could any free society survive for long if it were composed of persons like Goodman Brown after his dream, or would it turn into some form of absolutism or despotism, and soon be reduced to persecution on moral, religious, or political grounds?

[5] Although the materials of the story belong to Salem during the late seventeenth century—the location, one might remember, of the infamous witchcraft trials—it has many layers. It is a memorable study in spiritual deterioration and a vivid example of the need for trust and goodwill in human relationships. Without such will, life itself would soon resemble the life lived by Goodman Brown, whose vision makes his world bleak and forbidding—a place controlled by negation and death rather than understanding and acceptance.

❦ COMMENTARY ON THE ESSAY

This general review follows a normal pattern of exposition. The introduction briefly presents essential background, and it states a central idea about the timeliness of Hawthorne's ideas. Paragraph 2 deals with the problem of the dreamlike vagueness of the narrative. Paragraph 3 contains an explanation of the vagueness inasmuch as Hawthorne's point is to dramatize the way in which people become intolerant. Paragraph 4 treats the timeliness of this analysis in terms of important questions raised by the story. The last paragraph is a short tribute to the quality of Hawthorne's insights.

Throughout this sample review, the purpose is not to examine any of the points in great depth, but rather to give readers topics to consider in detail when they themselves consider the work.

Second Sample Essay: For a Specific Group
(Here, a Religious Group)

Hawthorne's "Young Goodman Brown"
and Today's Christians

[1]
Even though Hawthorne's allegorical story "Young Goodman Brown" is set in late seventeenth-century colonial Massachusetts, it has great significance for today's Christians.* The tale is about the shattering of the principal character's illusions about human beings as a result of his witnessing a nightmarish witches' Sabbath in a forest. Brown becomes a despairing person and deprives those around him of love and light. This material could easily be interpreted psychologically or politically, but the Christian context of the story invites discussion of Hawthorne's religious ideas. His significant message is both timely and biblically sound.†

[2]
The story is timely because it deals with—rather exposes—the development of religious intolerance. One would like to dismiss the topic as a dead issue in today's world. The reality is otherwise. Intolerance has not vanished along with seventeenth-century Salem, but it is still here and will continue to be as long as misperception and distrust like Brown's can exist. He sets up his own religious standards, and no one else can measure up. Surely this formula spells intolerance, no matter when it happens.

[3]
The Bible, a work that is at once both ancient and current, is the basis for "Young Goodman Brown." It is true that scripture can be used to justify intolerant views like those by which Goodman Brown judges his fellow Salem residents. We may presume that people in Brown's day, like many in our own, have often been urged to seek perfection (for example, Genesis 17:1; Matthew 5:48). Almost all the letters of Paul, together with the Pastoral and General epistles, give advice to Christians to purify life (see Romans 12; Ephesians 5:6; I Timothy 5:22; James 4:8). There is no shortage of such advice. Indeed, there is so much that one might believe, as Brown does, that persons seemingly ignoring it cannot continue to call themselves Christian.

[4]
More positively, however, the rigorous side of things seems to represent no more than a partial view of the biblical message. Nowhere does the Bible say that those who do not measure up should be condemned by *people*. The task of judgment, and even of vengeance if necessary, belongs to God alone (see Psalms 94:1 and Romans 12:19, for example). For human beings, the Bible constantly stresses forgiveness, and this is what Brown lacks. Here are only two of the many passages emphasizing forgiveness:

> When ye stand praying, forgive, if ye have ought against any; that your Father also which is in heaven may forgive you your trespasses. (Mark 11:25)

*Central idea.
†Thesis sentence.

Forbearing one another, and forgiving one another, if any man have a quarrel against any: even as Christ forgave you, so also do ye. (Colossians 3:13)

One can go beyond advice like this to examples such as those of the Good Samaritan (Luke 10:29–31) and the Samaritan woman at the Well (John 4:7–42). These people were outsiders, not members of the same community, yet Jesus regarded them lovingly.

[5]

<u>Charity, love, forgiveness, and toleration-these are virtues that people need today and that were needed in seventeenth-century Salem, but Goodman Brown ignores them totally.</u> He suffers from the "holier-than-thou" symptom that does nothing so well as to alienate others. It is no wonder that his offspring following him to his grave "carved no hopeful verse upon his tombstone, for his dying hour was gloom." Certainly we should all strive for perfection, but we should also leave judgment in greater hands, and rather spend our time working toward understanding. In "Young Goodman Brown," Hawthorne has dramatized this point vividly and powerfully.

❦ COMMENTARY ON THE ESSAY

This sample review is intended for an audience concerned about religious issues. As such, it considers the story not as a general work of art but as one with religious and moral implications. The essay works in two directions: first, as a presentation of arguments favoring religious tolerance; and second, as an attempt to supply enough biblical background to show that the views in Hawthorne's story are based in scripture. The aim of the review is thus just as much persuasion as exposition and argument.

The first paragraph introduces the central idea about the story's religious significance, concluding with the essay's thesis sentence. Paragraph 2 demonstrates that misperceptions such as Brown's can occur at any time; therefore, the story is about a permanent human condition. Paragraphs 3 and 4 deal with biblical passages that possibly have a bearing, first, on explaining Brown's conduct (3) and, second, criticizing it (4). This material is not the sort that one might bring out in an analysis of, say, the ideas in the work, because it deals more with the Bible than with the story. Nevertheless, it is appropriate here because a review is to be considered as a much freer form than an analysis. The last paragraph utilizes the negative example of Brown as an incentive for tolerance.

Although this sample review deals with religious issues, it does so because of the intended audience. For an audience with other interests, a different treatment would be appropriate, even for the same work of literature.

Third Sample Essay: A Personal Review
for a General Audience

Security and Hawthorne's "Young Goodman Brown"

[1]
The major prop of life is security and certainty. These elements of stability stem from confidence in the people around us, secure laws, a sound economy, hope, and trust in ourselves and in the world generally. The loss of any of of these stabilizing props destroys our security and may produce panic.* It is this kind of panic that Nathaniel Hawthorne portrays in his allegorical tale "Young Goodman Brown." The major character is young Brown, who is a resident of seventeenth-century colonial Salem. Deep in a nighttime forest, he witnesses a nightmarish satanic cult meeting, and because he sees his wife there together with the elders and dignitaries of the town, he loses the security that comes from confidence in others. His story makes one think about the importance of the many things—personal, political, and natural—that provide us with a secure outlook on life.†

[2]
Personal security can depend on almost as many situations as there are people. Vital to Brown is his belief in the purity of his wife, Faith. Many people similarly base their lives on their confidence in those around them. But much can happen to disturb such security. Friends on whom we count might not be helpful when we need them because we badly misjudged them. A serious illness of someone close may have a devastating effect on confidence in the continuity of life itself. And, like Brown, we might imprison ourselves in our own suspicions and never again be able to trust anyone else. Personal security is delicate, even though the example of Brown, who does not try to explore the truth of his shattered illusions, shows that efforts at understanding might help to restore personal security that is mortally threatened.

[3]
If personal security is fragile, political security is even more so. At election times, there are always claims and counterclaims, so that we are never absolutely sure about the political wisdom we follow. Like many people, Brown loses faith in the local dignitaries, and he can never participate again with confidence in church and home. Today, on a world scale, we have even greater problems with our security, for happenings abroad disturb financial security and also threaten our very lives with local hatreds and wars, which constantly verge on becoming big enough to cause the beginning of general wars. Certainly, political security is worth the many years of constant negotiating spent by diplomats in trying to gain it.

[4]
In the natural world, too, we assume a great deal on which we depend absolutely. We cannot drive around a blind corner without the confidence that the road will continue, even though we cannot see it before we make our turns. We normally assume that the sun will rise and set, that rain will fall, that crops will grow (or at least appear in stores and cafés), that the air will be breathable, and that the earth generally will be a good place. But often there are fires, tor-

*Central idea.
†Thesis sentence.

[4] nadoes, earthquakes, floods, hurricanes, and volcanic eruptions. What occurs to Goodman Brown is, to him, a psychological equivalent, for his world is shattered by the dreams (or nightmares) of a single night. Such events can make people doubt the very ground they walk on.

The upshot of Hawthorne's story is that security—confidence about the world and people—is subject to accident and also design. It is true, nevertheless, that people can work to make themselves more secure. Perhaps Brown's greatest flaw is that he apparently does not try to get to the bottom of [5] what he has seen. He accepts his vision without question and, with his security destroyed, he descends into a life of "gloom" and depression. It is the possibility that people can always try at least to make things better that provides a gauge by which to measure Brown and also ourselves. One should be grateful to Hawthorne for having pointed the way so memorably to these ideas.

᪥ COMMENTARY ON THE ESSAY

This sample review is a personal essay on a topic—security—suggested by Hawthorne's story. The material from "Young Goodman Brown" is thus introduced as a part, although a major part, of the train of thought. The method of development is primarily illustration.

Unlike the religiously based audience visualized for the second sample essay, the audience intended here is a general one concerned with many broad topics, such as the personal, political, and natural ones discussed. The goal is to cause readers to reconsider and redefine the topic of security.

Paragraph 1 introduces security as a topic, attempts a definition, relates the topic to Hawthorne's story, and concludes with the essay's thesis sentence. Even though "Young Goodman Brown" is a religious story about how the hero's perceptions of life are destroyed by the Devil, the body of the sample essay does not deal with the religious issues, but instead goes into three separate though connected topics. Paragraph 2 deals with the first of these—personal situations that threaten personal security. Paragraph 3 considers political threats, and paragraph 4 brings in references to threats from the forces of nature. The concluding paragraph includes additional references to Goodman Brown, relating his passiveness to a need for a more aggressive pursuit of security.

᪥ SPECIAL WRITING TOPICS FOR STUDYING THE WRITING OF REVIEWS

Write reviews on any one of the following topics, being sure to consider the audiences for whom the review is intended.

1. A review of *Trifles* for people interested in law and the sentencing of offenders
2. A review of "The Boxes" for a group of young mothers
3. A review of "Patterns" for a group of women whose husbands or sons have been killed in war or police work
4. A review of *The Bear* for people interested in humor and farce
5. A review of "The Cask of Amontillado" for fans of mysteries and horror stories
6. A review of "Cargoes" for a group of businesspeople
7. A review of "Dover Beach" for a group of philosophers
8. A review of "The Tyger" for a group of ministers
9. A review of "Desert Places" for a group of people interested in psychology
10. A review of "Rhine Boat Trip" for a group interested in World War II and the Holocaust

chapter 18

Writing the Research Essay:
Using Extra Resources for Understanding

Broadly, **research** is the act of systematic investigation, examination, and experimentation. It is the basic tool of intellectual inquiry for anyone engaged in any discipline—physics, chemistry, biology, psychology, anthropology, history, and literature, to name just a few disciplines. With research, our understanding and our civilization grow; without it, they die.

The beginning assumption of doing research is that the researcher is exploring new areas of knowledge. With each assignment, the researcher acquires not only the knowledge gained from the particular task but also the skills needed to undertake further research and thereby to gain further knowledge. Some research tasks are elementary, such as using a dictionary to discover the meaning of a word and thus aiding the understanding of an important passage. More involved research uses an array of resources: encyclopedias, biographies, introductions, critical studies, bibliographies, and histories. When you begin a research task, you usually have little or no knowledge about your topic, but with such resources it is possible to acquire a good deal of expert knowledge in a relatively short time.

While research is the animating spark of all disciplines, our topic here is **literary research**—the systematic use of primary and secondary sources in studying a literary problem. In doing literary research, you consult not only individual works themselves (*primary sources*) but also many other works that shed light on them and interpret them (*secondary sources*). Typical research tasks are to learn important facts about a work and about the period in which it was written; to learn about the lives, careers, and other works of authors; to discover and apply the comments and judgments of modern or earlier critics; to learn details that help explain the meaning of works; and to learn about critical and artistic taste.

☘ SELECTING A TOPIC

In most instances, your instructor assigns a research essay on a specific topic. Sometimes, however, the choice of a topic is left entirely up to you. For such assignments, it is helpful to know the types of research essays you might find most congenial. Here are some possibilities:

1. *A particular work.* You might treat character (for example, "The Character of Smirnov in *The Bear*" or "The Question of Whether Young Goodman Brown Is a Hero or a Dupe"), or tone, ideas, form, problems, and the like. A research paper on a single work is similar to an essay on the same work, except that the research paper takes into account more views and facts than those you are likely to have without the research. Please see the sample research essay, on Katherine Mansfield's "Miss Brill" (page 261) to see how materials may be handled for such an assignment.

2. *A particular author.* This essay is about an idea or some facet of style, imagery, setting, or tone of the author, tracing the origins and development of the topic through a number of different stories, poems, or plays. An example might be "The Idea of Sin and Guilt as Developed by Hawthorne" or "The Idea of the True Self as Developed by Frost in His Poetry before 1920." This type of essay is suitable for a number of shorter works, though it is also applicable for a single major work, such as a longer story, novel, or play.

3. *Comparison and contrast* (see Chapter 13). There are two types:

   a. *An idea or quality common to two or more authors.* Your intention might be to show points of similarity or contrast or else to show that one author's work may be read as a criticism of another's. Typical subjects would be "The Use of the Third-Person Limited Point of View by Hawthorne and Mansfield" or "The Theme of Love and Sexuality in Shakespeare, Chekhov, and Donne."

   b. *Different critical views of a particular work or body of works.* Sometimes much is to be gained from an examination of differing critical opinions on topics such as "The Meaning of Poe's 'The Cask of Amontillado,'" "Opposing Views of Hawthorne's 'Young Goodman Brown,'" or "Chekhov's Attitude Toward Women as Seen in *The Bear*." Such a study would attempt to determine the critical opinion and taste to which a work does or does not appeal, and it might also aim at conclusions about whether the work was or is in the advance or the rear guard of its time.

4. *The influence of an idea, author, philosophy, political situation, or artistic movement on specific works of an author or authors.* A paper on influences can be fairly direct, as in "Details of Black American Life as Reflected in Hughes's 'Negro,'"

or else more abstract and critical, as in "The Influence of Racial Oppression and the Goal of Racial Equality on the Speaker of Hughes's 'Negro.'"

5. *The origin of a particular work or type of work.* One avenue of research for such an essay might be to examine an author's biography to discover the germination and development of a work—for example, " 'Kubla Khan' as an Outgrowth of Coleridge's Reading." Another way of discovering origins might be to relate a work to a particular type or tradition: " 'The Cask of Amontillado' and Poe's Theories of the Short Story" or " 'Patterns' and Its Relationship to Antiwar Literature of World War I."

If you consider these types, an idea of what to write may come to you. Perhaps you have particularly liked one author or several authors. If so, you might start to think along the lines of types 1, 2, and 3. If you are interested in influences or in origins, then types 4 or 5 may suit you better.

If you still cannot decide on a topic after rereading the works you have liked, then you should carry your search for a topic into your school library. Look up your author or authors in the computer or card catalogue. Your first goal should be to find a relatively recent book-length critical study published by a university press. Look for a title indicating that the book is a general one dealing with the author's major works rather than just one work. Study those chapters relevant to the work or works that you have chosen. Most writers of critical studies describe their purpose and plan in their introductions or first chapters, so begin with the first part of the book. If there is no separate chapter on the primary text, use the index and go to the relevant pages. Reading in this way will give you enough knowledge about the issues and ideas raised by the work to enable you to select a promising topic. Once you make your decision, you are ready to develop a working bibliography.

🦌 SETTING UP A BIBLIOGRAPHY

The best way to develop a working bibliography of books and articles is to begin with major critical studies of the writer or writers. Again, go to the catalogue and find books that have been published by university presses. These books usually contain comprehensive bibliographies. Be careful to read the chapters on your primary work or works and to look for the footnotes or endnotes, for often you can save time if you record the names of books and articles listed in these notes. Then refer to the bibliographies included at the ends of the books, and select likely looking titles. Now, look at the dates of publication of the critical books. Let us suppose that you have been looking at three, published in 1963, 1987, and 1995. The chances are that the bibliography in a book published in 1995 will be complete up through about 1994, for the writer will usually have completed the manuscript at least a year before the book was published. What you should do then is to gather a bibliography of works published since 1994; you can safely assume that writers of critical works will have done the selecting for you of important works published before that time.

Learn to Use Bibliographical Guides

Fortunately for students doing literary research, the Modern Language Association (MLA) of America has been providing a complete bibliography of literary studies for years, not only in English and American literature but in the literature of many foreign languages. This is the *MLA International Bibliography of Books and Articles on the Modern Languages and Literatures (MLA Bibliography)*. The *MLA Bibliography* started achieving completeness in the late 1950s. By 1969 the project had grown so large that it was published in many parts, which are bound together in library editions. University and college libraries have sets of these bibliographies on open shelves or tables. Recently, they have become available on CD-ROM.

There are many other bibliographies useful for students doing literary research, such as the *Essay and General Literature Index*, the *International Index*, and various specific indexes. For most undergraduate and many graduate purposes, however, the *MLA Bibliography* is more than adequate. Remember that as you progress in your reading, the notes and bibliographies in the works you consult also will constitute an unfolding bibliography. For the sample research essay in this chapter, for example, a number of entries were discovered not from the bibliographies but from the reference lists in critical works.

The *MLA Bibliography* is conveniently organized by period and author. If your author is Katherine Mansfield, for example, look her up in *Volume I: British and Irish, Commonwealth, English, Caribbean, and American Literatures*, where you will also find references to authors such as Shakespeare, Poe, and Lowell. You will find most books and articles listed under the author's last name. In the *MLA Bibliography*, journal references are abbreviated, but a lengthy list explaining abbreviations appears at the beginning of the volume. Using the *MLA Bibliography*, begin with the most recent one and then go backward to your stopping point. Be sure to get the complete information, especially volume numbers and years of publication, for each article and book. You are now ready to find your sources and to take notes.

☞ ON-LINE LIBRARY SERVICES

Today, most libraries have their own computerized catalogues. In addition, many libraries are connected with a vast array of local, national, and even international libraries, so that by using various on-line services, you can extend your research far beyond the capacities of your own library. You can even use your own personal computer to gain access to the catalogues of large research libraries, provided that you have a modem, the right computer program, the correct entry information, the willingness and ability to follow the program codes, and patience and persistence. By using various "search engines" to gain access to sites on the World Wide Web, you can also discover special topics directly related to your subject—organizations devoted to making awards, for example, or clubs or other organizations that have been established in the home cities of particular authors, or works on topics inspired by such authors.

The ease with which you can gain access to the various libraries through a computer search is variable. Some library catalogues are friendly, whereas others require a certain amount of trial and error.[1] In many cases, you cannot determine exactly how to find what you are looking for without practice, for the words some libraries use to categorize holdings are not immediately apparent. In all cases, practice with the various systems is essential, for you cannot expect to get the most out of an electronic search the first time you try.

After you have gained access, you can ask for books by specific authors or for books about particular topics. If your author is Shakespeare, for example, you can ask for specific titles of his works or for books about him. A recent search for critical and interpretive works about Shakespeare in a large urban university library produced a list of 577 titles with accompanying bibliographical information. The same library listed 167 works dealing specifically with his best-known play, *Hamlet.* Another large library produced 2,412 titles on the criticism and interpretation of Shakespeare (not just in English but also in other languages). Once you have such materials on your screen, you can select and list only the titles that you think will be most useful to you.

Such a list comprises a fairly comprehensive search bibliography, which you can use when you physically enter the library to begin collecting and using materials. A major convenience is that many associated libraries, such as state colleges and urban public libraries, have pooled their resources. Thus, if you use the services of a network of libraries within your local county, you can go to another nearby library to use materials that are not accessible at your own college or branch. If distances are great, however, and your own library does not have a book that you think is important to your project, you can ask a librarian to get the book for you through the

---

[1]Libraries generally encourage access to their resources, however, so proper entry instructions are often attached to computer terminals, particularly for internal use. When you are hooked into catalogues of distant libraries, you will find that the computer screen itself contains easily followed instructions about what you need to do to continue your search.

IMPORTANT CONSIDERATIONS ABOUT COMPUTER-AIDED RESEARCH

You must always keep in mind that on-line catalogues can give you only what has been entered into them. If one library classifies a work under "criticism and interpretation" and another classifies it under "characters," a search of "criticism and interpretation" at the first library will find the work but a search at the second will not. Sometimes the inclusion of an author's life dates immediately following the name will throw off your search. Typographic errors in the system will cause additional search problems, although many search programs attempt to forestall such difficulties by providing "nearby" entries to enable you to determine whether incorrectly entered topics can prove fruitful for your further examination. Also, if you use on-line services, be careful to determine the year when the computerization began. Many libraries have a recent commencement date—1978, for example, or 1985. For completeness, therefore, you would need assistance in finding catalogue entries for items published before these years.

Just a few years ago, the broadness of scope that electronic searches provide for most undergraduate students doing research assignments was not possible; today, it is a commonplace. Even with the astounding possibilities of electronic resources, however, it is still necessary to take out actual books and articles—and read them and take notes on them—before you can begin and complete a research essay. The electronic services can help you locate materials, but they cannot do your reading, note taking, and writing. All that is still up to you, as it always has been.

Interlibrary Loan Service. Usually, with time, the libraries will accommodate as many of your needs as they can.

☞ TAKING NOTES AND PARAPHRASING MATERIAL

There are many ways of taking notes, including the on-the-spot use of computer notebooks, but the consensus is that the best method is to use note cards. If you have never used cards before, you might profit from consulting any one of a number of handbooks and special workbooks on research.[2] The principal advantage of cards is that they can be classified; numbered and renumbered; shuffled; tried out in one place, rejected, and then used in another place (or thrown away); and arranged in order when you start to write.

---

[2]See, for example, Melinda G. Kramer, Glenn Leggett, and C. David Mead, *Prentice Hall Handbook for Writers*, 12th ed. (Englewood Cliffs, NJ: Prentice Hall, 1995), 501–05.

Taking Careful Notes Is the Beginning of Good Research

WRITE THE SOURCE ON EACH CARD. As you take notes, write the source of your information on each card. This may seem bothersome, but it is easier than going back to the library to locate the correct source after you have begun your essay. You can save time if you take the complete data on one card—a "master card" for that source—and then create an abbreviation for the separate note cards you take from the source. Here is an example, which also includes the location where the reference was originally found (e.g., card catalogue, computer search, bibliography in a book, the *MLA Bibliography*, etc. Observe that the author's last name goes first.

Donovan, Josephine, ed. <u>Feminist</u>   PN
     <u>Literary Criticism: Explorations</u>   98
     <u>in Theory</u>.   .W64
Lexington: The University Press   F4
     of Kentucky, 1975.

DONOVAN

Card Catalogue, "Women"

If you take a number of notes from this book, the name *Donovan* will serve as identification. Be sure not to lose your complete master cards because you will need them when you prepare your list of works cited. If possible, record the complete bibliographical data in a computer file.

RECORD THE PAGE NUMBER FOR EACH NOTE. It would be hard to guess how much exasperation has been caused by the failure to record page numbers in notes. Be sure to get the page number down first, *before* you begin to take your note, and, to be doubly sure, write the page number again at the end of your note. If the detail goes from one page to the next in your source, record the exact spot where the page changes, as in this example:

Heilbrun and Stimson, in DONOVAN, pp. 63-64

[63] After the raising of the feminist consciousness
    it is necessary to develop/ [64] "the growth of
      moral perception" through anger and the correction
      of social inequity.

The reason for such care is that you may wish to use only a part of a note that you have taken, and when there are two pages, you will need to be accurate in locating what goes where.

RECORD ONLY ONE FACT OR OPINION ON A CARD.   Record only one major element on each card—one quotation, one paraphrase, one observation—*never two or more.* You might be tempted to fill up the entire card with many separate but unrelated details, but such a try at economy often gets you in trouble because you might want to use some of the details in other places. If you have only one entry per card, you will avoid such problems and also retain the freedom you need.

USE QUOTATION MARKS FOR ALL QUOTED MATERIAL.   In taking notes, it is extremely important to distinguish your source material from your own words. *Always put quotation marks around every direct quotation you copy verbatim from a source.* Make the quotation marks immediately, before you forget, so that you will always know that the words of your notes within quotation marks are the words of another writer.

Often, as you take a note, you can use some of your own words and some of the words from your source. In cases like this, you should be even more cautious. Put quotation marks around *every word* that you take directly from the source, even if your note looks like a picket fence. Later, when you begin writing your paper, your memory of what is yours and not yours will be dim, and if you use another's words in your own essay without proper acknowledgment, you are risking the charge of plagiarism. Most of the time, plagiarism is caused not by deliberate deception but rather by sloppy note taking.

Use Your Own Words to Paraphrase Material from Your Sources

When you take notes, it is best to paraphrase the sources. A paraphrase is a restatement in your own words, and because of this, it is actually a first step in the writing of the essay. A big problem in paraphrasing is to capture the idea in the source without copying words in the source. The best way is to read and reread the passage. Then, turn over the book or journal and write out the idea *in your own words* as accurately as you can. Once you have this note, compare it with the original and make corrections to improve your thought and emphasis. Add a short quotation if you believe it is needed, but be sure to use quotation marks. If your paraphrase is too close to the original, *throw out the note and try again.* This effort is worthwhile because often you can transfer all or some of your note directly to the appropriate place in your research paper.

To see the problems of paraphrasing, let us look at a paragraph of criticism and then see how a student doing research might take notes on it. The paragraph is by Richard F. Peterson, from an essay entitled "The Circle of Truth: The Stories of Katherine Mansfield and Mary Lavin," published in *Modern Fiction Studies* 24 (1978): 383–394. In the passage to be quoted, Peterson is considering the structures of two Mansfield stories, "Bliss" and "Miss Brill":

> "Bliss" and "Miss Brill" are flawed stories, but not because the truth they reveal about their protagonists is too brutal or painful for the tastes of the common reader. In each story, the climax of the narrative suggests an arranged reality that leaves a lasting impression, not of life, but of the author's cleverness. This strategy of arrangement for dramatic effect or revelation, unfortunately, is common in Katherine Mansfield's fiction. Too often in her stories a dropped remark at the right or wrong moment, a chance meeting or discovery, an intrusive figure in the shape of a fat man at a ball or in the Café de Madrid, a convenient death of a hired man or a stranger dying aboard a ship, or a *deus ex machina* in the form of two doves, a dill pickle, or a fly plays too much of a role in / [386] creating a character's dilemma or deciding the outcome of the narrative. 385–386

Because taking notes necessarily forces a shortening of this or any other criticism, it also requires you to discriminate, judge, interpret, and select; good note taking is no easy task. There are some things to guide you, however, when you go through the many sources you uncover.

KEEP THE PURPOSE OF YOUR RESEARCH ALWAYS IN THE FOREFRONT OF YOUR MIND. You may not know exactly what you are "fishing for" when you start to take notes, for you cannot prejudge what your essay will contain. Research is a form of discovery. But soon you will notice subjects and issues that your sources constantly explore. If you can accept one of these as your major topic or focus of interest, you may use that as your guide in all further note taking.

For example, suppose you start to take notes on criticism about Katherine Mansfield's "Miss Brill," and after a certain amount of reading, you decide to focus on the story's structure. This decision guides your further research and note taking. Thus, for example, Richard Peterson criticizes Mansfield's technique of arranging climaxes in her stories. With your topic being structure, it would therefore be appropriate to take a note on Peterson's judgment. The following note is adequate as a brief reminder of the content in the passage:

Peterson 385	structure: negative

Peterson claims that Mansfield creates climaxes that are too artificial, too unlifelike, giving the impression not of reality but of Mansfield's own "cleverness." 385

Let us now suppose that you want a fuller note, in the expectation that you need not just Peterson's general idea but also some of his supporting detail. Such a note might look like this:

Peterson 385   structure: negative

Peterson thinks that "Bliss" and "Miss Brill" are "flawed" because they have contrived endings that give the impression "not of life but of" Mansfield's "cleverness." She arranges things artificially, according to Peterson, to cause the endings in many other stories. Some of these things are chance remarks, discoveries, or meetings, together with other unexpected or chance incidents and objects. These contrivances make their stories imperfect. 385

In an actual research essay, any part of this note would be useful. The words are almost all the note taker's own, and the few quotations are within quotation marks. Note that Peterson, the critic, is properly recognized as the source of the criticism, so you could adapt the note easily when you are doing your writing. The key here is that your note taking should be guided by your developing plan for your essay.

Note taking is part of your thinking and composing process. You may not always know whether you will be able to use each note that you take, and you will always exclude many notes when you write your essay. You will always find, however, that taking notes is easier once you have determined your purpose.

TITLE YOUR NOTES. To help plan and develop the various parts of your essay, write a title for each of your notes, as in the examples in this chapter. This practice is a form of outlining. Let us continue discussing the structure of Mansfield's "Miss Brill," the actual subject of the sample research essay (pages 261–68). As you do your research, you discover that there is a divergence of critical thought about how the ending of the story should be understood. Here is a note about one of the diverging interpretations:

Daly 90   Last sentence

Miss Brill's "complete" "identification" with the shabby fur piece at the very end may cause readers to conclude that she is the one in tears but bravely does not recognize this fact, and also to conclude that she may never use the fur in public again because of her complete defeat. Everything may be for "perhaps the very last time."

Notice that the title classifies the topic of the note. If you use such classifications, a number of like-titled cards could underlie a section in your essay about how to understand the concluding sentence of "Miss Brill." In addition, once you decide to explore the last sentence, the topic itself will guide you in further study and note taking. (See the sample essay, in which paragraphs 19 to 24 concern this topic.)

HONOR YOUR OWN THOUGHTS; RECORD THEM AS THEY OCCUR TO YOU. As you take your notes, you will be developing your own responses and thoughts. Do not let these go, on the chance of remembering them later, but write them down *immediately*. Often you may notice a detail that your source does not mention, or you may get a hint for an idea that the critic does not develop. Often, too, you may get thoughts that can serve as "bridges" between details in your notes or as introductions or concluding observations. Be sure to title your comment and also to mark it as your own thought. Here is such a note, which is on the emphasis on character as opposed to action in "Miss Brill":

My Own	Last Sentence

> Mansfield's letter of Jan. 17, 1921, indicates that action as such was less significant in her scheme for the story than the sympathetic evocation of Miss Brill's observations, impressions, and moods. She wanted to reveal character.

Observe that in paragraph 5 of the sample research essay, the substance of this note (also a good deal of the language) is used to introduce new material once the passage from the Mansfield letter has been quoted.

SORT YOUR CARDS INTO CLASSIFIED GROUPS. If you have taken your notes well, your essay will have been forming in your mind already. The titles of your cards will suggest areas to be developed as you do your planning and initial drafting. Once you have assembled a stack of note cards derived from a reasonable number of sources (your instructor may have assigned a minimum number), you can sort them into groups according to the topics and titles. For the sample essay, after some shuffling and retitling, the cards were classified and then sorted into the following groups:

1. Writing and publication
2. The title: amusement and seriousness
3. General structure
4. Specific structures: season, time of day, levels of cruelty, Miss Brill's own "hierarchies" of unreality
5. The concluding paragraphs, especially the last sentence
6. Concluding remarks

If you look at the major sections of the sample essay, you will see that the topics are closely adapted from these groups of cards. In other words, the arrangement of the cards is an effective means of outlining and organizing a research essay.

MAKE LOGICAL ARRANGEMENTS OF THE CARDS IN EACH GROUP. There is still much to do with each group of cards. You cannot use the details as they happen to fall randomly in your stack. You need to decide which notes are relevant. You might also need to retitle some cards and use them elsewhere. Those that remain will have to be arranged in a logical order for you to find use for them in your essay.

Once you have your cards in order, you can write whatever comments or transitions are needed to move from detail to detail. Write this material directly on the cards, and be sure to use a different color ink so that you can distinguish later between the original note and what you add. Here is an example of such a "developed" notecard:

Magalaner 39   Structure, general

    Speaking of Mansfield's sense of form, and referring to "Miss Brill" as an example, Magalaner states that Mansfield has power to put together stories from "a myriad of threads into a rigidly patterned whole." 39

Some of these "threads" are the fall season, the time of day, examples of unkindness, the park bench sitters from the cupboards, and Miss Brill's stages of unreality (see Thorpe 661). Each of these is separate, but all work together to unify the story.

By adding such commentary to your notecards, you are also simplifying the writing of your first draft. In many instances, the note and the comment may be moved directly into the paper with minor adjustments (some of the content of this note appears in paragraph 6 of the sample essay, and almost all the topics introduced here are developed in paragraphs 9 to 14).

BE CREATIVE AND ORIGINAL: DO YOUR OWN THINKING AND WRITING. This is not to say that you can always transfer your notes directly into your essay. The major trap to avoid in a research paper is that your use of sources can become an end in itself and therefore a shortcut for your own thinking and writing. Often, students make the mistake of introducing details the way a master of ceremonies introduces performers in a variety show. This treatment is unfortunate because it is the *student* whose essay will be judged, even though the sources, like the performers, do all the work. Thus, it is important to be creative and original in a research essay and to do your own thinking and writing, even though you are relying heavily on your sources. Here are five ways in which research essays may be original:

1. *Your selection of material is original with you.* In each major section of your essay you will include many details from your sources. To be creative you should select different but related details and avoid overlapping or repetition. The essay will be judged on the basis of the thoroughness with which you make your point with different details (this in turn will represent the completeness of your research). Even though you are relying on published materials and cannot be original on that score, your selection can be original because you bring *these* materials together for the first time and because you emphasize some details and minimize others. Inevitably, your assemblage of details from your sources will be unique and therefore original.

2. *Your development of your essay is yours alone.* Your arrangement of your various points is an obvious area of originality: One detail seems naturally to precede another, and certain conclusions stem from certain details. As you present the details, conclusions, and arguments from your sources, you may also add your own original stamp by using supporting details that are different from those in your sources. You may also add your own emphasis to particular points—an emphasis that you do not find in your sources.

3. *Your words are yours and yours only.* Naturally, the words that you use will be original. Your topic sentences, for example, will all be your own. As you introduce details and conclusions, you will need to write "bridges" to get yourself from point to point. These may be introductory remarks or transitions. In other words, as you write, you are not just stringing things out but are actively tying thoughts together in a variety of creative ways. Your success in these efforts will constitute your greatest originality.

4. *Explaining and contrasting controversial views is an original presentation of material.* Closely related to your selection is that in your research you may have found conflicting or differing views on a topic. If you make a point to describe and distinguish these views and to explain the reasons for the differences, you are presenting material originally. To see how differing views may be handled, see paragraphs 19 through 21 of the sample essay.

5. *Your own insights and positions are uniquely your own.* There are three possibilities here, all related to how well you have learned the primary texts on which your research in secondary sources is based:

   a. *Weave your own interpretations and ideas into your essay; these are original.* An important part of taking notes is to make your own points precisely when they occur to you. Often you can expand these as truly original parts of your essay. Your originality does not need to be extensive; it may consist of no more than a single insight. Here is such a card, written during the research on the structure of "Miss Brill":

My Own	Miss Brill's unreality
It is ironic that the boy and girl sit down on the bench next to Miss Brill just when she is at the height of her fancies. By allowing her to overhear their insults, they introduce objective reality to her. The result is that she is plunged instantly from the height of rapture to the depth of pain.	

The originality here is built around the contrast between Miss Brill's exhilaration and her rapid and cruel deflation. The observation is not unusual or startling, but it nevertheless represents an attempt at original thought. When modified and adapted, the material of the note supplies much of paragraph 18 of the sample essay. You can see that here the development of a "my own" note card is an important part of the prewriting stage for a research essay.

b. *Filling gaps in the sources enables you to present original thoughts and insights.* As you read your secondary sources, you may realize that an obvious conclusion is not being made or that an important detail is not being stressed. Here is an area that you can develop on your own. Your conclusions may involve a particular interpretation or major point of comparison, or they may rest on a particularly important but understressed word or fact. For example, paragraphs 21 to 24 in the sample essay form an argument based on observations that critics have overlooked, or have neglected to mention, about the conclusion of "Miss Brill." In your research, whenever you find such a critical "vacuum" (assuming that you cannot read all the articles about some of your topics, where your discovery may already have been made a number of times), it is right to move in with whatever is necessary to fill it.

c. *By disputing your sources, you are being original.* Your sources may present arguments that you wish to dispute. As you develop your disagreement, you will be arguing originally, for you will be using details in a different way from that of the critic or critics whom you are disputing, and your conclusions will be your own. This area of originality is similar to the laying out of controversial critical views, except that you furnish one of the opposing views yourself. The approach is limited because it is difficult to find many substantive points of interpretation on which there are not already clearly delineated opposing views. Paragraph 13 of the sample research essay shows how a disagreement can lead to a different, if not original, interpretation.

❦ DOCUMENTING YOUR WORK

It is essential to acknowledge—to *document*—all sources from which you have *quoted* or *paraphrased* factual and interpretive information. If you do not give due acknowledgment, you run the risk of being challenged for presenting other people's work as your own. This practice is plagiarism. As the means of documentation, there are many reference systems, some using parenthetical references and others using footnotes or endnotes. Whatever system is used, documentation almost always includes a carefully prepared list of works cited or a bibliography.

We will first discuss the list of works cited and then review the two major reference systems for use in a research paper. Parenthetical references, preferred by the Modern Language Association (MLA) since 1984, are described in Joseph Gibaldi, *MLA Handbook for Writers of Research Papers,* 4th ed., 1995. Footnotes or endnotes, recommended by the MLA before 1984, are still widely required.

List of Works Cited (Bibliography)

The key to any reference system is a carefully prepared list of works cited that is included at the end of the essay. "Works Cited" means exactly that; the list should contain just those books and articles that you have actually *used* in your essay. If, however, your instructor requires that you use footnotes or endnotes, you can extend your concluding list to be a complete bibliography both of works cited and also of works consulted but not actually used. *Always, always, always, follow your instructor's directions.*

The list of works cited should include the following information, in each entry, in the form indicated. If you are using a word processor with the capacity to make italics, you may italicize book and article titles, but be sure to notify your instructor in advance.

For a Book

1. The author's name, last name first, followed by first name and middle name or initial. Period.
2. Title, underlined (or italicized). Period.
3. City of publication (not state or nation), colon; publisher (easily recognized abbreviations or key words may be used unless they seem awkward or strange; see the *MLA Handbook,* 218–20), comma; year of publication. Period.

For an Article

1. The author's name, last name first, followed by first name and middle name or initial. Period.
2. Title of article in quotation marks. Period.
3. Name of journal or periodical, underlined or italicized, followed by volume number in Arabic (*not* Roman) numbers with no punctuation, followed by the year of publication within parentheses, colon. For a daily paper or weekly magazine, omit the parentheses and cite the date in the British style followed by a colon (day, month, year; i.e., 29 Feb. 1988:). Inclusive page numbers (without any preceding "p." or "pp."). Period.

The list of works cited should be arranged alphabetically by author, with unsigned articles being listed by title. Bibliographical lists are begun at the left margin, with subsequent lines in hanging indention, so that the key locating word—usually the author's last name—can be easily seen. The many unpredictable and complex combinations, including ways to describe works of art, musical or other performances, and films, are detailed extensively in the *MLA Handbook* (104–82). Here are two model entries:

Book: Alpers, Antony. <u>The Life of Katherine Mansfield</u>. New York: Viking, 1980.
Article: Hankin, Cheryl. "Fantasy and the Sense of an Ending in the Work of Katherine Mansfield." <u>Modern Fiction Studies</u> 24 (1978): 465–74.

In Your Essay, Make Parenthetical References to Your List of Works Cited

Within the text of your research essay, refer *parenthetically* to the list of works cited. This parenthetical reference system is recommended in the *MLA Handbook* (183–205), and its principle is to provide documentation without asking readers to interrupt their reading to find footnotes or endnotes. Readers wanting to see the complete reference can easily find it in your list of works cited. With this system, you insert the author's last name and the relevant page number or numbers into the body of your essay. If the author's name is mentioned in the discussion, only the page number or numbers are given in parentheses. Here are two examples:

> Alexander Pope believed in the idea that the universe is a whole, a totally unified body, which provides a "viable benevolent system for the salvation of everyone who does good" (Kallich 24).

> Martin Kallich draws attention to Alexander Pope's belief in the idea that the universe is a whole, a totally unified body, which provides a "viable benevolent system for the salvation of everyone who does good" (24).

Learn the Systems for Making Footnotes and Endnotes

The most formal system of documentation still widely used is that of *footnotes* (references at the bottom of each page) or *endnotes* (references listed numerically at the end of the essay). If your instructor wants you to use one of these formats, do the following: Make a note the first time you quote or refer to a source, with the details ordered as outlined here:

For a Book

1. The author's name, first name or initials first, followed by middle name or initial, then last name, comma.
2. The title, underlined or italicized for a book, no punctuation. If you are referring to a work in a collection (article, story, poem), use quotation marks for that, but underline the title of the book. (Use a comma after the title if an editor, a translator, or an edition number follows.)
3. The name of the editor or translator, if relevant. Abbreviate "editor" or "edited by" as *ed.,* "editors" as *eds.* Use *trans.* for "translator" or "translated by."

4. The edition (if indicated), abbreviated thus: *2nd ed., 3rd ed.,* and so on.

5. The publication facts, in parentheses, without any preceding or following punctuation, in the following order:

   a. City (but *not* the state or nation) of publication, colon.

   b. Publisher (clear abbreviations are acceptable and desirable), comma.

   c. Year of publication, comma.

6. The page number(s) with no *p.* or *pp.,* for example, 65, 6–10, 15–19, 295–307, 311–16. If you are referring to longer works, such as novels or longer stories that may have division or chapter numbers, include these numbers for readers who may be using an edition different from yours.

For an Article

1. The author, first name or initials first, followed by middle name or initial, then last name, comma.

2. The title of the article, in quotation marks, comma.

3. The name of the journal, underlined or italicized, no punctuation.

4. The volume number, in Arabic numbers, no punctuation.

5. The year of publication in parentheses, colon. For newspaper and journal articles, omit the parentheses, and include day, month, and year (in the British style; i.e., 21 May 1996), colon.

6. The page number(s) with no *p.* or *pp.,* for example, 65, 6–10, 34–36, 98–102, 345–47.

For later notes to the same work, use the last name of the author as the reference unless you are referring to two or more works by the same author. Thus, if you refer to only one work by, say, Thomas Hardy, the name "Hardy" will be enough for all later references. Should you be referring to other works by Hardy, however, you will also need to make a short reference to the specific works to distinguish them, such as "Hardy, 'The Three Strangers'" and "Hardy, 'Channel Firing.'"

Footnotes are placed at the bottom of each page, and endnotes are included in separate pages at the end of the essay. The first lines of both footnotes and endnotes should be paragraph indented, and continuing lines should be flush with the left margin. Both endnote and footnote numbers are positioned slightly above the line (as superior numbers) like this: [12]. Generally, you may single-space footnotes and endnotes, and leave a space between them. Additionally, today's computer programs have specially designed and consecutively numbered footnote formats. These are generally acceptable, but be sure to make the proper agreements with your instructor. For more detailed coverage of footnoting practices, see the *MLA Handbook,* 242–56.

SAMPLE FOOTNOTES.   In the following examples, book titles and periodicals are shown underlined, as they would be in a typewritten or carefully handwritten essay:

[1]Blanche H. Gelfant, Women Writing in America: Voices in Collage (Hanover: UP of New England, for Dartmouth College, 1984), 110.
[2]Günter Grass, "Losses," Granta 42 (Winter 1992): 99.
[3]John O'Meara, "Hamlet and the Fortunes of Sorrowful Imagination: A reexamination of the Genesis and Fate of the Ghost," Cahiers Élisabéthains 35 (1989), 21.
[4]Grass 104.
[5]Gelfant 141.
[6]O'Meara 17.

As a principle, you do not need to repeat in a note any material that you have already mentioned in your own discourse. For example, if you recognize the author and title of your source, then the note should give no more than the data about publication. Here is an example:

In The Fiction of Katherine Mansfield, Marvin Magalaner points out that Mansfield was as skillful in the development of epiphanies (that is, the use of highly significant though perhaps unobtrusive actions or statements to reveal the depths of a particular character) as James Joyce himself, the "inventor" of the technique.[9]

[9](Carbondale: Southern Illinois UP, 1971) 130.

Learn About Other Reference Systems

Other reference systems and style manuals have been adopted by various disciplines (e.g., mathematics, medicine, psychology) to serve their own particular needs. If you receive no instructions from your instructors in other courses, you can adapt the systems described here. If you need to use the documentation methods of other fields, however, use the *MLA Handbook,* 256–61, particularly 260–61, for guidance about what style manual to select.

Accept Some Final Advice: Always Ask Your Instructor Whenever You're Not Sure What to Do

As long as all you want from a reference is the page number of a quotation or paraphrase, the parenthetical system described briefly here—and detailed fully in the *MLA Handbook*—is the most suitable and convenient one that you can use. However, you may wish to use footnotes or endnotes if you need to add more details, provide additional explanations, or refer your readers to other materials that you are not using.

Whatever method you follow, *you must always acknowledge sources properly.* Remember that whenever you begin to write and make references, you might forget a number of specific details about documentation, and you will certainly discover that you have many questions. Be sure then to ask your instructor.

☗ STRATEGIES FOR ORGANIZING IDEAS

INTRODUCTION. For a research essay, the introduction may be longer than for an ordinary essay because you need to relate your research to your topic. You may bring in relevant historical or biographical information (see, for example, the introduction of the sample essay). You might also summarize critical opinion or describe any relevant problems. The idea is to lead your reader into your topic by providing interesting and significant materials that you have found during your research. Obviously, you should include your usual guides—your central idea and your thesis sentence.

Because of the length of research essays, some instructors require a topic outline, which is in effect a brief table of contents. This pattern is observed in the sample essay. *Because an outline is a matter of choice with various instructors, be sure that you understand whether your instructor requires it.*

BODY AND CONCLUSION. Your development for both the body and the conclusion will be governed by your choice of subject. Consult the relevant chapters in this book about what to include for whatever approach or approaches you select (e.g., setting, point of view, character, or tone).

A research essay may be from five to fifteen or more pages. Clearly, an essay on only one work may be shorter than an essay on two or more. If you narrow your topic as suggested in the approaches described before, you can keep your paper within the assigned length. The sample research essay, for example, illustrates the first approach by being limited to the structural aspects of one story. Were you to write on characteristic structures in a number of other stories by Mansfield or any other writer (the second approach), you could limit your total number of pages by stressing comparative treatments and by avoiding excessive detail about problems pertaining to each and every story. In short, you will decide to include or exclude materials by compromising between the importance of the materials and the limits of your assignment.

Although you limit your topic in consultation with your instructor, you will be dealing not with one source alone but with many. Naturally these sources will provide you with details and also with many of your ideas. The problem is to handle the many strands without piling on too many details, and also without digressing. It is therefore important to keep your central idea foremost, for constantly stressing the central idea will help you in selecting relevant materials.

It must be emphasized and reemphasized that you need to distinguish between *your own work* and the *sources* you are using. Your readers will assume that everything you write is your own unless you indicate otherwise. Therefore, when blending your words with the ideas from sources, be clear about proper acknowledgments. Most commonly, if you are simply presenting details and facts, you can write straightforwardly and let parenthetical references suffice as your authority, as in the following sentence from the sample essay:

> While Cheryl Hankin suggests that the structuring is perhaps more "instinctive" than deliberate (474), Marvin Magalaner, using "Miss Brill" as an example, speaks of Mansfield's power to weave "a myriad of threads into a rigidly patterned whole" (39).

Here there can be no question about plagiarism, for the names of the authorities are acknowledged in full, the page numbers are specific, and the quotation marks clearly show the important word and phrase that are taken from the sources. If you grant recognition as recommended here, no confusion can result about the authority underlying your essay. Although the words belong to the writer of the essay, the parenthetical references clearly indicate that the sentence is derived from the two sources.

If you are using an interpretation that is unique to a particular writer, or if you are relying on a significant quotation from your source, you should make your acknowledgment as an essential part of your discussion, as in this sentence:

> Saralyn Daly, referring to Miss Brill as one of Mansfield's "isolatoes"—that is, solitary persons cut off from normal human contacts (88)—fears that the couple's callous insults have caused Miss Brill to face the outside world with her fur piece "perhaps for the very last time" (90).

Here the idea of the critic is singled out for special acknowledgment. If you indicate your sources in this way, no confusion can possibly arise about how you have used your sources.

Sample Research Essay
The Structure of Mansfield's "Miss Brill"°

I. INTRODUCTION
    A. THE WRITING OF "MISS BRILL"
    B. THE CHOICE OF THE NAME "BRILL"
    C. THE STORY'S STRUCTURE
II. SEASON AND TIME AS STRUCTURE
III. INSENSITIVE OR CRUEL ACTIONS AS STRUCTURE
IV. MISS BRILL'S "HIERARCHY OF UNREALITIES" AS STRUCTURE
V. THE STORY'S CONCLUSION
VI. CONCLUSION

I. Introduction

A. The Writing of "Miss Brill"

[1] Because Katherine Mansfield's "Miss Brill"—one of the eighty-eight short stories and fragments she wrote in her brief life (Magalaner 5)—succeeds so well as a portrait of the protagonist's inner life, it has become well known and has been frequently anthologized (Gargano). She apparently wrote it on the evening of November 11, 1920, when she was staying at Isola Bella, an island retreat in northern Italy where she had gone in her desperate search to overcome tuberculosis. In her own words, she describes the night of composition:

> Last night I walked about and saw the new moon with the old moon in her arms and the lights in the water and the hollow pools filled with stars—and lamented there was no God. But I came in and wrote Mill Brill instead; which is my insect Magnificat now and always. (Letters 594)

Her husband, J. Middleton Murry, who had remained in London, published the story in the November 26, 1920, issue of the journal Athenaeum, which he was then editing. In 1922, Mansfield Included "Miss Brill" in her collection entitled The Garden Party and Other Stories (Daly 134).

[2] She was particularly productive at the time of "Miss Brill" despite her illness, for she wrote a number of superb stories then. The others, as reported by her biographer Antony Alpers, were "The Lady's Maid," "The Young Girl," "The Daughters of the Late Colonel," and "The Life of Ma Parker" (304–05). All these stories share the common bond of "love and pity" rather than the "harshness or satire" that typifies many of her earlier stories (Alpers 305).

°See pages 336–39 for this story.

B. The Choice of the Name "Brill"

"Miss Brill," however, does contain at least a minor element of humor. James W. Gargano notes that the title character, Miss Brill, is named after a lowly flatfish, the brill. This fish, with notoriously poor vision, is related to the turbot and the whiting (it is the whiting that the rude girl compares to Miss Brill's fur piece). The Oxford English Dictionary records that the brill is "inferior in flavour" to the turbot. One may conclude that Mansfield, in choosing the name, wanted to minimize her heroine.

[3]

While Mansfield's use of the name suggests a small trick on poor Miss Brill, the story is not amusing but is rather poignant and powerful. Miss Brill is portrayed as one who has been excluded from "public history" (Gubar 31) because she lives exclusively in the "feminine world" (Maurois 337). Her main concerns, in other words, are not power and greatness but the privacy of personal moments, which may be upset by no more than a contemptuous giggle (Gubar 38). The poignancy of the story stems from Miss Brill's eagerness to be "part of a scene that ruthlessly excludes her" and thus makes her "the loneliest of all . . . [characters in] Katherine Mansfield's stories about lonely women" (Fullbrook 103). The story's power results from the feeling with which Mansfield renders the "inarticulate longings and the tumultuous feelings that lie beneath the surface of daily life" (McLaughlin 381). A mark of her skill is the way in which she enters the soul of the heroine and turns it "outward, for her reader to see and understand" (Magill 710), so much so that Claire Tomalin declares that the story is "conceived virtually as [a] dramatic" monologue (213). Mansfield's own description in writing "Miss Brill" bears out these claims, for it shows how deeply she tried to create the pathetic inner life of her character:

[4]

> In Miss Brill I choose not only the length of every sentence, but even the sound of every sentence. I choose the rise and fall of every paragraph to fit her, and to fit her on that day at that very moment. After I'd written it I read it aloud—numbers of times—just as one would play over a musical composition—trying to get it nearer to the expression of Miss Brill—until it fitted her. (Letter to Richard Murry of January 17, 1921, qtd. in Sewell, 5–6)

C. The Story's Structure

Mansfield's description strongly indicates that action in the story was less significant in her scheme than the sympathetic evocation of Miss Brill's mood and impressions—in other words, the depths of her character. Such a design might lead readers to conclude that the story is not so much formed as forming, a free rather than planned development. In reference to Mansfield's talent generally, Edward Wagenknecht reflects that the stories, including "Miss Brill," are "hardly even episodes or anecdotes. They offer reflections [instead] of some aspect of experience or express a mood" (163). In many ways, Wagenknecht's observation is true of "Miss Brill." The story seems to be built up from within the character, and it leaves the impression of an individual who experiences a "crisis in miniature," a "deep cut into time" in which life changes and all hopes and expectations are reversed (Hankin 465).

[5]

It follows that Mansfield's achievement in "Miss Brill" is to fashion a credible character in an especially pathetic and shattering moment. The story therefore embodies an intricate set of structures that simultaneously comple-

[6]

ment the movement downward.* Whatever the source of Mansfield's control over form, critics agree that her power was great. Marvin Magalaner, using "Miss Brill" as an example, speaks of Mansfield's weaving of "a myriad of threads into a rigidly patterned whole" (39). Noting the same control over form,

[6] Cheryl Hankin suggests that her structuring is perhaps more "instinctive" than deliberate (474). These complementary threads, stages, or "levels" of "unequal length" (Harmat uses the terms "niveaux" and "longueur inégale," 49, 51) are the fall season, the time of day, insensitive or cruel actions, Miss Brill's own unreal perceptions, and the final section or dénouement. †

II. Season and Time as Structure

A significant aspect of structure is Mansfield's use of season and times of day. The autumnal season is integral to the deteriorating circumstances of the heroine. In the first paragraph, for example, we learn that there is a "faint chill" in the air (is the word "chill" chosen to rhyme with "Brill"?), and this phrase is repeated in paragraph 10. Thus the author establishes autumn and the approaching end of the year as the beginning of the movement toward dashed hopes. This seasonal reference is also carried out when we read that

[7] "yellow leaves" are "down drooping" in the local Jardins Publiques (paragraph 6) and that leaves are drifting "now and again" from almost "nowhere, from the sky" (paragraph 1). It is the autumn cold that has caused Miss Brill to take out her bedraggled fur piece at which the young girl later is so amused. Thus the chill, together with the fur, forms a structural setting integrated with both the action and the mood of the story. The story both begins and ends with the fur (Sewell 25), which is the direct cause of Miss Brill's deep hurt at the end.

Like this seasonal structuring, the times of day parallel Miss Brill's darkening existence. At the beginning, the day is "brilliantly fine—the blue sky powdered with gold," and the light is "like white wine." This metaphorical language suggests the brightness and crispness of full sunlight. In paragraph 6, where

[8] we also learn of the yellow leaves, "the blue sky with gold-veined clouds" indicates that time has been passing as clouds accumulate during late afternoon. By the story's end, Miss Brill has returned to her "little dark room" (paragraph 18). In other words, the time moves from day to evening, from light to darkness, as an accompaniment to Miss Brill's psychological pain.

III. Insensitive or Cruel Actions as Structure

Mansfield's most significant structural device, which is not emphasized by critics, is the introduction of insensitive or cruel actions. It is as though the hurt felt by Miss Brill on the bright Sunday afternoon is also being felt by many others. Because she is the spectator who is closely related to Mansfield's nar-

[9] rative voice, Miss Brill is the filter through whom these negative examples reach the reader. Considering the patterns that emerge, one may conclude that Mansfield intends the beauty of the day and the joyousness of the band as an ironic contrast to the pettiness and insensitivity of the people in the park.

The first characters are a silent couple on Miss Brill's bench (paragraph 3)

[10] and the incompatible couple of the week before (paragraph 4). Because these seem no more than ordinary, they do not seem at first to be part of the story's

*Central idea.
†Thesis sentence.

[10] pattern of cruelty and rejection; but their incompatibility, suggested by their silence and one-way complaining, establishes a structural parallel with the young and insensitive couple who insult Miss Brill. Thus the first two couples prepare the way for the third, and all show behavior of increasing insensitivity.

[11] Almost unnoticed as a second level of negation is the vast group of "odd, silent, nearly all old" people filling "the benches and green chairs" (paragraph 5). They seem to be no more than a normal part of the Sunday afternoon landscape. But these people are significant structurally because the "dark little rooms—or even cupboards" that Miss Brill associates with them describe her own circumstances at the story's end (paragraphs 5,18). The reader may conclude from Miss Brill's quiet eavesdropping that she herself is one of these nameless and faceless ones, all of whom lead similar drab lives.

[12] Once Mansfield has set these levels for her heroine, she introduces examples of more active rejection and cruelty. The beautiful woman who throws down the bunch of violets is the first of these (paragraph 8). The causes of her scorn are not made clear, and Miss Brill does not know what to make of the incident; but the woman's actions indicate that she has been involved in a relationship that has ended bitterly.

[13] The major figure involved in rejection, who is important enough to be considered a structural double of Miss Brill, is the woman wearing the ermine toque (paragraph 8). She tries to please the "gentleman in grey," but this man insults her by blowing smoke in her face. It could be, as Peter Thorpe observes, that the woman is "obviously a prostitute" (661). More likely, from the conversation overheard by Miss Brill, the "ermine toque" has had a broken relationship with the gentleman. Being familiar with his Sunday habits, she deliberately comes to the park to meet him, as though by accident, to attempt a reconciliation. After her rejection, her hurrying off to meet someone "much nicer" (there is no such person, for Mansfield uses the phrase "as though" to introduce the ermine toque's departure) is her way of masking her hurt. Regardless of the exact situation, however, Mansfield makes it plain that the encounter demonstrates vulnerability, unkindness, and pathos.

[14] Once Mansfield establishes this major incident, she introduces two additional examples of insensitivity. At the end of paragraph 8, the hobbling old man "with long whiskers" is nearly knocked over by the troupe of four girls, who show arrogance if not contempt. The final examples involve Miss Brill herself. These are the apparent indifference of her students and that of the old invalid "who habitually sleeps" when she reads to him.

[15] Although "Miss Brill" is a brief story, Mansfield creates a large number of structural parallels to the sudden climax brought about by the insulting young couple. The boy and girl do not appear until the very end, in other words (paragraphs 11–14), but actions like theirs have been anticipated structurally in all previous parts of the story. Mansfield's speaker does not take us to the homes of the other victims as we follow Miss Brill into her poor lodgings, but the narrative invites us to conclude that the silent couple, the complaining wife and long-suffering husband, the unseen man rejected by the young woman, the ermine toque, and the funny gentleman, not to mention the many silent and withdrawn people sitting like statues in the park, all return to similar loneliness and personal pain.

IV. Miss Brill's "Hierarchy of Unrealities" as Structure

[16] The intricacy of the structure of "Miss Brill" does not end here. Of great importance is the structural development of the protagonist herself. Peter

[16] Thorpe notes a "hierarchy of unrealities" which govern the reader's increasing awareness of her plight (661). <u>By this measure, the story's actions progressively bring out Miss Brill's failures of perception and understanding—failures that in this respect make her like her namesake fish, the brill</u> (Gargano).

[17] These unrealities begin with Miss Brill's fanciful but harmless imaginings about her shabby fur piece. <u>This beginning sets up the pattern of her pathetic inner life</u>. When she imagines that the park band is a "single, responsive, and very sensitive creature" (Thorpe 661), we are to realize that she is simply making too much out of a band of ordinary musicians. Although she cannot interpret the actions of the beautiful young woman with the violets, she does see the encounter between the ermine toque and the gentleman in grey as an instance of rejection. Her response is correct, but then her belief that the band's drumbeats are sounding out "The Brute! The Brute!" indicates her vivid overdramatization of the incident. The "top of the hierarchy of unrealities" (Thorpe 661) is her fancy that she is an actor with a vital part in a gigantic drama played by all the people in the park. The most poignant aspect of this daydream is her imagining that someone would miss her if she were absent, for this fancy shows how far she is from reality.

[18] In light of this structure, or hierarchy, of unrealities, it is ironic that the boy and girl sit down next to her just when she is at the height of her fancy about her own importance. <u>When she hears the girl's insults, the couple introduces objective reality to her with a vengeance, and she is plunged from rapture to pain</u>. The following, and concluding, two paragraphs hence form a rapid dénouement to reflect her loneliness and despair.

V. The Story's Conclusion

[19] <u>Of unique importance in the structure of "Miss Brill" are the final two paragraphs—the conclusion, or dénouement—in which Miss Brill returns to her miserable little room</u>. This conclusion might easily be understood as a total, final defeat. For example, Saralyn Daly, referring to Miss Brill as one of Mansfield's "isolatoes"—that is, solitary persons cut off from normal human contacts (88)—fears that the couple's callous insults have caused Miss Brill to face the outside world with her fur piece "perhaps for the very last time" (90). Eudora Welty points out that Miss Brill is "defenseless and on the losing side" and that her defeat may be for "always" (87). Miss Brill's experience demonstrates a pattern described by Zinman as common in Mansfield's stories, in which the old are destroyed "by loneliness and sickness, by fear of death, by the thoughtless energy of the younger world around them" (457). With this disaster for the major character, the story may be fitted to the structuring of Mansfield stories observed by André Maurois: "moments of beauty suddenly broken by contact with ugliness, cruelty, or death" (342–43).

[20] <u>Because some critics have stated that Miss Brill's downfall is illogically sudden, they have criticized the conclusion</u>. Peterson, for example, complains that the ending is artificial and contrived because of the improbability that the young couple would appear at just that moment to make their insults (385). On much the same ground, Berkman declares that the ending is excessive, mechanical, and obvious (162, 175).

[21] <u>Cheryl Hankin, however, hints at another way in which the conclusion may be taken, a way that makes the story seem both ironic and grimly humorous</u>. In describing patterns to be found in Mansfield's stories, Hankin notes the following situation, which may account for the story's ending:

> [A]n impending disillusionment or change in expectations may be de-
> flected by the central character's transmutation of the experience into
> something positive. (466)

There is no question that the ending indicates that Miss Brill has been totally
shattered. Her deflation is shown by her quietness and dejection on returning
to her small "cupboard" room.

[22]   Mansfield's very last sentence, however, may be read as a way of indicating that Miss Brill is going back to her earlier habit of making reality over to
fit her own needs, in this respect indicating the "something positive" described
by Hankin:

> But when she put the lid on she thought she heard something crying.
> (paragraph 18)

It is hard to read this last sentence without finding irony and pathos in it. By
hearing "something crying" Miss Brill may likely be imagining that the fur piece,
and not she, has been hurt. One might remember that the thoughtless young
girl has laughed at the fur because it resembles a "fried whiting" (paragraph
14). The irony here is that Miss Brill, like the Boss in Mansfield's story "The
Fly," forgets about the pain of remembrance and slips back into customary defensive behavior.

[23]   This pattern of evasion is totally in keeping with Miss Brill's character.
Despite her poverty and loneliness, she has been holding a job (as a teacher
of English, presumably to French pupils), and has also been regularly performing her voluntary task of reading to the infirm old man. She has not had a life
filled with pleasure, but her Sunday afternoons of eavesdropping have enabled
her, through "the power of her imagination," to share the lives of many others
(Hanson and Gurr 81). Mansfield establishes this vicarious sociability as Miss
Brill's major strength, which Hanson and Gurr call "the saving grace of her life"
(81). Her method makes her both strange and pathetic, but nevertheless she
has been functioning. Within such a framework, the deflating insults of paragraphs 13 and 14 may be seen as another incentive for her to adjust by
strengthening her fancy, not abandoning it.

[24]   This is not to interpret the story's conclusion as an indication that Miss
Brill has shaken off the couple's insults. She is first and foremost a "victim"
(Zinman 457), if not of others, then of her own reality-modifying imagination;
but she is presented as a character who has positive qualities. Indeed, Mansfield herself expressed her own personal liking of Miss Brill (despite the name
"brill"). Her husband, J. Middleton Murry, shortly after receiving the story from
her for publication, sent her a letter in which he expressed his fondness for the
protagonist. In a return letter to him of November 21, 1920, Mansfield wrote
that she shared this fondness. She went on the same letter to say:

> One writes (one reason why is) because one does care so passionately
> that one must show it—one must declare one's love. (qtd. in Magalaner
> 17)

Surely the author could love her creation out of pity alone, but if she had
added an element of strength, such as the brave but sad ability to adjust to
"impossible and intolerable conditions" (Zinman 457), then her love would

have an additional cause. <u>Therefore it is plausible that the last sentence of</u> <u>"Miss Brill" shows the resumption of the heroine's way of surviving</u>.

VI. Conclusion

[25] <u>"Miss Brill" is a compact story intricately built up from a number of coex-</u> <u>isting structures</u>. It is alive, so much so that it justifies the tribute of Antony Alpers that it is a "minor masterpiece" (305). The structural contrast between the protagonist and the world around her is derived from a deeply felt dichotomy about life attributed to Mansfield herself, a sense that the human soul is beautiful, on the one hand, but that people are often vile, on the other (Moore 245). It is the vileness that Miss Brill seems to be avoiding at the end.

[26] The greater structure of "Miss Brill" is therefore a hard, disillusioned view of life itself, in which those who are lonely, closed out, and hurt are wounded even more. This pattern of exclusion not only affects the restricted lives of the lonely, but it also reaches directly into their minds and souls. Miss Brill's response is to retreat further and further into an inner world of unreality but also to continue life, even at an almost totally subdued level, within these confines. <u>It is Mansfield's "almost uncanny psychological insight"</u> (Hankin 467) <u>into the</u> <u>operation of this characteristic response that gives "Miss Brill" its structure and</u> <u>also accounts for its excellence</u>.

Works Cited

Alpers, Antony. <u>Katherine Mansfield, A Biography</u>. New York: Knopf, 1953.

Berkman, Sylvia. <u>Katherine Mansfield, A Critical Study</u>. New Haven: Yale UP (for Wellesley College), 1951.

"Brill." Oxford English Dictionary. 1933 ed.

Daly, Saralyn R. <u>Katherine Mansfield</u>. New York: Twayne, 1965.

Fullbrook, Kate. <u>Katherine Mansfield</u>. Bloomington and Indianapolis: Indiana UP, 1986.

Gargano, James W. "Mansfield's Miss Brill." <u>Explicator</u> 19. 2 (1960): item 10 (one page, unpaginated).

Gubar, Susan. "The Birth of the Artist as Heroine: (Re)production, the <u>Kunstler-</u> <u>roman</u> Tradition, and the Fiction of Katherine Mansfield." <u>The Representa-</u> <u>tion of Women in Fiction</u>. Ed. Carolyn Heilbrun and Margaret R. Higonnet. Selected Papers from the English Institute, 1981. Baltimore: Johns Hopkins UP, 1983, 19–58.

Hankin, Cheryl. "Fantasy and the Sense of an Ending in the Work of Katherine Mansfield." <u>Modern Fiction Studies</u> 24 (1978): 465–74.

Hanson, Clare, and Andrew Gurr. <u>Katherine Mansfield</u>. New York: St. Martin's, 1981.

Harmat, Andrée-Marie. "Essai D'Analyse Structurale D'Une Nouvelle Lyrique Anglaise: 'Miss Brill' de Katherine Mansfield." <u>Les Cahiers de la Nouvelle</u> 1 (1983): 49–74.

Heiney, Donald W. <u>Essentials of Contemporary Literature</u>. Great Neck: Barron's, 1954.

McLaughlin, Ann L. "The Same Job: The Shared Writing Aims of Katherine Mansfield and Virginia Woolf." <u>Modern Fiction Studies</u> 24 (1978): 369–82.

Magalaner, Marvin. <u>The Fiction of Katherine Mansfield</u>. Carbondale: Southern
    Illinois UP, 1971.

Magill, Frank N., ed. <u>English Literature: Romanticism to 1945</u>. Pasadena:
    Salem Softbacks, 1981.

Mansfield, Katherine. <u>Katherine Mansfield's Letters to John Middleton Murry,
    1913–1922</u>. Ed. John Middleton Murry. New York: Knopf, 1951. Cited as
    "Letters."

———. <u>The Short Stories of Katherine Mansfield.</u> New York: Knopf, 1967.

Maurois, André. <u>Points of View from Kipling to Graham Greene</u>. 1935. New
    York: Ungar, 1968.

Moore, Virginia. <u>Distinguished Women Writers</u>. 1934. Port Washington: Ken-
    nikat, 1962.

Peterson, Richard F. "The Circle of Truth: The Stories of Katherine Mansfield
    and Mary Lavin." <u>Modern Fiction Studies</u> 24 (1978): 383–94.

Sewell, Arthur. <u>Katherine Mansfield: A Critical Essay</u>. Auckland: Unicorn,
    1936.

Thorpe, Peter. "Teaching 'Miss Brill.'" <u>College English</u> 23 (1962): 661–63.

Tomalin, Claire. <u>Katherine Mansfield, A Secret Life</u>. New York: Knopf, 1988.

Wagenknecht, Edward. <u>A Preface to Literature</u>. New York: Holt, 1954.

Welty, Eudora. <u>The Eye of the Story: Selected Essays and Reviews</u>. New
    York: Random House, 1977.

Zinman, Toby Silverman. "The Snail Under the Leaf: Katherine Mansfield's Im-
    agery." <u>Modern Fiction Studies</u> 24 (1978): 457–64.

❦ COMMENTARY ON THE ESSAY

This essay fulfills an assignment of 2,500 to 3,000 words, with 15 to 25
sources. The bibliography was developed from a college library card catalogue, references in books of criticism (Magalaner, Daly, Berkman); the
MLA International Bibliography; and the *Essay and General Literature Index.*
The sources were found in a college library with selective, not exhaustive,
holdings, and in a local public library. There is only one rare source, an article (Harmat) obtained in photocopy form through interlibrary loan from
one of only two United States libraries holding the journal in which it appears. The location was made through the national OCLS on-line service.
For most semester-long or quarter-long courses, you will likely not have
time to add to your sources by this method, but the article in question refers
specifically to "Miss Brill," and it was therefore desirable to examine it.

The sources consist of books, articles, and chapters or portions of
books. One article (Sewell) has been published as a separate short mono-
graph. Also, one of the sources is the story "Miss Brill" itself (with locations

made by paragraph number) together with editions of Mansfield's letters and a collection of her stories. The sources are used for facts, interpretations, reinforcement of conclusions, and general guidance and authority. The essay also contains passages taking issue with certain conclusions in a few of the sources. All necessary thematic devices, including overall organization and transitions, are unique to the sample essay. Additional particulars about the handling of sources and developing a research essay are included in the discussion of note taking and related matters in this chapter.

The introduction to the sample essay contains essential details about the writing of the story and the title as well as a pointed summary of critical appraisals of the story itself. The idea explored here is that the story dramatizes Miss Brill's emotional responses first to exhilaration and then to pain. The central idea (paragraph 6) is built out of this idea, explaining that the movement of emotions in the story is accompanied by an intricate and complementary set of structures.

Sections II to V examine various elements of the story for their structural relationship to Miss Brill's emotions. Section II details the structural uses of the settings of autumn and times of day, pointing out how they parallel her experiences. The longest part, section III (paragraphs 9 to 15), is based on an idea not found in the sources—that a number of characters are experiencing difficulties and cruelties such as those that befall Miss Brill. Paragraph 10 cites the three couples of the story, paragraph 11 the silent old people, and paragraph 12 the woman with violets. Paragraph 13 is developed in disagreement with one of the sources, showing how a research essay may be original even though the sources form the basis for argument. Paragraph 14 contains brief descriptions of additional examples of insensitivity, two of them involving Miss Brill herself. Paragraph 15 both concludes and summarizes the story's instances of insensitivity and cruelty, emphasizing again parallels to Miss Brill's situation.

Section IV (paragraphs 16 to 18) is based on ideas about the story's structure found in one of the sources (Thorpe). It is hence more derivative than the previous section. Section V (paragraphs 19 to 24) is devoted to the dénouement of the story. Paragraphs 19 and 20 consider critical interpretations of the ending. In paragraph 21, however, a hint found in a source (Hankin) is used to interpret the story's final sentence. An argument in support of this original interpretation is developed in paragraphs 22 to 24, which conclude with a reference to Mansfield's own personal approval of the main character.

Section VI (paragraphs 25 and 26), the conclusion, relates the central idea to further biographical information and also to Mansfield's achievement in the story. Of the three sources used here, two are used earlier in the essay, and one (Moore) is new.

The list of works cited is the basis of all references in the essay, in accord with the *MLA Handbook for Writers of Research Papers*, 4th ed. By locating these references, a reader might readily examine, verify, and study any of the ideas and details drawn from the sources and developed in the essay.

❦ SPECIAL WRITING TOPICS FOR
UNDERTAKING RESEARCH ESSAYS

In beginning research on any of the following topics, follow the steps in research described in this chapter.

1. Common themes in a number of stories by Hawthorne, Poe, Hardy, or Mansfield
2. Various critical views of Chekhov's *The Bear*
3. Glaspell's use of the narrative material in *Trifles*
4. Hawthorne's use of religious and moral topic material
5. Shakespeare's imagery in the Sonnets
6. Views about women in Chopin, Glaspell, Mansfield, and Keats
7. Poe's view of the short story as represented in "The Cask of Amontillado" and a number of other stories

chapter 19

Writing Examinations on Literature

Succeeding on a literature examination is largely a result of intelligent and skillful preparation. Preparing means (1) studying the material assigned, in conjunction with the comments made in class by your instructor and by fellow students in discussion; (2) developing and reinforcing your own thoughts; (3) anticipating exam questions by creating and answering your own practice questions; and (4) understanding the precise function of the test in your education.

First, realize that the test is not designed either to trap you or to hold down your grade. The grade you receive is a reflection of your achievement in the course. If your grades are low, you can improve them by studying diligently and systematically. Those students who can easily do satisfactory work might do superior work if they improved their method of preparation. From whatever level you begin, you can increase your achievement by improving your method of study.

Your instructor has three major concerns in evaluating your tests (assuming the correct use of English): (1) to assess the extent of your command over the subject material of the course (How good is your retention?); (2) to assess how well you are able to think about the material (How well are you educating yourself?); and (3) to assess how well you respond to a question or deal with an issue.

⚕ ANSWER THE QUESTIONS ASKED

Many elements go into writing good answers on tests, but responsiveness is the most important. A major cause of low exam grades is that students really do not *answer* the questions asked. Does that failure seem surprising? The problem is that some students do no more than retell a story or restate an argument; they never confront the issues in the question. This common problem has been treated throughout this book. Therefore, if you are asked, "Why does . . . ," be sure to emphasize the *why* and to use the *does* only to exemplify the *why*. If the question is about *organization*, focus on organization. If a *problem* has been raised, deal with the problem. In short, always *respond directly* to the question or instruction. Compare the following two answers to the same question:

Question: How is the setting of Bierce's "An Occurrence at Owl Creek Bridge" important in the story's development?

A

The setting of Bierce's "An Occurrence at Owl Creek Bridge" is a major element in the development of the story. The first scene is on a railroad bridge in northern Alabama, and the action is that a man, Peyton Farquhar, is about to be hanged. He is a southerner who has been surrounded and captured by Union soldiers. They are ready to string him up and they have the guns and power, so he cannot escape. He is so scared that his own watch seems to sound loudly and slowly like a cannon. He also thinks about how he might escape once he is hanged, by freeing his hands and throwing off the noose that will be choking and killing him. The scene shifts to the week before, at Farquhar's plantation. A Union spy deceives Farquhar, thereby tempting him to try to sabotage the Union efforts to keep the railroad open. Because the spy tells Farquhar about the punishment, the reader assumes that Farquhar had tried the sabotage, was caught, and now is going to be hanged. The third scene is also at the bridge, but it is about what Farquhar

B

The setting of Bierce's "An Occurrence at Owl Creek Bridge" is a major element in the development of the story. The railroad bridge in northern Alabama, from which the doomed Peyton Farquhar will be hanged, is a frame for the story. The bridge, which begins as the real-life bridge in the first scene, becomes the bridge that the dying man imagines in the third. In between there is a brief scene at Farquhar's home, which took place a week before. The setting thus marks the progression of Farquhar's dying vision. He begins to distort and slow down reality—at the real bridge—when he realizes that there is no escape. The first indication of this distortion is that his watch seems to be ticking as slowly as a blacksmith's hammer. Once he is dropped from the bridge to be hanged, his perceptions slow down time so much that he imagines his complete escape before his death: falling into the water, freeing himself, being shot at, getting to shore, walking through a darkening forest, and returning home in beautiful morn-

sees and thinks in his own mind: He imagines that he has been hanged and then escapes. He thinks he falls into the creek, frees himself from the ropes, and makes it to shore, from which he makes the long walk home. His final thoughts are of his wife coming out of the house to meet him, with everything looking beautiful in the morning sunshine. Then we find out that all this was just in his mind, because we are back on the bridge, from which Farquhar is swinging, hanged, dead, with a broken neck.

ing sunshine. The final sentence brutally restores the real setting of the railroad bridge and makes clear that Farquhar is actually dead despite his imaginings. In all respects, therefore, the setting is essential to the story's development.

Column A begins well and introduces important details of the story's setting, but it does not address the question because it does not show how the details figure into the story's development. On the other hand, column B focuses directly on the connection between the locations and the changes in the protagonist's perceptions. Because of this emphasis, B is shorter than A; with the focus directly on the issue, there is no need for irrelevant narrative details. Thus, A is unresponsive and unnecessarily long, whereas B is responsive and includes details only if they exemplify the major points.

☝ PREPARATION

Your challenge is how best to prepare yourself to have a knowledgeable and ready mind at examination time. If you simply cram facts into your head for the examination in the hope that you can adjust to the questions, you will likely flounder. You need a systematic approach.

Read and Reread the Material on Which You Are to Be Examined

Above all, keep in mind that your preparation should begin as soon as the course begins, not on the night before the exam. Complete each assignment by the date it is due, for you will understand the classroom discussion only if you know the material (see also the guides for study in Chapter 1, pages 13–14). Then, about a week before the exam, review each assignment, preferably rereading everything completely. With this preparation, your study on the night before the exam will be fruitful and might be viewed as a climax of preparation, not the entire preparation.

Construct Your Own Questions:
Go on the Attack

To prepare yourself fully for an exam, read *actively*, not passively. Read with a goal, and *go on the attack* by anticipating test conditions—creating and answering your own practice questions. Don't waste time trying to guess the questions you think your instructor might ask. Guessing correctly might happen (and wouldn't you be happy if it did?), but do not turn your study into a game of chance. Instead, arrange the subject matter by asking yourself questions that help you get things straight.

How can you construct your own questions? It is not as hard as you might think. Your instructor may have announced certain topics or ideas to be tested on the exam, and you might develop questions from these, or you might apply general questions to the specifics of your assignments, as in the following examples:

1. *Ideas about a character and the interactions of characters* (see also Chapter 3). What is *A* like? How does *A* grow or change in the work? What does *A* learn or not learn that brings about the conclusion? To what degree does *A* represent a type or an idea? How does *B* influence *A*? Does a change in *C* bring about any corresponding change in *A*?

2. *Ideas about technical and structural questions.* These may be broad, covering everything from *point of view* (Chapter 6) to prosody and rhyme (Chapter 14). The best guide here is to study those technical aspects that have been discussed in class, for it is unlikely that you will be asked to go beyond the levels expected in classroom discussion.

3. *Ideas about events or situations.* What relationship does episode *A* have to situation *B*? Does *C's* thinking about situation *D* have any influence on the outcome of event *E*?

4. *Ideas about a problem* (see also Chapter 12). Why is character *A* or situation *X* this way and not that way? Is the conclusion justified by the ideas and events leading up to it?

Rephrase Your Notes as Questions

One of the best ways to construct questions is to adapt your classroom notes, because notes are the fullest record you have about your instructor's views. As you work with your notes, refer to passages from the text that were studied by the class or stressed by your instructor. If there is time, memorize as many important phrases or lines as you can; plan to incorporate these into your answers as evidence to support the points you make. Remember that it is useful to work not only with main ideas from your notes, but also with matters such as style, imagery, and organization.

Obviously, you cannot make questions from all your notes, and you will therefore need to select from those that seem most important. As an example, here is a short note from a classroom discussion of Shakespeare's *Hamlet*: "In a major respect, a study in how private problems get public, how a court conspiracy can produce disastrous national and even international consequences." Notice how you can devise practice questions from this note:

1. In what ways is *Hamlet* not only about private problems but also about public ones?
2. Why should the consequences of Claudius's murder of Hamlet's father be considered disastrous?

The principle shown here is that exam questions should never be asked just about *what* but should rather get into the issues of *why*. Observe that the first question therefore adapts the words *in what ways* to the phrasing of the note. For the second, the word *why* has been adapted. Either question forces pointed study, and neither asks you merely to describe events. Question 1 requires you to consider the wider political effects of Hamlet's hostility toward Claudius, including Hamlet's murder of Polonius and the subsequent madness of Ophelia. Question 2, with its emphasis on disaster, leads you to consider not only the ruination of the hopes and lives of those in the play but also the importance of young Fortinbras and the eventual establishment of Norwegian control over Denmark after Claudius and Hamlet are gone. If you spent fifteen or twenty minutes writing practice answers to these questions, you could be confident in taking an examination on the material, for it is likely that you could adapt your study answers to any exam question about the personal and political implications of Claudius's murder of his brother.

Practice Writing Questions
Even When Time Is Short

Whatever your subject, spend as much study time as possible making and answering your own questions. Remember also to work with your own remarks and the ideas you develop in the journal entries that you make when doing your regular assignments (see Chapter 1, pages 13–16). Many of these will give you additional ideas for your own questions, which you can practice along with the questions you develop from your notes.

Obviously, with limited study time, you will not be able to create your own questions and answers indefinitely. Even so, don't neglect asking and answering your own questions. If time is too short for full practice answers, write out the main heads, or topics, of an answer. When the press of time (or the need for sleep) no longer permits you to make even such a brief outline answer, keep thinking of questions and their answers on the way to the exam. *Never read passively or unresponsively, but always read with a creative, question-and-answer goal.* Think of studying as a prewriting experience.

The time you spend in this way will be valuable, for as you practice, you will develop control and therefore confidence. Often those who have difficulty with tests, or claim a phobia about them, prepare passively rather than actively. Your instructor's test questions compel responsiveness, thought, organization, and knowledgeable writing; but a passively prepared student is not ready for this challenge and therefore writes answers that are unresponsive and filled with summary. The grade for such a performance is low, and the student's fear of tests is reinforced. The best way to break such long-standing patterns of fear and uncertainty is active, creative study.

Study with a Classmate

Often the thoughts of another person can help you understand the material to be tested. Find a fellow student with whom you can work comfortably but also productively, for both of you together can help each other individually. In view of the need for steady preparation throughout a course, regular discussions about the material are a good idea. You might also make your joint study systematic by setting aside a specific evening or afternoon for work sessions. Many students have said that a major problem on the actual examination is their lack of familiarity with the way in which questions are phrased. Consequently, they need to interpret and understand the question before they begin answering it, and sometimes even may wind up by misunderstanding the question entirely. If you work with a fellow student, however, and trade questions, you will be gaining experience (and confidence) in dealing with this basic difficulty about exams. Working with someone else can be extremely rewarding, just as it can also be stimulating and instructive. Make the effort.

TWO BASIC TYPES OF QUESTIONS ABOUT LITERATURE

Generally, there are two types of questions on literature exams. Keep them in mind as you prepare. The first type is *factual*, or *mainly objective*, and the second is *general, comprehensive, broad*, or *mainly subjective*. Except for multiple-choice questions, very few questions are purely objective in a literature course.

Anticipate the Kinds of Factual Questions
That Might Be Asked

MULTIPLE-CHOICE QUESTIONS ASK YOU TO PICK THE MOST ACCURATE AND LIKELY ANSWERS.   Multiple-choice questions are mainly factual. Your instructor will most likely use them for short quizzes, usually on days when an assignment is due, to make sure that you are keeping up with the reading. Multiple-choice questions test your knowledge of facts and your ingenuity in perceiving subtleties of phrasing. On a literature exam, however, this type of question is rare.

IDENTIFICATION QUESTIONS ASK FOR ACCURACY, EXPLANATION, AND SOME INTERPRETATION.   Identification questions are more interesting and challenging because they require you both to know details and also to develop thoughts about them. This type of question will frequently be used as a check on the depth and scope of your reading. In fact, an entire exam could be composed of only identification questions, each demanding perhaps five minutes to write. Here are some typical examples of what you might be asked to identify:

1. *A character.* To identify a character, it is necessary to describe briefly the character's position, main activity, and significance. Let us assume that Montresor is the character to be identified. Our answer should state that he is the narrator of "The Cask of Amontillado" (position) who invites Fortunato into his wine vaults on the pretext of testing the quality of some new Amontillado wine (main activity). He is therefore the major cause of the action, and he embodies one of the story's themes, that the desire for revenge makes human beings diabolically cruel (significance). Under the category of "significance," of course, you might develop as many ideas as you have time for, but the short example here is a general model for most examinations.

2. *Incidents or situations.* To identify an incident or a situation (for example, "A woman mourns the death of her husband"), first describe the circumstances and the principal character involved in them (Mrs. Popov's reaction to her widowhood in Chekhov's play *The Bear*), and then try to demonstrate its significance in the work. That is, in *The Bear*, Mrs. Popov is mourning the death of her husband, and in the course of the play, Chekhov uses her feelings to show amusingly that life with real emotion is stronger than duty to the dead.

3. *Things, places, and dates.* Your instructor may ask you to identify a hair ribbon (Hawthorne's "Young Goodman Brown") or a beach (Arnold's "Dover Beach") or the date of Lowell's "Patterns" (1916). For dates, you may be given a leeway of five or ten years. What is important about a date is not so much exactness as historical and intellectual perspective. The date of "Patterns," for example, was the third year of World War I, and the poem consequently reflects a reaction against the protracted and senseless loss of life in war (even though details of the poem itself suggest an eighteenth-century war). To claim

"World War I" as the date of the poem would likely be acceptable as an answer if it happens that you cannot remember the exact date.

4. *Quotations.* You should remember enough of the text to identify a passage taken from it, or at least to make an informed guess. Generally, you should (1) locate the quotation, if you remember it, or else describe the probable location; (2) show the ways in which the quotation is typical of the content and style of the work you have read; and (3) describe the importance of the passage. If you suffer a momentary lapse of memory, write a reasoned and careful explanation of your guess. Even if your guess is wrong, the knowledge and cogency of your explanation should give you points.

TECHNICAL AND ANALYTICAL QUESTIONS AND PROBLEMS REQUIRE YOU TO RELATE KNOWLEDGE AND TECHNICAL UNDERSTANDING TO THE ISSUE. In a scale of ascending importance, the third and most difficult type of factual question relates to those matters with which this book has been concerned: technique, analysis, and problems. You might be asked to discuss the *setting, images, point of view,* or *important idea* of a work; you might be asked about the *tone* of a story or poem; or you might be asked to *explicate* a poem that may or may not be duplicated for your benefit (if it is not duplicated, woe to students who have not studied their assignments). Questions like these assume that you have technical knowledge, and they also ask you to examine the text within the limitations imposed by the terms.

Obviously, technical questions occur more frequently in advanced courses than in elementary ones, and the questions become more subtle as the courses become more advanced. Instructors of elementary courses may ask about ideas and problems but will likely not use many of the others unless they state their intentions to do so in advance, or unless technical terms have been studied in class.

Questions of this type are fairly long, perhaps allowing from fifteen to twenty-five minutes for each. If you have two or more of these questions, try to space your time sensibly; do not devote eighty percent of your time to one question and leave only twenty percent for the rest.

Understand How Your Responses to Factual Questions Will Be Judged and Graded

IDENTIFICATION QUESTIONS PROBE YOUR UNDERSTANDING AND APPLICATION OF FACTS. In all factual questions, your instructor is testing (1) your factual command and (2) your quickness in relating a part to the whole. Thus, suppose you are identifying the incident "a man kills a canary." It is correct to say that Glaspell's play *Trifles* is the location of the incident, that the murdered farmer John Wright was the killer, and that the canary belonged to his wife. Knowledge of these details clearly establishes that you know the facts. But a strong answer must go further. Even in the brief time you have for short answers, you should always connect the facts (1) to major causation in the work, (2) to an important idea or ideas, (3) to the development of the work, and (4) for a quotation, to the style. Time is short and you must be selective, but if you can make your answer move from facts to significance, you will always fashion superior responses. Along these lines, let us look at an answer identifying the action from *Trifles:*

> The action is from Glaspell's *Trifles.* The man who kills the bird is John Wright, and the owner is Mrs. Wright. The killing is important because it is shown as the final indignity in Mrs. Wright's desperate life, and it prompts her to strangle Wright in his sleep. It is thus the cause not only of the murder but also of the investigation bringing the officers and their wives onstage. In fact, the wringing of the bird's neck makes the play possible because it is the wives who discover the dead bird, and this discovery is the means by which Glaspell highlights them as the major characters in the play. Because the husband's brutal act shows how bleak the life of Mrs. Wright actually was, it dramatizes the lonely plight of women in a male-dominated way of life like that on the Wright farm. The discovery also raises the issue of legality and morality, because the two wives decide to conceal the evidence, therefore protecting Mrs. Wright from conviction and punishment.

Any of the points in this answer could be developed as a separate essay, but the paragraph is successful as a short answer because it goes beyond fact to deal with significance. Clearly, such answers are possible at the time of an exam only if you have devoted considerable thought to the various exam works beforehand. The more thinking and practicing you do before an exam, the better your answers will be. Remember this advice as an axiom: *You cannot write superior answers if you do not think extensively before the exam.* By studying well beforehand, you will be able to reduce surprise to an absolute minimum.

LONGER FACTUAL QUESTIONS PROBE YOUR KNOWLEDGE AND YOUR ABILITY TO ORGANIZE YOUR THOUGHTS. More extended factual questions also require more thoroughly developed organization. Remember that for these questions, your knowledge of essay writing is important, because the quality of your composition will determine a major share of your instructor's evaluation of your answers. It is therefore best to take several minutes to gather your thoughts together before you begin to write, because *a ten-minute planned answer is preferable to a twenty-five-minute unplanned answer.* You do not need to write every possible fact on each particular question. Of greater importance is the use to which you put the facts that you know and the organization of your answer. Use a sheet of scratch paper to jot down the facts that you remember and your ideas about them in relation to the question. Then put them together, phrase a thesis sentence, and use your facts to exemplify and support your thesis.

It is always necessary to begin your answer pointedly, using key words or phrases from the question or direction if possible, so that your answer will have thematic shape. You should never begin an answer with "Because" and then go on from there without referring again to the question. To be most responsive during the short time available for an exam, you should use the question as your guide for your answer. Let us suppose that you have the following question on your test: "How does Glaspell use details in *Trifles* to reveal the character of Minnie Wright?" The most common way to go astray on such a question—and the easiest thing to do also—is to concentrate on Mrs. Wright's character rather than on how Glaspell uses detail to bring out her character. The word *how* makes a vast difference in the nature of the final answer, and hence a good method on the exam is to duplicate key phrases in the question to ensure that you make your major points clear. Here is an opening sentence that uses the key words and phrases (italicized here) from the question to direct thought and provide focus:

> Glaspell *uses details* of setting, marital relationships, and personal habits *to reveal the character of Mrs. Wright* as a person of great but unfulfilled potential whom anger has finally overcome.

Because this sentence repeats the key phrases from the question and also because it promises to show *how* the details are to be focused on the character, it suggests that the answer to follow will be responsive.

General or Comprehensive Questions Require You to Connect a Number of Works to Broader Matters of Idea and Technique

General or comprehensive questions are particularly important on final examinations, when your instructor is testing your total comprehension of the course material. Considerable time is usually allowed for answering this type of question, which can be phrased in a number of ways:

1. A *direct question* asking about philosophy, underlying attitudes, main ideas, characteristics of style, backgrounds, and so on. Here are some possible questions in this category:

   What use do _____, _____, and _____ make of the topic of _____?

   Define and characterize the short story as a genre of literature.

   Explain the use of dialogue by Hawthorne and Maupassant.

   Contrast the technique of point of view as used by _____, _____, and _____.

2. A *"comment" question*, often based on an extensive quotation, borrowed from a critic or written by your instructor for the occasion, asking about a broad class of writers, a literary movement, or the like. Your instructor may ask you to treat this question broadly (taking in many writers) or else to apply the quotation to a specific writer.

3. A *"suppose" question*, such as "What advice might Minnie Wright of *Trifles* give the speakers of Lowell's 'Patterns' and Keats's 'Bright Star'?" or "What might the speaker of Rossetti's poem 'Echo' say if she learned that her dead lover was Goodman Brown of Hawthorne's 'Young Goodman Brown'?" Although "suppose" questions might seem whimsical at first sight, they have a serious design and should prompt original and radical thinking. The first question, for example, should cause a test writer to bring out, from Minnie Wright's perspective, that the love of both speakers was not actual, but potential. She would likely sympathize with the speaker of "Patterns," but she might also say that the lost married life might not have been as ideal as the speaker assumes. For the speaker of "Bright Star," a male, Mrs. Wright might say that the steadfast love he seeks should also be linked to kindness and toleration as well as passion.

Although "suppose" questions (and answers) are speculative, the need to respond to them requires a detailed consideration of the works involved, and in this respect the "suppose" question is a salutary means of learning. It is of course difficult to prepare for a "suppose" question, which you can therefore regard as a test not only of your knowledge but also of your inventiveness and ingenuity.

Understand How Your Responses to General and Comprehensive Questions Will Be Judged and Graded

When answering broad, general questions, you are dealing with an unstructured situation, and not only must you supply an *answer* but—equally important—you also must also create a *structure* within which your answer can have meaning. You might say that you make up your own specific question out of the original general question. If you were asked to consider the role of women as seen in works by Lowell, Maupassant, and Glaspell, for example, you would structure the question by focusing a number of clearly defined topics. A possible way to begin answering such a question might be this:

Lowell, Maupassant, and Glaspell present a view of female resilence by demonstrating the inner control, endurance, and power of adaptation of their major characters.

With this sort of focus, you would be able to proceed point by point, introducing supporting data as you form your answer.

As a general rule, the best method for answering a comprehensive question is comparison-contrast (see also Chapter 13). The reason is that in dealing with, say, a general question on Rossetti, Chekhov, and Keats, it is too easy to write *three* separate essays rather than *one*. Thus, you should try to create a topic such as "The treatment of real or idealized love" or "The difficulties in male-female relationships," and then to develop your answer point by point rather than writer by writer. By creating your answer in this way, you can bring in references to each or all of the writers as they become relevant. If you were to treat each writer separately, your comprehensive answer would lose focus and effectiveness, and it would be needlessly repetitive.

Remember that in judging your response to a general question, your instructor is interested in seeing (1) how effectively you perceive and explain the significant issues in the question, (2) how intelligently and clearly you organize your answer, and (3) how persuasively you use materials from the work as supporting evidence.

Bear in mind that in answering comprehensive questions, you don't have complete freedom. What you have is the *freedom to create your own structure*. The underlying idea of the comprehensive, general question is that you possess special knowledge and insights that cannot be discovered by more factual questions. You must therefore formulate your own responses to the material and introduce evidence that reflects your own insights and command of information.

Two final words: Good luck.

appendix a

Critical Approaches Important in the Study of Literature

A number of critical theories or approaches for understanding and interpreting literature are available to critics and students alike. Many of these have been developed during the twentieth century to create a discipline of literary studies comparable with disciplines in the natural and social sciences. Literary critics have often borrowed liberally from other disciplines (e.g., history, psychology, anthropology) but have primarily aimed at developing literature as a study in its own right.

At the heart of the various critical approaches are many fundamental questions: What is literature? What does it do? Is its concern only to tell stories, or is it to express emotions? Is it private? Public? How does it get its ideas across? What more does it do than express ideas? How valuable was literature in the past, and how valuable is it now? What can it contribute to intellectual, artistic, and social history? To what degree is literature an art, as opposed to an instrument for imparting knowledge? How is literature used, and how and why is it misused? What theoretical and technical expertise may be invoked to enhance literary studies?

Questions such as these indicate that criticism is concerned not only with reading and interpreting stories, poems, and plays, but also with establishing theoretical understanding. Because of such extensive aims, you will understand that a full explanation and illustration of the approaches would fill the pages of a long book. The following descriptions are therefore intended as no more than brief introductions. Bear in mind that in the hands of skilled critics, the approaches are so subtle, sophisticated, and complex that they are not only critical stances but also philosophies.

Although the various approaches provide widely divergent ways to study literature and literary problems, they reflect major tendencies rather than absolute straitjacketing. Not every approach is appropriate for every work, nor are the approaches always mutually exclusive. Even the most devoted practitioners of the methods do not pursue them rigidly. In addition, some of the approaches are more "user-friendly" for certain types of discovery than others. To a degree at least, most critics therefore utilize methods that technically belong to one or more of the other approaches. A critic stressing the topical/historical approach, for example, might introduce the close study of a work that is associated with the method of the New Criticism. Similarly, a psychoanalytical critic might include details about archetypes. In short, a great deal of criticism is *pragmatic* or *eclectic* rather than rigid.

The approaches to be considered here are these: moral/intellectual; topical/historical; New Critical/formalist; structuralist; feminist; economic determinist/Marxist; psychological/psychoanalytic; archetypal/symbolic/ mythic; deconstructionist; and reader-response.

The object of learning about these approaches, like everything in this book, is to help you develop your own reading and writing. Accordingly, following each of the descriptions there is a brief paragraph showing how Hawthorne's story "Young Goodman Brown" (page 327) might be considered in the light of the particular approach. The paragraph following the discussion of structuralism, for example, shows how the structuralist approach can be applied to Goodman Brown and his story, and so also with the feminist approach, the economic determinist approach, and the others. Whenever you are doing your own writing about literature, you are free to use the various approaches as part or all of your assignment, as you believe the approach may help you.

☙ MORAL/INTELLECTUAL

The moral/intellectual approach is concerned with content and values (see also Chapter 7). The approach is as old as literature itself, for literature is a traditional mode of imparting morality, philosophy, and religion. The concern in moral/intellectual criticism is not only to discover meaning but also to determine whether works of literature are both *true* and *significant*.

To study literature from the moral/intellectual perspective is therefore to determine whether a work conveys a lesson or a message and whether it can help readers lead better lives and improve their understanding of the world: What ideas does the work contain? How strongly does the work bring forth its ideas? What application do the ideas have to the work's characters and situations? How may the ideas be evaluated intellectually? Morally? Discussions based on such questions do not imply that literature is primarily a medium of moral and intellectual exhortation. Ideally, moral/ intellectual criticism should differ from sermonizing to the degree that readers should always be left with their own decisions about whether they wish to assimilate the content of a work and about whether this content is personally or morally acceptable.

Sophisticated critics have sometimes demeaned the moral/intellectual approach on the grounds that "message hunting" reduces a work's artistic value by treating it like a sermon or political speech; but the approach will be valuable as long as readers expect literature to be applicable to their own lives.

Example

"Young Goodman Brown" raises the issue of how an institution designed for human elevation, such as the religious system of colonial Salem, can be so ruinous. Does the failure result from the system itself or from the people who misunderstand it? Is what is true of religion as practiced by Brown also true of social and political institutions? Should any religious or political philosophy be given greater credence than goodwill and mutual trust? One of the major virtues of "Young Goodman Brown" is that it provokes questions like these but at the same time provides a number of satisfying answers. A particularly important one is that religious and moral beliefs should not be used to justify the condemnation of others. Another important answer is that attacks made from the refuge of a religion or group, such as Brown's puritanical judgment, is dangerous because it enables the judge to condemn without thought and without personal responsibility.

ᛘ TOPICAL/HISTORICAL

This traditional approach stresses the relationship of literature to its historical period, and for this reason it has had a long life. Although much literature may be applicable to many places and times, much of it also directly reflects the intellectual and social worlds of the authors. When was the work written? What were the circumstances that produced it? What major issues does it deal with? How does it fit into the author's career? Keats's poem "On First Looking Into Chapman's Homer," for example, is his excited response to his reading of one of the major literary works of Western civilization. Hardy's "Channel Firing" is an acerbic response to continued armament and preparation for war during the twentieth century.

The topical/historical approach investigates relationships of this sort, including the elucidation of words and concepts that today's readers may not immediately understand. Obviously, the approach requires the assistance of footnotes, dictionaries, library catalogues, histories, and handbooks.

A common criticism of the topical/historical approach is that in the extreme, it deals with background knowledge rather than with literature itself. It is possible, for example, for a topical/historical critic to describe a writer's life, the period of the writer's work, and the social and intellectual ideas of the time—all without ever considering the meaning, importance, and value of the work itself.

A reaction against such an unconnected use of historical details is the so-called *New Historicism*. This approach justifies the introduction of historical knowledge by integrating it with the understanding of particular texts. Readers of Arnold's "Dover Beach," for example, sometimes find it difficult fully to comprehend Arnold's statement "The Sea of Faith / Was once, too, at the full, . . ." If knowledge of the "Higher Criticism" of the Bible can be introduced, however, as a method established in Arnold's time by which the Bible was considered as a historical document rather than the absolute uncontaminated word of God, then the sense of his idea can be clarified. Because the introduction of such historical material is designed to facilitate the reading of the poem—and also the reading of other literature of the period—the New Historicism represents an integration of knowledge and interpretation. As a principle, New Historicism entails the acquisition of as much historical information as possible, because our knowledge of the relationship of literature to its historical period can never be complete. The practitioner of New Historicism must always seek new information on the grounds that it will be found to be relevant to literary works.

Example

"Young Goodman Brown" is an allegorical story by Nathaniel Hawthorne (1804–1864), a New England writer who probed deeply into the relationships between religion and guilt. His ancestors had been involved in religious persecutions, including the Salem witch trials, and he, living 150 years afterward, wanted to analyze the weaknesses and uncertainties of the sin-dominated religion of the earlier period, a tradition of which he was a resentful heir. Not surprisingly, therefore, "Young Goodman Brown" takes place in Puritan colonial Salem, and Hawthorne's implied judgments are those of a severe critic of how the harsh old religion destroyed personal and family relationships. Although the immediate concerns of the story belong to a vanished age, Hawthorne's treatment is still valuable because it is still timely.

☙ NEW CRITICAL/FORMALIST

New Criticism has been a dominant force in twentieth-century literary studies. To the degree that it focuses upon literary texts as formal works of art, it departs from the traditional topical/historical approach. The objection raised by New Critics is that as topical/historical critics consider literary history, they evade direct contact with actual texts.

The inspiration for the formalist or New Critical approach was the French practice of explication de texte, a method that emphasizes detailed examination and explanation. The New Criticism is at its most brilliant in the formal analysis of smaller units such as entire poems and short passages. For the analysis of larger structures, the New Criticism also utilizes a number of techniques that form the basis for chapters in this book. Discussions of point of view, tone, plot, character, and structure, for example, are formal ways of looking at literature that are derived from the New Criticism.

The aim of the formalist study of literature is to provide readers not only with the means of explaining the content of works (What, specifically, does a work say?) but also with the insights needed for evaluating the artistic quality of individual works and writers (How well is it said?). A major aspect of New Critical thought is that content and form—including all ideas, ambiguities, subtleties, and even apparent contradictions—were originally within the conscious or subconscious control of the author. There are no accidents. It does not necessarily follow, however, that today's critic is able to define the author's intentions exactly, for such intentions require knowledge of biographical details that are irretrievably lost. Each literary work therefore takes on its own existence and identity, and the critic's work is to discover a reading or readings that explain the facts of the text. Note that the New Critic does not claim infallible interpretations and does not exclude the validity of multiple readings of the same work.

Dissenters from the New Criticism have noted a tendency by New Critics to ignore relevant knowledge that history and biography can bring to literary studies. In addition, the approach has been subject to the charge that stressing the explication of texts alone fails to deal with literary value and appreciation. In other words, the formalist critic, in explaining the meaning of literature, sometimes neglects the reasons for which readers find literature stimulating and valuable.

Example

A major aspect of Hawthorne's "Young Goodman Brown" is that the details are so vague and dreamlike that many readers are uncertain about what is happening. The action is a nighttime walk by the protagonist, Young Goodman Brown, into a deep forest where he encounters a mysterious satanic ritual that leaves him bitter and misanthropic. This much seems clear, but the precise nature of Brown's experience is not clear, nor is the identity of the stranger (father, village elder, devil) who accompanies Brown as he begins his walk. At the story's end Hawthorne's narrator states that the whole episode may have been no more than a dream or nightmare. Yet when morning comes, Brown walks back into town as though returning from an overnight trip, and he recoils in horror from his fellow villagers, including his wife Faith (paragraph 70). Could his attitude result from nothing more than a nightmare?

Even at the story's end these uncertainties remain. For this reason one may conclude that Hawthorne deliberately creates the uncertainties to reveal how persons like Brown build defensive walls of judgment around themselves. The story thus implies that the real source of Brown's anger is as vague as his nocturnal walk, but he doesn't understand it in this way. Because Brown's vision and judgment are absolute, he rejects everyone around him, even if the cost is a life of bitter suspicion and spiritual isolation.

⚘ STRUCTURALIST

The principle of structuralism stems from the attempt to find relationships and connections among elements that appear to be separate and discrete. Just as physical science reveals unifying universal principles of matter such as gravity and the forces of electromagnetism (and is constantly searching for a "unified field theory"), structuralism attempts to discover the forms unifying all literature. Thus a structural description of Maupassant's "The Necklace" stresses that the main character, Mathilde, is an *active* protagonist who undergoes a *test* (or series of tests) and emerges with a victory, though not the kind she had originally hoped for. The same might be said of Mrs. Popov and Smirnov in Chekhov's *The Bear*. If this same kind of structural view is applied to Bierce's "An Occurrence at Owl Creek Bridge," the protagonist is defeated in the test. Generally, the structural approach applies such patterns to other works of literature to determine that some protagonists are active or submissive, that they pass or fail their tests, or that they succeed or fail at other encounters. The key is that many apparently unrelated works reveal many common patterns or contain similar structures with important variations.

The structural approach is important because it enables critics to discuss works from widely separate cultures and historical periods. In this respect, critics have followed the leads of modern anthropologists, most notably Claude Lévi-Strauss (1908–1990). Along such lines, critics have undertaken the serious examination of folk and fairy tales. Some of the groundbreaking structuralist criticism, for example, was devoted to the structural principles underlying folktales of Russia. The method also bridges popular and serious literature, making little distinction between the two insofar as the description of the structures is concerned. Indeed, structuralism furnishes an ideal approach for comparative literature, and the method also enables critics to consolidate genres such as modern romances, detective tales, soap operas, and film.

Like the New Criticism, structuralism aims at comprehensiveness of description, and many critics would insist that the two are complementary and not separate. A distinction is that the New Criticism is at its best in dealing with smaller units of literature, whereas structuralism is best in the analysis of narratives and therefore larger units such as novels, myths, and stories. Because structuralism shows how fiction is organized into various typical situations, the approach merges with the *archetypal* approach, and at times it is difficult to find any distinctions between structuralism and archetypalism.

Structuralism, however, deals not just with narrative structures but also with structures of any type, wherever they occur. For example, structuralism makes great use of linguistics. Modern linguistic scholars have determined that there is a difference between "deep structures" and "surface structures" in language. A structuralist analysis of style, therefore, emphasizes how writers utilize such structures. The structuralist interpretation of language also perceives distinguishing types or "grammars" of language that are recurrent in various types of literature. Suppose, for example, that you encounter opening passages like the following:

> Once upon a time a young prince fell in love with a young princess. He decided to tell her of his love, and early one morning he left his castle on his white charger, riding toward her castle home high in the mountains.

> Early that morning, Alan had found himself thinking about Anne. He had believed her when she said she loved him, but his feelings about her were not certain, and his thinking had left him still unsure.

The words of these two passages create different and distinct frames of reference. One is a fairy tale of the past, the other a modern internalized reflection of feeling. The passages therefore demonstrate how language itself fits into predetermined patterns or structures. Similar uses of language structures can be associated with other types of literature.

Example

Young Goodman Brown is a hero who is passive, not active. He is a *witness*, a *receiver* rather than a *doer*. His only action—taking his trip in the forest—occurs at the story's beginning. After that point, he no longer acts but instead is acted upon, and what he sees puts his life's beliefs to a test. Of course, many protagonists undergo similar testing (such as rescuing victims and slaying particularly terrible dragons), and they emerge triumphant. Not so with Goodman Brown. He is a responder who allows himself to be victimized by his own perceptions—or misperceptions. Despite all his previous experiences with his wife and with the good people of his village, he generalizes too hastily. He lets the single disillusioning experience of his nightmare govern his entire outlook on others, and thus he fails his test and turns his entire life into failure.

₹ FEMINIST

The feminist approach holds that most of our literature presents a masculine-patriarchal view in which the role of women is negated or at best minimized. As an adjunct of the feminist movement in politics, the feminist critique of literature seeks to raise consciousness about the importance and unique nature of women in literature.

Specifically, the feminist view attempts (1) to show that writers of traditional literature have ignored women and have also transmitted misguided and prejudiced views of them, (2) to stimulate the creation of a critical milieu that reflects a balanced view of the nature and value of women, (3) to recover the works of women writers of past times and to encourage the publication of present women writers so that the literary canon can be expanded to recognize women as thinkers and artists, and (4) to urge transformations in the language so as to eliminate inequities and inequalities that result from linguistic distortions.

In form, the feminist perspective seeks to evaluate various literary works from the standpoint of the presentation of women. For works such as "The Necklace" (story), "Patterns" (poem), and *The Bear* (play), a feminist critique focuses on how such works treat women and also on either the shortcomings or enlightenment of the author as a result of this treatment: How important are the female characters, how individual in their own right? Are they credited with their own existence and their own character? In their relationships with men, how are they treated? Are they given equal status? Ignored? Patronized? Demeaned? Pedestalized? How much interest do the male characters exhibit about women's concerns?

Example

At the beginning of "Young Goodman Brown," Brown's wife, Faith, is only peripheral. In the traditional patriarchal spirit of wife-as-adjunct, she asks her husband to stay at home and take his journey at another time. Hawthorne does not give her the intelligence or dignity, however, to let her explain her concern (or might he not have been interested in what she had to say?), and she therefore remains in the background with her pink hair ribbon as her distinguishing characteristic. During the midforest satanic ritual she appears again and is given power, but only the power to cause her husband to go astray. Once she is led in as a novice in the practice of demonism, her husband falls right in step. Unfortunately, by following her, Brown can conveniently excuse himself from guilt by claiming that "she" had made him do it, just as Eve, in some traditional views of the fall of humankind, compelled Adam to eat the apple (Genesis 3:16–17). Hawthorne's attention to the male hero, in other words, permits him to distort the female's role.

☞ ECONOMIC DETERMINIST/MARXIST

The concept of cultural and economic determinism is one of the major political ideas of the last century. Karl Marx (1818–1883) emphasized that the primary influence on life was economic, and he saw society as an opposition between the capitalist and working classes. The literature that emerged from this kind of analysis features individuals in the grips of the class struggle. Often called "proletarian literature," it emphasizes persons of the lower class—the poor and oppressed who spend their lives in endless drudgery and misery, and whose attempts to rise above their disadvantages usually result in renewed suppression.

Marx's political ideas were never widely accepted in the United States and have faded still more after the political breakup of the Soviet Union, but the idea of economic determinism (and the related term *Social Darwinism*) is still credible. As a result, much literature can be judged from an economic perspective: What is the economic status of the characters? What happens to them as a result of this status? How do they fare against economic and political odds? What other conditions stemming from their class does the writer emphasize (e.g., poor education, poor nutrition, poor health care, inadequate opportunity)? To what extent does the work fail by overlooking the economic, social, and political implications of its material? In what other ways does economic determinism affect the work? How should readers consider the story in today's developed or underdeveloped world? Seemingly, Hawthorne's story "Young Goodman Brown," which we have used for analysis in these discussions, has no economic implications, but an economically oriented discussion might take the following turns:

Example

"Young Goodman Brown" is a fine story just as it is. It deals with the false values instilled by the skewed acceptance of sin-dominated religion, but it overlooks the economic implications of this situation. One suspects that the real story in the little world of Goodman Brown's Salem should be about survival and the disruption that an alienated member of society can produce. After Brown's condemnation and distrust of others forces him into his own shell of sick imagination, Hawthorne does not consider how such a disaffected character would injure the economic and public life of the town. Consider this, just for a moment: Why would the people from whom Brown recoils in disgust want to deal with him in business or personal matters? In town meetings, would they want to follow his opinions on crucial issues of public concern and investment? Would his preoccupation with sin and damnation make him anything more than a horror in his domestic life? Would his wife, Faith, be able to discuss household management with him, or how to take care of the children? All these questions of course are pointed toward another story—a story that

Hawthorne did not write. They also indicate the shortcomings of Hawthorne's approach, because it is clear that the major result of Young Goodman Brown's selfish preoccupation with evil would be a serious disruption of the economic and political affairs of his small community.

🦌 PSYCHOLOGICAL/PSYCHOANALYTIC

The scientific study of the mind is a product of psychodynamic theory as established by Sigmund Freud (1856–1939) and of the psychoanalytic method practiced by his followers. Psychoanalysis provided a new key to the understanding of character by claiming that behavior is caused by hidden and unconscious motives. It was greeted as a virtual revelation, and not surprisingly it had a profound effect on twentieth-century literature.

In addition, its popularity produced a psychological/psychoanalytic approach to criticism.[1] Some critics use the approach to explain fictional characters, as in the landmark interpretation by Freud and Ernest Jones that Shakespeare's Hamlet suffers from an Oedipus complex. Still other critics use it as a way of analyzing authors and the artistic process. For example, John Livingston Lowes's *The Road to Xanadu* presents a detailed examination of the mind, reading, and neuroses of Coleridge, the author of "Kubla Khan" (page 353).

Critics using the psychoanalytic approach treat literature somewhat like information about patients in therapy. In the work itself, what are the obvious and hidden motives that cause a character's behavior and speech? How much background (e.g., repressed childhood trauma, adolescent memories) does the author reveal about a character? How purposeful is this information with regard to the character's psychological condition? How much is important in the analysis and understanding of the character?

In the consideration of authors, critics utilizing the psychoanalytic model consider questions like these: What particular life experiences explain characteristic subjects or preoccupations? Was the author's life happy? Miserable? Upsetting? Solitary? Social? Can the death of someone in the author's family be associated with melancholy situations in that author's work? (All eleven brothers and sisters of the English poet Thomas Gray, for example, died before reaching adulthood. Gray was the only one to survive. In his poetry, Gray often deals with death, and he is therefore considered as one of the "Graveyard School" of eighteenth-century poets. A psychoanalytical critic might make much of this connection.)

---

[1]See also Chapter 3: Writing About Character: The People in Literature.

Example

At the end of "Young Goodman Brown," Hawthorne's major character is no longer capable of normal existence. His nightmare should be read as a symbol of what in reality would have been lifelong mental subjection to the type of puritanical religion that emphasizes sin and guilt. Such preoccupation with sin is no hindrance to psychological health if the preoccupied people are convinced that God forgives them and grants them mercy. In their dealings with others, they remain healthy as long as they believe that other people have the same sincere trust in divine forgiveness. If their own faith is weak and uncertain, however, and they cannot believe in forgiveness, then they are likely to project their own guilt—really a form of personal terror—onto others. They remain conscious of their own sins, but they find it easy to claim that others are sinful—even those who are spiritually spotless, and even their own family, who should be dearest to them. When this process of projection occurs, such people have created the rationale of condemning others because of their own guilt. The price that they pay is a life of gloom, a fate that Hawthorne designates for Goodman Brown after the nightmare about demons in human form.

ARCHETYPAL/SYMBOLIC/MYTHIC

The archetypal approach, derived from the work of the Swiss psychoanalyst Carl Jung (1875–1961), presupposes that human life is built up out of patterns, or *archetypes* ("first molds" or "first patterns"), that are similar throughout various cultures and historical times.[2] The approach is similar to the structuralist analysis of literature, for both approaches stress the connections that may be discovered in literature written in different times and in vastly different locations in the world.

In literary evaluation, the archetypal approach is used to support the claim that the very best literature is grounded in archetypal patterns. The archetypal critic therefore looks for archetypes such as God's creation of human beings, the sacrifice of a hero, or the search for paradise. How does an individual story, poem, or play fit into any of the archetypal patterns? What truths does this correlation provide (particularly truths that cross historical, national, and cultural lines)? How closely does the work fit the archetype? What variations can be seen? What meaning or meanings do the connections have?

The most tenuous aspect of archetypal criticism is Jung's assertion that the recurring patterns provide evidence for a "universal human consciousness" that all of us, by virtue of our humanity, still retain in our minds and in our very blood.

[2]Symbolism is also considered in Chapter 10.

Not all critics accept the hypothesis of a universal human consciousness, but they nevertheless consider the approach important for comparisons and contrasts (see Chapter 13). Many human situations, such as adolescence, dawning love, the search for success, the reconciliation with one's mother and father, and the encroachment of age and death, are similar in structure and can be analyzed as archetypes. For example, the following situations can be seen as a pattern or archetype of initiation: A young man discovers the power of literature and understanding ("On First Looking Into Chapman's Homer"); a man determines the importance of truth and fidelity amidst uncertainty ("Dover Beach"); a man and woman fall in love despite their wishes to remain independent (*The Bear*); a woman gains strength and integrity because of previously unrealized inner resources ("The Necklace"). The archetypal approach encourages the analysis of variations on the same theme, as in Glaspell's *Trifles,* when the two women develop their impromptu cover-up of the crime (one sort of initiation) and also begin to assert their freedom of thought and action independent of their husbands (another sort of initiation).

Example

In the sense that Young Goodman Brown undergoes a change from psychological normality to rigidity, the story is a reverse archetype of the initiation ritual. According to the archetype of successful initiation, initiates seek to demonstrate their worthiness to become full-fledged members of society. Telemachus in Homer's *Odyssey,* for example, is a young man who in the course of the epic goes through the initiation rituals of travel, discussion, and battle. But in "Young Goodman Brown," we see initiation in reverse, for just as there is an archetype of successful initiation, Brown's initiation leads him into failure. In the private areas of life on which happiness depends, he falls short. He sees evil in his fellow villagers, condemns his own minister, and shrinks even from his own family. His life is one of despair and gloom. His suspicions are those of a Puritan of long ago, but the timeliness of Hawthorne's story is that the archetype of misunderstanding and condemnation has not changed. Today's headlines of misery and war are produced by the same kind of intolerance that is exhibited by Goodman Brown.

🕯 DECONSTRUCTIONIST

The *deconstructionist* approach—which deconstructionists explain not as an approach but rather as a performance—was developed by the French critic Jacques Derrida (b. 1930). In the 1970s and 1980s, it became a major but also controversial mode of criticism. As a literary theory, deconstructionism produces a type of analysis that stresses ambiguity and contradiction.

A major principle of deconstructionism is that Western thought has been *logocentric;* that is, Western philosophers have based their ideas on the assumption that central truth is knowable and entire (this view is incorrect, according to a deconstructionist). The deconstructionist view is instead that there is no central truth because circumstances and time, which are changeable and sometimes arbitrary, govern the world of the intellect. This analysis leads to the declaration "All interpretation is misinterpretation." That is, literary works cannot be encapsulated as organically unified entireties, and therefore there is not *one correct interpretation* but only *interpretations,* each one possessing its own validity.

In "deconstructing" a work, therefore, the deconstructionist critic raises questions about what other critics have claimed about the work: Is a poem accepted as a model of classicism? Then it also exhibits qualities of romanticism. Is a story about a young Native American's flight from school commonly taken as a criticism of modern urban life? Then it may also be taken as a story of the failure of youth. In carrying out such criticism, deconstructionist critics place heavy emphasis on the ideas contained in terms such as *ambivalence, discrepancy, enigma, uncertainty, delusion, indecision,* and *lack of resolution,* among others.

The deconstructionist attack on "correct," "privileged," or "accepted" readings is also related to the principle that language, and therefore literature, is unstable. "Linguistic instability" means that the understanding of words can never be exact or comprehensive because there is a never-ending *play* between the words in a text and their many shades of meaning, including possible future meanings. That is, the words do not remain constant and produce a definite meaning, but instead call forth the possibility of "infinite substitutions" of meaning. Each work of literature is therefore ambiguous and uncertain because its full meaning is constantly *deferred.* This infinite play or semantic tension renders language unstable and makes correct or accepted readings impossible.

It is fair to state that deconstructionism, among all the literary theories, has received intense criticism that has sometimes bordered on discrediting the theory entirely. A number of critics find that the position is elusive and vague. They grant that literary works are often ambiguous, uncertain, and apparently contradictory, but explain that the cause of these conditions is not linguistic instability but rather authorial intention. They also point out that the deconstructionist linguistic analysis is derivative, unoriginal, and incorrect. In addition, critics claim that the deconstructionist linguistic position simply does not support deconstructionist assertions about linguistic instability. Critics also draw attention to the contradiction that deconstructionism cannot follow its major premise about there being no "privileged readings" because it must recognize the privileged readings in order to invalidate or "subvert" them.

Example

There are many uncertainties in the details of "Young Goodman Brown." If one starts with the stranger on the path, one might conclude that he could be Brown's father, because he recognizes Brown immediately and speaks to him jovially. On the other hand, the stranger could be the devil (he is recognized as such by Goody Cloyse) because of his wriggling walking stick. After disappearing, the stranger also takes on the characteristics of an omniscient cult leader and seer, because at the satanic celebration he knows all the secret sins committed by Brown's neighbors and the community of greater New England. Additionally, he might represent a perverted conscience whose aim is to mislead and befuddle people by steering them into the holier-than-thou judgmentalism that Brown adopts. This method would be truly diabolical—to use religion in order to bring people to their own damnation. That the stranger is an evil force is therefore clear, but the pathways of his evil are not as clear. He seems to work his mission of damnation by reaching souls like that of Goodman Brown through means ordinarily attributed to conscience. If the stranger represents a satanic conscience, what are we to suppose that Hawthorne is asserting about what is considered real conscience?

⚛ READER-RESPONSE

The theory of reader-response is rooted in *phenomenology*, a branch of philosophy that deals with "the understanding of how things appear." The phenomenological idea of knowledge is that reality is to be found not in the external world itself but rather in the mental *perception* of externals. That is, all that we human beings can know—actual *knowledge*—is our collective and personal understanding of the world and our conclusions about it.

As a consequence of the phenomenological concept, reader-response theory holds that the reader is a necessary third party in the author-text-reader relationship that constitutes the literary work. The work, in other words, is not fully created until readers make a *transaction* with it by assimilating it and *actualizing* it in the light of their own knowledge and experience. The representative questions of the theory are these: What does this work mean to me, in my present intellectual and moral makeup? What particular aspects of my life can help me understand and appreciate the work? How can the work improve my understanding and widen my insights? How can my increasing understanding help me understand the work more deeply? The theory is that the free interchange or transaction that such questions bring about leads toward interest and growth so that readers can assimilate literary works and accept them as part of their lives.

As an initial way of reading, the reader-response method may be personal and anecdotal. In addition, by stressing response rather than interpretation, one of the leading exponents of the method (Stanley Fish) has raised the extreme question about whether texts, by themselves, have objective identity. These aspects have been cited as both a shortcoming and an inconsequentiality of the method.

It is therefore important to stress that the reader-response theory is *open*. It permits beginning readers to bring their own personal reactions to literature, but it also aims to increase the discipline and skills of readers. The more that readers bring to literature through their interests and disciplined studies, the more "competent" and comprehensive their responses will be. With cumulative experience, the disciplined reader will habitually adjust to new works and respond to them with increasing skill. If the works require special knowledge in fields such as art, politics, science, philosophy, religion, or morality, then competent readers will seek out such knowledge and utilize it in developing their responses. Also, because students experience many similar intellectual and cultural disciplines, it is logical to conclude that responses will tend not to diverge but rather to coalesce; agreements result not from personal but from cultural similarities. The reader-response theory, then, can and should be an avenue toward informed and detailed understanding of literature, but the initial emphasis is the *transaction* between readers and literary works.

Example

"Young Goodman Brown" is worrisome because it shows so disturbingly that good intentions may cause harmful results. I think that a person with too high a set of expectations is ripe for disillusionment, just as Goodman Brown is. When people don't measure up to this person's standard of perfection, they can be thrown aside as though they are worthless. They may be good, but their past mistakes make it impossible for the person with high expectations to endure them. I have seen this situation occur among some of my friends and acquaintances, particularly in romantic relationships. Goodman Brown makes the same kind of misjudgment, expecting perfection and turning sour when he learns about flaws. It is not that he is not a good man, because he is shown at the start as a person of belief and stability. He uncritically accepts his nightmare revelation that everyone else is evil, however (including his parents), and he finally distrusts everyone because of this baseless suspicion. He cannot look at his neighbors without avoiding them like an "anathema," and he turns away from his own wife "without a greeting" (paragraph 70). Brown's problem is that he equates being human with being unworthy. By such a distorted standard of judgment, all of us fail, and that is what makes the story so disturbing.

appendix b

The Integration of Quotations and Other Important Details, and the Use of Tenses in Writing About Literature

In establishing evidence for the points you make in your essays and essay examinations, you constantly need to refer to various parts of stories, plays, and poems. You also need to include shorter and longer quotations and to keep time sequences straight within works. In addition, you may need to refer to biographical and historical details that have a bearing on the work or works you are studying. So that your own writing may flow as accurately and naturally as possible, it is most important for you to be able to integrate these references and time distinctions clearly and easily.

DISTINGUISH YOUR THOUGHTS FROM THOSE OF YOUR AUTHOR. Ideally, your essays should reflect your own thought as it is prompted and illustrated by an author's work. In a typical discussion of literature, you are constantly introducing paraphrase, general interpretations, observations, and independent applications of everything being discussed. It is not easy to keep these various elements integrated and to keep confusion from arising. Often the major problem is that it is hard for your reader to figure out when *your* ideas have stopped and your *author's* have begun. You must therefore arrange things to make the distinction clear, but you must also blend your materials so that your reader may follow you easily. Let us see an example of how such problems may be handled. Here, the writer being discussed is the Romantic poet William Wordsworth (1770–1850). The passage moves from reference to Wordsworth's ideas—really a paraphrase—to an independent application of the idea:

> [1] In the "Preface to the Lyrical Ballads," Wordsworth states that the language of poetry should be the same as that of prose. [2] That is, poetic diction should not be artificial or contrived in any sense, but should consist of the words normally used by people in their everyday lives (lines 791–793). [3] If one follows this principle in poetry, then it would be improper to refer to the sun as anything but *the sun*. [4] To call it a *heavenly orb* or the *source of golden gleams* would be inadmissible because these phrases are not used in common speech.

Here the first two sentences paraphrase Wordsworth's ideas about poetic diction, the second going so far as to locate a passage where Wordsworth develops the idea. The third and fourth sentences apply Wordsworth's idea to examples chosen by the writer. The blending is provided by the transitional clause, "If one follows this principle in poetry," and the reader is thus not confused about who is saying what.

INTEGRATE MATERIAL BY USING QUOTATION MARKS. You often find it necessary to use short quotations from your author to illustrate your ideas and interpretations. Here the problem of distinguishing your thoughts from the author's is solved by quotation marks. In such an internal quotation, you may treat prose and poetry in the same way. If a poetic quotation extends from the end of one line to the beginning of another, however, indicate the line break with a virgule (/), and use a capital letter to begin the next line, as in the following:

> Wordsworth states that in his boyhood all of nature seemed like his own personal property. Rocks, mountains, and woods were almost like food to him, and he claimed that "the sounding cataract / Haunted . . . [him] like a passion" (lines 76–80).

BLEND QUOTATIONS INTO YOUR OWN SENTENCES. Making internal quotations still creates the problem of blending materials, however, for quotations should never be brought in unless you prepare your reader for them in some way. *Do not*, for example, bring in quotations in the following manner:

> Alexander Pope's pastoral sky is darkened by thick clouds, bringing a feeling of gloom that is associated with the same feeling that can be sensed at a funeral. "See gloomy clouds obscure the cheerful day."

This abrupt quotation throws the reader off balance because it is not blended into the previous sentence. It is better to prepare the reader to move from the discourse to the quotation, as in the following revision:

Alexander Pope's pastoral scene is marked by sorrow and depression, as though the spectator, who is asked to "see gloomy clouds obscure the cheerful day," is present at a funeral.

Here the quotation is made an actual part of the sentence. This sort of blending is satisfactory, provided that the quotation is brief.

INDENT AND BLOCK LONG QUOTATIONS.   The standard for how to place quotations should be not to quote within a sentence any passage longer than twenty or twenty-five words (but consult your instructor, for the exact number of words allowable may vary). Quotations of greater length demand so much separate attention that they interfere with your own sentence. It is possible but not desirable to have one of your sentences conclude with a quotation, but you should never make an extensive quotation in the *middle* of a sentence. By the time you finish such an unwieldy sentence, your reader will have lost sight of how it began. When your quotation is long, you should make a point of introducing it and setting it off separately as a block.

The physical layout of block quotations should be as follows: Leave three blank lines between your own discourse and the quotation. Double-space the quotation (like the rest of your essay), and indent it five spaces from your left margin to distinguish it from your own writing. You might use fewer spaces for longer lines of poetry, but the standard should always be to create a balanced, neat page. After the quotation, leave a three-line space again, and resume your own discourse. Here is a specimen, from an essay about Wordsworth's "Lines Written in Early Spring":

In "Lines Written in Early Spring" Wordsworth develops an idea that the world of nature is linked directly to the moral human consciousness. He speaks of no religious systems or books of moral values. Instead, he derives his ideas directly from his experience, assuming that the world was made for the joy of the living creatures in it, including human beings ("man"), and that anyone disturbing that power of joy is violating "Nature's holy plan" itself. Wordsworth's moral criticism, in other words, is derived from his faith in the integrity of creation:

> If this belief from heaven be sent,
> If such be Nature's holy plan,
> Have I not reason to lament
> What man has made of man?
>   (lines 21–24)

This concept that morality and life are inextricably joined is the most interesting and engaging aspect of the poem. It seems to encourage a live-and-let-live attitude toward others, however, not an active program of direct outreach and help.

When quoting lines of poetry, always remember to quote them *as lines*. Do not run them together. When you create such block quotations, as in the preceding example, you do *not* need quotation marks.

Today, computer usage is becoming a more established means of preparing papers, and therefore computer styling is becoming prominent in the handling of the matters discussed here. If you have a style feature such as "Poem Text" or "Nest Paragraph," each of which sets block quotations apart from "Normal" text, you may certainly make use of the feature. Explain to your instructor, however, to make sure that your computer corresponds to expectations established in your class.

USE THREE SPACED PERIODS (AN *ELLIPSIS*) TO SHOW OMISSIONS. Whether your quotation is long or short, you will often need to change some of the material in it to conform to your own sentence requirements. You might wish to omit something from the quotation that is not essential to your point. Indicate such omissions with three spaced periods (. . .), as follows:

> Under the immediate threat of death, Farquhar's perceptions are sharpened and heightened. In actuality there is "swirling water . . . racing madly beneath his feet," but it is his mind that is racing swiftly, and he accordingly perceives that a "piece of dancing driftwood . . . down the current" moves so slowly that he believes the stream is "sluggish."

If your quotation is very brief, however, do not use spaced periods, as they might be more of a hindrance than a help. For example, do not use the three spaced periods in a quotation like this:

> Keats asserts that ". . . a thing of beauty . . ." always gives joy.

Instead, make your quotation without the ellipsis:

> Keats asserts that "a thing of beauty" always gives joy.

USE SQUARE BRACKETS TO INSERT YOUR OWN EXPLANATIONS WITHIN QUOTATIONS. If you add words of your own to integrate the quotation into your own train of discourse or to explain words that may seem obscure, put square brackets around these words, as in the following passage:

> In the "Tintern Abbey Lines," Wordsworth refers to a trance-like state, in which the "affections gently lead . . . [him] on." He is unquestionably describing a state of extreme relaxation, for he mentions that the "motion of . . . human

blood [was] / Almost suspended [i.e., his pulse slowed]" and that in these states he considered himself to be "a living soul" (lines 42–49).

DO NOT CHANGE YOUR SOURCE.   Always reproduce your source exactly. Although most anthologies modernize the spelling of older writers, the works of British authors may include words like *tyre* and *labour*. Also, you may encounter "old-spelling" editions in which all words are spelled exactly as they were centuries ago. Your principle should be *to duplicate everything exactly as you find it*, even if this means spelling words like *achieve* as *atchieve* or *joke* as *joak*. A student once took the liberty of amending the word *an* to "and" in the construction "an I were" in an Elizabethan text. The result was inaccurate, because in introductory clauses, *an* really meant *if* (or *and if*) and not *and*. Difficulties like this one are rare, but you can avoid them if you reproduce the text as you find it. Should you think that something is either misspelled or confusing as it stands, you may do one of two things:

1. Clarify or correct the confusing word or phrase within brackets, as in the following:

   In 1714, fencing was considered a "Gentlemany [i.e., gentlemanly] subject."

2. Use the word *sic* (Latin for *thus*, meaning "It is this way in the text") immediately after the problematic word or obvious mistake:

   He was just "finning [sic] his way back to health" when the next disaster struck.

DO NOT OVERQUOTE.   A word of caution: *Do not use too many quotations.* You will be judged on your own thought and on the continuity and development of your own essay. It is tempting to include many quotations on the theory that you need to use examples from the text to illustrate and support your ideas. Naturally, it is important to introduce examples, but realize that too many quotations can disturb the flow of *your own* thought. If your essay consists of many illustrations linked together by no more than your introductory sentences, how much thinking have you actually shown? Try, therefore, to create your own discussion, using examples appropriately to connect your thought to the text or texts you are analyzing.

USE THE PRESENT TENSE OF VERBS WHEN REFERRING TO ACTIONS AND IDEAS IN A WORK.   Literary works spring into life with each and every reading. You may thus assume that everything happening takes place in the present, and when writing about literature, you should use the *present tense of verbs*. It is correct to say "Mathilde and her husband *work* and *economize* [not "*worked* and *economized*"] for ten years to pay off the 18,000-franc debt that they *undertake* [not "*undertook*"] to pay for the lost necklace."

When you consider an author's ideas, the present tense is also proper, on the principle that the words of an author are just as alive and current today (and tomorrow) as they were at the moment of writing—even if this same author has been dead for hundreds or even thousands of years.

Because it is incorrect to shift tenses inappropriately, you may encounter a problem when you want to refer to actions that have occurred prior to the time of the main action. An instance occurs in Bierce's "An Occurrence at Owl Creek Bridge," where the narrator explains an event that occurred shortly before the time of the action. In such a situation, it is important to keep details in order, and thus you may use the past tense as long as you keep the relationship clear between past and present, as in this example: "Farquhar *had clearly planned* to blow up the bridge after the Union spy *spoke* to him, and hence he *is therefore now living* his last moments on earth." This use of the past influencing the present is acceptable because it corresponds to the cause-and-effect relationship brought out in the story.

A problem also arises when you introduce historical or biographical details about a work or an author. It is appropriate to use the *past tense* for such details as long as they actually do belong to the past. Thus it is correct to state that "Shakespeare **lived** from 1564 to 1616" or that "Shakespeare **wrote** *Hamlet* in about 1599–1600." It is also permissible to mix past and present tenses when you are treating historical facts about a literary work and are also considering it as a living text. Of prime importance is to keep things straight. Here is a paragraph example showing how past and present tenses may be used when appropriate:

> Because *Hamlet* **was** first **performed** in about 1600, Shakespeare most probably **wrote** it shortly before this time. In the play, a tragedy, Shakespeare **treats** an act of vengeance, but more importantly he **demonstrates** the difficulty of ever learning the exact truth. The hero, Prince Hamlet, **is** the focus of this difficulty, for the task of revenge **is assigned** to him by the Ghost of his father. Though the Ghost **claims** that his brother, Claudius, **is** his murderer, Hamlet **is** not able to verify this claim.

Here, the historical details are presented in the past tense, but all the details about the play *Hamlet*, including Shakespeare as the creating author whose ideas and words are still alive, are considered in the present.

As a general principle, you will be right most of the time if you use the present tense exclusively for literary details and the past tense for historical details. When in doubt, however, *consult your instructor.*

appendix c

Works Used for Sample Essays and References

STORIES

Ambrose Bierce (1842–1914?)

An Occurrence at Owl Creek Bridge   1891

A man stood upon a railroad bridge in northern Alabama, looking down into the swift water twenty feet below. The man's hands were behind his back, the wrists bound with a cord. A rope closely encircled his neck. It was attached to a stout cross-timber above his head and the slack fell to the level of his knees. Some loose boards laid upon the sleepers supporting the metals of the railway supplied a footing for him and his executioners—two private soldiers of the Federal army, directed by a sergeant who in civil life may have been a deputy sheriff. At a short remove upon the same temporary platform was an officer in the uniform of his rank, armed. He was a captain. A sentinel at each end of the bridge stood with his rifle in the position known as "support," that is to say, vertical in front of the left shoulder, the hammer resting on the forearm thrown straight across the chest—a formal and unnatural position, enforcing an erect carriage of the body. It did not appear to be the duty of these two men to know what was occurring at the center of the bridge; they merely blockaded the two ends of the foot planking that traversed it.

Beyond one of the sentinels nobody was in sight; the railroad ran straight away into a forest for a hundred yards, then, curving, was lost to view. Doubtless there was an outpost farther along. The other bank of the stream was open ground—a gentle acclivity topped with a stockade of vertical tree trunks, loopholed for rifles, with a single embrasure through which protruded the muzzle of a brass cannon commanding the bridge. Midway of the slope between the bridge and fort were the spectators—a single company of infantry in line, at "parade rest," the butts of the rifles on the ground, the barrels inclining slightly backward against the right shoulder, the hands crossed upon the stock. A lieutenant stood at the right of the line, the point of his sword upon the ground, his left hand resting upon his right. Excepting the group of four at the center of the bridge, not a man moved. The company faced the bridge, staring stonily, motionless. The sentinels, facing the banks of the stream, might have been statues to adorn the bridge. The captain stood with folded arms, silent, observing the work of his subordinates, but making no sign. Death is a dignitary who when he comes announced is to be received with formal manifestations of respect, even by those most familiar with him. In the code of military etiquette silence and fixity are forms of deference.

The man who was engaged in being hanged was apparently about thirty-five years of age. He was a civilian, if one might judge from his habit, which was that of a planter. His features were good—a straight nose, firm mouth, broad forehead, from which his long, dark hair was combed straight back, falling behind his ears to the collar of his well-fitting frock coat. He wore a mustache and pointed beard, but no whiskers; his eyes were large and dark gray, and had a kindly expression which one would hardly have expected in one whose neck was in the hemp. Evidently this was no vulgar assassin. The liberal military code makes provision for hanging many kinds of persons, and gentlemen are not excluded.

The preparations being complete, the two private soldiers stepped aside and each drew away the plank upon which he had been standing. The sergeant turned to the captain, saluted and placed himself immediately behind that officer, who in turn moved apart one pace. These movements left the condemned man and the sergeant standing on the two ends of the same plank, which spanned three of the cross-ties of the bridge. The end upon which the civilian stood almost, but not quite, reached a fourth. This plank had been held in place by the weight of the captain; it was now held by that of the sergeant. At a signal from the former the latter would step aside, the plank would tilt and the condemned man go down between two ties. The arrangement commended itself to his judgment as simple and effective. His face had not been covered nor his eyes bandaged. He looked a moment at his "unsteadfast footing," then let his gaze wander to the swirling water of the stream racing madly beneath his feet. A piece of dancing drift-wood caught his attention and his eyes followed it down the current. How slowly it appeared to move! What a sluggish stream!

He closed his eyes in order to fix his last thoughts upon his wife and children. The water, touched to gold by the early sun, the brooding mists under the banks at some distance down the stream, the fort, the soldiers, the piece of driftwood— all had distracted him. And now he became conscious of a new disturbance. Striking through the thought of his dear ones was a sound which he could neither ignore nor understand, a sharp, distinct, metallic percussion like the stroke of a blacksmith's hammer upon the anvil; it had the same ringing quality. He wondered what it was, and whether immeasurably distant or near by—it seemed both. Its recurrence was regular, but as slow as the tolling of a death knell. He awaited each stroke with impatience and—he knew not why—apprehension. The intervals of silence grew progressively longer; the delays became maddening. With their greater infrequency the sounds increased in strength and sharpness. They hurt his ear like the thrust of a knife; he feared he would shriek. What he heard was the ticking of his watch.

5

He unclosed his eyes and saw again the water below him. "If I could free my hands," he thought, "I might throw off the noose and spring into the stream. By diving I could evade the bullets and, swimming vigorously, reach the bank, take to the woods and get away home. My home, thank God, is as yet outside their lines; my wife and little ones are still beyond the invader's farthest advance."

As these thoughts, which have here to be set down in words, were flashed into the doomed man's brain rather than evolved from it the captain nodded to the sergeant. The sergeant stepped aside.

II

Peyton Farquhar was a well-to-do planter, of an old and highly respected Alabama family. Being a slave owner and like other slave owners a politician he was naturally an original secessionist and ardently devoted to the Southern cause. Circumstances of an imperious nature, which it is unnecessary to relate here, had prevented him from taking service with the gallant army that had fought the disastrous campaigns ending with the fall of Corinth,° and he chafed under the inglorious restraint, longing for the release of his energies, the larger life of the soldier, the opportunity for distinction. That opportunity, he felt, would come, as it comes to all in war time. Meanwhile he did what he could. No service was too humble for him to perform in aid of the South, no adventure too perilous for him to undertake if consistent with the character of a civilian who was at heart a soldier, and who in good faith and without too much qualification assented to at least a part of the frankly villainous dictum that all is fair in love and war.

One evening while Farquhar and his wife were sitting on a rustic bench near the entrance to his grounds, a grayclad soldier rode up to the gate and asked for a drink of water. Mrs. Farquhar was only too happy to serve him with her own white hands. While she was fetching the water her husband approached the dusty horseman and inquired eagerly for news from the front.

10   "The Yanks are repairing the railroads," said the man, "and are getting ready for another advance. They have reached the Owl Creek bridge, put it in order and built a stockade on the north bank. The commandant has issued an order, which is posted everywhere, declaring that any civilian caught interfering with the railroad, its bridges, tunnels or trains will be summarily hanged. I saw the order."

"How far is it to the Owl Creek bridge?" Farquhar asked.

"About thirty miles."

"Is there no force on this side of the creek?"

"Only a picket post half a mile out, on the railroad, and a single sentinel at this end of the bridge."

15   "Suppose a man—a civilian and student of hanging—should elude the picket post and perhaps get the better of the sentinel," said Farquhar, smiling, "what could he accomplish?"

The soldier reflected "I was there a month ago," he replied "I observed that the flood of last winter had lodged a great quantity of driftwood against the wooden pier at this end of the bridge. It is now dry and would burn like tow."

Corinth: In the northeast corner of Mississippi, near the Alabama state line, Corinth was the site of a battle in 1862 won by the Union army.

The lady had now brought the water, which the soldier drank. He thanked her ceremoniously, bowed to her husband and rode away. An hour later, after nightfall, he repassed the plantation, going northward in the direction from which he had come. He was a Federal scout.

III

As Peyton Farquhar fell straight downward through the bridge he lost consciousness and was as one already dead. From this state he was awakened—ages later, it seemed to him—by the pain of a sharp pressure upon his throat, followed by a sense of suffocation. Keen, poignant agonies seemed to shoot from his neck downward through every fiber of his body and limbs. These pains appeared to flash along well-defined lines of ramification and to beat with an inconceivably rapid periodicity. They seemed like streams of pulsating fire heating him to an intolerable temperature. As to his head, he was conscious of nothing but a feeling of fullness—of congestion. These sensations were unaccompanied by thought. The intellectual part of his nature was already effaced; he had power only to feel, and feeling was torment. He was conscious of motion. Encompassed in a luminous cloud, of which he was now merely the fiery heart, without material substance, he swung through unthinkable arcs of oscillation, like a vast pendulum. Then all at once, with terrible suddenness, the light about him shot upward with the noise of a loud plash; a frightful roaring was in his ears, and all was cold and dark. The power of thought was restored; he knew that the rope had broken and he had fallen into the stream. There was no additional strangulation; the noose about his neck was already suffocating him and kept the water from his lungs. To die of hanging at the bottom of a river!—the idea seemed to him ludicrous. He opened his eyes in the darkness and saw above him a gleam of light, but how distant, how inaccessible! He was still sinking, for the light became fainter and fainter until it was a mere glimmer. Then it began to grow and brighten, and he knew that he was rising toward the surface—knew it with reluctance, for he was now very comfortable. "To be hanged and drowned," he thought, "that is not so bad; but I do not wish to be shot. No; I will not be shot; that is not fair."

He was not conscious of an effort, but a sharp pain in his wrist apprised him that he was trying to free his hands. He gave the struggle his attention, as an idler might observe the feat of a juggler, without interest in the outcome. What splendid effort—what magnificent, what superhuman strength! Ah, that was a fine endeavor! Bravo! The cord fell away; his arms parted and floated upward, the hands dimly seen on each side in the growing light. He watched them with a new interest as first one and then the other pounced upon the noose at his neck. They tore it away and thrust it fiercely aside, its undulations resembling those of a water snake. "Put it back, put it back!" He thought he shouted these words to his hands, for the undoing of the noose had been succeeded by the direst pang that he had yet experienced. His neck ached horribly; his brain was on fire; his heart, which had been fluttering faintly, gave a great leap, trying to force itself out at his mouth. His whole body was racked and wrenched with an insupportable anguish! But his disobedient hands gave no heed to the command. They beat the water vigorously with quick, downward strokes, forcing him to the surface. He felt his head emerge; his eyes were blinded by the sunlight; his chest expanded convulsively, and with a supreme and crowning agony his lungs engulfed a great draught of air, which instantly he expelled in a shriek!

20   He was now in full possession of his physical senses. They were indeed, preternaturally keen and alert. Something in the awful disturbance of his organic system had so exalted and refined them that they made record of things never before perceived. He felt the ripples upon his face and heard their separate sounds as they struck. He looked at the forest on the bank of the stream, saw the individual trees, the leaves and the veining of each leaf—saw the very insects upon them: the locusts, the brilliant-bodied flies, the gray spiders stretching their webs from twig to twig. He noted the prismatic colors in all the dewdrops upon a million blades of grass. The humming of the gnats that danced above the eddies of the stream, the beating of the dragon flies' wings, the strokes of the water-spiders' legs, like oars which had lifted their boat—all these made audible music. A fish slid along beneath his eyes and he heard the rush of its body parting the water.

He had come to the surface facing down the stream; in a moment the visible world seemed to wheel slowly round, himself the pivotal point, and he saw the bridge, the fort, the soldiers upon the bridge, the captain, the sergeant, the two privates, his executioners. They were in silhouette against the blue sky. They shouted and gesticulated, pointing at him. The captain had drawn his pistol, but did not fire; the others were unarmed. Their movements were grotesque and horrible, their forms gigantic.

Suddenly he heard a sharp report and something struck the water smartly within a few inches of his head, spattering his face with spray. He heard a second report, and saw one of the sentinels with his rifle at his shoulder, a light cloud of blue smoke rising from the muzzle. The man in the water saw the eye of the man on the bridge gazing into his own through the sights of the rifle. He observed that it was a gray eye and remembered having read that gray eyes were keenest, and that all famous marksmen had them. Nevertheless, this one had missed.

A counter-swirl had caught Farquhar and turned him half round; he was again looking into the forest on the bank opposite the fort. The sound of a clear, high voice in a monotonous singsong now rang out behind him and came across the water with a distinctness that pierced and subdued all other sounds, even the beating of the ripples in his ears. Although no soldier, he had frequented camps enough to know the dread significance of that deliberate, drawling, aspirated chant; the lieutenant on shore was taking a part in the morning's work. How coldly and pitilessly—with what an even, calm intonation, presaging, and enforcing tranquillity in the men—with what accurately measured intervals fell those cruel words:

"Attention, company! . . . Shoulder arms! . . . Ready! . . . Aim! . . . Fire!"

25   Farquhar dived—dived as deeply as he could. The water roared in his ears like the voice of Niagara, yet he heard the dulled thunder of the volley and, rising again toward the surface, met shining bits of metal, singularly flattened, oscillating slowly downward. Some of them touched him on the face and hands, then fell away, continuing their descent. One lodged between his collar and neck; it was uncomfortably warm and he snatched it out.

As he rose to the surface, gasping for breath, he saw that he had been a long time under water; he was perceptibly farther down stream—nearer to safety. The soldiers had almost finished reloading; the metal ramrods flashed all at once in the sunshine as they were drawn from the barrels, turned in the air; and thrust into their sockets. The two sentinels fired again, independently and ineffectually.

The hunted man saw all this over his shoulder; he was now swimming vigorously with the current. His brain was as energetic as his arms and legs; he thought with the rapidity of lightning.

"The officer," he reasoned, "will not make that martinet's error a second time. It is as easy to dodge a volley as a single shot. He has probably already given the command to fire at will. God help me, I cannot dodge them all!"

An appalling plash within two yards of him was followed by a loud, rushing sound, *diminuendo,* which seemed to travel back through the air to the fort and died in an explosion which stirred the very river to its deeps! A rising sheet of water curved over him, fell down upon him, blinded him, strangled him! The cannon had taken a hand in the game. As he shook his head free from the commotion of the smitten water he heard the deflected shot humming through the air ahead, and in an instant it was cracking and smashing the branches in the forest beyond.

They will not do that again," he thought; "the next time they will use a charge of grape. I must keep my eye upon the gun; the smoke will apprise me—the report arrives too late; it lags behind the missile. That is a good gun." 30

Suddenly he felt himself whirled round and round—spinning like a top. The water, the banks, the forests, the now distant bridge, fort and men—all were commingled and blurred. Objects were represented by their colors only; circular horizontal streaks of color—that was all he saw. He had been caught in a vortex and was being whirled on with a velocity of advance and gyration that made him giddy and sick. In a few moments he was flung upon the gravel at the foot of the left bank of the stream—the southern bank—and behind a projecting point which concealed him from his enemies. The sudden arrest of his motion, the abrasion of one of his hands on the gravel, restored him, and he wept with delight. He dug his fingers into the sand, threw it over himself in handfuls and audibly blessed it. It looked like diamonds, rubies, emeralds; he could think of nothing beautiful which it did not resemble. The trees upon the bank were giant garden plants; he noted a definite order in their arrangement, inhaled the fragrance of their blooms. A strange, roseate light shone through the spaces among their trunks and the wind made in their branches the music of Æolian harps. He had no wish to perfect his escape—was content to remain in that enchanting spot until retaken.

A whiz and rattle of grapeshot among the branches high above his head roused him from his dream. The baffled cannoneer had fired him a random farewell. He sprang to his feet, rushed up the sloping bank, and plunged into the forest.

All that day he traveled, laying his course by the rounding sun. The forest seemed interminable; nowhere did he discover a break in it, not even a woodman's road. He had not known that he lived in so wild a region. There was something uncanny in the revelation.

By nightfall he was fatigued, footsore, famishing. The thought of his wife and children urged him on. At last he found a road which led him in what he knew to be the right direction. It was as wide and straight as a city street, yet it seemed untraveled. No fields bordered it, no dwelling anywhere. Not so much as the barking of a dog suggested human habitation. The black bodies of the trees formed a straight wall on both sides, terminating on the horizon in a point, like a diagram in a lesson in perspective. Overhead, as he looked up through this rift in the wood, shone great golden stars looking unfamiliar and grouped in strange constellations. He was sure they were arranged in some order which had a secret and malign significance. The wood on either side was full of singular noises, among which—once, twice, and again—he distinctly heard whispers in an unknown tongue.

35   His neck was in pain and lifting his hand to it found it horribly swollen. He knew that it had a circle of black where the rope had bruised it. His eyes felt congested; he could no longer close them. His tongue was swollen with thirst; he relieved its fever by thrusting it forward from between his teeth into the cold air. How softly the turf had carpeted the untraveled avenue—he could no longer feel the roadway beneath his feet!

Doubtless, despite his suffering, he had fallen asleep while walking, for now he sees another scene—perhaps he has merely recovered from a delirium. He stands at the gate of his own home. All is as he left it, and all bright and beautiful in the morning sunshine. He must have traveled the entire night. As he pushes open the gate and passes up the wide white walk, he sees a flutter of female garments; his wife, looking fresh and cool and sweet, steps down from the veranda to meet him. At the bottom of the steps she stands waiting, with a smile of ineffable joy, an attitude of matchless grace and dignity. Ah, how beautiful she is! He springs forward with extended arms. As he is about to clasp her he feels a stunning blow upon the back of the neck; a blinding white light blazes all about him with a sound like the shock of a cannon—then all is darkness and silence!

Peyton Farquhar was dead; his body, with a broken neck, swung gently from side to side beneath the timbers of the Owl Creek bridge.

Kate Chopin (1851–1904)

The Story of an Hour   1894

Knowing that Mrs. Mallard was afflicted with a heart trouble, great care was taken to break to her as gently as possible the news of her husband's death.

It was her sister Josephine who told her, in broken sentences: veiled hints that revealed in half concealing. Her husband's friend Richards was there, too, near her. It was he who had been in the newspaper office when intelligence of the railroad disaster was received, with Brently Mallard's name leading the list of "killed." He had only taken the time to assure himself of its truth by a second telegram, and had hastened to forestall any less careful, less tender friend in bearing the sad message.

She did not hear the story as many women have heard the same, with a paralyzed inability to accept its significance. She wept at once, with sudden, wild abandonment, in her sister's arms. When the storm of grief had spent itself she went away to her room alone. She would have no one follow her.

There stood, facing the open window, a comfortable, roomy armchair. Into this she sank, pressed down by a physical exhaustion that haunted her body and seemed to reach into her soul.

She could see in the open square before her house the tops of trees that were all aquiver with the new spring life. The delicious breath of rain was in the air. In the street below a peddler was crying his wares. The notes of a distant song which some one was singing reached her faintly, and countless sparrows were twittering in the eaves.

There were patches of blue sky showing here and there through the clouds that had met and piled one above the other in the west facing her window.

She sat with her head thrown back upon the cushion of the chair, quite motionless, except when a sob came up into her throat and shook her, as a child who has cried itself to sleep continues to sob in its dreams.

She was young, with a fair, calm face, whose lines bespoke repression and even a certain strength. But now there was a dull stare in her eyes, whose gaze was fixed away off yonder on one of those patches of blue sky. It was not a glance of reflection, but rather indicated a suspension of intelligent thought.

There was something coming to her and she was waiting for it, fearfully. What was it? She did not know; it was too subtle and elusive to name. But she felt it, creeping out of the sky, reaching toward her through the sounds, the scents, the color that filled the air.

Now her bosom rose and fell tumultuously. She was beginning to recognize this thing that was approaching to possess her, and she was striving to beat it back with her will—as powerless as her two white slender hands would have been.

When she abandoned herself a little whispered word escaped her slightly parted lips. She said it over and over under her breath: "free, free, free!" The vacant stare and the look of terror that had followed it went from her eyes. They stayed keen and bright. Her pulses beat fast, and the coursing blood warmed and relaxed every inch of her body.

She did not stop to ask if it were or were not a monstrous joy that held her. A clear and exalted perception enabled her to dismiss the suggestion as trivial.

She knew that she would weep again when she saw the kind, tender hands folded in death; the face that had never looked save with love upon her, fixed and gray and dead. But she saw beyond that bitter moment a long procession of years to come that would belong to her absolutely. And she opened and spread her arms out to them in welcome.

There would be no one to live for during those coming years; she would live for herself. There would be no powerful will bending hers in that blind persistence with which men and women believe they have a right to impose a private will upon a fellow-creature. A kind intention or a cruel intention made the act seem no less a crime as she looked upon it in that brief moment of illumination.

And yet she had loved him—sometimes. Often she had not. What did it matter! What could love, the unsolved mystery, count for in face of this possession of self assertion which she suddenly recognized as the strongest impulse of her being!

"Free! Body and soul free!" she kept whispering.

Josephine was kneeling before the closed door with her lips to the keyhole, imploring for admission. "Louise, open the door! I beg; open the door—you will make yourself ill. What are you doing, Louise? For heaven's sake open the door."

"Go away. I am not making myself ill." No; she was drinking in a very elixir of life through that open window.

Her fancy was running riot along those days ahead of her. Spring days, and summer days, and all sorts of days that would be her own. She breathed a quick prayer that life might be long. It was only yesterday she had thought with a shudder that life might be long.

20   She arose at length and opened the door to her sister's importunities. There was a feverish triumph in her eyes, and she carried herself unwittingly like a goddess of Victory. She clasped her sister's waist, and together they descended the stairs. Richards stood waiting for them at the bottom.

Some one was opening the front door with a latchkey. It was Brently Mallard who entered, a little travel-stained, composedly carrying his grip-sack and umbrella. He had been far from the scene of accident, and did not even know there had been one. He stood amazed at Josephine's piercing cry: at Richards' quick motion to screen him from the view of his wife.

But Richards was too late.

When the doctors came they said she had died of heart disease—of joy that kills.

Thomas Hardy (1840–1928)

The Three Strangers   ·   1888

Among the few features of agricultural England which retain an appearance but little modified by the lapse of centuries may be reckoned the high, grassy and furzy downs, coombs, or ewe-leases, as they are indifferently called, that fill a large area of certain counties in the south and southwest. If any mark of human occupation is met with hereon, it usually takes the form of the solitary cottage of some shepherd.

Fifty years ago such a lonely cottage stood on such a down, and may possibly be standing there now. In spite of its loneliness, however, the spot, by actual measurement, was not more than five miles from a county-town. Yet that affected it little. Five miles of irregular upland, during the long inimical seasons, with their sleets, snows, rains, and mists, afford withdrawing space enough to isolate a Timon or a Nebuchadnezzar; much less, in fair weather, to please that less repellent tribe, the poets, philosophers, artists, and others who "conceive and meditate of pleasant things."

Some old earthen camp or barrow, some clump of trees, at least some starved fragment of ancient hedge is usually taken advantage of in the erection of these forlorn dwellings. But, in the present case, such a kind of shelter had been disregarded. Higher Crowstairs, as the house was called, stood quite detached and undefended.

The only reason for its precise situation seemed to be the crossing of two footpaths at right angles hard by, which may have crossed there and thus for a good five hundred years. Hence the house was exposed to the elements on all sides. But, though the wind up here blew unmistakably when it did blow, and the rain hit hard whenever it fell, the various weathers of the winter season were not quite so formidable on the coomb as they were imagined to be by dwellers on low ground. The raw rimes were not so pernicious as in the hollows, and the frosts were scarcely so severe. When the shepherd and his family who tenanted the house were pitied for their sufferings from the exposure, they said that upon the whole they were less inconvenienced by "wuzzes and flames" (hoarses and phlegms) than when they had lived by the stream of a snug neighboring valley.

The night of March 28, 182–, was precisely one of the nights that were wont to call forth these expressions of commiseration. The level rainstorm smote walls, slopes, and hedges like the clothyard shafts of Senlac and Crécy. Such sheep and outdoor animals as had no shelter stood with their buttocks to the winds; while the tails of little birds trying to roost on some scraggy thorn were blown inside-out like umbrellas. The gable-end of the cottage was stained with wet, and the eavesdroppings flapped against the wall. Yet never was commiseration for the shepherd more misplaced. For that cheerful rustic was entertaining a large party in glorification of the christening of his second girl.

The guests had arrived before the rain began to fall, and they were all now assembled in the chief or living room of the dwelling. A glance into the apartment at eight o'clock on this eventful evening would have resulted in the opinion that it was as cozy and comfortable a nook as could be wished for in boisterous weather. The calling of its inhabitant was proclaimed by a number of highly polished sheep crooks without stems that were hung ornamentally over the fireplace, the curl of each shining crook varying from the antiquated type engraved in the patriarchal pictures of old family Bibles to the most approved fashion of the last local sheep-fair. The room was lighted by half a dozen candles having wicks only a trifle smaller than the grease which enveloped them, in candlesticks that were never used but at highdays, holy-days, and family feasts. The lights were scattered about the room, two of them standing on the chimney piece. This position of candles was in itself significant. Candles on the chimney piece always meant a party.

On the hearth, in front of a back-brand to give substance, blazed a fire of thorns, that crackled "like the laughter of the fool."

Nineteen persons were gathered here. Of these, five women, wearing gowns of various bright hues, sat in chairs along the wall; girls shy and not shy filled the window-bench; four men, including Charley Jake the hedge-carpenter, Elijah New the parish-clerk, and John Pitcher, a neighboring dairyman, the shepherd's father-in-law, lolled in the settle; a young man and maid, who were blushing over tentative *pourparlers* on a life-companionship, sat beneath the corner-cupboard; and an elderly engaged man of fifty or upward moved restlessly about from spots where his betrothed was not to the spot where she was. Enjoyment was pretty general, and so much the more prevailed in being unhampered by conventional restrictions. Absolute confidence in each other's good opinion begat perfect ease, while the finishing stroke of manner, amounting to a truly princely serenity, was lent to the majority by the absence of any expression or trait denoting that they wished to get on in the world, enlarge their minds, or do any eclipsing thing whatever—which nowadays

5

so generally nips the bloom and *bonhomie* of all except the two extremes of the social scale.

Shepherd Fennel had married well, his wife being a dairyman's daughter from a vale at a distance, who brought fifty guineas in her pocket—and kept them there, till they should be required for ministering to the needs of a coming family. This frugal woman had been somewhat exercised as to the character that should be given to the gathering. A sit-still party had its advantages; but an undisturbed position of ease in chairs and settles was apt to lead on the men to such an unconscionable deal of toping that they would sometimes fairly drink the house dry. A dancing-party was the alternative; but this, while avoiding the foregoing objection on the score of good drink, had a counterbalancing disadvantage in the matter of good victuals, the ravenous appetites engendered by the exercise causing immense havoc in the buttery. Shepherdess Fennel fell back upon the intermediate plan of mingling short dances with short periods of talk and singing, so as to hinder any ungovernable rage in either. But this scheme was entirely confined to her own gentle mind: the shepherd himself was in the mood to exhibit the most reckless phases of hospitality.

The fiddler was a boy of those parts, about twelve years of age, who had a wonderful dexterity in jigs and reels, though his fingers were so small and short as to necessitate a constant shifting for the high notes, from which he scrambled back to the first position with sounds not of unmixed purity of tone. At seven the shrill tweedle-dee of this youngster had begun, accompanied by a booming ground-bass from Elijah New, the parish-clerk, who had thoughtfully brought with him his favorite musical instrument, the serpent. Dancing was instantaneous, Mrs. Fennel privately enjoining the players on no account to let the dance exceed the length of a quarter of an hour.

10   But Elijah and the boy, in the excitement of their position, quite forgot the injunction. Moreover, Oliver Giles, a man of seventeen, one of the dancers, who was enamored of his partner, a fair girl of thirty-three rolling years, had recklessly handed a new crown-piece to the musicians, as a bribe to keep going as long as they had muscle and wind. Mrs. Fennel, seeing the steam begin to generate on the countenances of her guests, crossed over and touched the fiddler's elbow and put her hand on the serpent's mouth. But they took no notice, and fearing she might lose her character of genial hostess if she were to interfere too markedly, she retired and sat down helpless. And so the dance whizzed on with cumulative fury, the performers moving in their planet-like courses, direct and retrograde, from apogee to perigee, till the hand of the well-kicked clock at the bottom of the room had traveled over the circumference of an hour.

While these cheerful events were in course of enactment within Fennel's pastoral dwelling, an incident having considerable bearing on the party had occurred in the gloomy night without. Mrs. Fennel's concern about the growing fierceness of the dance corresponded in point of time with the ascent of a human figure to the solitary hill of Higher Crowstairs from the direction of the distant town. This personage strode on through the rain without a pause, following the little-worn path which, further on in its course, skirted the shepherd's cottage.

It was nearly the time of full moon, and on this account, though the sky was lined with a uniform sheet of dripping cloud, ordinary objects out of doors were readily visible. The sad, wan light revealed the lonely pedestrian to be a man of supple frame; his gait suggested that he had somewhat passed the period of perfect and instinctive agility, though not so far as to be otherwise than rapid of motion when occasion required. At a rough guess, he might have been about forty years of age. He appeared tall, but a recruiting sergeant, or other person accustomed to the judging of men's heights by the eye, would have discerned that this was chiefly owing to his gauntness, and that he was not more than five-feet eight or nine.

Notwithstanding the regularity of his tread, there was caution in it, as in that of one who mentally feels his way; and despite the fact that it was not a black coat nor a dark garment of any sort that he wore, there was something about him which suggested that he naturally belonged to the black-coated tribes of men. His clothes were of fustian, and his boots hobnailed, yet in his progress he showed not the mud-accustomed bearing of hobnailed and fustianed peasantry.

By the time that he had arrived abreast of the shepherd's premises the rain came down, or rather came along, with yet more determined violence. The outskirts of the little settlement partially broke the force of wind and rain, and this induced him to stand still. The most salient of the shepherd's domestic erections was an empty sty at the forward corner of his hedgeless garden, for in these latitudes the principle of masking the homelier features of your establishment by a conventional frontage was unknown. The traveler's eye was attracted to this small building by the pallid shine of the wet slates that covered it. He turned aside, and, finding it empty, stood under the pent-roof for shelter.

While he stood, the boom of the serpent within the adjacent house, and the 15 lesser strains of the fiddler, reached the spot as an accompaniment to the surging hiss of the flying rain on the sod, its louder beating on the cabbage-leaves of the garden, on the eight or ten beehives just discernible by the path, and its dripping from the eaves into a row of buckets and pans that had been placed under the walls of the cottage. For at Higher Crowstairs, as at all such elevated domiciles, the grand difficulty of housekeeping was an insufficiency of water; and a casual rainfall was utilized by turning out, as catchers, every utensil that the house contained. Some queer stories might be told of the contrivances for economy in suds and dishwaters that are absolutely necessitated in upland habitations during the droughts of summer. But at this season there were no such exigencies; a mere acceptance of what the skies bestowed was sufficient for an abundant store.

At last the notes of the serpent ceased and the house was silent. This cessation of activity aroused the solitary pedestrian from the reverie into which he had elapsed, and, emerging from the shed, with an apparently new intention, he walked up the path to the house-door. Arrived here, his first act was to kneel down on a large stone beside the row of vessels, and to drink a copious draught from one of them. Having quenched his thirst, he rose and lifted his hand to knock, but paused with his eye upon the panel. Since the dark surface of the wood revealed absolutely nothing, it was evident that he must be mentally looking through the door, as if he wished to measure thereby all the possibilities that a house of this sort might include, and how they might bear upon the question of his entry.

In his indecision he turned and surveyed the scene around. Not a soul was anywhere visible. The garden path stretched downward from his feet, gleaming like the track of a snail; the roof of the little well (mostly dry), the well-cover, the top rail of the garden-gate, were varnished with the same dull liquid glaze; while, far away in the vale, a faint whiteness of more than usual extent showed that the rivers were high in the meads. Beyond all this winked a few bleared lamplights through the beating drops—lights that denoted the situation of the county-town from which he had appeared to come. The absence of all notes of life in that direction seemed to clinch his intentions, and he knocked at the door.

Within, a desultory chat had taken the place of movement and musical sound. The hedge-carpenter was suggesting a song to the company, which nobody just then was inclined to undertake, so that the knock afforded a not unwelcome diversion.

"Walk in!" said the shepherd, promptly.

20   The latch clicked upward, and out of the night our pedestrian appeared upon the door-mat. The shepherd arose, snuffed two of the nearest candles, and turned to look at him.

Their light disclosed that the stranger was dark in complexion and not unprepossessing as to feature. His hat, which for a moment he did not remove, hung low over his eyes, without concealing that they were large, open, and determined, moving with a flash rather than a glance round the room. He seemed pleased with his survey, and, baring his shaggy head, said, in a rich, deep voice: "The rain is so heavy, friends, that I ask leave to come in and rest awhile."

"To be sure, Stranger," said the shepherd. "And faith, you've been lucky in choosing your time, for we are having a bit of a fling for a glad cause—though, to be sure, a man could hardly wish that glad cause to happen more than once a year."

"Nor less," spoke up a woman. "For 'tis best to get your family over and done with, as soon as you can, so as to be all the earlier out of the fag o't."

"And what may be this glad cause?" asked the stranger.

25   "A birth and christening," said the shepherd.

The stranger hoped his host might not be made unhappy either by too many or too few of such episodes and, being invited by a gesture to a pull at the mug, he readily acquiesced. His manner, which, before entering, had been so dubious, was now altogether that of a careless and candid man.

"Late to be traipsing athwart this coomb—hey?" said the engaged man of fifty.

"Late it is, Master, as you say.—I'll take a seat in the chimney corner, if you have nothing to urge against it, Ma'am; for I am a little moist on the side that was next the rain."

Mrs. Shepherd Fennel assented, and made room for the self-invited comer, who, having got completely inside the chimney corner, stretched out his legs and arms with the expansiveness of a person quite at home.

30   "Yes, I am rather cracked in the vamp," he said freely, seeing that the eyes of the shepherd's wife fell upon his boots, "and I am not well fitted either. I have had some rough times lately, and have been forced to pick up what I can get in the way of wearing, but I must find a suit better fit for working-days when I reach home."

"One of hereabouts?" she inquired.

"Not quite that—further up the country."

"I thought so. And so be I; and by your tongue you come from my neighborhood."

"But you would hardly have heard of me," he said quickly. "My time would be long before yours, Ma'am, you see."

35   This testimony to the youthfulness of his hostess had the effect of stopping her cross-examination.

"There is only one thing more wanted to make me happy," continued the newcomer, "and that is a little baccy, which I am sorry to say I am out of."

"I'll fill your pipe," said the shepherd.

"I must ask you to lend me a pipe likewise."

"A smoker, and no pipe about 'ee?"

"I have dropped it somewhere on the road."

40

The shepherd filled and handed him a new clay pipe, saying, as he did so, "Hand me your baccy-box—I'll fill that too, now I am about it."

The man went through the movement of searching his pockets.

"Lost that too?" said his entertainer, with some surprise.

"I am afraid so," said the man with some confusion. "Give it to me in a screw of paper." Lighting his pipe at the candle with a suction that drew the whole flame into the bowl, he resettled himself in the corner and bent his looks upon the faint steam from his damp legs, as if he wished to say no more.

Meanwhile the general body of guests had been taking little notice of this visi- 45
tor by reason of an absorbing discussion in which they were engaged with the band about a tune for the next dance. The matter being settled, they were about to stand up when an interruption came in the shape of another knock at the door.

At sound of the same the man in the chimney corner took up the poker and began stirring the brands as if doing it thoroughly were the one aim of his existence; and a second time the shepherd said, "Walk in!" In a moment another man stood upon the straw-woven door-mat. He too was a stranger.

This individual was one of a type radically different from the first. There was more of the commonplace in his manner, and a certain jovial cosmopolitanism sat upon his features. He was several years older than the first arrival, his hair being slightly frosted, his eyebrows bristly, and his whiskers cut back from his cheeks. His face was rather full and flabby, and yet it was not altogether a face without power. A few grog-blossoms marked the neighborhood of his nose. He flung back his long drab greatcoat, revealing that beneath it he wore a suit of cinder-gray shade throughout, large heavy seals, of some metal or other that would take a polish, dangling from his fob as his only personal ornament. Shaking the water drops from his low-crowned glazed hat, he said, "I must ask for a few minutes' shelter, comrades, or I shall be wetted to my skin before I get to Casterbridge."

"Make yourself at home, Master," said the shepherd, perhaps a trifle less heartily than on the first occasion. Not that Fennel had the least tinge of niggardliness in his composition; but the room was far from large, spare chairs were not numerous, and damp companions were not altogether desirable at close quarters for the women and girls in their bright-colored gowns.

However, the second comer, after taking off his greatcoat, and hanging his hat on a nail in one of the ceiling-beams as if he had been specially invited to put it there, advanced and sat down at the table. This had been pushed so closely into the chimney corner, to give all available room to the dancers, that its inner edge grazed the elbow of the man who had ensconced himself by the fire; and thus the two strangers were brought into close companionship. They nodded to each other by way of breaking the ice of unacquaintance, and the first stranger handed his neighbor the family mug—a huge vessel of brown ware, having its upper edge worn away like a threshold by the rub of whole generations of thirsty lips that had gone the way of all flesh, and bearing the following inscription burnt upon its rotund side in yellow letters:

THERE IS NO FUN
UNTIL i CUM.

The other man, nothing loth, raised the mug to his lips, and drank on, and on, and on—till a curious blueness overspread the countenance of the shepherd's wife, who had regarded with no little surprise the first stranger's free offer to the second of what did not belong to him to dispense.

50   "I knew it!" said the toper to the shepherd with much satisfaction. "When I walked up your garden before coming in, and saw the hives all of a row, I said to myself, 'Where there's bees there's honey, and where there's honey there's mead.' But mead of such a truly comfortable sort as this I really didn't expect to meet in my older days." He took yet another pull at the mug, till it assumed an ominous elevation.

"Glad you enjoy it!" said the shepherd, warmly.

"It is goodish mead," assented Mrs. Fennel, with an absence of enthusiasm which seemed to say that it was possible to buy praise for one's cellar at too heavy a price. "It is trouble enough to make—and really I hardly think we shall make any more. For honey sells well, and we ourselves can make shift with a drop o' small mead and metheglin for common use from the comb-washings."

"Oh, but you'll never have the heart!" reproachfully cried the stranger in cinder-gray, after taking up the mug a third time and setting it down empty. "I love mead, when 'tis old like this, as I love to go to church o' Sundays, or to relieve the needy any day of the week."

"Ha, ha, ha!" said the man in the chimney corner, who, in spite of the taciturnity induced by the pipe of tobacco, could not or would not refrain from this slight testimony to his comrade's humor.

55   Now the old mead of those days, brewed of the purest first-year or maiden honey, four pounds to the gallon—with its due complement of white of eggs, cinnamon, ginger, cloves, mace, rosemary, yeast, and processes of working, bottling, and cellaring—tasted remarkably strong; but it did not taste so strong as it actually was. Hence, presently, the stranger in cinder-gray at the table, moved by its creeping influence, unbuttoned his waistcoat, threw himself back in his chair, spread his legs, and made his presence felt in various ways.

"Well, well, as I say," he resumed, "I am going to Casterbridge, and to Casterbridge I must go. I should have been almost there by this time; but the rain drove me into your dwelling, and I'm not sorry for it."

"You don't live in Casterbridge?" said the shepherd.

"Not as yet; though I shortly mean to move there."

"Going to set up in trade, perhaps?"

60   "No, no," said the shepherd's wife. "It is easy to see that the gentleman is rich, and don't want to work at anything."

The cinder-gray stranger paused, as if to consider whether he would accept that definition of himself. He presently rejected it by answering, "Rich is not quite the word for me, Dame. I do work, and I must work. And even if I only get to Casterbridge by midnight I must begin work there at eight tomorrow morning. Yes, het or wet, blow or snow, famine or sword, my day's work tomorrow must be done."

"Poor man! Then, in spite o' seeming, you be worse off than we," replied the shepherd's wife.

"'Tis the nature of my trade, men and maidens. 'Tis the nature of my trade more than my poverty. . . . But really and truly I must up and off, or I shan't get a lodging in the town." However, the speaker did not move, and directly added, "There's time for one more draught of friendship before I go; and I'd perform it at once if the mug were not dry."

"Here's a mug o' small," said Mrs. Fennel. "Small, we call it, though to be sure 'tis only the first wash o' the combs."

"No," said the stranger, disdainfully. "I won't spoil your first kindness by par-taking o' your second."   65

"Certainly not," broke in Fennel. "We don't increase and multiply every day, and I'll fill the mug again." He went away to the dark place under the stairs where the barrel stood. The shepherdess followed him.

"Why should you do this?" she said, reproachfully, as soon as they were alone. "He's emptied it once, though it held enough for ten people; and now he's not contented wi' the small, but must needs call for more o' the strong! And a stranger unbeknown to any of us. For my part, I don't like the look o' the man at all."

"But he's in the house, my honey; and 'tis a wet night, and a christening. Daze it, what's a cup of mead more or less? There'll be plenty more next bee-burning."

"Very well—this time, then," she answered, looking wistfully at the barrel. "But what is the man's calling, and where is he one of, that he should come in and join us like this?"

"I don't know. I'll ask him again."   70

The catastrophe of having the mug drained dry at one pull by the stranger in cinder-gray was effectually guarded against this time by Mrs. Fennel. She poured out his allowance in a small cup, keeping the large one at a discreet distance from him. When he had tossed off his portion the shepherd renewed his inquiry about the stranger's occupation.

The latter did not immediately reply, and the man in the chimney corner, with sudden demonstrativeness, said, "Anybody may know my trade—I'm a wheelwright."

"A very good trade for these parts," said the shepherd.

"And anybody may know mine—if they've the sense the find it out," said the stranger in cinder-gray.

"You may generally tell what a man is by his claws," observed the hedge-carpenter, looking at his own hands. "My fingers be as full of thorns as an old pin-cushion is of pins."   75

The hands of the man in the chimney corner instinctively sought the shade, and he gazed into the fire as he resumed his pipe. The man at the table took up the hedge-carpenter's remark, and added smartly, "True; but the oddity of my trade is that, instead of setting a mark upon me, it sets a mark upon my cus-tomers."

No observation being offered by anybody in elucidation of this enigma, the shepherd's wife once more called for a song. The same obstacles presented them-selves as at the former time—one had no voice, another had forgotten the first verse. The stranger at the table, whose soul had now risen to a good working temperature, relieved the difficulty by exclaiming that, to start the company, he would sing him-self. Thrusting one thumb into the armhole of his waistcoat, he waved the other hand in the air, and, with an extemporizing gaze at the shining sheepcrooks above the mantelpiece, began:

> *O my trade it is the rarest one,*
>> *Simple shepherds all—*
> *My trade is a sight to see;*
> *For my customers I tie, and take them up on high,*
> *And waft 'em to a far countree!*

The room was silent when he had finished the verse—with one exception, that of the man in the chimney corner, who at the singer's word, "Chorus!" joined him in a deep bass voice of musical relish:

And waft 'em to a far countree!

Oliver Giles, John Pitcher the dairyman, the parish-clerk, the engaged man of fifty, the row of young women against the wall, seemed lost in thought not of the gayest kind. The shepherd looked meditatively on the ground, the shepherdess gazed keenly at the singer, and with some suspicion; she was doubting whether this stranger were merely singing an old song from recollection, or was composing one there and then for the occasion. All were as perplexed at the obscure revelation as the guests at Belshazzar's Feast, except the man in the chimney corner, who quietly said, "Second verse, stranger," and smoked on.

The singer thoroughly moistened himself from his lips inward, and went on with the next stanza as requested:

> *My tools are but common ones,*
>   *Simple shepherds all—*
> *My tools are no sight to see:*
> *A little hempen string, and a post whereon to swing,*
> *Are implements enough for me!*

Shepherd Fennel glanced round. There was no longer any doubt that the stranger was answering his question rhythmically. The guests one and all started back with suppressed exclamations. The young woman engaged to the man of fifty fainted halfway, and would have proceeded, but finding him wanting in alacrity for catching her she sat down trembling.

80   "Oh, he's the———!" whispered the people in the background, mentioning the name of an ominous public officer. "He's come to do it! 'Tis to be at Casterbridge jail tomorrow—the man for sheep-stealing—the poor clockmaker we heard of, who used to live at Shottsford and had no work to do—Timothy Summers, whose family were astarving, and so he went out of Shottsford by the highroad, and took a sheep in open daylight, defying the farmer and the farmer's wife and the farmer's lad, and every man jack among 'em. He" (and they nodded toward the stranger of the deadly trade) "is come from up the country to do it because there's not enough to do in his own county-town, and he's got the place here now our own county-man's dead; he's going to live in the same cottage under the prison wall."

The stranger in cinder-gray took no notice of this whispered string of observations, but again wetted his lips. Seeing that his friend in the chimney corner was the only one who reciprocated his joviality in any way, he held out his cup toward that appreciative comrade, who also held out his own. They clinked together, the eyes of the rest of the room hanging upon the singer's actions. He parted his lips for the third verse; but at that moment another knock was audible upon the door. This time the knock was faint and hesitating.

The company seemed scared; the shepherd looked with consternation toward the entrance, and it was with some effort that he resisted his alarmed wife's deprecatory glance, and uttered for the third time the welcoming words, "Walk in!"

The door was gently opened, and another man stood upon the mat. He, like those who had preceded him, was a stranger. This time it was a short, small personage, of fair complexion, and dressed in a decent suit of dark clothes.

"Can you tell me the way to————?" he began: when, gazing round the room to observe the nature of the company among whom he had fallen, his eyes lighted on the stranger in cinder-gray. It was just at the instant when the latter, who had thrown his mind into his song with such a will that he scarcely heeded the interruption, silenced all whispers and inquiries by bursting into his third verse:

> *Tomorrow is my working day,*
> > *Simple shepherds all—*
> *Tomorrow is a working day for me:*
> *For the farmer's sheep is slain, and the lad who did it ta'en,*
> *And on his soul may God ha' merc-y!*

The stranger in the chimney corner, waving cups with the singer so heartily that his mead splashed over on the hearth, repeated in his bass voice as before:

> *And on his soul may God ha' merc-y!*

All this time the third stranger had been standing in the doorway. Finding   85
now that he did not come forward or go on speaking, the guests particularly regarded him. They noticed to their surprise that he stood before them the picture of abject terror—his knees trembling, his hand shaking so violently that the door-latch by which he supported himself rattled audibly: his white lips were parted, and his eyes fixed on the merry officer of justice in the middle of the room. A moment more and he had turned, closed the door, and fled.

"What a man can it be?" said the shepherd.

The rest, between the awfulness of their late discovery and the odd conduct of this third visitor, looked as if they knew not what to think, and said nothing. Instinctively they withdrew further and further from the grim gentleman in their midst, whom some of them seemed to take for the Prince of Darkness himself, till they formed a remote circle, an empty space of floor being left between them and him—

> . . . *circulas, cujus centrum diabolus.*°

The room was so silent—though there were more than twenty people in it—that nothing could be heard but the patter of the rain against the window-shutters, accompanied by the occasional hiss of a stray drop that fell down the chimney into the fire, and the steady puffing of the man in the corner, who had now resumed his pipe of long clay.

The stillness was unexpectedly broken. The distant sound of a gun reverberated through the air—apparently from the direction of the county-town.

"Be jiggered!" cried the stranger who had sung the song, jumping up.

"What does that mean?" asked several.   90

"A prisoner escaped from the jail—that's what it means."

---

circulas . . . diabolus: circles, whose center [is] the devil.

All listened. The sound was repeated, and none of them spoke but the man in the chimney corner, who said quietly, "I've often been told that in this county they fire a gun at such times; but I never heard it till now."

"I wonder if it is *my* man?" murmured the personage in cinder-gray.

"Surely it is!" said the shepherd involuntarily. "And surely we've zeed him! That little man who looked in at the door by now, and quivered like a leaf when he zeed ye and heard your song!"

95   "His teeth chattered, and the breath went out of his body," said the dairyman.

"And his heart seemed to sink within him like a stone," said Oliver Giles.

"And he bolted as if he'd been shot at," said the hedge-carpenter.

"True—his teeth chattered, and his heart seemed to sink; and he bolted as if he'd been shot at," slowly summed up the man in the chimney corner.

"I didn't notice it," remarked the hangman.

100   "We were all awondering what made him run off in such a fright," faltered one of the women against the wall, "and now 'tis explained!"

The firing of the alarm-gun went on at intervals, low and sullenly, and their suspicions became a certainty. The sinister gentleman in cinder-gray roused himself. "Is there a constable here?" he asked, in thick tones. "If so, let him step forward."

The engaged man of fifty stepped quavering out from the wall, his betrothed beginning to sob on the back of the chair.

"You are a sworn constable?"

"I be, Sir."

105   "Then pursue the criminal at once, with assistance, and bring him back here. He can't have gone far."

"I will, Sir, I will—when I've got my staff. I'll go home and get it, and come sharp here, and start in a body."

"Staff!—never mind your staff; the man'll be gone!"

"But I can't do nothing without my staff—can I, William, and John, and Charles Jake? No; for there's the king's royal crown apainted on en in yaller and gold, and the lion and the unicorn, so as when I raise en up and hit my prisoner, 'tis made a lawful blow thereby. I wouldn't 'tempt to take up a man without my staff— no, not I. If I hadn't the law to gie me courage, why, instead o' my taking up him he might take up me!"

"Now, I'm a king's man myself, and can give you authority enough for this," said the formidable officer in gray. "Now then, all of ye, be ready. Have ye any lanterns?"

110   "Yes—have ye any lanterns?—I demand it!" said the constable.

"And the rest of you able-bodied—"

"Able-bodied men—yes—the rest of ye!" said the constable.

"Have you some good stout staves and pitchforks—"

"Staves and pitchforks—in the name o' the law! And take 'em in yer hands and go in quest, and do as we in authority tell ye!"

115   Thus aroused, the men prepared to give chase. The evidence was, indeed, though circumstantial, so convincing, that but little argument was needed to show the shepherd's guests that after what they had seen it would look very much like connivance if they did not instantly pursue the unhappy third stranger, who could not as yet have gone more than a few hundred yards over such uneven country.

A shepherd is always well provided with lanterns; and, lighting these hastily, and with hurdle-staves in their hands, they poured out of the door, taking a direction along the crest of the hill, away from the town, the rain having fortunately a little abated.

Disturbed by the noise, or possibly by unpleasant dreams of her baptism, the child who had been christened began to cry heart-brokenly in the room overhead. These notes of grief came down through the chinks of the floor to the ears of the women below, who jumped up one by one, and seemed glad of the excuse to ascend and comfort the baby, for the incidents of the last half-hour greatly oppressed them. Thus in the space of two or three minutes the room on the ground-floor was deserted quite.

But it was not for long. Hardly had the sound of footsteps died away when a man returned round the corner of the house from the direction the pursuers had taken. Peeping in at the door, and seeing nobody there, he entered leisurely. It was the stranger of the chimney corner, who had gone out with the rest. The motive of his return was shown by his helping himself to a cut piece of skimmer-cake that lay on a ledge beside where he had sat, and which he had apparently forgotten to take with him. He also poured out half a cup more mead from the quantity that remained, ravenously eating and drinking these as he stood. He had not finished when another figure came in just as quietly—his friend in cinder-gray.

"Oh—you here?" said the latter, smiling. "I thought you had gone to help in the capture." And this speaker also revealed the object of his return by looking solicitously round for the fascinating mug of old mead.

"And I thought you had gone," said the other, continuing his skimmer-cake   *120* with some effort.

"Well, on second thoughts, I felt there were enough without me," said the first confidentially, "and such a night as it is, too. Besides, 'tis the business o' the Government to take care of its criminals—not mine."

"True; so it is. And I felt as you did, that there were enough without me."

"I don't want to break my limbs running over the humps and hollows of this wild country."

"Nor I neither, between you and me."

"These shepherd-people are used to it—simple-minded souls, you know,   *125* stirred up to anything in a moment. They'll have him ready for me before the morning, and no trouble to me at all."

"They'll have him, and we shall have saved ourselves all labor in the matter."

"True, true. Well, my way is to Casterbridge; and 'tis as much as my legs will do to take me that far. Going the same way?"

"No, I am sorry to say! I have to get home over there" (he nodded indefinitely to the right), "and I feel as you do, that it is quite enough for my legs to do before bedtime."

The other had by this time finished the mead in the mug, after which, shaking hands heartily at the door, and wishing each other well, they went their several ways.

In the meantime the company of pursuers had reached the end of the hog's-   *130* back elevation which dominated this part of the down. They had decided on no particular plan of action; and, finding that the man of the baleful trade was no longer in their company, they seemed quite unable to form any such plan now. They descended in all directions down the hill, and straightway several of the party fell into the snare set by Nature for all misguided midnight ramblers over this part of the cretaceous formation. The "lanchets," or flint slopes, which belted the escarpment at intervals of a dozen yards, took the less cautious ones unawares, and losing their footing on the rubbly steep they slid sharply downward, the lanterns rolling from their hands to the bottom, and there lying on their sides till the horn was scorched through.

When they had again gathered themselves together, the shepherd, as the man who knew the country best, took the lead, and guided them round these treacherous inclines. The lanterns, which seemed rather to dazzle their eyes and warn the fugitive than to assist them in the exploration, were extinguished, due silence was observed; and in this more rational order they plunged into the vale. It was a grassy, briery, moist defile, affording some shelter to any person who had sought it; but the party perambulated it in vain, and ascended on the other side. Here they wandered apart, and after an interval closed together again to report progress. At the second time of closing in they found themselves near a lonely ash, the single tree on this part of the coomb, probably sown there by a passing bird some fifty years before. And here, standing a little to one side of the trunk, as motionless as the trunk itself appeared the man they were in quest of, his outline being well defined against the sky beyond. The band noiselessly drew up and faced him.

"Your money or your life!" said the constable sternly to the still figure.

"No, no," whispered John Pitcher. "'Tisn't our side ought to say that. That's the doctrine of vagabonds like him, and we be on the side of the law."

"Well, well," replied the constable, impatiently; "I must say something, mustn't I? and if you had all the weight o' this undertaking upon your mind, perhaps you'd say the wrong thing, too!—Prisoner at the bar, surrender in the name of the Father—the Crown, I mane!"

135   The man under the tree seemed now to notice them for the first time, and, giving them no opportunity whatever for exhibiting their courage, he strolled slowly toward them. He was, indeed, the little man, the third stranger; but his trepidation had in a great measure gone.

"Well, travelers," he said, "did I hear you speak to me?"

"You did; you've got to come and be our prisoner at once!" said the constable. "We arrest 'ee on the charge of not biding in Casterbridge jail in a decent proper manner to be hung tomorrow morning. Neighbors, do your duty, and seize the culprit!"

On hearing the charge, the man seemed enlightened, and, saying not another word, resigned himself with preternatural civility to the search-party, who, with their staves in their hands, surrounded him on all sides, and marched him back toward the shepherd's cottage.

It was eleven o'clock by the time they arrived. The light shining from the open door, a sound of men's voices within, proclaimed to them as they approached the house that some new events had arisen in their absence. On entering they discovered the shepherd's living-room to be invaded by two officers from Casterbridge jail, and a well-known magistrate who lived at the nearest county-seat, intelligence of the escape having become generally circulated.

"Gentlemen," said the constable, "I have brought back your man—not with- *140*
out risk and danger; but everyone must do his duty! He is inside this circle of able-
bodied persons, who have lent me useful aid, considering their ignorance of Crown
work.—Men, bring forward your prisoner!" And the third stranger was led to the
light.

"Who is this?" said one of the officials.

"The man," said the constable.

"Certainly not," said the turnkey; and the first corroborated his statement.

"But how can it be otherwise?" asked the constable. "Or why was he so terrified at sight o' the singing instrument of the law who sat there?" Here he related the
strange behavior of the third stranger on entering the house during the hangman's
song.

"Can't understand it," said the officer coolly. "All I know is that it is not the *145*
condemned man. He's quite a different character from this one; a gauntish fellow,
with dark hair and eyes, rather good-looking, and with a musical bass voice that if
you heard it once you'd never mistake as long as you lived."

"Why, souls—'twas the man in the chimney corner!"

"Hey—what?" said the magistrate, coming forward after inquiring particulars
from the shepherd in the background. "Haven't you got the man after all?"

"Well, Sir," said the constable, "he's the man we were in search of, that's true;
and yet he's not the man we were in search of. For the man we were in search of was
not the man we wanted, Sir, if you understand my everyday way; for 'twas the man
in the chimney corner!"

"A pretty kettle of fish altogether!" said the magistrate. "You had better start
for the other man at once."

The prisoner now spoke for the first time. The mention of the man in the chim- *150*
ney corner seemed to have moved him as nothing else could do. "Sir," he said, stepping forward to the magistrate, "take no more trouble about me. The time is come
when I may as well speak. I have done nothing; my crime is that the condemned
man is my brother. Early this afternoon I left home at Shottsford to tramp it all the
way to Casterbridge jail to bid him farewell. I was benighted, and called here to rest
and ask the way. When I opened the door I saw before me the very man, my brother,
that I thought to see in the condemned cell at Casterbridge. He was in this chimney
corner; and jammed close to him, so that he could not have got out if he had tried,
was the executioner who'd come to take his life, singing a song about it and not
knowing that it was his victim who was close by, joining in to save appearances. My
brother looked a glance of agony at me, and I know he meant, 'Don't reveal what
you see; my life depends on it.' I was so terror-struck that I could hardly stand, and,
not knowing what I did, I turned and hurried away."

The narrator's manner and tone had the stamp of truth, and his story made a
great impression on all around. "And do you know where your brother is at the present time?" asked the magistrate.

"I do not. I have never seen him since I closed this door."

"I can testify to that, for we've been between ye ever since," said the constable.

"Where does he think to fly to?—what is his occupation?"

"He's a watch-and-clock-maker, Sir." *155*

" 'A said 'a was a wheelwright—a wicked rogue," said the constable.

"The wheels of clocks and watches he meant, no doubt," said Shepherd Fennel. "I thought his hands were palish for's trade."

"Well, it appears to me that nothing can be gained by retaining this poor man in custody," said the magistrate; "your business lies with the other, unquestionably."

And so the little man was released off-hand; but he looked nothing the less sad on that account, it being beyond the power of magistrate or constable to raze out the written troubles in his brain, for they concerned another whom he regarded with more solicitude than himself. When this was done, and the man had gone his way, the night was found to be so far advanced that it was deemed useless to renew the search before the next morning.

160   Next day, accordingly, the quest for the clever sheep-stealer became general and keen, to all appearance at least. But the intended punishment was cruelly disproportioned to the transgression, and the sympathy of a great many country-folk in that district was strongly on the side of the fugitive. Moreover, his marvelous coolness and daring in hob-and-nobbing with the hangman, under the unprecedented circumstances of the shepherd's party, won their admiration. So that it may be questioned if all those who ostensibly made themselves so busy in exploring woods and fields and lanes were quite so thorough when it came to the private examination of their own lofts and outhouses. Stories were afloat of a mysterious figure being occasionally seen in some old overgrown trackway or other, remote from turnpike roads, but when a search was instituted in any of these suspected quarters nobody was found. Thus the days and weeks passed without tidings.

In brief, the bass-voiced man of the chimney corner was never recaptured. Some said that he went across the sea, others that he did not, but buried himself in the depths of a populous city. At any rate, the gentleman in cinder-gray never did his morning's work at Casterbridge, nor met anywhere at all, for business purposes, the genial comrade with whom he had passed an hour of relaxation in the lonely house on the coomb.

The grass has long been green on the graves of Shepherd Fennel and his frugal wife; the guests who made up the christening parry have mainly followed their entertainers to the tomb; the baby in whose honor they all had met is a matron in the sere and yellow leaf. But the arrival of the three strangers at the shepherd's that night, and the details connected therewith, is a story as well-known as ever in the country about Higher Crowstairs.

Nathaniel Hawthorne (1804–1864)

# *Young Goodman Brown*												1835

Young Goodman Brown came forth at sunset, into the street of Salem village,° but put his head back, after crossing the threshold, to exchange a parting kiss with his young wife. And Faith, as the wife was aptly named, thrust her own pretty head into the street, letting the wind play with the pink ribbons of her cap, while she called to Goodman Brown.

"Dearest heart," whispered she, softly and rather sadly, when her lips were close to his ear, "prithee, put off your journey until sunrise, and sleep in your own bed tonight. A lone woman is troubled with such dreams and such thoughts, that she's afeared of herself, sometimes. Pray, tarry with me this night, dear husband, of all nights in the year!"

"My love and my Faith," replied young Goodman Brown, "of all nights in the year; this one night must I tarry away from thee. My journey, as thou callest it, forth and back again, must needs be done 'twixt now and sunrise. What, my sweet, pretty wife, dost thou doubt me already, and we but three months married!"

"Then God bless you!" said Faith with the pink ribbons, "and may you find all well, when you come back."

"Amen!" cried Goodman Brown. "Say thy prayers, dear Faith, and go to bed   5 at dusk, and no harm will come to thee."

So they parted; and the young man pursued his way, until, being about to turn the corner by the meeting-house, he looked back and saw the head of Faith still peeping after him, with a melancholy air, in spite of her pink ribbons.

"Poor little Faith!" thought he, for his heart smote him. "What a wretch am I, to leave her on such an errand! She talks of dreams, too. Methought, as she spoke, there was trouble in her face, as if a dream had warned her what work is to be done tonight. But no, no! 'twould kill her to think it. Well, she's a blessed angel on earth; and after this one night, I'll cling to her skirts and follow her to Heaven."

With this excellent resolve for the future, Goodman Brown felt himself justified in making more haste on his present evil purpose. He had taken a dreary road, darkened by all the gloomiest trees of the forest, which barely stood aside to let the narrow path creep through, and closed immediately behind. It was all as lonely as could be; and there is this peculiarity in such a solitude, that the traveller knows not who may be concealed by the innumerable trunks and the thick boughs overhead; so that, with lonely footsteps, he may yet be passing through an unseen multitude.

"There may be a devilish Indian behind every tree," said Goodman Brown to himself; and he glanced fearfully behind him, as he added, "What if the devil himself should be at my very elbow!"

Salem village: in Massachusetts, about fifteen miles north of Boston. The time of the story is the seventeenth or early eighteenth century.

10   His head being turned back, he passed a crook of the road, and looking forward again, beheld the figure of a man, in grave and decent attire, seated at the foot of an old tree. He arose at Goodman Brown's approach, and walked onward, side by side with him.

  "You are late, Goodman Brown," said he. "The clock of the Old South° was striking, as I came through Boston; and that is full fifteen minutes agone."

  "Faith kept me back a while," replied the young man, with a tremor in his voice, caused by the sudden appearance of his companion, though not wholly unexpected.

  It was now deep dusk in the forest, and deepest in that part of it where these two were journeying. As nearly as could be discerned, the second traveller was about fifty years old, apparently in the same rank of life as Goodman Brown, and bearing a considerable resemblance to him, though perhaps more in expression than features. Still, they might have been taken for father and son. And yet, though the elder person was as simply clad as the younger, and as simple in manner too, he had an indescribable air of one who knew the world, and would not have felt abashed at the governor's dinner-table, or in King William's° court, were it possible that his affairs should call him thither. But the only thing about him that could be fixed upon as remarkable, was his staff, which bore the likeness of a great black snake, so curiously wrought, that it might almost be seen to twist and wriggle itself like a living serpent. This, of course, must have been an ocular deception, assisted by the uncertain light.

  "Come, Goodman Brown!" cried his fellow-traveller, "this is a dull pace for the beginning of a journey. Take my staff, if you are so soon weary."

15   "Friend," said the other, exchanging his slow pace for a full stop, "having kept covenant by meeting thee here, it is my purpose now to return whence I came. I have scruples, touching the matter thou wot'st of."°

  "Sayest thou so?" replied he of the serpent, smiling apart. "Let us walk on, nevertheless, reasoning as we go, and if I convince thee not, thou shalt turn back. We are but a little way in the forest, yet."

  "Too far, too far!" exclaimed the goodman, unconsciously resuming his walk. "My father never went into the woods on such an errand, nor his father before him. We have been a race of honest men and good Christians, since the days of the martyrs.° And shall I be the first of the name of Brown that ever took this path and kept—"

  "Such company, thou wouldst say," observed the elder person, interrupting his pause. "Well said, Goodman Brown! I have been as well acquainted with your family as ever a one among the Puritans; and that's no trifle to say. I helped your grandfather, the constable, when he lashed the Quaker woman so smartly through the streets of Salem. And it was I that brought your father a pitch-pine knot, kindled

  Old South: The Old South Church, in Boston, is still there.
  King William: William III was king of England from 1688 to 1701 (the time of the story). William IV was king from 1830 to 1837 (the period when Hawthorne wrote the story).
  thou wot'st: you know (thou knowest).
  days of the martyrs: the period of martyrdom of Protestants in England during the reign of Queen Mary (1553–1558).

at my own hearth, to set fire to an Indian village, in King Philip's war.° They were my good friends, both; and many a pleasant walk have we had along this path, and returned merrily after midnight. I would fain be friends with you, for their sake."

"If it be as thou sayest," replied Goodman Brown, "I marvel they never spoke of these matters. Or, verily, I marvel not, seeing that the least rumor of the sort would have driven them from New England. We are a people of prayer, and good works to boot, and abide no such wickedness."

"Wickedness or not," said the traveller with twisted staff, "I have a very general acquaintance here in New England. The deacons of many a church have drunk the communion wine with me; the selectmen, of divers towns, make me their chairman; and a majority of the Great and General Court are firm supporters of my interest. The governor and I, too—but these are state secrets." 20

"Can this be so!" cried Goodman Brown, with a stare of amazement at his undisturbed companion. "Howbeit, I have nothing to do with the governor and council; they have their own ways, and are no rule for a simple husbandman like me. But, were I to go on with thee, how should I meet the eye of that good old man, our minister, at Salem village? Oh, his voice would make me tremble, both Sabbath-day and lecture-day!"

Thus far, the elder traveller had listened with due gravity, but now burst into a fit of irrepressible mirth, shaking himself so violently, that his snakelike staff actually seemed to wriggle in sympathy.

"Ha! ha! ha!" shouted he, again and again; then composing himself, "Well, go on, Goodman Brown, go on; but, prithee, don't kill me with laughing!"

"Well, then, to end the matter at once," said Goodman Brown, considerably nettled, "there is my wife, Faith. It would break her dear little heart; and I'd rather break my own!"

"Nay, if that be the case," answered the other, "e'en go thy ways, Goodman Brown. I would not, for twenty old women like the one hobbling before us, that Faith should come to any harm." 25

As he spoke, he pointed his staff at a female figure on the path, in whom Goodman Brown recognized a very pious and exemplary dame, who had taught him his catechism in youth, and was still his moral and spiritual adviser, jointly with the minister and Deacon Gookin.

"A marvel, truly, that Goody° Cloyse should be so far in the wilderness, at night-fall!" said he. "But, with your leave, friend, I shall take a cut through the woods, until we have left this Christian woman behind. Being a stranger to you, she might ask whom I was consorting with, and whither I was going."

"Be it so," said his fellow-traveller. "Betake you to the woods, and let me keep the path."

Accordingly, the young man turned aside, but took care to watch his companion, who advanced softly along the road, until he had come within a staff's length of

King Philip's war: This war (1675–1676), infamous for the atrocities committed by the New England settlers, resulted in the suppression of Indian tribal life and prepared the way for unlimited settlement of New England by European immigrants. "Philip" was the English name of Chief Metacomet of the Wampanoag tribe.

Goody: shortened form of "goodwife," a respectful name for a married woman of low rank. A "Goody Cloyse" was one of the women sentenced to execution by Hawthorne's great-grandfather, Judge John Hathorne.

the old dame. She, meanwhile, was making the best of her way, with singular speed for so aged a woman, and mumbling some indistinct words, a prayer, doubtless, as she went. The traveller put forth his staff, and touched her withered neck with what seemed the serpent's tail.

30   "The devil!" screamed the pious old lady.

"Then Goody Cloyse knows her old friend?" observed the traveller, confronting her, and leaning on his writhing stick.

"Ah, forsooth, and is it your worship, indeed?" cried the good dame. "Yea, truly is it, and in the very image of my old gossip,° Goodman Brown, the grandfather of the silly fellow that now is. But, would your worship believe it? My broomstick hath strangely disappeared, stolen, as I suspect, by that unhanged witch, Goody Cory,° and that, too, when I was all anointed with the juice of smallage and cinquefoil and wolf's-bane—"°

"Mingled with fine wheat and the fat of a new-born babe," said the shape of old Goodman Brown.

"Ah, your worship knows the recipe," cried the old lady, cackling aloud. "So, as I was saying, being all ready for the meeting, and no horse to ride on, I made up my mind to foot it; for they tell me there is a nice young man to be taken into communion tonight. But now your good worship will lend me your arm, and we shall be there in a twinkling."

35   "That can hardly be," answered her friend. "I will not spare you my arm, Goody Cloyse, but here is my staff, if you will."

So saying, he threw it down at her feet, where, perhaps, it assumed life, being one of the rods which its owner had formerly lent to the Egyptian Magi.° Of this fact, however, Goodman Brown could not take cognizance. He had cast up his eyes in astonishment, and looking down again, beheld neither Goody Cloyse nor the serpentine staff, but his fellow-traveller alone, who waited for him as calmly as if nothing had happened.

"That old woman taught me my catechism!" said the young man; and there was a world of meaning in this simple comment.

They continued to walk onward, while the elder traveller exhorted his companion to make good speed and persevere in the path, discoursing so aptly, that his arguments seemed rather to spring up in the bosom of his auditor, than to be suggested by himself. As they went he plucked a branch of maple, to serve for a walking-stick, and began to strip it of the twigs and little boughs, which were wet with evening dew. The moment his fingers touched them, they became strangely withered and dried up, as with a week's sunshine. Thus the pair proceeded, at a good free pace, until suddenly, in a gloomy hollow of the road, Goodman Brown sat himself down on the stump of a tree, and refused to go any farther.

"Friend," said he, stubbornly, "my mind is made up. Not another step will I budge on this errand. What if a wretched old woman do choose to go to the devil,

---

gossip: from "good sib" or "good relative."

Goody Cory: the name of a woman who was also sent to execution by Judge Hathorne.

smallage and cinquefoil and wolf's-bane: plants commonly used by witches in making ointments.

lent to the Egyptian Magi: See Exodus 7:10–12.

when I thought she was going to Heaven! Is that any reason why I should quit my dear Faith, and go after her?"

"You will think better of this by and by," said his acquaintance, composedly.   *40*
"Sit here and rest yourself a while; and when you feel like moving again, there is my staff to help you along."

Without more words, he threw his companion the maple stick, and was as speedily out of sight as if he had vanished into the deepening gloom. The young man sat a few moments by the roadside, applauding himself greatly, and thinking with how clear a conscience he should meet the minister, in his morning walk, nor shrink from the eye of good old Deacon Gookin. And what calm sleep would be his, that very night, which was to have been spent so wickedly, but purely and sweetly now, in the arms of Faith! Amidst these pleasant and praiseworthy meditations, Goodman Brown heard the tramp of horses along the road, and deemed it advisable to conceal himself within the verge of the forest, conscious of the guilty purpose that had brought him thither, though now so happily turned from it.

On came the hoof-tramps and the voices of the riders, two grave old voices, conversing soberly as they drew near. These mingled sounds appeared to pass along the road, within a few yards of the young man's hiding-place; but owing, doubtless, to the depth of the gloom, at that particular spot, neither the travellers nor their steeds were visible. Though their figures brushed the small boughs by the wayside, it could not be seen that they intercepted, even for a moment, the faint gleam from the strip of bright sky, athwart which they must have passed. Goodman Brown alternately crouched and stood on tiptoe, pulling aside the branches, and thrusting forth his head as far as he durst, without discerning so much as a shadow. It vexed him the more, because he could have sworn, were such a thing possible, that he recognized the voices of the minister and Deacon Gookin, jogging° along quietly, as they were wont to do, when bound to some ordination or ecclesiastical council. While yet within hearing, one of the riders stopped to pluck a switch.

"Of the two, reverend Sir," said the voice like the deacon's, "I had rather miss an ordination dinner than tonight's meeting. They tell me that some of our community are to be here from Falmouth and beyond, and others from Connecticut and Rhode Island; besides several of the Indian powwows,° who, after their fashion, know almost as much deviltry as the best of us. Moreover, there is a goodly young woman to be taken into communion."

"Mighty well, Deacon Gookin" replied the solemn old tones of the minister. "Spur up, or we shall be late. Nothing can be done, you know, until I get on the ground."

The hoofs clattered again, and the voices, talking so strangely in the empty air,   *45*
passed on through the forest, where no church had ever been gathered, nor solitary Christian prayed. Whither, then, could these holy men be journeying, so deep into the heathen wilderness? Young Goodman Brown caught hold of a tree, for support, being ready to sink down on the ground, faint and over-burthened with the heavy

---

jogging: riding a horse at a slow trot; not to be confused with the current meaning of "jogging," which refers to running slowly on foot.

powwows: a Narragansett Indian word describing a ritual ceremony of dancing, incantation, and magic.

sickness of his heart. He looked up to the sky, doubting whether there really was a Heaven above him. Yet, there was the blue arch, and the stars brightening in it.

"With Heaven above, and Faith below, I will yet stand firm against the devil!" cried Goodman Brown.

While he still gazed upward, into the deep arch of the firmament, and had lifted his hands to pray, a cloud, though no wind was stirring, hurried across the zenith, and hid the brightening stars. The blue sky was still visible, except directly overhead, where this black mass of cloud was sweeping swiftly northward. Aloft in the air, as if from the depths of the cloud, came a confused and doubtful sound of voices. Once, the listener fancied that he could distinguish the accents of town's people of his own, men and women, both pious and ungodly, many of whom he had met at the communion-table, and had seen others rioting at the tavern. The next moment, so indistinct were the sounds, he doubted whether he had heard aught but the murmur of the old forest, whispering without a wind. Then came a stronger swell of those familiar tones, heard daily in the sunshine, at Salem village, but never, until now, from a cloud at night. There was one voice, of a young woman, uttering lamentations, yet with an uncertain sorrow, and entreating for some favor, which, perhaps, it would grieve her to obtain. And all the unseen multitude, both saints and sinners, seemed to encourage her onward.

"Faith!" shouted Goodman Brown, in a voice of agony and desperation; and the echoes of the forest mocked him, crying—"Faith! Faith!" as if bewildered wretches were seeking her, all through the wilderness.

The cry of grief, rage, and terror was yet piercing the night, when the unhappy husband held his breath for a response. There was a scream, drowned immediately in a louder murmur of voices fading into far-off laughter, as the dark cloud swept away, leaving the clear and silent sky above Goodman Brown. But something fluttered lightly down through the air, and caught on the branch of a tree. The young man seized it and beheld a pink ribbon.

50   "My Faith is gone!" cried he, after one stupefied moment. "There is no good on earth, and sin is but a name. Come, devil! for to thee is this world given."

And maddened with despair, so that he laughed loud and long, did Goodman Brown grasp his staff and set forth again, at such a rate, that he seemed to fly along the forest path, rather than to walk or run. The road grew wilder and drearier, and more faintly traced, and vanished at length, leaving him in the heart of the dark wilderness, still rushing onward, with the instinct that guides mortal man to evil. The whole forest was peopled with frightful sounds; the creaking of the trees, the howling of wild beasts, and the yell of Indians; while, sometimes, the wind tolled like a distant church bell, and sometimes gave a broad roar around the traveller, as if all Nature were laughing him to scorn. But he was himself the chief horror of the scene, and shrank not from its other horrors.

"Ha! ha! ha!" roared Goodman Brown, when the wind laughed at him. "Let us hear which will laugh loudest! Think not to frighten me with your deviltry! Come witch, come wizard, come Indian powwow, come devil himself! and here comes Goodman Brown. You may as well fear him as he fear you!"

In truth, all through the haunted forest, there could be nothing more frightful than the figure of Goodman Brown. On he flew, among the black pines, brandishing his staff with frenzied gestures, now giving vent to an inspiration of horrid blasphemy, and now shouting forth such laughter, as set all the echoes of the forest laughing like demons around him. The fiend in his own shape is less hideous than when he rages in the breast of man. Thus sped the demoniac on his course, until, quivering among the trees, he saw a red light before him, as when the felled trunks and branches of a clearing have been set on fire, and throw up their lurid blaze against the sky, at the hour of midnight. He paused, in a lull of the tempest that had driven him onward, and heard the swell of what seemed a hymn, rolling solemnly from a distance, with the weight of many voices. He knew the tune. It was a familiar one in the choir of the village meeting-house. The verse died heavily away, and was lengthened by a chorus, not of human voices, but of all the sounds of the benighted wilderness, pealing in awful harmony together. Goodman Brown cried out; and his cry was lost to his own ear, by its unison with the cry of the desert.

In the interval of silence, he stole forward, until the light glared full upon his eyes. At one extremity of an open space, hemmed in by the dark wall of the forest, arose a rock, bearing some rude, natural resemblance either to an altar or a pulpit, and surrounded by four blazing pines, their tops aflame, their stems untouched, like candles at an evening meeting. The mass of foliage, that had overgrown the summit of the rock, was all on fire, blazing high into the night, and fitfully illuminating the whole field. Each pendent twig and leafy festoon was in a blaze. As the red light arose and fell, a numerous congregation alternately shone forth, then disappeared in shadow, and again grew, as it were, out of the darkness, peopling the heart of the solitary woods at once.

"A grave and dark-clad company!" quoth Goodman Brown.

55

In truth, they were such. Among them, quivering to-and-fro, between gloom and splendor, appeared faces that would be seen, next day, at the council-board of the province, and others which, Sabbath after Sabbath, looked devoutly heavenward, and benignantly over the crowded pews, from the holiest pulpits in the land. Some affirm that the lady of the governor was there. At least, there were high dames well known to her, and wives of honored husbands, and widows a great multitude, and ancient maidens, all of excellent repute, and fair young girls, who trembled lest their mothers should espy them. Either the sudden gleams of light, flashing over the obscure field, bedazzled Goodman Brown, or he recognized a score of the church members of Salem village, famous for their especial sanctity. Good old Deacon Gookin had arrived, and waited at the skirts of that venerable saint, his reverend pastor. But, irreverently consorting with these grave, reputable, and pious people, these elders of the church, these chaste dames and dewy virgins, there were men of dissolute lives and women of spotted fame, wretches given over to all mean and filthy vice, and suspected even of horrid crimes. It was strange to see, that the good shrank not from the wicked, nor were the sinners abashed by the saints. Scattered, also, among their pale-faced enemies, were the Indian priests, or powwows, who had often scared their native forest with more hideous incantations than any known to English witchcraft.

"But, where is Faith?" thought Goodman Brown; and, as hope came into his heart, he trembled.

Another verse of the hymn arose, a slow and mournful strain, such as the pious love, but joined to words which expressed all that our nature can conceive of sin, and darkly hinted at far more. Unfathomable to mere mortals is the lore of fiends. Verse after verse was sung, and still the chorus of the desert swelled between, like the deepest tone of a mighty organ. And, with the final peal of that dreadful anthem, there came a sound, as if the roaring wind, the rushing streams, the howling beasts, and every other voice of the unconverted wilderness were mingling and according with the voice of guilty man, in homage to the prince of all. The four blazing pines threw up a loftier flame, and obscurely discovered shapes and visages of horror on the smoke-wreaths, above the impious assembly. At the same moment, the fire on the rock shot redly forth, and formed a glowing arch above its base, where now appeared a figure. With reverence be it spoken, the apparition bore no slight similitude, both in garb and manner, to some grave divine of the New England churches.

"Bring forth the converts!" cried a voice, that echoed through the field and rolled into the forest.

60   At the word, Goodman Brown stepped forth from the shadow of the trees, and approached the congregation, with whom he felt a loathful brotherhood, by the sympathy of all that was wicked in his heart. He could have well-nigh sworn, that the shape of his own dead father beckoned him to advance, looking downward from a smoke-wreath, while a woman, with dim features of despair, threw out her hand to warn him back. Was it his mother? But he had no power to retreat one step, nor to resist, even in thought, when the minister and good old Deacon Gookin seized his arms, and led him to the blazing rock. Thither came also the slender form of a veiled female, led between Goody Cloyse, that pious teacher of the catechism, and Martha Carrier, who had received the devil's promise to be queen of hell. A rampant hag was she! And there stood the proselytes, beneath the canopy of fire.

"Welcome, my children," said the dark figure, "to the communion of your race! Ye have found, thus young, your nature and your destiny. My children, look behind you!"

They turned; and flashing forth, as it were, in a sheet of flame, the fiend-worshippers were seen; the smile of welcome gleamed darkly on every visage.

"There," resumed the sable form, "are all whom ye have reverenced from youth. Ye deemed them holier than yourselves, and shrank from your own sin, contrasting it with their lives of righteousness and prayerful aspirations heavenward. Yet, here are they all, in my worshipping assembly! This night it shall be granted you to know their secret deeds; how hoary-bearded elders of the church have whispered wanton words to the young maids of their households; how many a woman, eager for widow's weeds, has given her husband a drink at bedtime, and let him sleep his last sleep in her bosom; how beardless youths have made haste to inherit their father's wealth; and how fair damsels—blush not, sweet ones!—have dug little graves in the garden, and bidden me, the sole guest, to an infant's funeral. By the sympathy of your human hearts for sin, ye shall scent out all the places—whether in church, bed-chamber, street, field, or forest—where crime has been committed, and shall exult to behold the whole earth one stain of guilt, one mighty blood-spot. Far more than this! It shall be yours to penetrate, in every bosom, the deep mystery of sin, the fountain of all wicked arts, and which inexhaustibly supplies more evil impulses than human power—than my power, at its utmost!—can make manifest in deeds. And now, my children, look upon each other."

They did so; and, by the blaze of the hell-kindled torches, the wretched man beheld his Faith, and the wife her husband, trembling before that unhallowed altar.

"Lo! there ye stand, my children," said the figure, in a deep and solemn tone, almost sad, with its despairing awfulness, as if his once angelic nature° could yet mourn for our miserable race. Depending upon one another's hearts, ye had still hoped that virtue were not all a dream! Now are ye undeceived!—Evil is the nature of mankind. Evil must be your only happiness. Welcome, again, my children, to the communion of your race!" 65

Welcome!" repeated the fiend-worshippers, in one cry of despair and triumph.

And there they stood, the only pair, as it seemed, who were yet hesitating on the verge of wickedness, in this dark world. A basin was hollowed, naturally, in the rock. Did it contain water, reddened by the lurid light? or was it blood? or, perchance, a liquid flame? Herein did the Shape of Evil dip his hand, and prepare to lay the mark of baptism upon their foreheads, that they might be partakers of the mystery of sin, more conscious of the secret guilt of others, both in deed and thought, than they could now be of their own. The husband cast one look at his pale wife, and Faith at him. What polluted wretches would the next glance show them to each other, shuddering alike at what they disclosed and what they saw!

"Faith! Faith!" cried the husband. "Look up to Heaven, and resist the Wicked One!"

Whether Faith obeyed, he knew not. Hardly had he spoken, when he found himself amid calm night and solitude, listening to a roar of the wind, which died heavily away through the forest He staggered against the rock, and felt it chill and damp, while a hanging twig, that had been all on fire, besprinkled his cheek with the coldest dew.

The next morning, young Goodman Brown came slowly into the street of Salem village staring around him like a bewildered man. The good old minister was taking a walk along the grave-yard, to get an appetite for breakfast and meditate his sermon, and bestowed a blessing, as he passed, on Goodman Brown. He shrank from the venerable saint, as if to avoid an anathema. Old Deacon Gookin was at domestic worship, and the holy words of his prayer were heard through the open window. "What God doth the wizard pray to?" quoth Goodman Brown. Goody Cloyse, that excellent old Christian, stood in the early sunshine, at her own lattice, catechising a little girl, who had brought her a pint of morning's milk. Goodman Brown snatched away the child, as from the grasp of the fiend himself. Turning the corner by the meetinghouse, he spied the head of Faith, with the pink ribbons, gazing anxiously forth, and bursting into such joy at the sight of him that she skipt along the street, and almost kissed her husband before the whole village. But Goodman Brown looked sternly and sadly into her face, and passed on without a greeting. 70

Had Goodman Brown fallen asleep in the forest, and only dreamed a wild dream of a witch-meeting?

Be it so, if you will. But, alas! it was a dream of evil omen for young Goodman Brown. A stern, a sad, a darkly meditative, a distrustful, if not a desperate man did he become, from the night of that fearful dream. On the Sabbath day, when the congregation were singing a holy psalm, he could not listen, because an anthem of

once angelic nature: Lucifer ("light carrier"), another name for the Devil, led the traditional revolt of the angels and was thrown into hell as his punishment. See Isaiah 14:12-15.

sin rushed loudly upon his ear, and drowned all the blessed strain. When the minister spoke from the pulpit, with power and fervid eloquence, and with his hand on the open Bible, of the sacred truths of our religion, and of saint-like lives and triumphant deaths, and of future bliss or misery unutterable, then did Goodman Brown turn pale, dreading lest the roof should thunder down upon the gray blasphemer and his hearers. Often, awaking suddenly at midnight, he shrank from the bosom of Faith, and at morning or eventide, when the family knelt down in prayer, he scowled, and muttered to himself, and gazed sternly at his°wife, and turned away. And when he had lived long, and was borne to his grave, a hoary corpse, followed by Faith, an aged woman, and children and grandchildren, a goodly procession, besides neighbors not a few, they carved no hopeful verse upon his tombstone; for his dying hour was gloom.

Katherine Mansfield (1888–1923)

Miss Brill °   1920

Although it was so brilliantly fine—the blue sky powdered with gold and great spots of light like white wine splashed over the Jardins Publiques°—Miss Brill was glad that she had decided on her fur. The air was motionless, but when you opened your mouth there was just a faint chill, like a chill from a glass of iced water before you sip, and now and again a leaf came drifting—from nowhere, from the sky. Miss Brill put up her hand and touched her fur. Dear little thing! It was nice to feel it again. She had taken it out of its box that afternoon, shaken out the moth-powder, given it a good brush, and rubbed the life back into the dim little eyes. "What has been happening to me?" said the sad little eyes. Oh, how sweet it was to see them snap at her again from the red eiderdown! . . . But the nose, which was of some black composition, wasn't at all firm. It must have had a knock, somehow. Never mind—a little dab of black sealing-wax when the time came—when it was absolutely necessary. . . . Little rogue! Yes, she really felt like that about it. Little rogue biting its tail just by her left ear. She could have taken it off and laid it on her lap and stroked it. She felt a tingling in her hands and arms, but that came from walking, she supposed. And when she breathed, something light and sad—no, not sad, exactly—something gentle seemed to move in her bosom.

There were a number of people out this afternoon, far more than last Sunday. And the band sounded louder and gayer. That was because the Season had begun. For although the band played all the year round on Sundays, out of season it was never the same. It was like some one playing with only the family to listen; it didn't

Miss Brill: Brill is the name of a common deep-sea flatfish.
Jardins Publiques: public gardens or park. The setting of the story is apparently a French seaside town.

care how it played if there weren't any strangers present. Wasn't the conductor wearing a new coat, too? She was sure it was new. He scraped with his foot and flapped his arms like a rooster about to crow, and the bandsmen sitting in the green rotunda blew out their cheeks and glared at the music. Now there came a little "flutey" bit—very pretty!—a little chain of bright drops. She was sure it would be repeated. It was; she lifted her head and smiled.

Only two people shared her "special" seat: a fine old man in a velvet coat, his hands clasped over a huge carved walking-stick, and a big old woman, sitting upright, with a roll of knitting on her embroidered apron. They did not speak. This was disappointing, for Miss Brill always looked forward to the conversation. She had become really quite expert, she thought, at listening as though she didn't listen, at sitting in other people's lives just for a minute while they talked round her.

She glanced, sideways, at the old couple. Perhaps they would go soon. Last Sunday, too, hadn't been as interesting as usual. An Englishman and his wife, he wearing a dreadful Panama hat and she button boots. And she'd gone on the whole time about how she ought to wear spectacles; she knew she needed them; but that it was no good getting any; they'd be sure to break and they'd never keep on. And he'd been so patient. He'd suggested everything—gold rims, the kind that curved round your ears, little pads inside the bridge. No, nothing would please her. "They'll always be sliding down my nose!" Miss Brill had wanted to shake her.

The old people sat on the bench, still as statues. Never mind, there was always   5
the crowd to watch. To and fro, in front of the flower-beds and the band rotunda, the couples and groups paraded, stopped to talk, to greet, to buy a handful of flowers from the old beggar who had his tray fixed to the railings. Little children ran among them, swooping and laughing; little boys with big white silk bows under their chins, little girls, little French dolls, dressed up in velvet and lace. And sometimes a tiny staggerer came suddenly rocking into the open from under the trees, stopped, stared, as suddenly sat down "flop," until its small high-stepping mother, like a young hen, rushed scolding to its rescue. Other people sat on the benches and green chairs, but they were nearly always the same, Sunday after Sunday, and—Miss Brill had often noticed—there was something funny about nearly all of them. They were odd, silent, nearly all old, and from the way they stared they looked as though they'd just come from dark little rooms or even—even cupboards!

Behind the rotunda the slender trees with yellow leaves down drooping, and through them just a line of sea, and beyond the blue sky with gold-veined clouds.

Tum-tum-tum tiddle-um! tiddle-um! tum tiddle-um tum ta! blew the band.

Two young girls in red came by and two young soldiers in blue met them, and they laughed and paired and went off arm-in-arm. Two peasant women with funny straw hats passed, gravely, leading beautiful smoke-coloured donkeys. A cold, pale nun hurried by. A beautiful woman came along and dropped her bunch of violets, and a little boy ran after to hand them to her, and she took them and threw them away as if they'd been poisoned. Dear me! Miss Brill didn't know whether to admire that or not! And now an ermine toque° and a gentleman in grey met just in front of her. He was tall, stiff, dignified, and she was wearing the ermine toque she'd bought when her hair was yellow. Now everything, her hair, her face, even her eyes, was

---

ermine toque: close-fitting hat made of the white fur of an ermine; here the phrase stands for the woman wearing the hat.

the same colour as the shabby ermine, and her hand, in its cleaned glove, lifted to dab her lips, was a tiny yellowish paw. Oh, she was so pleased to see him—delighted! She rather thought they were going to meet that afternoon. She described where she'd been—everywhere, here, there, along by the sea. The day was so charming—didn't he agree? And wouldn't he, perhaps? . . . But he shook his head, lighted a cigarette, slowly breathed a great deep puff into her face, and, even while she was still talking and laughing, flicked the match away and walked on. The ermine toque was alone; she smiled more brightly than ever. But even the band seemed to know what she was feeling and played more softly, played tenderly, and the drum beat, "The Brute! The Brute!" over and over. What would she do? What was going to happen now? But as Miss Brill wondered, the ermine toque turned, raised her hand as though she'd seen some one else, much nicer, just over there, and pattered away. And the band changed again and played more quickly, more gaily than ever, and the old couple on Miss Brill's seat got up and marched away, and such a funny old man with long whiskers hobbled along in time to the music and was nearly knocked over by four girls walking abreast.

Oh, how fascinating it was! How she enjoyed it! How she loved sitting here, watching it all! It was like a play. It was exactly like a play. Who could believe the sky at the back wasn't painted? But it wasn't till a little brown dog trotted on solemn and then slowly trotted off, like a little "theatre" dog, a little dog that had been drugged, that Miss Brill discovered what it was that made it so exciting. They were all on the stage. They weren't only the audience, not only looking on; they were acting. Even she had a part and came every Sunday. No doubt somebody would have noticed if she hadn't been there; she was part of the performance after all. How strange she'd never thought of it like that before! And yet it explained why she made such a point of starting from home at just the same time each week—so as not to be late for the performance—and it also explained why she had quite a queer, shy feeling at telling her English pupils how she spent her Sunday afternoons. No wonder! Miss Brill nearly laughed out loud. She was on the stage. She thought of the old invalid gentleman to whom she read the newspaper four afternoons a week while he slept in the garden. She had got quite used to the frail head on the cotton pillow, the hollowed eyes, the open mouth and the high pinched nose. If he'd been dead she mightn't have noticed for weeks; she wouldn't have minded. But suddenly he knew he was having the paper read to him by an actress! "An actress!" The old head lifted; two points of light quivered in the old eyes. "An actress—are ye?" And Miss Brill smoothed the newspaper as though it were the manuscript of her part and said gently: "Yes, I have been an actress for a long time."

10   The band had been having a rest. Now they started again. And what they played was warm, sunny, yet there was just a faint chill—a something, what was it?—not sadness—no, not sadness—a something that made you want to sing. The tune lifted, lifted, the light shone; and it seemed to Miss Brill that in another moment all of them, all the whole company, would begin singing. The young ones, the laughing ones who were moving together, they would begin, and the men's voices, very resolute and brave, would join them. And then she too, she too, and the others on the benches—they would come in with a kind of accompaniment—something low, that scarcely rose or fell, something so beautiful—moving. . . . And Miss Brill's eyes filled with tears and she looked smiling at all the other members of the company.

Yes, we understand, we understand, she thought—though what they understood she didn't know.

Just at that moment a boy and girl came and sat down where the old couple had been. They were beautifully dressed; they were in love. The hero and heroine, of course, just arrived from his father's yacht. And still soundlessly singing, still with that trembling smile, Miss Brill prepared to listen.

"No, not now," said the girl, "Not here, I can't."

"But why? Because of that stupid old thing at the end there?" asked the boy. "Why does she come here at all—who wants her? Why doesn't she keep her silly old mug at home?"

"It's her fu-fur which is so funny," giggled the girl. "It's exactly like a fried whiting."

"Ah, be off with you!" said the boy in an angry whisper. Then: "Tell me, ma petite chérie—"   15

"No, not here," said the girl. "Not *yet*."

On her way home she usually bought a slice of honeycake at the baker's. It was her Sunday treat. Sometimes there was an almond in her slice, sometimes not. It made a great difference. If there was an almond it was like carrying home a tiny present—a surprise—something that might very well not have been there. She hurried on the almond Sundays and struck the match for the kettle in quite a dashing way.

But to-day she passed the baker's by, climbed the stairs, went into the little dark room—her room like a cupboard—and sat down on the red eiderdown. She sat there for a long time. The box that the fur came out of was on the bed. She unclasped the necklet quickly; quickly, without looking, laid it inside. But when she put the lid on she thought she heard something crying.

Frank O'Connor (1903–1966)

First Confession   1951

All the trouble began when my grandfather died and my grandmother—my father's mother—came to live with us. Relations in the one house are a strain at the best of times, but, to make matters worse, my grandmother was a real old countrywoman and quite unsuited to the life in town. She had a fat, wrinkled old face, and, to Mother's great indignation, went round the house in bare feet—the boots had her crippled, she said. For dinner she had a jug of porter° and a pot of potatoes with—

---

porter: a dark-brown beer.

sometimes—a bit of salt fish, and she poured out the potatoes on the table and ate them slowly, with great relish, using her fingers by way of a fork.

Now, girls are supposed to be fastidious, but I was the one who suffered most from this. Nora, my sister, just sucked up to the old woman for the penny she got every Friday out of the old-age pension, a thing I could not do. I was too honest, that was my trouble; and when I was playing with Bill Connell, the sergeant-major's son, and saw my grandmother steering up the path with the jug of porter sticking out from beneath her shawl I was mortified. I made excuses not to let him come into the house, because I could never be sure what she would be up to when we went in.

When Mother was at work and my grandmother made the dinner I wouldn't touch it. Nora once tried to make me, but I hid under the table from her and took the bread-knife with me for protection. Nora let on to be very indignant (she wasn't, of course, but she knew Mother saw through her, so she sided with Gran) and came after me. I lashed out at her with the bread-knife, and after that she left me alone. I stayed there till Mother came in from work and made my dinner, but when Father came in later Nora said in a shocked voice: "Oh, Dadda, do you know what Jackie did at dinner time?" Then, of course, it all came out; Father gave me a flaking; Mother interfered, and for days after that he didn't speak to me and Mother barely spoke to Nora. And all because of that old woman! God knows, I was heart-scalded.

Then, to crown my misfortune, I had to make my first confession and communion. It was an old woman called Ryan who prepared us for these. She was about the one age with Gran; she was well-to-do, lived in a big house on Montenotte, wore a black cloak and bonnet, and came every day to school at three o'clock when we should have been going home, and talked to us of hell. She may have mentioned the other place as well, but that could only have been by accident, for hell had the first place in her heart.

5   She lit a candle, took out a new half-crown, and offered it to the first boy who would hold one finger—only one finger!—in the flame for five minutes by the school clock. Being always very ambitious I was tempted to volunteer, but I thought it might look greedy. Then she asked were we afraid of holding one finger—only one finger!—in a little candle flame for five minutes and not be afraid of burning all over in roasting hot furnaces for all eternity. "All eternity! Just think of that! A whole lifetime goes by and it's nothing, not even a drop in the ocean of your sufferings." The woman was really interesting about hell, but my attention was all fixed on the half-crown. At the end of the lesson she put it back in her purse. It was a great disappointment; a religious woman like that, you wouldn't think she'd bother about a thing like a half-crown.

Another day she said she knew a priest who woke one night to find a fellow he didn't recognize leaning over the end of his bed. The priest was a bit frightened—naturally enough—but he asked the fellow what he wanted, and the fellow said in a deep, husky voice that he wanted to go to confession. The priest said it was an awkward time and wouldn't it do in the morning, but the fellow said that last time he went to confession, there was one sin he kept back, being ashamed to mention it, and now it was always on his mind. Then the priest knew it was a bad case, because the fellow was after making a bad confession and committing a mortal sin. He got up to dress, and just then the cock crew in the yard outside, and—lo and behold!—when the priest looked round there was no sign of the fellow, only a smell of burning timber, and when the priest looked at his bed didn't he see the print of two hands burned in it? That was because the fellow had made a bad confession. This story made a shocking impression on me.

But the worst of all was when she showed us how to examine our conscience. Did we take the name of the Lord, our God, in vain? Did we honour our father and our mother? (I asked her did this include grandmothers and she said it did.) Did we love our neighbours as ourselves? Did we covet our neighbour's goods? (I thought of the way I felt about the penny that Nora got every Friday.) I decided that, between one thing and another, I must have broken the whole ten commandments, all on account of that old woman, and so far as I could see, so long as she remained in the house I had no hope of ever doing anything else.

I was scared to death of confession. The day the whole class went I let on to have a toothache, hoping my absence wouldn't be noticed; but at three o'clock, just as I was feeling safe, along comes a chap with a message from Mrs. Ryan that I was to go to confession myself on Saturday and be at the chapel for communion with the rest. To make it worse, Mother couldn't come with me and sent Nora instead.

Now, that girl had ways of tormenting me that Mother never knew of. She held my hand as we went down the hill, smiling sadly and saying how sorry she was for me, as if she were bringing me to the hospital for an operation.

"Oh, God help us!" she moaned. "Isn't it a terrible pity you weren't a good boy? Oh, Jackie, my heart bleeds for you! How will you ever think of all your sins? Don't forget you have to tell him about the time you kicked Gran on the shin."   *10*

"Lemme go!" I said, trying to drag myself free of her. "I don't want to go to confession at all."

"But sure, you'll have to go to confession, Jackie," she replied in the same regretful tone. "Sure, if you didn't the parish priest would be up to the house, looking for you. 'Tisn't, God knows, that I'm not sorry for you. Do you remember the time you tried to kill me with the bread-knife under the table? And the language you used to me? I don't know what he'll do with you at all, Jackie. He might have to send you up to the bishop."

I remember thinking bitterly that she didn't know the half of what I had to tell—if I told it. I knew I couldn't tell it, and understood perfectly why the fellow in Mrs. Ryan's story made a bad confession; it seemed to me a great shame that people wouldn't stop criticizing him. I remember that steep hill down to the church, and the sunlit hillsides beyond the valley of the river, which I saw in the gaps between the houses like Adam's last glimpse of Paradise.°

Then, when she had manœuvered me down the long flight of steps to the chapel yard, Nora suddenly changed her tone. She became the raging malicious devil she really was.

"There you are!" she said with a yelp of triumph, hurling me through the church door. "And I hope he'll give you the penitential psalms, you dirty little caffler."   *15*

I knew then I was lost, given up to eternal justice. The door with the coloured-glass panels swung shut behind me, the sunlight went out and gave place to deep shadow, and the wind whistled outside so that the silence within seemed to crackle like ice under my feet. Nora sat in front of me by the confession box. There were a couple of old women ahead of her, and then a miserable-looking poor devil came

Adam's last glimpse of Paradise: Genesis 3:23–24.

and wedged me in at the other side, so that I couldn't escape even if I had the courage. He joined his hands and rolled his eyes in the direction of the roof, muttering aspirations in an anguished tone, and I wondered had he a grandmother too. Only a grandmother could account for a fellow behaving in that heartbroken way, but he was better off than I, for he at least could go and confess his sins; while I would make a bad confession and then die in the night and be continually coming back and burning people's furniture.

Nora's turn came, and I heard the sound of something slamming, and then her voice as if butter wouldn't melt in her mouth, and then another slam, and out she came. God, the hypocrisy of women! Her eyes were lowered, her head was bowed, and her hands were joined very low down on her stomach, and she walked up the aisle to the side altar looking like a saint. You never saw such an exhibition of devotion, and I remembered the devilish malice with which she had tormented me all the way from our door, and wondered were all religious people like that, really. It was my turn now. With the fear of damnation in my soul I went in, and the confessional door closed of itself behind me.

It was pitch-dark and I couldn't see the priest or anything else. Then I really began to be frightened. In the darkness it was a matter between God and me, and He had all the odds. He knew what my intentions were before I even started; I had no chance. All I had ever been told about confession got mixed up in my mind, and I knelt to one wall and said: "Bless me, father, for I have sinned; this is my first confession." I waited for a few minutes, but nothing happened, so I tried it on the other wall. Nothing happened there either. He had me spotted all right.

It must have been then that I noticed the shelf at about one height with my head. It was really a place for grown-up people to rest their elbows, but in my distracted state I thought it was probably the place you were supposed to kneel. Of course, it was on the high side and not very deep, but I was always good at climbing and managed to get up all right. Staying up was the trouble. There was room only for my knees, and nothing you could get a grip on but a sort of wooden moulding a bit above it. I held on to the moulding and repeated the words a little louder, and this time something happened all right. A slide was slammed back; a little light entered the box, and a man's voice said: "Who's there?"

20   "'Tis me, father," I said for fear he mightn't see me and go away again. I couldn't see him at all. The place the voice came from was under the moulding, about level with my knees, so I took a good grip of the moulding and swung myself down till I saw the astonished face of a young priest looking up at me. He had to put his head on one side to see me, and I had to put mine on one side to see him, so we were more or less talking to one another upside-down. It struck me as a queer way of hearing confessions, but I didn't feel it my place to criticize.

"Bless me, father, for I have sinned; this is my first confession," I rattled off all in one breath, and swung myself down the least shade more to make it easier for him.

"What are you doing up there?" he shouted in an angry voice, and the strain the politeness was putting on my hold of the moulding, and the shock of being addressed in such an uncivil tone, were too much for me. I lost my grip, tumbled, and hit the door an unmerciful wallop before I found myself flat on my back in the middle of the aisle. The people who had been waiting stood up with their mouths open. The priest opened the door of the middle box and came out, pushing his biretta back from his forehead; he looked something terrible. Then Nora came scampering down the aisle.

"Oh, you dirty little caffler!" she said. "I might have known you'd do it. I might have known you'd disgrace me. I can't leave you out of my sight for one minute."

Before I could even get to my feet to defend myself she bent down and gave me a clip across the ear. This reminded me that I was so stunned I had even forgotten to cry, so that people might think I wasn't hurt at all, when in fact I was probably maimed for life. I gave a roar out of me.

"What's all this about?" the priest hissed, getting angrier than ever and pushing Nora off me. "How dare you hit the child like that, you little vixen?"   25

"But I can't do my penance with him, father," Nora cried, cocking an outraged eye up to him.

"Well, go and do it, or I'll give you some more to do," he said, giving me a hand up. "Was it coming to confession you were, my poor man?" he asked me.

"'Twas, father," said I with a sob.

"Oh," he said respectfully, "a big hefty fellow like you must have terrible sins. Is this your first?"

"'Tis, father," said I.   30

"Worse and worse," he said gloomily. "The crimes of a lifetime. I don't know will I get rid of you at all today. You'd better wait now till I'm finished with these old ones. You can see by the looks of them they haven't much to tell."

"I will, father," I said with something approaching joy.

The relief of it was really enormous. Nora stuck out her tongue at me from behind his back, but I couldn't even be bothered retorting. I knew from the very moment that man opened his mouth that he was intelligent above the ordinary. When I had time to think, I saw how right I was. It only stood to reason that a fellow confessing after seven years would have more to tell than people that went every week. The crimes of a lifetime, exactly as he said. It was only what he expected, and the rest was the cackle of old women and girls with their talk of hell, the bishop, and the penitential psalms. That was all they knew. I started to make my examination of conscience, and barring the one bad business of my grandmother it didn't seem so bad.

The next time, the priest steered me into the confession box himself and left the shutter back the way I could see him get in and sit down at the further side of the grille from me.

"Well, now," he said, "what do they call you?"   35

"Jackie, father," said I.

"And what's a-trouble to you, Jackie?"

"Father," I said, feeling I might as well get it over while I had him in good humour, "I had it all arranged to kill my grandmother."

He seemed a bit shaken by that, all right, because he said nothing for quite a while.

"My goodness," he said at last, "that'd be a shocking thing to do. What put   40
that into your head?"

"Father," I said, feeling very sorry for myself, "she's an awful woman."

"Is she?" he asked. "What way is she awful?"

"She takes porter, father," I said, knowing well from the way Mother talked of it that this was a mortal sin, and hoping it would make the priest take a more favourable view of my case.

"Oh, my!" he said, and I could see he was impressed.

45 "And snuff, father," said I.

"That's a bad case, sure enough, Jackie," he said.

"And she goes round in her bare feet, father," I went on in a rush of self-pity, "and she knows I don't like her, and she gives pennies to Nora and none to me, and my da sides with her and flakes me, and one night I was so heartscalded I made up my mind I'd have to kill her."

"And what would you do with the body?" he asked with great interest.

"I was thinking I could chop that up and carry it away in a barrow I have," I said.

50 "Begor, Jackie," he said, "do you know you're a terrible child?"

"I know, father," I said, for I was just thinking the same thing myself. "I tried to kill Nora too with a bread-knife under the table, only I missed her."

"Is that the little girl that was beating you just now?" he asked.

"'Tis, father."

"Someone will go for her with a bread-knife one day, and he won't miss her," he said rather cryptically. "You must have great courage. Between ourselves, there's a lot of people I'd like to do the same to but I'd never have the nerve. Hanging is an awful death."

55 "Is it, father?" I asked with the deepest interest—I was always very keen on hanging. "Did you ever see a fellow hanged?"

"Dozens of them," he said solemnly. "And they all died roaring."

"Jay!" I said.

"Oh, a horrible death!" he said with great satisfaction. "Lots of fellows I saw killed their grandmothers too, but they all said 'twas never worth it."

He had me there for a full ten minutes talking, and then walked out the chapel yard with me. I was genuinely sorry to part with him, because he was the most entertaining character I'd ever met in the religious line. Outside, after the shadow of the church, the sunlight was like the roaring of waves on a beach; it dazzled me; and when the frozen silence melted and I heard the screech of trams on the road my heart soared. I knew now I wouldn't die in the night and come back, leaving marks on my mother's furniture. It would be a great worry to her, and the poor soul had enough.

60 Nora was sitting on the railing, waiting for me, and she put on a very sour puss when she saw the priest with me. She was made jealous because a priest had never come out of the church with her.

"Well," she asked coldly, after he left me, "what did he give you?"

"Three Hail Marys," I said.

"Three Hail Marys," she repeated incredulously. "You mustn't have told him anything."

"I told him everything," I said confidently.

65 "About Gran and all?"

"About Gran and all."

(All she wanted was to be able to go home and say I'd made a bad confession.)

"Did you tell him you went for me with the bread-knife?" she asked with a frown.

"I did to be sure."

"And he only gave you three Hail Marys?"   *70*

"That's all."

She slowly got down from the railing with a baffled air. Clearly, this was beyond her. As we mounted the steps back to the main road she looked at me suspiciously.

"What are you sucking?" she asked.

"Bullseyes."

"Was it the priest gave them to you?"   *75*

"'Twas."

"Lord God," she wailed bitterly, "some people have all the luck! 'Tis no advantage to anybody trying to be good. I might just as well be a sinner like you."

Edgar Allan Poe (1809–1849)

The Cask of Amontillado   1846

The thousand injuries of Fortunato I had borne as I best could; but when he ventured upon insult, I vowed revenge. You, who so well know the nature of my soul, will not suppose, however, that I gave utterance to a threat. *At length* I would be avenged: this was a point definitively settled—but the very definitiveness with which it was resolved, precluded the idea of risk. I must not only punish, but punish with impunity. A wrong is unredressed when retribution overtakes its redresser. It is equally unredressed when the avenger fails to make himself felt as such to him who has done the wrong.

It must be understood, that neither by word nor deed had I given Fortunato cause to doubt my good-will. I continued, as was my wont, to smile in his face, and he did not perceive that my smile *now* was at the thought of his immolation.

He had a weak point—this Fortunato—although in other regards he was a man to be respected and even feared. He prided himself on his connoisseurship in wine. Few Italians have the true virtuoso spirit. For the most part their enthusiasm is adopted to suit the time and opportunity—to practice imposture upon the British and Austrian millionaires. In painting and gemmary Fortunato, like his countrymen, was a quack—but in the matter of old wines he was sincere. In this respect I did not differ from him materially: I was skillful in the Italian vintages myself, and bought largely whenever I could.

It was about dusk, one evening during the supreme madness of the carnival season, that I encountered my friend. He accosted me with excessive warmth, for he had been drinking much. The man wore motley. He had on a tight-fitting parti-striped dress, and his head was surmounted by the conical cap and bells. I was so pleased to see him, that I thought I should never have done wringing his hand.

5   I said to him: "My dear Fortunato, you are luckily met. How remarkably well you are looking today! But I have received a pipe of what passes for Amontillado, and I have my doubts."

"How?" said he. "Amontillado? A pipe? Impossible! And in the middle of the carnival!"

"I have my doubts," I replied; "and I was silly enough to pay the full Amontillado price without consulting you in the matter. You were not to be found, and I was fearful of losing a bargain."

"Amontillado!"

"I have my doubts."

10   "Amontillado!"

"And I must satisfy them."

"Amontillado!"

"As you are engaged, I am on my way to Luchesi. If anyone has a critical turn, it is he: He will tell me—"

"Luchesi cannot tell Amontillado from Sherry."

15   "And yet some fools will have it that his taste is a match for your own."

"Come, let us go."

"Whither?"

"To your vaults."

"My friend, no; I will not impose upon your good nature. I perceive you have an engagement. Luchesi—"

20   "I have no engagement;—come."

"My friend, no. It is not the engagement, but the severe cold with which I perceive you are afflicted. The vaults are insufferably damp. They are encrusted with nitre."

"Let us go, nevertheless. The cold is merely nothing. Amontillado! You have been imposed upon. And as for Luchesi, he cannot distinguish Sherry from Amontillado."

Thus speaking, Fortunato possessed himself of my arm. Putting on a mask of black silk, and drawing a *roquelaure*° closely about my person, I suffered him to hurry me to my palazzo.

There were no attendants at home; they had absconded to make merry in honor of the time. I had told them that I should not return until the morning, and had given them explicit orders not to stir from the house. These orders were sufficient, I well knew, to insure their immediate disappearance, one and all, as soon as my back was turned.

25   I took from their sconces two flambeaux, and giving one to Fortunato, bowed him through several suites of rooms to the archway that led into the vaults. I passed down a long and winding staircase, requesting him to be cautious as he followed. We came at length to the foot of the descent, and stood together on the damp ground of the catacombs of the Montresors.

roquelaure: a type of cloak.

The gait of my friend was unsteady, and the bells upon his cap jingled as he strode.

"The pipe?" said he.

"It is farther on," said I; "but observe the white webwork which gleams from these cavern walls."

He turned toward me, and looked into my eyes with two filmy orbs that distilled the rheum of intoxication.

"Nitre?" he asked, at length. 30

"Nitre," I replied. "How long have you had that cough?"

"Ugh! ugh! ugh!—ugh! ugh! ugh!—ugh! ugh! ugh!—ugh! ugh! ugh!—ugh! ugh! ugh!"

My poor friend found it impossible to reply for many minutes.

"It is nothing," he said at last.

"Come," I said, with decision, "we will go back; your health is precious. You 35 are rich, respected, admired, beloved; you are happy, as once I was. You are a man to be missed. For me it is no matter. We will go back; you will be ill, and I cannot be responsible. Besides, there is Luchesi—"

"Enough," he said; "the cough is a mere nothing; it will not kill me. I shall not die of a cough."

"True—true," I replied; "and, indeed, I had no intention of alarming you unnecessarily; but you should use all proper caution. A draught of this Medoc will defend us from the damps."

Here I knocked off the neck of a bottle which I drew from a long row of its fellows that lay upon the mould.

"Drink," I said, presenting him the wine.

He raised it to his lips with a leer. He paused and nodded to me familiarly, 40 while his bells jingled.

"I drink," he said, "to the buried that repose around us."

"And I to your long life."

He again took my arm, and we proceeded.

"These vaults," he said, "are extensive."

"The Montresors," I replied, "were a great and numerous family." 45

"I forget your arms."

"A huge human foot *d'or*, in a field azure; the foot crushes a serpent rampant whose fangs are imbedded in the heel."

"And the motto?"

"Nemo me impune lacessit."°

"Good!" he said. 50

The wine sparkled in his eyes and the bells jingled. My own fancy grew warm with the Medoc. We had passed through walls of piled bones, with casks and puncheons intermingling, into the inmost recesses of the catacombs. I paused again, and this time I made bold to seize Fortunato by an arm above the elbow.

"The nitre!" I said; "see, it increases. It hangs like moss upon the vaults. We are below the river's bed. The drops of moisture trickle among the bones. Come, we will go back ere it is too late. Your cough—"

Nemo me impune lacessit: No one attacks me with impunity.

"It is nothing," he said; "let us go on. But first, another draught of the Medoc."

I broke and reached him a flagon of De Grâve. He emptied it at a breath. His eyes flashed with a fierce light. He laughed and threw the bottle upward with a gesticulation I did not understand.

55   I looked at him in surprise. He repeated the movement—a grotesque one.

"You do not comprehend?" he said.

"Not I," I replied.

"Then you are not of the brotherhood."

"How?"

60   "You are not of the Masons."

"Yes, yes," I said; "yes, yes."

"You? Impossible! A Mason?"

"A Mason," I replied.

"A sign," he said.

65   "It is this," I answered, producing a trowel from beneath the folds of my *roquelaure*.

"You jest," he exclaimed, recoiling a few paces. "But let us proceed to the Amontillado."

"Be it so," I said, replacing the tool beneath the cloak, and again offering him my arm. He leaned upon it heavily. We continued our route in search of the Amontillado. We passed through a range of low arches, descended, passed on, and descending again, arrived at a deep crypt, in which the foulness of the air caused our flambeaux rather to glow than flame.

At the most remote end of the crypt there appeared another less spacious. Its walls had been lined with human remains, piled to the vault overhead, in the fashion of the great catacombs of Paris. Three sides of this interior crypt were still ornamented in this manner. From the fourth the bones had been thrown down, and lay promiscuously upon the earth, forming at one point a mound of some size. Within the wall thus exposed by the displacing of the bones, we perceived a still interior recess, in depth about four feet, in width three, in height six or seven. It seemed to have been constructed for no especial use within itself, but formed merely the interval between two of the colossal supports of the roof of the catacombs, and was backed by one of their circumscribing walls of solid granite.

It was in vain that Fortunato, uplifting his dull torch, endeavored to pry into the depth of the recess. Its termination the feeble light did not enable us to see.

70   "Proceed," I said; "herein is the Amontillado. As for Luchesi—"

"He is an ignoramus," interrupted my friend, as he stepped unsteadily forward, while I followed immediately at his heels. In an instant he had reached the extremity of the niche, and finding his progress arrested by the rock, stood stupidly bewildered. A moment more and I had fettered him to the granite. In its surface were two iron staples, distant from each other about two feet, horizontally. From one of these depended a short chain, from the other a padlock. Throwing the links about his waist, it was but the work of a few seconds to secure it. He was too much astounded to resist. Withdrawing the key I stepped back from the recess.

"Pass your hand," I said, "over the wall; you cannot help feeling the nitre. Indeed it is *very* damp. Once more let me *implore* you to return. No? Then I must positively leave you. But I must first render you all the little attentions in my power."

"The Amontillado!" ejaculated my friend, not yet recovered from his astonishment.

"True," I replied; "the Amontillado."

As I said these words I busied myself among the pile of bones of which I have   *75* before spoken. Throwing them aside, I soon uncovered a quantity of building stone and mortar. With these materials and with the aid of my trowel, I began vigorously to wall up the entrance of the niche.

I had scarcely laid the first tier of the masonry when I discovered that the intoxication of Fortunato had in a great measure worn off. The earliest indication I had of this was a low moaning cry from the depth of the recess. It was *not* the cry of a drunken man. There was then a long and obstinate silence. I laid the second tier, and the third, and the fourth; and then I heard the furious vibrations of the chain. The noise lasted for several minutes, during which, that I might hearken to it with the more satisfaction, I ceased my labors and sat down upon the bones. When at last the clanking subsided, I resumed the trowel, and finished without interruption the fifth, the sixth, and the seventh tier. The wall was now nearly upon a level with my breast. I again paused, and holding the flambeaux over the mason-work, threw a few feeble rays upon the figure within.

A succession of loud and shrill screams, bursting suddenly from the throat of the chained form, seemed to thrust me violently back. For a brief moment I hesitated—I trembled. Unsheathing my rapier, I began to grope with it about the recess; but the thought of an instant reassured me. I placed my hand upon the solid fabric of the catacombs, and felt satisfied. I reapproached the wall. I replied to the yells of him who clamored. I reechoed—I aided—I surpassed them in volume and in strength. I did this, and the clamorer grew still.

It was now midnight, and my task was drawing to a close. I had completed the eighth, the ninth, and the tenth tier. I had finished a portion of the last and the eleventh; there remained but a single stone to be fitted and plastered in. I struggled with its weight; I placed it partially in its destined position. But now there came from out the niche a low laugh that erected the hairs upon my head. It was succeeded by a sad voice, which I had difficulty in recognizing as that of the noble Fortunato. The voice said—

"Ha! ha! ha!—he! he!—a very good joke indeed—an excellent jest. We will have many a rich laugh about it at the palazzo—he! he! he!—over our wine—he! he! he!"

"The Amontillado!" I said.   *80*

"He! he! he!—he! he! he!—yes, the Amontillado. But is it not getting late? Will not they be awaiting us at the palazzo, the Lady Fortunato and the rest? Let us be gone."

"Yes," I said, "let us be gone."

"For the love of God, Montresor!"

"Yes," I said, "for the love of God!"

But to these words I hearkened in vain for a reply. I grew impatient. I called   *85* aloud:

"Fortunato!"

No answer. I called again:

"Fortunato!"

No answer still. I thrust a torch through the remaining aperture and let it fall within. There came forth in return only a jingling of the bells. My heart grew sick— on account of the dampness of the catacombs. I hastened to make an end of my labor. I forced the last stone into its position. I plastered it up. Against the new masonry I reerected the old rampart of bones. For the half of a century no mortal has disturbed them. *In pace requiescat!°*

In pace requiescat: May he rest in peace.

POEMS

Matthew Arnold (1822–1888)

Dover Beach   1849

The sea is calm to-night.
The tide is full, the moon lies fair
Upon the straits:—on the French coast the light
Gleams and is gone; the cliffs of England stand,
Glimmering and vast, out in the tranquil bay.   5
Come to the window, sweet is the night air!
Only, from the long line of spray
Where the sea meets the moon-blanched land,
Listen! You can hear the grating roar
Of pebbles which the waves draw back, and fling,   10
At their return, up the high strand,
Begin, and cease, and then again begin,
With tremulous cadence slow, and bring
The eternal note of sadness in.

Sophocles long ago   15
Heard it on the Ægean, and it brought
Into his mind the turbid ebb and flow
Of human misery; we
Find also in the sound a thought,
Hearing it by this distant northern sea.   20
The Sea of Faith
Was once, too, at the full, and round earth's shore
Lay like the folds of a bright girdle furled.
But now I only hear
Its melancholy, long, withdrawing roar,   25
Retreating, to the breath
Of the night wind, down the vast edges drear
And naked shingles of the world.

Ah, love, let us be true
To one another! for the world, which seems   30
To lie before us like a land of dreams,
So various, so beautiful, so new,
Hath really neither joy, nor love, nor light,
Nor certitude, nor peace, nor help for pain;
And we are here as on a darkling plain   35
Swept with confused alarms of struggle and flight
Where ignorant armies clash by night.

William Blake (1757–1827)

The Tyger°   1794

Tyger! Tyger! burning bright
In the forests of the night,
What immortal hand or eye
Could frame thy fearful symmetry?

5   In what distant deeps or skies
Burnt the fire of thine eyes?
On what wings dare he aspire?
What the hand, dare seize the fire?

And what shoulder, & what art,
10 Could twist the sinews of thy heart?
And when thy heart began to beat,
What dread hand? & what dread feet?

What the hammer? what the chain?
In what furnace was thy brain?
15 What the anvil? what dread grasp
Dare its deadly terrors clasp?

When the stars threw down their spears,
And water'd heaven with their tears,
Did he smile his work to see?
20 Did he who made the Lamb make thee?

Tyger! Tyger! burning bright
In the forests of the night,
What immortal hand or eye
Dare frame thy fearful symmetry?

Tyger: Tyger here means not only a tiger but a larger wild cat.

Samuel Taylor Coleridge (1772–1834)

Kubla Khan   1816

In Xanadu did Kubla Kahn
A stately pleasure dome decree:
Where Alph, the sacred river, ran
Through caverns measureless to man
 Down to a sunless sea.   *5*
So twice five miles of fertile ground
With walls and towers were girdled round:
And there were gardens bright with sinuous rills,
Where blossomed many an incense-bearing tree;
And here were forests ancient as the hills,   *10*
Enfolding sunny spots of greenery.

But oh! that deep romantic chasm which slanted
Down the green hill athwart a cedarn cover!
A savage place! as holy and enchanted
As e'er beneath a waning moon was haunted   *15*
By woman wailing for her demon lover!
And from this chasm, with ceaseless turmoil seething,
As if this earth in fast thick pants were breathing,
A mighty fountain momently was forced:
Amid whose swift half-intermitted burst   *20*
Huge fragments vaulted like rebounding hail,
Or chaffy grain beneath the thresher's flail;
And 'mid these dancing rocks at once and ever
It flung up momently the sacred river.
Five miles meandering with a mazy motion   *25*
Through wood and dale the sacred river ran,
Then reached the caverns measureless to man,
And sank in tumult to a lifeless ocean:
And 'mid this tumult Kubla heard from far
Ancestral voices prophesying war!   *30*
 The shadow of the dome of pleasure
 Floated midway on the waves;
 Where was heard the mingled measure
 From the fountain and the caves.
It was a miracle of rare device,   *35*
A sunny pleasure dome with caves of ice!

 A damsel with a dulcimer
 In a vision once I saw:

It was an Abyssinian maid,
40   And on her dulcimer she played,
          Singing of Mount Abora.
Could I revive within me
Her symphony and song,
To such a deep delight 'twould win me,
45   That with music loud and long,
I would build that dome in air,
That sunny dome! those caves of ice!
And all who heard should see them there,
And all should cry, Beware! Beware!
50   His flashing eyes, his floating hair!
Weave a circle round him thrice,
And close your eyes with holy dread,
For he on honeydew hath fed,
And drunk the milk of Paradise.

Robert Frost (1875–1963)

Desert Places   1936

Snow falling and night falling fast, oh, fast
In a field I looked into going past,
And the ground almost covered smooth in snow,
But a few weeds and stubble showing last.

5   The woods around it have it—it is theirs.
All animals are smothered in their lairs.
I am too absent-spirited to count;
The loneliness includes me unawares.

And lonely as it is that loneliness
10   Will be more lonely ere it will be less—
A blanker whiteness of benighted snow
With no expression, nothing to express.

They cannot scare me with their empty spaces
Between stars—on stars where no human race is.
15   I have it in me so much nearer home
To scare myself with my own desert places.

Thomas Hardy (1840–1928)

Channel Firing 1914

That night your great guns unawares,
Shook all our coffins as we lay,
And broke the chancel window squares.
We thought it was the Judgment-day

And sat upright. While drearisome 5
Arose the howl of wakened hounds:
The mouse let fall the altar-crumb,
The worms drew back into the mounds.

The glebe cow drooled. Till God called, "No;
It's gunnery practice out at sea 10
Just as before you went below;
The world is as it used to be:

"All nations striving strong to make
Red war yet redder. Mad as hatters
They do no more for Christés sake 15
Than you who are helpless in such matters.

"That this is not the judgment-hour
For some of them's a blessed thing,
For if it were they'd have to scour
Hell's floor for so much threatening . . . 20

"Ha, ha. It will be warmer when
I blow the trumpet (if indeed
I ever do; for you are men,
And rest eternal sorely need)."

So down we lay again. "I wonder, 25
Will the world ever saner be,"
Said one, "than when He sent us under
In our indifferent century!"

And many a skeleton shook his head.
"Instead of preaching forty year," 30
My neighbor Parson Thirdly said,
"I wish I had stuck to pipes and beer."

Again the guns disturbed the hour,
Roaring their readiness to avenge,
As far inland as Stourton Tower, 35
And Camelot, and starlit Stonehenge.

Langston Hughes (1902–1967)

Negro   1958

I am a Negro:
    Black as the night is black,
    Black like the depths of my Africa.

I've been a slave:
5   Caesar told me to keep his door-steps clean.
    I brushed the boots of Washington.

I've been a worker:
    Under my hand the pyramids arose.
    I made mortar for the Woolworth Building

10 I've been a singer:
    All the way from Africa to Georgia
    I carried my sorrow songs.
    I made ragtime.

I've been a victim:
15   The Belgians cut off my hands in the Congo.
    They lynch me still in Mississippi.

I am a Negro:
    Black as the night is black,
    Black like the depths of my Africa.

John Keats (1795–1821)

Bright Star   1819

Bright star! would I were steadfast as thou art—
    Not in lone splendor hung aloft the night,
And watching, with eternal lids apart,
    Like Nature's patient, sleepless eremite,°

eremite: hermit

The moving waters at their priestlike task 5
   Of pure ablution round earth's human shores,
Or gazing on the new soft-fallen mask
   Of snow upon the mountains and the moors;
No—yet still steadfast, still unchangeable,
   Pillowed upon my fair love's ripening breast, 10
To feel forever its soft fall and swell,
   Awake forever in a sweet unrest,
Still, still to hear her tender-taken breath,
And so live ever—or else swoon to death.

Irving Layton (b. 1912)

Rhine Boat Trip°   1977

The castles on the Rhine
are all haunted
by the ghosts of Jewish mothers
looking for their ghostly children

And the clusters of grapes 5
in the sloping vineyards
are myriads of blinded eyes
staring at the blind sun

The tireless Lorelei°
can never comb from their hair 10
the crimson beards
of murdered rabbis

However sweetly they sing
one hears only
the low wailing of cattle-cars° 15
moving invisibly across the land

   Rhine Boat Trip: The Rhine, Germany's best-known river, is virtually synonymous with German national history.
   Lorelei: mythical shore nymphs who lured passing rivermen to their doom; subject of a famous poem by Heinrich Heine (1797–1856).
   cattle-cars: During the Holocaust in World War II, the Nazis crowded their victims together into cattle cars and transported them by rail to concentration and extermination camps in Germany and neighboring countries.

Amy Lowell (1874–1925)

Patterns   1916

I walk down the garden paths,
And all the daffodils
Are blowing, and the bright blue squills.
I walk down the patterned garden-paths
5   In my stiff, brocaded gown.
With my powdered hair and jewelled fan,
I too am a rare
Pattern. As I wander down
The garden paths.

10   My dress is richly figured,
And the train
Makes a pink and silver stain
On the gravel, and the thrift
Of the borders.
15   Just a plate of current fashion
Tripping by in high-heeled, ribboned shoes.
Not a softness anywhere about me,
Only whalebone° and brocade.
And I sink on a seat in the shade

20   Of a lime tree. For my passion
Wars against the stiff brocade.
The daffodils and squills
Flutter in the breeze
As they please.
25   And I weep;
For the lime-tree is in blossom
And one small flower has dropped upon my bosom.

And the plashing of waterdrops
In the marble fountain
30   Comes down the garden-paths.
The dripping never stops.
Underneath my stiffened gown
Is the softness of a woman bathing in a marble basin,
A basin in the midst of hedges grown
35   So thick, she cannot see her lover hiding.
But she guesses he is near,

---

whalebone: used as a stiffener in tightly laced corsets.

And the sliding of the water
Seems the stroking of a dear
Hand upon her.
What is Summer in a fine brocaded gown!   *40*
I should like to see it lying in a heap upon the ground.
All the pink and silver crumpled up on the ground.
I would be the pink and silver as I ran along the paths,
And he would stumble after,
Bewildered by my laughter.   *45*
I should see the sun flashing from his sword-hilt and buckles on his shoes.
I would choose
To lead him in a maze along the patterned paths,
A bright and laughing maze for my heavy-booted lover.
Till he caught me in the shade,   *50*
And the buttons of his waistcoat bruised my body as he clasped me,
Aching, melting, unafraid.
With the shadows of the leaves and the sundrops,
And the plopping of the waterdrops,
All about us in the open afternoon—   *55*
I am very like to swoon
With the weight of this brocade,
For the sun sifts through the shade.

Underneath the fallen blossom
In my bosom,   *60*
Is a letter I have hid.
It was brought to me this morning by a rider from the Duke.
Madam, we regret to inform you that Lord Hartwell
Died in action Thursday se'nnight.°
As I read it in the white, morning sunlight,   *65*
The letters squirmed like snakes.
"Any answer, Madam," said my footman.
"No," I told him.
"See that the messenger takes some refreshment.

No, no answer."   *70*
And I walked into the garden,
Up and down the patterned paths,
In my stiff, correct brocade.
The blue and yellow flowers stood up proudly in the sun,
Each one.   *75*
I stood upright too,
Held rigid to the pattern
By the stiffness of my gown.
Up and down I walked.
Up and down.   *80*

---

se'nnight: i.e., a week ago (seven nights) last Thursday.

In a month he would have been my husband.
In a month, here, underneath this lime,
We would have broken the pattern;
He for me, and I for him,
He as Colonel, I as Lady,
On this shady seat.
He had a whim
That sunlight carried blessing.
And I answered, "It shall be as you have said."
Now he is dead.

In Summer and in Winter I shall walk
Up and down
The patterned garden-paths
In my stiff, brocaded gown.
The squills and daffodils
Will give place to pillared roses, and to asters, and to snow.
I shall go
Up and down,
In my gown.
Gorgeously arrayed,
Boned and stayed.
And the softness of my body will be guarded from embrace
By each button, hook, and lace.
For the man who should loose me is dead,
Fighting with the Duke in Flanders,°
In a pattern called a war.
Christ! What are patterns for?

Flanders: a place of frequent warfare in Belgium. The speaker's clothing (lines 5, 6) suggests the time of the Duke of Marlborough's Flanders campaigns of 1702–1710. The Battle of Waterloo (1815) was also fought nearby under the Duke of Wellington. During World War I, fierce fighting against the Germans occurred in Flanders in 1914 and 1915, with great loss of life.

John Masefield (1878–1967)

Cargoes   1902

Quinquereme° of Nineveh° from distant Ophir,°
Rowing home to haven in sunny Palestine,
With a cargo of ivory,
And apes and peacocks,°
Sandalwood, cedarwood,° and sweet white wine.   5

Stately Spanish galleon coming from the Isthmus,°
Dipping through the Tropics by the palm-green shores,
With a cargo of diamonds,
Emeralds, amethysts,
Topazes, and cinnamon, and gold moidores.°   10

Dirty British coaster with a salt-caked smoke-stack,
Butting through the Channel in the mad March days,
With a cargo of Tyne coal,°
Road-rails, pig-lead,
Firewood, iron-ware, and cheap tin trays.   15

quinquereme: the largest of the ancient ships. It was powered by three tiers of oars and was named "quinquereme" because five men operated each vertical oar station. The top two oars were each taken by two men, while one man alone took the bottom oar.

Nineveh: capital of ancient Assyria, an "exceeding great city" (Jonah 3:3).

Ophir: Ophir probably was in Africa and was known for its gold (1 Kings 10:22; 1 Chron. 29:4). Masefield echoes some of the biblical verses in lines 4 and 5.

apes and peacocks: 1 Kings 10:22 and 2 Chron. 9:21.

cedarwood: 1 Kings 9:11.

Isthmus: the Isthmus of Panama.

moidores: coins used in Portugal and Brazil at the time the New World was being explored.

Tyne coal: coal from Newcastle upon Tyne, in northern England, renowned for its coal production.

Wilfred Owen (1893–1918)

Anthem for Doomed Youth   1920

What passing-bells° for these who die as cattle?
Only the monstrous anger of the guns.
Only the stuttering rifles' rapid rattle
Can patter out their hasty orisons.°
5   No mockeries for them from prayers or bells,
Nor any voice of mourning save the choirs—
The shrill, demented choirs of wailing shells;
And bugles calling for them from sad shires.°

What candles may be held to speed them all?
10   Not in the hands of boys, but in their eyes
Shall shine the holy glimmers of good-byes.
The pallor of girls' brows shall be their pall;
Their flowers the tenderness of patient minds,
And each slow dusk a drawing-down of blinds.

passing-bells: church bells that are tolled at the entry of a funeral cortege into a church
cemetery.
    orisons: prayers.
    shires: British counties.

William Shakespeare (1564–1616)

Sonnet 73: That Time of Year
Thou Mayest in Me Behold   1609

That time of year thou mayest in me behold,
When yellow leaves, or none, or few do hang
Upon those boughs which shake against the cold,
Bare ruined choirs, where late the sweet birds sang.
In me thou seest the twilight of such day,   5
As after Sunset fadeth in the West;
Which by and by black night doth take away,
Death's second self that seals up all in rest.
In me thou seest the glowing of such fire,
That on the ashes of his youth doth lie,   10
As the death bed, whereon it must expire,
Consumed with that which it was nourished by.
  This thou perceiv'st, which makes thy love more strong.
  To love that well, which thou must leave ere long.

Sonnet 116: Let Me Not
to the Marriage of True Minds   1609

Let me not to the marriage of true minds
Admit impediments; love is not love
Which alters when it alteration finds
Or bends with the remover to remove.
O no, it is an ever fixèd mark   5
That looks on tempests and is never shaken;
It is the star to every wandering bark
Whose worth's unknown, although his height be taken.
Love's not Time's fool, though rosy lips and cheeks
Within his bending sickle's compass come;   10
Love alters not with his brief hours and weeks.
But bears it out even to the edge of doom:
  If this be error and upon me proved,
  I never writ, nor no man ever loved.

Shelly Wagner (b. ca. 1950)

The Boxes   1991

When I told the police I couldn't find you,
they began a search that included everything—
even the boxes in the house:
the footlockers of clothes in the attic,
the hamper in the bathroom,
and the Chinese lacquered trunk by the sofa.
They made me raise every lid.
I told them you would never stay in a box,
not with all the commotion.
You would have jumped out,
found your flashlight
and joined the search.

Poor Thomas, taking these men
who don't know us
through our neighbors' garages
where you never played,
hoping they were right
and we were wrong
and he would find you and
snatch you home by the hand

so the police cars could
get out of our driveway
and the divers would
get out of our river
because it was certainly
past our bedtime.
We would double-bolt our doors
like always,
say longer prayers than usual
and go to bed. But during the night
I would have sat till morning
beside my sleeping boys.

But that's not what happened.
Thomas is still here, now older.
I still go to his room
when he is sleeping
just to look at him.
I still visit the cemetery,

not as often,
but the urge is the same: *40*
to lie down on the grass,
put my arm around the hump of ground
and tell you, "Get out of this box!
Put a stop to this commotion. Come home.
You should be in bed."   *45*

PLAYS

Anton Chekhov (1860–1904)

The Bear: A Joke in One Act   1888

CAST OF CHARACTERS

Mrs. Popov.   *A widow of seven months,* MRS. POPOV *is small and pretty, with dimples. She is a landowner. At the start of the play, she is pining away in memory of her dead husband.*

Grigory Stepanovich Smirnov.   *Easily angered and loud,* SMIRNOV *is older. He is a landowner, too, and a man of substance.*

Luka.   LUKA *is* MRS. POPOV'S *footman (a servant whose main tasks were to wait table and attend the carriages, in addition to general duties). He is old enough to feel secure in telling* MRS. POPOV *what he thinks.*

Gardener, Coachman, Workmen, *who enter at the end.*

SCENE. *The drawing room of* MRS. POPOV'S *country home.*

*[*MRS. POPOV, *in deep mourning, does not remove her eyes from a photograph.]*

LUKA.   It isn't right, madam . . . you're only destroying yourself. . . . The chambermaid and the cook have gone off berry picking; every living being is rejoicing; even the cat knows how to be content, walking around the yard catching birds, and you sit in your room all day as if it were a convent, and you don't take pleasure in anything. Yes, really! Almost a year has passed since you've gone out of the house!

MRS. POPOV.   And I shall never go out. . . . What for? My life is already ended. *He* lies in his grave; I have buried myself in these four walls . . . we are both dead.

LUKA.   There you go again! Your husband is dead, that's as it was meant to be, it's the will of God, may he rest in peace. . . . You've done your mourning and that will do. You can't go on weeping and mourning forever. My wife died when her time came, too. . . . Well? I grieved, I wept for a month, and that was enough for her; the old lady wasn't worth a second more. [*Sighs.*] You've forgotten all your neighbors. You don't go anywhere or accept any calls. We live, so to speak, like spiders. We never see the light. The mice have eaten my uniform. It isn't as if there weren't any nice neighbors—the district is full of them . . . there's a regiment stationed at Riblov, such officers—they're like candy—you'll never get your fill of them! And in the barracks, never a Friday goes by without a dance; and, if you please, the military band plays music every day. . . . Yes, madam, my dear lady: you're young, beautiful, in the full bloom of youth—if only you took a little pleasure in life . . . Beauty doesn't last forever, you know! In ten years' time, you'll be wanting to wave your fanny in front of the officers—and it will be too late.

MRS. POPOV.   [*Determined.*] I must ask you never to talk to me like that! You know that when Mr. Popov died, life lost all its salt for me. It may seem to you that I am alive, but that's only conjecture! I vowed to wear mourning to my grave and not to see the light of day. . . . Do you hear me? May his departed spirit see how much I love him. . . . Yes, I know, it's no mystery to you that he was often mean to me, cruel . . . and even unfaithful, but I shall remain true to the grave and show him I know how to love. There, beyond the grave, he will see me as I was before his death. . . .

LUKA.   Instead of talking like that, you should be taking a walk in the garden   5
or have Toby or Giant harnessed and go visit some of the neighbors . . .

MRS. POPOV.   Ai! [*She weeps.*]

LUKA.   Madam! Dear lady! What's the matter with you! Christ be with you!

MRS. POPOV.   Oh, how he loved Toby! He always used to ride on him to visit the Korchagins or the Vlasovs. How wonderfully he rode! How graceful he was when he pulled at the reins with all his strength! Do you remember? Toby, Toby! Tell them to give him an extra bag of oats today.

LUKA.   Yes, madam.

[*Sound of loud ringing.*]

MRS. POPOV.   [*Shudders.*] Who's that? Tell them I'm not at home!   10

LUKA.   Of course, madam. [*He exits.*]

MRS. POPOV.   [*Alone. Looks at the photograph.*] You will see, Nikolai, how much I can love and forgive . . . my love will die only when I do, when my poor heart stops beating. [*Laughing through her tears.*] Have you no shame? I'm a good girl, a virtuous little wife. I've locked myself in and I'll be true to you to the grave, and you . . . aren't you ashamed, you chubby cheeks? You deceived me, you made scenes, for weeks on end you left me alone . . .

LUKA.   [*Enters, alarmed.*] Madam, somebody is asking for you. He wants to see you. . . .

MRS. POPOV.   But didn't you tell them that since the death of my husband, I don't see anybody?

LUKA.   I did, but he didn't want to listen; he spoke about some very impor-   15
tant business.

MRS. POPOV.   I am *not at home!*

LUKA.   That's what I told him . . . but . . . the devil . . . he cursed and pushed past me right into the room . . . he's in the dining room right now.

MRS. POPOV.   [*Losing her temper.*] Very well, let him come in . . . such manners! [*Luka goes out.*] How difficult these people are! What does he want from me? Why should he disturb my peace? [*Sighs.*] But it's obvious I'll have to go live in a convent. . . . [*Thoughtfully.*] Yes, a convent. . . .

SMIRNOV.   [*Enters while speaking to* LUKA.] You idiot, you talk too much. . . . Ass! [*Sees* MRS. POPOV *and changes to dignified speech.*] Madam, may I introduce myself: retired lieutenant of the artillery and landowner, Grigory Stepanovich Smirnov! I feel the necessity of troubling you about a highly important matter. . . .

MRS. POPOV.   [*Refusing her hand.*] What do you want?   20

SMIRNOV.   Your late husband, whom I had the pleasure of knowing, has remained in my debt for two twelve-hundred-ruble notes. Since I must pay the interest at the agricultural bank tomorrow, I have come to ask you, madam, to pay me the money today.

MRS. POPOV.   One thousand two hundred. . . . And why was my husband in debt to you?

SMIRNOV.   He used to buy oats from me.

MRS. POPOV.   [*Sighing, to* LUKA.] So, Luka, don't you forget to tell them to give Toby an extra bag of oats.

[LUKA *goes out.*]

[*To* SMIRNOV.] If Nikolai, my husband, was in debt to you, then it goes without saying that I'll pay; but please excuse me today. I haven't any spare cash. The day after tomorrow, my steward will be back from town and I will give him instructions to pay you what is owed; until then I cannot comply with your wishes. . . . Besides, today is the anniversary—exactly seven months ago my husband died, and I'm in such a mood that I'm not quite disposed to occupy myself with money matters.

25   SMIRNOV.   And I'm in such a mood that if I don't pay the interest tomorrow, I'll be owing so much that my troubles will drown me. They'll take away my estate!

MRS. POPOV.   You'll receive your money the day after tomorrow.

SMIRNOV.   I don't want the money the day after tomorrow. I want it today.

MRS. POPOV.   You must excuse me. I can't pay you today.

SMIRNOV.   And I can't wait until after tomorrow.

30   MRS. POPOV.   What can I do, if I don't have it now?

SMIRNOV.   You mean to say you can't pay?

MRS. POPOV.   I can't pay. . . .

SMIRNOV.   Hm! Is that your last word?

MRS. POPOV.   That is my last word.

35   SMIRNOV.   Positively the last?

MRS. POPOV.   Positively.

SMIRNOV.   Thank you very much. We'll make a note of that. [*Shrugs his shoulders.*] And people want me to be calm and collected! Just now, on the way here, I met a tax officer and he asked me: why are you always so angry, Grigory Stepanovich? Goodness' sake, how can I be anything but angry? I need money desperately . . . I rode out yesterday early in the morning, at daybreak, and went to see all my debtors; and if only one of them had paid his debt . . . I was dog-tired, spent the night God knows where—a Jewish tavern beside a barrel of vodka. . . . Finally I got here, fifty miles from home, hoping to be paid, and you treat me to a "mood." How can I help being angry?

MRS. POPOV.   It seems to me that I clearly said: My steward will return from the country and then you will be paid.

SMIRNOV.   I didn't come to your steward, but to you! What the hell, if you'll pardon the expression, would I do with your steward?

40   MRS. POPOV.   Excuse me, my dear sir, I am not accustomed to such profane expressions nor to such a tone. I'm not listening to you any more. [*Goes out quickly.*]

SMIRNOV.   [*Alone.*] Well, how do you like that? "A mood.". . . "Husband died seven months ago"! Must I pay the interest or mustn't I? I ask you: Must I pay, or must I not? So, your husband's dead, and you're in a mood and all that finicky stuff . . . and your steward's away somewhere; may he drop dead. What do you want me to do? Do you think I can fly away from my creditors in a balloon or something? Or should I run and bash my head against the wall? I go to Gruzdev—and he's not at home; Yaroshevich is hiding, with Kuritsin it's a quarrel to the death and I almost throw him out the window; Mazutov has diarrhea, and this one is in a "mood." Not one of these swine wants to pay me! And all because I'm too nice to them. I'm a sniveling idiot, I'm spineless, I'm an old lady! I'm too delicate with them! So, just you wait! You'll find out what I'm like! I won't let you play around with me, you devils! I'll stay and stick it out until she pays. Rrr! . . . How furious I am today, how furious! I'm shaking inside from rage and I can hardly catch my breath. . . . Damn it! My God, I even feel sick! [*He shouts.*] Hey, you!

LUKA.   [*Enters.*] What do you want?

SMIRNOV.   Give me some beer or some water! [*LUKA exits.*] What logic is there in this! A man needs money desperately, it's like a noose around his neck—and she won't pay because, you see, she's not disposed to occupy herself with money matters! . . . That's the logic of a woman! That's why I never did like and do not like to talk to women. I'd rather sit on a keg of gunpowder than talk to a woman. Brr! . . . I even have goose pimples, this broad has put me in such a rage! All I have to do is see one of those spoiled bitches from a distance, and I get so angry it gives me a cramp in the leg. I just want to shout for help.

LUKA.   [*Entering with water.*] Madam is sick and won't see anyone.

SMIRNOV.   Get out! [*LUKA goes.*] Sick and won't see anyone! No need to see   45
me . . . I'll stay and sit here until you give me the money. You can stay sick for a week, and I'll stay for a week. . . . If you're sick for a year, I'll stay a year. I'll get my own back, dear lady! You can't impress me with your widow's weeds and your dimpled cheeks . . . we know all about those dimples! [*Shouts through the window.*] Semyon, unharness the horses! We're not going away quite yet! I'm staying here! Tell them in the stable to give the horses some oats! You brute, you let the horse on the left side get all tangled up in the reins again! [*Teasing.*] "Never mind" . . . I'll give you a never mind! [*Goes away from the window.*] Shit! The heat is unbearable and nobody pays up. I slept badly last night and on top of everything else this broad in mourning is "in a mood" . . . my head aches . . . [*Drinks, and grimaces.*] Shit! This is water! What I need is a drink! [*Shouts.*] Hey, you!

LUKA.   [*Enters.*] What is it?

SMIRNOV.   Give me a glass of vodka. [*LUKA goes out.*] Oaf! [*Sits down and examines himself.*] Nobody would say I was looking well! Dusty all over, boots dirty, unwashed, unkept, straw on my waistcoat. . . . The dear lady probably took me for a robber. [*Yawns.*] It's not very polite to present myself in a drawing room looking like this; oh well; who cares? . . . I'm not here as a visitor but as a creditor, and there's no official costume for creditors.

LUKA.   [*Enters with vodka.*] You're taking liberties, my good man. . . .

SMIRNOV.   [*Angrily.*] What?

LUKA.   I . . . nothing . . . I only . . .   50

SMIRNOV.   Who are you talking to? Shut up!

LUKA.   [*Aside.*] The devil sent this leech. An ill wind brought him. . . . [*LUKA goes out.*]

SMIRNOV.   Oh how furious I am! I'm so mad I could crush the whole world into a powder! I even feel faint! [*Shouts.*] Hey, you!

MRS. POPOV.   [*Enters, eyes downcast.*] My dear sir, in my solitude, I have long ago grown unaccustomed to the masculine voice and I cannot bear shouting. I must request you not to disturb my peace and quiet!

SMIRNOV.   Pay me my money and I'll go.   55

MRS. POPOV.   I told you in plain language: I haven't any spare cash now; wait until the day after tomorrow.

SMIRNOV.   And I also told you respectfully, in plain language: I don't need the money the day after tomorrow, but today. If you don't pay me today, then tomorrow I'll have to hang myself.

MRS. POPOV.   But what can I do if I don't have the money? You're so strange!

SMIRNOV.   Then you won't pay me now? No?

60   MRS. POPOV.   I can't. . . .

SMIRNOV.   In that case, I can stay here and wait until you pay. . . . [*Sits down.*] You'll pay the day after tomorrow? Excellent! In that case I'll stay here until the day after tomorrow. I'll sit here all that time . . . [*Jumps up.*] I ask you: Have I got to pay the interest tomorrow, or not? Or do you think I'm joking?

MRS. POPOV.   My dear sir, I ask you not to shout! This isn't a stable!

SMIRNOV.   I wasn't asking you about a stable but about this: Do I have to pay the interest tomorrow or not?

MRS. POPOV.   You don't know how to behave in the company of a lady!

65   SMIRNOV.   No, I don't know how to behave in the company of a lady!

MRS. POPOV.   No, you don't! You are an ill-bred, rude man! Respectable people don't talk to a woman like that!

SMIRNOV.   Ach, it's astonishing! How would you like me to talk to you? In French, perhaps? [*Lisps in anger.*] Madame, je vous prie°. . . how happy I am that you're not paying me the money. . . . Ah, pardon, I've made you uneasy! Such lovely weather we're having today! And you look so becoming in your mourning dress. [*Bows and scrapes.*]

MRS. POPOV.   That's rude and not very clever!

SMIRNOV.   [*Teasing.*] Rude and not very clever! I don't know how to behave in the company of ladies. Madam, in my time I've seen far more women than you've seen sparrows. Three times I've fought duels over women; I've jilted twelve women, nine have jilted me! Yes! There was a time when I played the fool; I became sentimental over women, used honeyed words, fawned on them, bowed and scraped. . . . I loved, suffered, sighed at the moon; I became limp, melted, shivered. . . . I loved passionately, madly, every which way, devil take me, I chattered away like a magpie about the emancipation of women, ran through half my fortune as a result of my tender feelings; but now, if you will excuse me, I'm on to your ways! I've had enough! Dark eyes, passionate eyes, ruby lips, dimpled cheeks; the moon, whispers, bated breath—for all that I wouldn't give a good goddamn. Present company excepted, of course, but all women, young and old alike, are affected clowns, gossips, hateful, consummate liars to the marrow of their bones, vain, trivial, ruthless, outrageously illogical, and as far as this is concerned [*taps on his forehead.*], well, excuse my frankness, any sparrow could give pointers to a philosopher in petticoats! Look at one of those romantic creatures: muslin, ethereal demigoddess, a thousand raptures, and you look into her soul—a common crocodile! [*Grips the back of a chair; the chair cracks and breaks.*] But the most revolting part of it all is that this crocodile imagines that she has, above everything, her own privilege, a monopoly on tender feelings. The hell with it—you can hang me upside down by that nail if a woman is capable of loving anything besides a lapdog. All she can do when she's in love is slobber! While

Madame, je vous prie: Madam, I beg you.

the man suffers and sacrifices, all her love is expressed in playing with her skirt and trying to lead him around firmly by the nose. You have the misfortune of being a woman, you know yourself what the nature of a woman is like. Tell me honestly: Have you ever in your life seen a woman who is sincere, faithful, and constant? You never have! Only old and ugly ladies are faithful and constant! You're more liable to meet a horned cat or a white woodcock than a faithful woman!

MRS. POPOV.   Pardon me, but in your opinion, who is faithful and constant in   *70*
love? The man?

SMIRNOV.   Yes, the man!

MRS. POPOV.   The man! [*Malicious laugh.*] Men are faithful and constant in love! That's news! [*Heatedly.*] What right have you to say that? Men are faithful and constant! For that matter, as far as I know, of all the men I have known and now know, my late husband was the best. . . . I loved him passionately, with all my being, as only a young intellectual woman can love; I gave him my youth, my happiness, my life, my fortune; he was my life's breath; I worshipped him as if I were a heathen, and . . . and, what good did it do—this best of men himself deceived me shamelessly at every step of the way. After his death, I found his desk full of love letters; and when he was alive—it's terrible to remember—he used to leave me alone for weeks at a time, and before my eyes he flirted with other women and deceived me. He squandered my money, made a mockery of my feelings . . . and, in spite of all that, I loved him and was true to him . . . and besides, now that he is dead, I am still faithful and constant. I have shut myself up in these four walls forever and I won't remove these widow's weeds until my dying day. . . .

SMIRNOV.   [*Laughs contemptuously.*] Widow's weeds! . . . I don't know what you take me for! As if I didn't know why you wear that black outfit and bury yourself in these four walls! Well, well! It's no secret, so romantic! When some fool of a poet passes by this country house, he'll look up at your window and think: "Here lives the mysterious Tamara, who, for the love of her husband, buried herself in these four walls." We know these tricks!

MRS. POPOV.   [*Flaring.*] What? How dare you say that to me?

SMIRNOV.   You may have buried yourself alive, but you haven't forgotten to   *75*
powder yourself!

MRS. POPOV.   How dare you use such expressions with me?

SMIRNOV.   Please don't shout. I'm not your steward! You must allow me to call a spade a spade. I'm not a woman and I'm used to saying what's on my mind! Don't you shout at me!

MRS. POPOV.   I'm not shouting, you are! Please leave me in peace!

SMIRNOV.   Pay me my money and I'll go.

MRS. POPOV.   I won't give you any money!   *80*

SMIRNOV.   Yes, you will.

MRS. POPOV.   To spite you, I won't pay you anything. You can leave me in peace!

SMIRNOV.   I don't have the pleasure of being either your husband or your fiancé, so please don't make scenes! [*Sits down.*] I don't like it.

MRS. POPOV.   [*Choking with rage.*] You're sitting down?

SMIRNOV.   Yes, I am.   *85*

MRS. POPOV.   I ask you to get out!

SMIRNOV.   Give me my money. . . [*Aside.*] Oh, I'm so furious! Furious!

MRS. POPOV.   I don't want to talk to impudent people! Get out of here! [*Pause.*] You're not going? No?

SMIRNOV.   No.

90   MRS. POPOV.   No?

SMIRNOV.   No!

MRS. POPOV.   We'll see about that. [*Rings.*]

[*LUKA enters.*]

Luka, show the gentleman out.

LUKA.   [*Goes up to SMIRNOV.*] Sir, will you please leave, as you have been asked. You mustn't . . .

SMIRNOV.   [*Jumping up.*] Shut up! Who do you think you're talking to? I'll make mincemeat out of you!

95   LUKA.   [*His hand to his heart.*] Oh my God! Saints above! [*Falls into chair.*] Oh, I feel ill! I feel ill! I can't catch my breath!

MRS. POPOV.   Where's Dasha? Dasha! [*She shouts.*] Dasha! Pelagea! Dasha! [*She rings.*]

LUKA.   Oh! They've all gone berry picking . . . there's nobody at home . . . I'm ill! Water!

MRS. POPOV.   Will you please get out!

SMIRNOV.   Will you please be more polite?

100   MRS. POPOV.   [*Clenches her fist and stamps her feet.*] You're nothing but a crude bear! A brute! A monster!

SMIRNOV.   What? What did you say?

MRS. POPOV.   I said that you were a bear, a monster!

SMIRNOV.   [*Advancing toward her.*] Excuse me, but what right do you have to insult me?

MRS. POPOV.   Yes, I am insulting you . . . so what? Do you think I'm afraid of you?

105   SMIRNOV.   And do you think just because you're one of those romantic creations, that you have the right to insult me with impunity? Yes? I challenge you!

LUKA.   Lord in Heaven! Saints above! . . . Water!

SMIRNOV.   Pistols!

MRS. POPOV.   Do you think just because you have big fists and you can bellow like a bull, that I'm afraid of you? You're such a bully!

SMIRNOV.   I challenge you! I'm not going to let anybody insult me, and I don't care if you are a woman, a delicate creature!

110   MRS. POPOV.   [*Trying to get a word in edgewise.*] Bear! Bear! Bear!

SMIRNOV.   It's about time we got rid of the prejudice that only men must pay for their insults! Devil take it, if women want to be equal, they should behave as equals! Let's fight!

MRS. POPOV.   You want to fight! By all means!

SMIRNOV.   This minute!

MRS. POPOV.   This minute! My husband had some pistols. . . . I'll go and get them right away. [*Goes out hurriedly and then returns.*] What pleasure I'll have putting a bullet through that thick head of yours! The hell with you! [*She goes out.*]

115   SMIRNOV.   I'll shoot her down like a chicken! I'm not a little boy or a sentimental puppy. I don't care if she is delicate and fragile.

LUKA. Kind sir! Holy father! [*kneels.*] Have pity on a poor old man and go away from here! You've frightened her to death and now you're going to shoot her? SMIRNOV. [*Not listening to him.*] If she fights, then it means she believes in equality of rights and emancipation of women. Here the sexes are equal! I'll shoot her like a chicken! But what a woman! [*Imitates her.*] "The hell with you! . . . I'll put a bullet through that thick head of yours! . . ." What a woman! How she blushed, her eyes shone . . . she accepted my challenge! To tell the truth, it was the first time in my life I've seen a woman like that. . . .

LUKA. Dear sir, please go away! I'll pray to God on your behalf as long as I live!

SMIRNOV. That's a woman for you! A woman like that I can understand! A real woman! Not a sour-faced nincompoop but fiery, gunpowder! Fireworks! I'm even sorry to have to kill her!

LUKA. [*Weeps.*] Dear sir . . . go away!   120

SMIRNOV. I positively like her! Positively! Even though she has dimpled cheeks, I like her! I'm almost ready to forget about the debt. . . . My fury has diminished. Wonderful woman!

MRS. POPOV. [*Enters with pistols.*] Here they are, the pistols. Before we fight, you must show me how to fire. . . . I've never had a pistol in my hands before . . .

LUKA. Oh dear Lord, for pity's sake. . . . I'll go and find the gardener and the coachman. . . . What did we do to deserve such trouble? [*Exit.*]

SMIRNOV. [*Examining the pistols.*] You see, there are several sorts of pistols . . . there are special dueling pistols, the Mortimer with primers. Then there are Smith and Wesson revolvers, triple action with extractors . . . excellent pistols! . . . they cost a minimum of ninety rubles a pair. . . . You must hold the revolver like this . . . [*Aside.*] What eyes, what eyes! A woman to set you on fire!

MRS. POPOV. Like this?   125

SMIRNOV. Yes, like this . . . then you cock the pistol . . . take aim . . . put your head back a little . . . stretch your arm out all the way . . . that's right . . . then with this finger press on this little piece of goods . . . and that's all there is to do . . . but the most important thing is not to get excited and aim without hurrying . . . try to keep your arm from shaking.

MRS. POPOV. Good . . . it's not comfortable to shoot indoors. Let's go into the garden.

SMIRNOV. Let's go. But I'm giving you advance notice that I'm going to fire into the air.

MRS. POPOV. That's the last straw! Why?

SMIRNOV. Why? . . . Why . . . because it's my business, that's why.   130

MRS. POPOV. Are you afraid? Yes? Aahhh! No, sir. You're not going to get out of it that easily! Be so good as to follow me! I will not rest until I've put a hole through your forehead . . . that forehead I hate so much! Are you afraid?

SMIRNOV. Yes. I'm afraid.

MRS. POPOV. You're lying! Why don't you want to fight?

SMIRNOV. Because . . . because you . . . because I like you.

MRS. POPOV. [*Laughs angrily.*] He likes me! He dares say that he likes me!   135
[*Points to the door.*] Out!

SMIRNOV. [*Loads the revolver in silence, takes cap and goes; at the door, stops for half a minute while they look at each other in silence; then he approaches* MRS. POPOV *hesi-*

tantly.] Listen. . . . Are you still angry? I'm extremely irritated, but, do you understand me, how can I express it . . . the fact is, that, you see, strictly speaking. . . [*He shouts.*] Is it my fault, really, for liking you? [*Grabs the back of a chair, which cracks and breaks.*] Why the hell do you have such fragile furniture! I like you! Do you understand? I . . . I'm almost in love with you!

MRS. POPOV.   Get away from me—I hate you!

SMIRNOV.   God, what a woman! I've never in my life seen anything like her! I'm lost! I'm done for! I'm caught like a mouse in a trap!

MRS. POPOV.   Stand back or I'll shoot!

140   SMIRNOV.   Shoot! You could never understand what happiness it would be to die under the gaze of those wonderful eyes, to be shot by a revolver which was held by those little velvet hands. . . . I've gone out of my mind! Think about it and decide right away, because if I leave here, then we'll never see each other again! Decide . . . I'm a nobleman, a respectable gentleman, of good family. I have an income of ten thousand a year. . . . I can put a bullet through a coin tossed in the air . . . I have some fine horses. . . . Will you be my wife?

MRS. POPOV.   [*Indignantly brandishes her revolver.*] Let's fight! I challenge you!

SMIRNOV.   I'm out of my mind . . . I don't understand anything . . . [*Shouts.*] Hey, you, water!

MRS. POPOV.   [*Shouts.*] Let's fight!

SMIRNOV.   I've gone out of my mind. I'm in love like a boy, like an idiot! [*He grabs her hand, she screams with pain.*] I love you! [*Kneels.*] I love you as I've never loved before! I've jilted twelve women, nine women have jilted me, but I've never loved one of them as I love you. . . . I'm weak, I'm a limp rag. . . . I'm on my knees like a fool, offering you my hand. . . . Shame, shame! I haven't been in love for five years, I vowed I wouldn't; and suddenly I'm in love, like a fish out of water. I'm offering my hand in marriage. Yes or no? You don't want to? You don't need to! [*Gets up and quickly goes to the door.*]

145   MRS. POPOV.   Wait!

SMIRNOV.   [*Stops.*] Well?

MRS. POPOV.   Nothing . . . you can go . . . go away . . . wait . . . No, get out, get out! I hate you! But—don't go! Oh, if you only knew how furious I am, how angry! [*Throws revolver on table.*] My fingers are swollen from that nasty thing. . . . [*Tears her handkerchief furiously.*] What are you waiting for? Get out!

SMIRNOV.   Farewell!

MRS. POPOV.   Yes, yes, go away! [*Shouts.*] Where are you going? Stop. . . . Oh, go away! Oh, how furious I am! Don't come near me! Don't come near me!

150   SMIRNOV.   [*Approaching her.*] How angry I am with myself! I'm in love like a student. I've been on my knees. . . . It gives me the shivers. [*Rudely.*] I love you! A lot of good it will do me to fall in love with you! Tomorrow I've got to pay the interest, begin the mowing of the hay. [*Puts his arm around her waist.*] I'll never forgive myself for this. . . .

MRS. POPOV.   Get away from me! Get your hands away! I . . . hate you! I . . . challenge you!

[*Prolonged kiss, LUKA enters with an ax, the GARDENER with a rake, the COACHMAN with a pitchfork, and WORKMEN with cudgels.*]

LUKA.　[*Catches sight of the pair kissing.*] Lord in heaven! [*Pause.*]

MRS. POPOV.　[*Lowering her eyes.*] Luka, tell them in the stable not to give Toby any oats today.

CURTAIN

Susan Glaspell (1882–1948)

Trifles　　　　　1916

CAST OF CHARACTERS

George Henderson, *county attorney*
Henry Peters, *sheriff*
Lewis Hale, *a neighboring farmer*
Mrs. Peters
Mrs. Hale

SCENE. *The kitchen in the now abandoned farmhouse of* JOHN WRIGHT, *a gloomy kitchen, and left without having been put in order—unwashed pans under the sink, a loaf of bread outside the breadbox, a dish-towel on the table—other signs of incompleted work. At the rear the outer door opens and the* SHERIFF *comes in followed by the* COUNTY ATTORNEY *and* HALE. *The* SHERIFF *and* HALE *are men in middle life, the* COUNTY ATTORNEY *is a young man; all are much bundled up and go at once to the stove. They are followed by the two women—the* SHERIFF'S *wife first; she is a slight wiry woman, a thin nervous face.* MRS. HALE *is larger and would ordinarily be called more comfortable looking, but she is disturbed now and looks fearfully about as she enters. The women have come in slowly, and stand close together near the door.*

COUNTY ATTORNEY.　[*Rubbing his hands.*] This feels good. Come up to the fire, ladies.

MRS. PETERS.　[*After taking a step forward.*] I'm not—cold.

SHERIFF.　[*Unbuttoning his overcoat and stepping away from the stove as if to mark the beginning of official business.*] Now, Mr. Hale, before we move things about, you explain to Mr. Henderson just what you saw when you came here yesterday morning.

COUNTY ATTORNEY.　By the way, has anything been moved? Are things just as you left them yesterday?

SHERIFF.　[*Looking about.*] It's just the same. When it dropped below zero last night I thought I'd better send Frank out this morning to make a fire for us—no use getting pneumonia with a big case on, but I told him not to touch anything except the stove—and you know Frank.　　5

COUNTY ATTORNEY.   Somebody should have been left here yesterday.

SHERIFF.   Oh—yesterday. When I had to send Frank to Morris Center for that man who went crazy—I want you to know I had my hands full yesterday. I knew you could get back from Omaha by today and as long as I went over everything here myself—

COUNTY ATTORNEY.   Well, Mr. Hale, tell just what happened when you came here yesterday morning.

HALE.   Harry and I had started to town with a load of potatoes. We came along the road from my place and as I got here I said, "I'm going to see if I can't get John Wright to go in with me on a party telephone." I spoke to Wright about it once before and he put me off, saying folks talked too much anyway, and all he asked was peace and quiet—I guess you know about how much he talked himself; but I thought maybe if I went to the house and talked about it before his wife, though I said to Harry that I didn't know as what his wife wanted made much difference to John—

10   COUNTY ATTORNEY.   Let's talk about that later, Mr. Hale. I do want to talk about that, but tell now just what happened when you got to the house.

HALE.   I didn't hear or see anything; I knocked at the door, and still it was all quiet inside. I knew they must be up, it was past eight o'clock. So I knocked again, and I thought I heard somebody say, "Come in." I wasn't sure, I'm not sure yet, but I opened the door—this door [*Indicating the door by which the two women are still standing.*] and there in that rocker—[*Pointing to it.*] sat Mrs. Wright.

[*They all look at the rocker.*]

COUNTY ATTORNEY.   What—was she doing?

HALE.   She was rockin' back and forth. She had her apron in her hand and was kind of—pleating it.

COUNTY ATTORNEY.   And how did she—look?

15   HALE.   Well, she looked queer.

COUNTY ATTORNEY.   How do you mean—queer?

HALE.   Well, as if she didn't know what she was going to do next. And kind of done up.

COUNTY ATTORNEY.   How did she seem to feel about your coming?

HALE.   Why, I don't think she minded—one way or other. She didn't pay much attention. I said, "How do, Mrs. Wright, it's cold, ain't it?" And she said, "Is it?"—and went on kind of pleating at her apron. Well, I was surprised; she didn't ask me to come up to the stove, or to set down, but just sat there, not even looking at me, so I said, "I want to see John." And then she—laughed. I guess you would call it a laugh. I thought of Harry and the team outside, so I said a little sharp: "Can't I see John?" "No," she says, kind o' dull like. "Ain't he home?" says I. "Yes," says she, "he's home." "Then why can't I see him?" I asked her, out of patience. "'Cause he's dead," says she. "*Dead?*" says I. She just nodded her head, not getting a bit excited, but rockin' back and forth. "Why—where is he?" says I, not knowing what to say. She just pointed upstairs—like that. [*Himself pointing to the room above.*] I got up, with the idea of going up there. I walked from there to here—then I says, "What did he die of?" "He died of a rope round his neck," says she, and just went on pleatin' at her apron. Well, I went out and called Harry. I thought I might—need help. We went upstairs and there he was lyin'—

COUNTY ATTORNEY.   I think I'd rather have you go into that upstairs, where   *20*
you can point it all out. Just go on now with the rest of the story.

HALE.   Well, my first thought was to get that rope off. It looked . . . [*Stops, his
face twitches.*] . . . but Harry, he went up to him, and he said, "No, he's dead all right,
and we'd better not touch anything." So we went back downstairs. She was still sitting that same way. "Has anybody been notified?" I asked. "No," says she, uncon-
cerned. "Who did this, Mrs. Wright?" said Harry. He said it businesslike—and she
stopped pleatin' of her apron. "I don't know," she says. "You don't *know*?" says
Harry. "No," says she. "Weren't you sleepin' in the bed with him?" says Harry.
"Yes," says she, "but I was on the inside." "Somebody slipped a rope round his neck
and strangled him and you didn't wake up?" says Harry. "I didn't wake up," she
said after him. We must 'a looked as if we didn't see how that could be, for after a
minute she said, "I sleep sound." Harry was going to ask her more questions but I
said maybe we ought to let her tell her story first to the coroner, or the sheriff, so
Harry went fast as he could to Rivers' place, where there's a telephone.

COUNTY ATTORNEY.   And what did Mrs. Wright do when she knew that you
had gone for the coroner?

HALE.   She moved from that chair to this one over here [*Pointing to a small
chair in the corner.*] and just sat there with her hands held together and looking down.
I got a feeling that I ought to make some conversation, so I said I had come in to see
if John wanted to put in a telephone, and at that she started to laugh, and then she
stopped and looked at me—scared. [*The COUNTY ATTORNEY, who has had his notebook
out, makes a note.*] I dunno, maybe it wasn't scared. I wouldn't like to say it was. Soon
Harry got back, and then Dr. Lloyd came, and you, Mr. Peters, and so I guess that's
all I know that you don't.

COUNTY ATTORNEY.   [*Looking around.*] I guess we'll go upstairs first—and
then out to the barn and around there. [*To the SHERIFF.*] You're convinced that there
was nothing important here—nothing that would point to any motive.

SHERIFF.   Nothing here but kitchen things.   *25*

[*The COUNTY ATTORNEY, after again looking around the kitchen, opens the door of a cupboard closet. He gets up on a chair and looks on a shelf. Pulls his hand away, sticky.*]

COUNTY ATTORNEY.   Here's a nice mess.

[*The women draw nearer.*]

MRS. PETERS.   [*To the other woman.*] Oh, her fruit; it did freeze. [*To the LAWYER.*]
She worried about that when it turned so cold. She said the fire'd go out and her jars
would break.

SHERIFF.   Well, can you beat the women! Held for murder and worryin' about
her preserves.

COUNTY ATTORNEY.   I guess before we're through she may have something
more serious than preserves to worry about.

HALE.   Well, women are used to worrying over trifles.   *30*

[*The two women move a little closer together.*]

COUNTY ATTORNEY.   [*With the gallantry of a young politician.*] And yet, for all
their worries, what would we do without the ladies? [*The women do not unbend. He
goes to the sink, takes a dipperful of water from the pail and pouring it into a basin, washes*

his hands. Starts to wipe them on the roller-towel, turns it for a cleaner place.] Dirty towels! [*Kicks his foot against the pans under the sink.*] Not much of a housekeeper, would you say, ladies?

MRS. HALE. [*Stiffly.*] There's a great deal of work to be done on a farm.

COUNTY ATTORNEY. To be sure. And yet [*With a little bow to her.*] I know there are some Dickson county farmhouses which do not have such roller towels.

[*He gives it a pull to expose its full length again.*]

MRS. HALE. Those towels get dirty awful quick. Men's hands aren't always as clean as they might be.

35 COUNTY ATTORNEY. Ah, loyal to your sex, I see. But you and Mrs. Wright were neighbors. I suppose you were friends, too.

MRS. HALE. [*Shaking her head.*] I've not seen much of her of late years. I've not been in this house—it's more than a year.

COUNTY ATTORNEY. And why was that? You didn't like her?

MRS. HALE. I liked her all well enough. Farmers' wives have their hands full, Mr. Henderson. And then—

COUNTY ATTORNEY. Yes?

40 MRS. HALE. [*Looking about.*] It never seemed a very cheerful place.

COUNTY ATTORNEY. No—it's not cheerful. I shouldn't say she had the homemaking instinct.

MRS. HALE. Well, I don't know as Wright had, either.

COUNTY ATTORNEY. You mean that they didn't get on very well?

MRS. HALE. No, I don't mean anything. But I don't think a place'd be any cheerfuller for John Wright's being in it.

45 COUNTY ATTORNEY. I'd like to talk more of that a little later. I want to get the lay of things upstairs now.

[*He goes to the left, where three steps lead to a stair door.*]

SHERIFF. I suppose anything Mrs. Peters does'll be all right. She was to take in some clothes for her, you know, and a few little things. We left in such a hurry yesterday.

COUNTY ATTORNEY. Yes, but I would like to see what you take, Mrs. Peters, and keep an eye out for anything that might be of use to us.

MRS. PETERS. Yes, Mr. Henderson.

[*The women listen to the men's steps on the stairs, then look about the kitchen.*]

MRS. HALE. I'd hate to have men coming into my kitchen, snooping around and criticizing.

[*She arranges the pans under the sink which the LAWYER had shoved out of place.*]

50 MRS. PETERS. Of course it's no more than their duty.

MRS. HALE. Duty's all right, but I guess that deputy sheriff that came out to make the fire might have got a little of this on. [*Gives the roller towel a pull.*] Wish I'd thought of that sooner. Seems mean to talk about her for not having things slicked up when she had to come away in such a hurry.

MRS. PETERS. [*Who had gone to a small table in the left rear corner of the room, and lifted one end of a towel that covers a pan.*] She had bread set.

[*Stands still.*]

MRS. HALE. [*Eyes fixed on a loaf of bread beside the breadbox, which is on a low shelf at the other side of the room. Moves slowly toward it.*] She was going to put this in there. [*Picks up loaf, then abruptly drops it. In a manner of returning to familiar things.*] It's a shame about her fruit. I wonder if it's all gone. [*Gets up on the chair and looks.*] I think there's some here that's all right, Mrs. Peters. Yes—here; [*Holding it toward the window.*] this is cherries, too. [*Looking again.*] I declare I believe that's the only one. [*Gets down, bottle in her hand. Goes to the sink and wipes it off on the outside.*] She'll feel awful bad after all her hard work in the hot weather. I remember the afternoon I put up my cherries last summer.

[*She puts the bottle on the big kitchen table, center of the room. With a sigh, is about to sit down in the rocking-chair. Before she is seated realizes what chair it is; with a slow look at it, steps back. The chair which she has touched rocks back and forth.*]

MRS. PETERS. Well, I must get those things from the front room closet. [*She goes to the door at the right, but after looking into the other room, steps back.*] You coming with me, Mrs. Hale? You could help me carry them.

[*They go in the other room; reappear, MRS. PETERS carrying a dress and skirt, MRS. HALE following with a pair of shoes.*]

MRS. PETERS. My, it's cold in there. 55

[*She puts the clothes on the big table, and hurries to the stove.*]

MRS. HALE. [*Examining the skirt.*] Wright was close. I think maybe that's why she kept so much to herself. She didn't even belong to the Ladies Aid. I suppose she felt she couldn't do her part, and then you don't enjoy things when you feel shabby. She used to wear pretty clothes and be lively, when she was Minnie Foster, one of the town girls singing in the choir. But that—oh, that was thirty years ago. This all you was to take in?

MRS. PETERS. She said she wanted an apron. Funny thing to want, for there isn't much to get you dirty in jail, goodness knows. But I suppose just to make her feel more natural. She said they was in the top drawer in this cupboard. Yes, here. And then her little shawl that always hung behind the door. [*Opens stair door and looks.*] Yes, here it is.

[*Quickly shuts door leading upstairs.*]

MRS. HALE. [*Abruptly moving toward her.*] Mrs. Peters?
MRS. PETERS. Yes, Mrs. Hale?
MRS. HALE. Do you think she did it? 60
MRS. PETERS. [*In a frightened voice.*] Oh, I don't know.
MRS. HALE. Well, I don't think she did. Asking for an apron and her little shawl. Worrying about her fruit.
MRS. PETERS. [*Starts to speak, glances up, where footsteps are heard in the room above. In a low voice.*] Mr. Peters says it looks bad for her. Mr. Henderson is awful sarcastic in a speech and he'll make fun of her sayin' she didn't wake up.
MRS. HALE. Well, I guess John Wright didn't wake when they was slipping that rope under his neck.

65   MRS. PETERS.   No, it's strange. It must have been done awful crafty and still. They say it was such a—funny way to kill a man, rigging it all up like that.

MRS. HALE.   That's just what Mr. Hale said. There was a gun in the house. He says that's what he can't understand.

MRS. PETERS.   Mr. Henderson said coming out that what was needed for the case was a motive; something to show anger, or—sudden feeling.

MRS. HALE.   [*Who is standing by the table.*] Well, I don't see any signs of anger around here. [*She puts her hand on the dish towel which lies on the table, stands looking down at table, one half of which is clean, the other half messy.*] It's wiped to here. [*Makes a move as if to finish work, then turns and looks at loaf of bread outside the breadbox. Drops towel. In that voice of coming back to familiar things.*] Wonder how they are finding things upstairs. I hope she had it a little more red-up° up there. You know, it seems kind of *sneaking*. Locking her up in town and then coming out here and trying to get her own house to turn against her!

MRS. PETERS.   But Mrs. Hale, the law is the law.

70   MRS. HALE.   I s'pose 'tis. [*Unbuttoning her coat.*] Better loosen up your things. Mrs. Peters. You won't feel them when you go out.

[*MRS. PETERS takes off her fur tippet,° goes to hang it on hook at back of room, stands looking at the under part of the small corner table.*]

MRS. PETERS.   She was piecing a quilt.

[*She brings the large sewing basket and they look at the bright pieces.*]

MRS. HALE.   It's log cabin pattern. Pretty, isn't it? I wonder if she was goin' to quilt it or just knot it?

[*Footsteps have been heard coming down the stairs. The SHERIFF enters followed by HALE and the COUNTY ATTORNEY.*]

SHERIFF.   They wonder if she was going to quilt it or just knot it!

[*The men laugh; the women look abashed.*]

COUNTY ATTORNEY.   [*Rubbing his hands over the stove.*] Frank's fire didn't do much up there, did it? Well, let's go out to the barn and get that cleared up.

[*The men go outside.*]

75   MRS. HALE.   [*Resentfully.*] I don't know as there's anything so strange, our takin' up our time with little things while we're waiting for them to get the evidence. [*She sits down at the big table smoothing out a block with decision.*] I don't see as it's anything to laugh about.

MRS. PETERS.   [*Apologetically.*] Of course they've got awful important things on their minds.

[*Pulls up a chair and joins MRS. HALE at the table.*]

MRS. HALE.   [*Examining another block.*] Mrs. Peters, look at this one. Here. this is the one she was working on, and look at the sewing! All the rest of it has been so

red-up: neat, arranged in order.
tippet: scarf-like garment of fur or wool for the neck and shoulders.

nice and even. And look at this! It's all over the place! Why, it looks as if she didn't know what she was about!

[*After she has said this they look at each other, then start to glance back at the door. After an instant MRS. HALE has pulled at a knot and ripped the sewing.*]

MRS. PETERS.   Oh, what are you doing, Mrs. Hale?

MRS. HALE.   [*Mildly.*] Just pulling out a stitch or two that's not sewed very good. [*Threading a needle.*] Bad sewing always made me fidgety.

MRS. PETERS.   [*Nervously.*] I don't think we ought to touch things.   80

MRS. HALE.   I'll just finish up this end. [*Suddenly stopping and leaning forward.*] Mrs. Peters?

MRS. PETERS.   Yes, Mrs. Hale?

MRS. HALE.   What do you suppose she was so nervous about?

MRS. PETERS.   Oh—I don't know. I don't know as she was nervous. I sometimes sew awful queer when I'm just tired. [*MRS. HALE starts to say something, looks at MRS. PETERS, then goes on sewing.*] Well I must get these things wrapped up. They may be through sooner than we think. [*Putting apron and other things together.*] I wonder where I can find a piece of paper, and string.

MRS. HALE.   In that cupboard, maybe.   85

MRS. PETERS.   [*Looking in cupboard.*] Why, here's a birdcage. [*Holds it up.*] Did she have a bird, Mrs. Hale?

MRS. HALE.   Why, I don't know whether she did or not—I've not been here for so long. There was a man around last year selling canaries cheap, but I don't know as she took one; maybe she did. She used to sing real pretty herself.

MRS. PETERS.   [*Glancing around.*] Seems funny to think of a bird here. But she must have had one, or why would she have a cage? I wonder what happened to it.

MRS. HALE.   I s'pose maybe the cat got it.

MRS. PETERS.   No, she didn't have a cat. She's got that feeling some people   90
have about cats—being afraid of them. My cat got in her room and she was real upset and asked me to take it out.

MRS. HALE.   My sister Bessie was like that. Queer, ain't it?

MRS. PETERS.   [*Examining the cage.*] Why, look at this door. It's broke. One hinge is pulled apart.

MRS. HALE.   [*Looking too.*] Looks as if someone must have been rough with it.

MRS. PETERS.   Why, yes.

[*She brings the cage forward and puts it on the table.*]

MRS. HALE.   I wish if they're going to find any evidence they'd be about it. I   95
don't like this place.

MRS. PETERS.   But I'm awful glad you came with me, Mrs. Hale. It would be lonesome for me sitting here alone.

MRS. HALE.   It would, wouldn't it? [*Dropping her sewing.*] But I tell you what I do wish, Mrs. Peters. I wish I had come over sometimes when *she* was here. I—[*Looking around the room.*] I—wish I had.

MRS. PETERS.   But of course you were awful busy, Mrs. Hale—your house and your children.

MRS. HALE.   I could've come. I stayed away because it weren't cheerful—and that's why I ought to have come. I—I've never liked this place. Maybe because it's down in a hollow and you don't see the road. I dunno what it is, but it's a lonesome place and always was. I wish I had come over to see Minnie Foster sometimes. I can see now—

[*Shakes her head.*]

100   MRS. PETERS.   Well, you mustn't reproach yourself, Mrs. Hale. Somehow we just don't see how it is with other folks until—something comes up.

MRS. HALE.   Not having children makes less work—but it makes a quiet house, and Wright out to work all day, and no company when he did come in. Did you know John Wright, Mrs. Peters?

MRS. PETERS.   Not to know him; I've seen him in town. They say he was a good man.

MRS. HALE.   Yes—good; he didn't drink, and kept his word as well as most, I guess, and paid his debts. But he was a hard man, Mrs. Peters. Just to pass the time of day with him—[*Shivers.*] Like a raw wind that gets to the bone. [*Pauses, her eye falling on the cage.*] I should think she would 'a wanted a bird. But what do you suppose went with it?

MRS. PETERS.   I don't know, unless it got sick and died.

[*She reaches over and swings the broken door, swings it again, both women watch it.*]

105   MRS. HALE.   You weren't raised round here, were you? [*MRS. PETERS shakes her head.*] You didn't know—her?

MRS. PETERS.   Not till they brought her yesterday,

MRS. HALE.   She—come to think of it, she was kind of like a bird herself—real sweet and pretty, but kind of timid and—fluttery. How—she—did—change. [*Silence; then as if struck by a happy thought and relieved to get back to everyday things.*] Tell you what, Mrs. Peters, why don't you take the quilt in with you? It might take up her mind.

MRS. PETERS.   Why, I think that's a real nice idea, Mrs. Hale. There couldn't possibly be any objection to it, could there? Now, just what would I take? I wonder if her patches are in here—and her things.

[*They look in the sewing basket.*]

MRS. HALE.   Here's some red. I expect this has got sewing things in it. [*Brings out a fancy box.*] What a pretty box. Looks like something somebody would give you. Maybe her scissors are in here. [*Opens box. Suddenly puts her hand to her nose.*] Why— [*MRS. PETERS bends nearer, then turns her face away.*] There's something wrapped up in this piece of silk.

110   MRS. PETERS.   Why, this isn't her scissors.

MRS. HALE.   [*Lifting the silk.*] Oh, Mrs. Peters—it's—

[*MRS. PETERS bends closer.*]

MRS. PETERS.   It's the bird.

MRS. HALE.   [*Jumping up.*] But, Mrs. Peters—look at it! Its neck! Look at its neck! It's all—other side *to*.

MRS. PETERS.   Somebody—wrung—its—neck.

[*Their eyes meet. A look of growing comprehension, of horror. Steps are heard outside. MRS. HALE slips box under quilt pieces, and sinks into her chair. Enter SHERIFF and COUNTY ATTORNEY. MRS. PETERS rises.*]

COUNTY ATTORNEY. [*As one turning from serious things to little pleasantries.*]   *115*
Well, ladies, have you decided whether she was going to quilt it or knot it?

MRS. PETERS.   We think she was going to—knot it.

COUNTY ATTORNEY.   Well, that's interesting, I'm sure. [*Seeing the bird-cage.*]
Has the bird flown?

MRS. HALE. [*Putting more quilt pieces over the box.*] We think the—cat got it.

COUNTY ATTORNEY.   [*Preoccupied.*] Is there cat?

[*MRS. HALE glances in a quick covert way at MRS. PETERS.*]

MRS. PETERS.   Well, not *now*. They're superstitious, you know. They leave.   *120*

COUNTY ATTORNEY. [*To SHERIFF PETERS, continuing an interrupted conversation.*] No sign at all of anyone having come from the outside. Their own rope. Now
let's go up again and go over it piece by piece. [*They start upstairs.*] It would have to
have been someone who knew just the—

[*MRS. PETERS sits down. The two women sit there not looking at one another, but as if peering into something and at the same time holding back. When they talk now it is in the manner of feeling their way over strange ground, as if afraid of what they are saying, but as if
they cannot help saying it.*]

MRS. HALE.   She liked the bird. She was going to bury it in that pretty box.

MRS. PETERS. [*In a whisper.*] When I was a girl—my kitten—there was a boy
took a hatchet, and before my eyes—and before I could get there—[*Covers her face an
instant.*] If they hadn't held me back I would have—[*Catches herself, looks upstairs
where steps are heard, falters weakly.*]—hurt him.

MRS. HALE.   [*With a slow look around her.*] I wonder how it would seem never
to have had any children around. [*Pause.*] No, Wright wouldn't like the bird—a
thing that sang. She used to sing. He killed that, too.

MRS. PETERS. [*Moving uneasily.*] We don't know who killed the bird.   *125*

MRS. HALE.   I knew John Wright.

MRS. PETERS.   It was an awful thing was done in this house that night, Mrs.
Hale. Killing a man while he slept, slipping a rope around his neck that choked the
life out of him.

MRS. HALE.   His neck. Choked the life out of him.

[*Her hand goes out and rests on the birdcage.*]

MRS. PETERS. [*With rising voice.*] We don't know who killed him. We don't
know.

MRS. HALE. [*Her own feeling not interrupted.*] If there'd been years and years   *130*
of nothing, then a bird to sing to you, it would be awful—still, after the bird was
still.

MRS. PETERS. [*Something within her speaking.*] I know what stillness is. When
we homesteaded in Dakota, and my first baby died—after he was two years old, and
me with no other then—

MRS. HALE. [*Moving.*] How soon do you suppose they'll be through, looking
for the evidence?

MRS. PETERS.   I know what stillness is. [*Pulling herself back.*] The law has got to
punish crime, Mrs. Hale.

MRS. HALE. [*Not as if answering that.*] I wish you'd seen Minnie Foster when she wore a white dress with blue ribbons and stood up there in the choir and sang. [*A look around the room.*] Oh, I wish I'd come over here once in a while! That was a crime! That was a crime! Who's going to punish that?

135   MRS. PETERS. [*Looking upstairs.*] We mustn't—take on.

MRS. HALE. I might have known she needed help! I know how things can be—for women. I tell you, it's queer, Mrs. Peters. We live close together and we live far apart. We all go through the same things—it's all just a different kind of the same thing. [*Brushes her eyes; noticing the bottle of fruit, reaches out for it.*] If I was you I wouldn't tell her her fruit was gone. Tell her it *ain't*. Tell her it's all right. Take this in to prove it to her. She—she may never know whether it was broke or not.

MRS. PETERS. [*Takes the bottle, looks about for something to wrap it in; takes petticoat from the clothes brought from the other room, very nervously begins winding this around the bottle. In a false voice.*] My, it's a good thing the men couldn't hear us. Wouldn't they just laugh! Getting all stirred up over a little thing like a—dead canary. As if that could have anything to do with—with—wouldn't they *laugh*!

[*The men are heard coming down stairs.*]

MRS. HALE. [*Under her breath.*] Maybe they would—maybe they wouldn't.

COUNTY ATTORNEY. No, Peters, it's all perfectly clear except a reason for doing it. But you know juries when it comes to women. If there was some definite thing. Something to show—something to make a story about—a thing that would connect up with this strange way of doing it—

[*The women's eyes meet for an instant. Enter HALE from outer door.*]

140   HALE. Well, I've got the team° around. Pretty cold out there.

COUNTY ATTORNEY. I'm going to stay here a while by myself. [*To the SHERIFF.*] You can send Frank out for me, can't you? I want to go over everything. I'm not satisfied that we can't do better.

SHERIFF. Do you want to see what Mrs. Peters is going to take in?

[*The COUNTY ATTORNEY goes to the table, picks up the apron, laughs.*]

COUNTY ATTORNEY. Oh, I guess they're not very dangerous things the ladies have picked out. [*Moves a few things about, disturbing the quilt pieces which cover the box. Steps back.*] No, Mrs. Peters doesn't need supervising. For that matter, a sheriff's wife is married to the law. Ever think of it that way, Mrs. Peters?

MRS. PETERS. Not—just that way.

145   SHERIFF. [*Chuckling.*] Married to the law. [*Moves toward the other room.*] I just want you to come in here a minute, George. We ought to take a look at these windows.

COUNTY ATTORNEY. [*Scoffingly.*] Oh, windows!

SHERIFF. We'll be right out, Mr. Hale.

[*HALE goes outside. The SHERIFF follows the COUNTY ATTORNEY into the other room. Then MRS. HALE rises, hands tight together, looking intensely at MRS. PETERS, whose eyes make a slow turn, finally meeting MRS. HALE'S. A moment MRS. HALE holds her, then her own eyes*]

team: a team of horses for drawing a sleigh or wagon.

point the way to where the box is concealed. Suddenly MRS. PETERS *throws back quilt pieces and tries to put the box in the bag she is wearing. It is too big. She opens box, starts to take bird out, cannot touch it, goes to pieces, stands there helpless. Sound of a knob turning in the other room.* MRS. HALE *snatches the box and puts it in the pocket of her big coat. Enter* COUNTY ATTORNEY *and* SHERIFF.]

COUNTY ATTORNEY.   [*Facetiously.*] Well, Henry, at least we found out that she was not going to quilt it. She was going to—what is it you call it, ladies?

MRS. HALE.   [*Her hand against her pocket.*] We call it—knot it, Mr. Henderson.

CURTAIN

A Glossary of Important Terms

This glossary presents brief definitions of terms and concepts discussed in the text (usually boldfaced). Page references indicate where readers may find additional detail and illustration, together with discussions about how the concepts can be utilized in studying and writing about literature.

Accent or **beat,** The heavy stresses or accents in lines of poetry. The number of accents or beats in a line usually dictates the meter of the line (five beats in a pentameter line, four in a tetrameter line, etc.), 185

Accented rhyme. See *Heavy-stress rhyme.*

Accented syllable, A syllable receiving a major, or heavy, stress, 185

Acute accent, In scansion, the prime mark (´) indicating a heavy stress, 185

Allegory, A complete narrative that may also be applied to a parallel set of moral, philosophical, political, religious, or social situations, 139–51, 142–43

Alliteration, The repetition of identical consonant sounds (most often the sounds beginning words) in close proximity (e.g., "pensive poets," "grown gray"), 184, 192

Allusion, Unacknowledged references and quotations. Authors assume that readers will recognize the original sources and relate their meaning to the new context. 144

Amphibrach, A three-syllable foot consisting of a light, heavy, and light stress, 189

Amphimacer or **cretic,** A three-syllable foot consisting of a heavy, light, and heavy stress, 189

Analytical sentence outline, A scheme or plan for an essay, arranged according to topics (A, B, C, etc.) and with the topics expressed in sentences, 26–27

Analyzed rhyme. See *Inexact rhyme.*

Anapest, A three-syllable foot consisting of two light stresses climaxed by a heavy stress, 188

Antagonist, The person, idea, force, or general set of circumstances opposing the *protagonist;* an essential element of *plot,* 57

Anticipation. See *Procatalepsis.*

Archetypal/Symbolic/Mythic critical approach, An interpretive literary approach explaining literature in terms of archetypal patterns (e.g., God's creation of human beings, the search for paradise, the initiation of a young person), 293–94

Assonance, The repetition of identical vowel sounds in different words in close proximity, as in the d*ee*p gr*ee*n s*ea*, 184, 191

Atmosphere or **mood,** The emotional aura invoked by a work, 69–70

Auditory images, References to sounds, 120–21

Authorial symbol. See *Contextual symbol.*

Authorial voice, The voice or persona used by authors when seemingly speaking for themselves. The use of the term makes it possible to discuss a narration or presentation without identifying the ideas absolutely with those of the author. See also *Speaker, Point of view,* and *Third-person point of view,* 97, 110

Bacchius or **Bacchic,** A three-syllable foot consisting of a light stress followed by two heavy stresses, as in "a new song" and "the old ways," 189

Ballad, Ballad Measure, A narrative poem composed of quatrains in *ballad measure;* that is, a pattern of iambic tetrameter alternating with iambic trimeter and rhyming *x-a-x-a,* 194

Beast fable, A fable featuring animals with human characteristics, 143

Beat. See *Accent.*

Brainstorming, The exploration, discovery, and development of details to be used in a composition, 18–22

Breve, A mark in the shape of a bowl-like half circle (˘) to indicate a light stress or unaccented syllable, 185

Cacophony, Meaning "bad sound," *cacophony* refers to words combining sharp or harsh sounds. 192–93

Cadence group, A coherent word group spoken as a single rhythmical unit, such as a noun phrase ("our sacred honor") or prepositional phrase ("of parting day"), 188

Caesura, caesurae, The pause(s) or juncture(s) separating phrases within lines of poetry, an important aspect of poetic *rhythm,* 188–91

Central idea, (1) The thesis or main idea of an essay. (2) The theme of a literary work, 22–24

Character, An extended verbal representation of a human being, the inner self that determines thought, speech, and behavior, 22, 53–65

Climax (Greek for *ladder*), The high point of *conflict* and tension preceding the resolution of a story or play; the point of decision, of inevitability and no return. The climax is sometimes merged with the *crisis* in the consideration of dramatic and narrative structure. 83–84

Close reading, The detailed study of a poem or passage, designed to explain characters, ideas, style, setting, etc., 210–16

Close-up (film), A camera view of an actor's head and upper body, designed to emphasize the psychological makeup and reactions of the character being portrayed; contrasted with *long shot,* 222

Comparison-contrast, A technique of analyzing two or more works in order to determine similarities and differences in topic, treatment, and quality, 173–82

Complication, A stage of narrative and dramatic structure in which the major *conflicts* are brought out; the *rising action of a drama,* 83

Conflict, The opposition between two characters, between large groups of people, or between *protagonists* and larger forces such as natural objects, ideas, modes of behavior, public opinion, and the like. Conflict may also be internal and psychological, involving choices facing a *protagonist.* It is the essence of *plot.* 77–78

Consonant sounds or consonant segments, Consonant sounds are produced as a result of the touching or close proximity of the tongue or the lips in relation to the teeth or palate (e.g., *m, n, p, f, sh, ch*); to be compared with *vowel sounds,* 192

Contextual, private, or authorial symbol, A symbol which is derived not from common historical, cultural, or religious materials, but which is rather developed within the context of an individual work. See also *Cultural Symbol.* 141

Cosmic irony (irony of fate), Situational irony that is connected to a pessimistic or fatalistic view of life, 151

Cretic. See *Amphimacer.*

Crisis, The point of uncertainty and tension—the turning point—that results from the conflicts and difficulties brought about through the complications of the plot. The crisis leads to the climax—that is, to the decision made by the protagonist to resolve the conflict. Sometimes the crisis and the climax are considered as two elements of the same stage of plot development. 83

Cultural or universal symbol, A symbol that is recognized and shared as a result of a common political, social, and cultural heritage. See also *Contextual symbol.* 140–41

Dactyl, A three-syllable foot consisting of a heavy stress followed by two lights, as in each word of the phrase "notable quotable parables," 188

Deconstructionist critical approach, An interpretive literary approach that rejects absolute interpretations and stresses ambiguities and contradictions, 294–96

Dénouement (untying) or **resolution,** The final stage of plot development, in which mysteries are explained, characters find their destinies, and the work is completed. Usually the dénouement is done as speedily as possible, for it occurs after all conflicts are ended. 84

Dilemma, A situation presenting a character with two choices, each one of which is unacceptable, dangerous, or even lethal, 77

Dimeter, A line of two metrical feet, 186

Dipody, dipodic foot, or **syzygy,** A strong beat that creates a single foot out of two normal feet—usually iambs or trochees—so that a "galloping" or "rollicking" rhythm results, 189

Documentation, Granting recognition to the ideas and words of others, either through textual, parenthetical, or footnote references, 254–60

Double entendre ("double meaning"), Deliberate ambiguity, often sexual and usually humorous, 157

Double rhyme. See *Trochaic rhyme.*

Drama, An individual play; also plays considered as a group; one of the three major genres of imaginative literature, 3

Dramatic irony, A special kind of situational irony in which a character perceives his or her plight in a limited way while the audience and one or more of the other characters understand it entirely, 158

Dramatic or objective point of view, A third-person narration reporting speech and action, but excluding commentary on the actions and thoughts of the characters, 97–98, 100, 110

Dynamic character, A character who undergoes adaptation, change, or growth, unlike the *static character,* who remains constant. In a *short story,* there is usually only one dynamic character, whereas in a *novel* there may be many. 57

Echoic words, Words echoing the actions they describe, such as *buzz, bump,* and *slap;* important in the device of *onomatopoeia,* 192

Economic Determinist/Marxist critical approach, An interpretive literary approach based on the theories of Karl Marx (1818–1883), stressing that literature is to be judged from an economic perspective, 291–92

Editing. See *Montage.*

Enclosing setting. See *Framing setting.*

End-stopped line, A line ending in a full pause, usually indicated with a period or semicolon, 190

Enjambement or run-on line, A line having no end punctuation but running over to the next line, 190

Epic, A long narrative poem elevating character, speech, and action, 3

Essay, A short and tightly organized written composition dealing with a topic such as a character, setting, or point of view, 16–42

Euphony, Meaning "good sound," *euphony* refers to word groups containing consonants that permit an easy and pleasant flow of spoken sound. See also *cacophony.* 192–93

Exact rhyme, Rhyming words in which both the vowel and consonant sounds rhyme; also called *perfect rhyme.* It is important to note that rhymes result from *sound* rather than spelling; words do not have to be spelled the same way or look alike to rhyme. 193

Examination, A written or oral test or inquiry designed to discover a person's understanding and capacity to deal with a particular topic or set of topics, 271–82

Exposition, The stage of dramatic or narrative structure which introduces all things necessary for the development of the plot. 83

Eye rhyme or sight rhyme, Words which seem to rhyme because parts of them are spelled identically but pronounced differently (e.g., *bear, fear; fury, bury; stove, shove; wonder, yonder*). 193

Fable, A brief *story* illustrating a moral truth, most often associated with the ancient Greek writer Aesop, 143

Falling rhyme, Trochaic rhymes, such as *dying* and *crying,* and also dactylic rhymes, such as *flattery* and *battery,* and *slippery* and *frippery,* 190

Feet. See *Foot.*

Feminist critical approach, An interpretive literary approach designed to raise consciousness about the importance and unique nature of women in literature, 290

Fiction, *Narratives* based in the imagination of the author, not in literal, reportorial facts; one of the three major genres of imaginative literature, 3

Figurative language, Words and expressions that conform to a particular pattern or form, such as *metaphor, simile,* and *parallelism,* 3, 111, 128–38

Figures. See *Figurative language.*

Figures of Speech. See *Figurative language.*

Film script, The written dramatic text on which a film is based, including directions for movement and expression, 220–21

Film, Motion pictures, movies, 217–30

First-person point of view, The use of an "I," or first-person, speaker or narrator who tells about things that he/she has seen, done, spoken, heard, thought, and also learned about in other ways, 95–96, 100, 110

Flashback, A method of narration in which past events are introduced into a present action, 94–85

Flat character, A character, usually minor, who is not individual, but rather useful and structural, static and unchanging; distinguished from *round character,* 57–58

Foot, feet, A measured combination of heavy and light *stresses,* such as the iamb, which contains a light and a heavy stress, 185

Formal substitution. See *Substitution.*

Formalist critical approach. See *New Critical/Formalist critical approach.*

Framing (enclosing) setting, The same features of topic or setting used at both the beginning and ending of a work so as to "frame" or "enclose" the work, 69

Freewriting. See *Brainstorming.*

Graph, Graphics (spelling), Writing or spelling; the appearance of words on a page, as opposed to their actual sounds, 184

Gustatory images, References to impressions of taste, 120–21

Haiku, A poetic form derived from Japanese, traditionally containing three lines of 5, 7, and 5 syllables, in that order, 3

Half rhyme. See *Inexact rhyme.*

Heavy-stress rhyme or rising rhyme, A rhyme, such as rhyming iambs or anapests, ending with a strong stress. The rhymes may be produced with one syllable words, like *sky* and *fly,* or with multisyllabic words in which the accent falls on the last syllable, such as *decline* and *confine.* 185, 194

Heptameter or the septenary, A line consisting of seven metrical feet, 186

Hero, heroine, The major male and female *protagonists* in a narrative or drama. The terms are often used to describe leading characters in adventures and romances. 57

Hexameter, A line consisting of six metrical feet, 186

Historical critical approach, See *Topical/Historical critical approach.*

Hovering accent. See *Spondee.*

Hyperbole or overstatement, A rhetorical figure in which emphasis is achieved through exaggeration, 157

Iamb, A two-syllable *foot* consisting of a light stress followed by a heavy stress (e.g., *the winds, a book, she might*), 186

Idea, A concept, thought, opinion, or belief; in literature, a unifying, centralizing conception or theme, 107–117

Identical rhyme, The use of the same words in rhyming positions, such as *veil* and *veil*, or *stone* and *stone*, 194

Image, Imagery, Images are references that trigger the mind to fuse together memories of sights (*visual*), sounds (*auditory*), tastes (*gustatory*), smells (*olfactory*), and sensations of touch (*tactile*). "Image" refers to a single mental creation. "Imagery" refers to images throughout a work or throughout the works of a writer or group of writers. Images may be *literal* (descriptive and pictorial) and *metaphorical* (figurative and suggestive). 3, 118–27

Imaginative literature, Literature based in the imagination of the writer; the genres of imaginative literature are *fiction, poetry,* and *drama, 2–3, passim*

Imperfect foot, A metrical foot consisting of a single syllable, either heavily or lightly stressed, 188

Inexact rhyme, Rhymes that are created from words with similar but not identical sounds. In most of these instances, either the vowel segments are different while the consonants are the same, or vice versa. This type of rhyme is variously called *slant rhyme, near rhyme, half rhyme, off rhyme, analyzed rhyme,* or *suspended rhyme.* 194

Intellectual critical approach. See *Topical/Intellectual critical approach.*

Irony, Broadly, a means of indirection. Language that states the opposite of what is intended is *verbal irony.* The placement of characters in a state of ignorance is *dramatic irony,* while an emphasis on powerlessness is *situational irony.* 70, 156–58

Irony of fate. See *Cosmic irony.*

Irony of situation. See *Situational irony.*

Journal, A notebook or word-processor file for recording responses and observations that, for purposes of writing, may be used in the development of essays, 13–16

Kinesthetic images, Words describing human or animal motion and activity, 121

Kinetic images, Words describing general motion, 121

Light stress, In speech and in metrical scansion, the less emphasized syllables, as in Shakespeare's "That time of year," in which *that* and *of* are pronounced less emphatically than *time* and *year,* 185

Limited point of view or **limited-omniscient point of view,** A third-person narration in which the actions and thoughts of the protagonist are the focus of attention, 98, 100

Literary research. See *Research.*

Literature, Written or oral compositions that tell stories, dramatize situations, express emotions, and analyze and advocate ideas. Literature is designed to engage readers emotionally as well as intellectually, with the major genres being *fiction, poetry, drama,* and *nonfiction prose,* and with many separate sub-forms. 3, *passim*

Long shot (film), A distant camera view, including not only characters but also their surroundings; to be contrasted with a *close-up, 222*

Major mover, A major participant in a work's action who either causes things to happen or who is the subject of major events. If the first-person narrator is also a major mover, such as the *protagonist,* that fact gives first-hand authenticity to the narration. 100

Marxist critical approach. See *Economic Determinist/Marxist critical approach.*

Mechanics of verse. See *Prosody.*

Metaphor ("carrying out a change"), *Figurative language* that describes something as though it actually were something else, thereby enhancing understanding and insight, 128–38

Meter, The number of feet within a line of traditional verse, such as *iambic pentameter* referring to a line containing five *iambs,* 186–91

Metrical foot. See *Foot.*

Metrics. See *Prosody.*

Monometer, A line consisting of one metrical foot, 186

Montage or **editing,** The editing or assembling of the various camera "takes," or separately filmed scenes, to make a continuous film, 220–22

Mood. See *Atmosphere.*

Moral/Intellectual critical approach, An interpretive literary approach that is concerned primarily with content and values, 284–85

Music of poetry. See *Prosody.*

Myth, Mythology, Mythos, A *myth* is a story that deals with the relationships of gods to humanity, or with battles among heroes. A myth may also be a set of beliefs or assumptions among societies. *Mythology* refers collectively to all the stories and beliefs, either of a single group or number of groups. A system of beliefs and religious or historical doctrine is a *mythos,* 3, 143

Mythic critical approach. See *Archetypal/Symbolic/Mythic critical approach.*

Narration, The relating or recounting of a sequence of events or actions. Whereas a narration may be reportorial and historical, *narrative fiction* is primarily creative and imaginative. See also *Prose fiction.* 3

Narrative fiction. See *Prose fiction.*

Narrator. See *Speaker.*

Near rhyme. See *Inexact rhyme.*

New Critical/Formalist critical approach, An interpretive literary approach based on the French practice of *explication de texte,* stressing the form and details of literary works, 286–88

Nonfiction prose, A genre consisting of essays, articles, and books about real as opposed to fictional occurrences and objects; one of the major genres of literature, 3

Novel, A long work of prose fiction, 3

Objective point of view. See *Dramatic point of view.*

Octameter , A line of eight metrical feet, 186

Off rhyme, See *Inexact rhyme.*

Olfactory imagery, Images referring to impressions of smell, 120–21

Omniscient point of view, A *third-person narrative* in which the *speaker* or *narrator,* with no apparent limitations, may describe intentions, actions, reactions, locations, and speeches of any or all of the characters, and may also describe their innermost thoughts (when necessary), 98, 100

Onomatopoeia, A blending of consonant and vowel sounds designed to imitate or suggest the activity being described, 192

Outline. See *Analytical sentence outline.*

Overstatement. See *Hyperbole.*

Parable, A short *allegory* designed to illustrate a religious truth, most often associated with Jesus as recorded in the Gospels, 3, 143

Paraphrase, A brief restatement, in one's own words, of all or part of a literary work; a précis, 248–49

Pentameter, A line of five metrical feet, 196

Perfect rhyme. See *Exact rhyme.*

Persona. See *Speaker.*

Phonetic, phonetics, The actual pronunciation of sounds, as distinguished from spelling or *graphics,* 184

Plausibility. See *Probability.*

Plot, The plan or groundwork for a story or a play, with the actions resulting from believable and authentic human responses to a *conflict.* It is causation, conflict, response, opposition, and interaction that make a plot out of a series of actions, 76–82

Poem, poet, poetry, A variable literary genre which is, foremost, characterized by the rhythmical qualities of language. While poems may be short (including *epigrams* and *haiku* of just a few lines) or long (*epics* of thousands of lines), the essence of poetry is compression, economy, and force, in contrast with the expansiveness of prose. There is no bar to the topics that poets may consider, and poems may range from the personal and lyric to the public and discursive. A *poem* is one poetic work. A *poet* is a person who writes poems. *Poetry* may refer to the poems of one writer, to poems of a number of writers, to all poems generally, or to the aesthetics of poetry considered as an art. 3

Point of view, The *speaker, voice, narrator,* or *persona* of a work; the position from which details are perceived and related; a centralizing mind or intelligence; not to be confused with *opinion* or *belief,* 22, 91–106

Point-of-view character, The central figure or *protagonist* in a *limited-point-of-view narration,* the character about whom events turn, the focus of attention in the narration, 98

Private or **contextual symbol.** See *Cultural symbol.*

Probability or **plausibility,** The standard that literature should be concerned with what is likely, common, normal, and usual, 58–59

Problem, A question or issue about the interpretation or understanding of a work, 165–72

Procatalepsis or **anticipation,** A rhetorical strategy whereby the writer raises an objection and then answers it; the idea is to strengthen an argument by anticipating and forestalling objections, 167–68

Prose fiction, Imaginative prose narratives (short stories and novels) that focus on one or a few characters who undergo a change or development as they interact with other characters and deal with their problems, 3

Prosody, The sounds and rhythms of poetry, 183–209

Protagonist, The central character and focus of interest in a narrative or drama, 57

Psychological/Psychoanalytic critical approach, An interpretive literary approach stressing how psychology may be used in the explanation of both authors and literary works, 292–93

Pyrrhic, A metrical foot consisting of two unaccented syllables, 188

Quatrain, (1) A four-line stanza or poetic unit. (2) In an *English* or *Shakespearean* sonnet, a group of four lines united by rhyme, 194

Reader-Response critical approach, An interpretive literary approach based in the proposition that literary works are not fully created until readers make "transactions" with them by "actualizing" them in the light of their own knowledge and experience, 296-97

Realism or **verisimilitude,** The use of true, lifelike, or probable situations and concerns. Also, the theory underlying the use of reality in literature, 58–59

Representative character, A *flat character* with the qualities of all other members of a group (i.e., clerks, cowboys, detectives, etc.); a *stereotype,* 57

Research, literary, The systematic use of primary and secondary sources for assistance in studying a literary problem, 241–70

Resolution. See *Dénouement.*

Response, A reader's intellectual and emotional reactions to a literary work, 43–52

Review, A free-ranging essay on a literary work, 231–40

Rhetorical figure. See *Figurative language.*

Rhetorical substitution. See *Substitution.*

Rhyme, The repetition of identical or closely related sounds in the syllables of different words, most often in concluding syllables at the ends of lines, 184, 193–95

Rhyme scheme, A pattern of rhyme, usually indicated by the assignment of a letter of the alphabet to each rhyming sound, as in *a b b a* as the rhyming pattern of the first quatrain of an Italian or Petrarchan sonnet, 194–95

Rhythm, The varying speed, intensity, elevation, pitch, loudness, and expressiveness of speech, especially poetry, 185–91

Rising rhyme. See *Heavy-stress rhyme.*

Romance, (1) Lengthy Spanish and French *stories* of the sixteenth and seventeenth centuries. (2) Modern formulaic *stories* describing the growth of an impulsive, passionate, and powerful love relationship, 3

Round character, A character who profits from experience and undergoes a change or development; usually but not necessarily the protagonist, 56–57

Run-on line. See *Enjambement.*

Scan, scansion, The act of determining the prevailing *rhythm* of a poem, 185

Second-person point of view, A narration in which a second-person listener ("you") is the protagonist and the speaker is someone (e.g., doctor, parent, rejected lover, etc.) with knowledge that the protagonist does not possess or understand about his or her own actions, 96–97, 100

Segment, The smallest meaningful unit of sound, such as the *l, uh,* and *v* sounds making up the word "love." Segments are to be distinguished from spellings. 184

Selective recollection. See *Flashback.*

Septenary. See *Heptameter*.

Setting, The natural, manufactured, and cultural environment in which characters live and move, including all their possessions, homes, ways of life, and assumptions, 66–75

Short story, A compact, concentrated work of narrative fiction that may also contain description, dialogue, and commentary. Poe used the term "brief prose tale" for the short story, and emphasized that it should create a powerful and unified impact. 3

Sight rhyme. See *Eye rhyme*.

Simile, A figure of comparison, using "like" with nouns and "as" with clauses, as in "the trees were bent by the wind *like actors bowing after a performance*," 128-38

Situational irony or irony of situation, A type of *irony* emphasizing that human beings are enmeshed in forces beyond their comprehension and control, 157

Slant rhyme, An *inexact rhyme* in which the concluding consonant sounds (but not the vowels) are identical, as in "should" and "food," "slim" and "ham." See also *Inexact rhyme*. 194

Sound, The phonetics of language, collectively and separately considered. See also *Prosody*. 3

Speaker, The *narrator* of a story or poem, the *point of view*, often an independent character who is completely imagined and consistently maintained by the author. In addition to narrating the essential events of the work (justifying status as the *narrator*), the speaker may also introduce other aspects of his or her knowledge, and may interject judgments and opinions. Often the character of the speaker is of as much interest as the actions or incidents. 91–92

Spondee, A two-syllable foot consisting of successive, equally heavy accents (e.g., *slow time, men's eyes*). 187

Stanza, A group of poetic lines corresponding to paragraphs in prose; stanzaic meters and rhymes are usually repeating and systematic. 194

Static character, A character who undergoes no change; contrasted with a *dynamic character*, 57

Stereotype, A character who is so ordinary and unoriginal that he or she seems to have been cast in a mold; a *representative* character, 58

Stock character, A *flat character* in a standard role with standard *traits*, such as the irate police captain, the bored hotel clerk, the sadistic criminal, etc.; a *stereotype*, 57

Story, A narrative, usually fictional, centering on a major character, and rendering a complete action, 3

Stress, The emphasis given to a syllable, either strong or light. See also *Accent*. 185

Strong-stress rhythm. See *Accentual rhythm*.

Structuralist critical approach, An interpretive literary approach attempting to find relationships and similarities among elements that appear to be separate and discrete, 288–89

Structure, The arrangement and placement of materials in a work, 82–90

Substitution, *Formal substitution* is the use of an actual variant foot within a line, such as an anapest being used in place of an iamb. *Rhetorical substitution* is the manipulation of the caesura to create the effect of a series of differing feet. 190–91

Suspended rhyme. See *Inexact rhyme*.

Syllable, A separately pronounced part of a word (e.g., the *sing* and *ing* parts of "singing") or, in some cases, a complete word (e.g., *the, when, flounced*), 184

Symbol, symbolism, A specific word, idea, or object that may stand for ideas, values, persons, or ways of life, 22, 139–51

Syzygy. See *Dipody*.

Tactile imagery, Images of touch and responses to touch, 121

Tenor, The ideas conveyed in a *metaphor* or *simile*. See also *Vehicle*. 130

Tense, The use of verb tenses as an aspect of *point of view*, conveying immediacy or distance, psychological engagement or uninvolvement, 99

Tetrameter, A line of four metrical feet, 186

Thesis sentence or thesis statement, An introductory sentence which names the topics to be developed in the body of an essay, 24–25

Third-person point of view, A third-person method of narration (i.e., *she, he, it, they, them*, etc.), in which the speaker or narrator is not a part of the story, unlike the involvement of the narrator of a *first-person point of view*. Because the third-person speaker may exhibit great knowledge and understanding, together with other qualities of character, he or she is often virtually identified with the author, but this identification is not easily decided. See also *Authorial voice, Omniscient point of view*. 97–98

Third-person objective point of view. See *Dramatic point of view.*

Tone, The techniques and modes of presentation that reveal or create attitudes, 152–64

Topic sentence, The sentence determining or introducing the subject matter of a paragraph. 25–26

Topical/Historical critical approach, An interpretive literary approach that stresses the relationship of literature to its historical period, 285–86

Trait, traits, A typical mode of behavior; the study of major traits provides a guide to the description of character. 54

Trimeter, A line of three metrical feet, 186

Triple rhyme. See *Dactylic rhyme.*

Trochaic (double) rhyme, Rhyming trochees such as *flower* and *shower,* 194

Trochee, trochaic, A two-syllable foot consisting of a heavy stress followed by a light stress (e.g., running, singing, eating), 187

Unaccented syllable, A syllable receiving a light stress, 185, 194

Understatement, The deliberate underplaying or undervaluing of an assertion or idea to create emphasis, 156

Universal symbol. See *Cultural symbol.*

Unreliable speaker, A fictional narrator who may have ulterior motives or whose intelligence is limited. The account of an unreliable speaker is therefore unreliable and subject to interpretation, 96

Unstressed syllable. See *Light stress.*

Value, values, The attachment of worth, significance, and desirability to an *idea* so that the *idea* is judged not only for its significance as thought but also for its importance as a goal, ideal, or standard, 108

Vehicle, The specific words of a *metaphor or simile.* See also *Tenor.* 130

Verbal irony, Language stressing the importance of an idea by stating the opposite of what is meant, 156–57

Verisimilitude ("like truth"), A characteristic whereby the setting, circumstances, characters, dialogue, actions, and outcomes in a work are designed to seem true, lifelike, real, plausible, and probable. See also *Realism.* 58–59

Versification. See *Prosody.*

Virgule, A slash mark (/) used in scansion to mark the boundaries of poetic feet, 185

Visual image, Language describing visible objects and situations, 120

Voice. See *Speaker.*

Vowel sounds or **vowel segments,** Meaningful continuant sounds produced by the resonation of the voice in the space between the tongue and the top of the mouth, such as the *ee* in *feel,* the *eh* in *bet,* and the *oo* in *cool,* 185

Index of Authors, Directors, Topics, and Chapter Titles

Works are listed alphabetically under the name of the author or director, although films are also listed by title. Anonymous works, collectively-authored works, and works of unknown authorship or directorship are indexed under the titles. For brief definitions of important terms and concepts used in the text, please consult the preceding *Glossary*.